Praise for Stupidparty Math v. Myth

"The book is exhaustively researched by a political junkie: Andendall manages to cover everything from voter fraud and global warming to Keynesian economics and creationism. The pugnacious prose is accompanied by a series of visual aids, which include satirical cartoons, humorous pie charts and a puzzle about the 'Stupidparty.' Often hilarious, the actual analysis provided can be very astute; for instance, with genuine empirical rigor and élan, Chapter 11 ('Environmental Stewardship = Better Capitalism') dissects the problem of disenfranchised farmers as a political constituency."

—Kirkus Reviews

"With wit and cynicism, Andendall turns a critical eye on the Republican Party, contributing important insight to an ongoing political debate. Stupidparty Math v. Myth: Unmasking the Destructive Forces Eroding American Democracy, from its title to its format, is a curious experience. Patrick M. Andendall, author of this colorful, well-designed, and fun e-book, has assembled a coherent fact-filled guide to how he believes the Republican Party became the 'Stupid Party' and how this has dire consequences for politics in this country. Throughout 'Stupidparty,' the graphics, illustrations, and cartoons are outstanding, colorful, and make it so much easier to digest the often complex information. Andendall should be applauded for his attempt to make a serious point: the American political system needs functioning political parties, and, with the way the Republican Party is currently operating, America does not have that."

—Clarion Review

"[Pat] is a man of ideas and convictions and has taken them seriously enough to write long and hard about his values and vision. He's not intimidated by 'party think' and doesn't believe in empty slogans and vitriolic rhetoric. I hope he won't take offense at my calling him thoughtful and brave—willing to put his ideas out there, knowing that in some quarters he will be denounced just for deviating a few degrees from the conventional 'wisdom' by those who are twisting their Party into a pale imitation of what it once was. Read this book and admire him for having the guts to write it, get it out there."

—Danny Schechter, "the news dissector" and recipient of the Society of Professional Journalists' 2001 Award for Excellence in Documentary Journalism

STUPIDPARTY
MATH V. MYTH

UNMASKING THE DESTRUCTIVE FORCES
ERODING AMERICAN DEMOCRACY

PATRICK M. ANDENDALL

Cover image: Vasily Koren': *The Four Horsemen of the Apocalypse.* From the first Russian engraved Bible, 1692–1696. http://www.protos7.ru/Apokaliptika/RusApoka/Istor1.htm. Pushkin State Museum of Fine Arts, Moscow

http://commons.wikimedia.org/wiki/File:KorenRiders.jpg

This work is in the public domain in the United States, and those countries with a copyright term of life of the author plus 100 years or less.

Published by Fact Over Fiction Publishing, Ltd.

Library of Congress Control Number: TBA
ISBN: 978-0-9960739-0-5 (softcover edition)
ISBN: 978-0-9960739-1-2 (eBook edition)

Printed in the United States

Editor: Margaret A. Harrell

A very special acknowledgement to my editor, Margaret Harrell, with an expertise and unique talent, no doubt burgeoning through her fascinating life experiences, and working with truly notable writers, goes beyond the call of duty. Fate brought her to my assistance.

End of Times—The Four Horses of Apocalypse
I awoke with a vivid vision, or was it a dream?

And I saw, and behold a white horse. And he that sat on him had calculated that he would forever be a ruler and would set forth and conquer Myth with the use of Math.

And there went out another horse, that was red. And power was given to him that sat thereon to take Science to mankind, and that he must prevent raging winds, hell's furnace, and plagues by allowing research to inoculate against witchcraft.

And I beheld, and lo a black horse. And he that sat on him had a pair of balances in his hand. On one side sat facts and on the other untruths, and never again would the two be held equivalent.

And I looked, and behold a pale horse. And his name that sat on him was Knowledge, and Ignorance followed behind. And as the power of Math, Science, and Facts was given to Knowledge, so he trampled over Ignorance, and deep into the earth this conquered beast did disperse.

Inspired by the Book of Revelations, the last book of the New Testament.

How This Book Works

This book was originally designed to be read as an ebook to enable the reader to quickly jump to any of the more than 1500 citations. There are "Blue" hyperlinks, mainly for attribution; "Olive Green" hyperlinks, mainly to allow the reader to explore various topics more thoroughly; and "Rusty Red" hyperlinks, usually to add some levity to sometimes rather disturbing material. On occasion the narrative simply provides a link in order keep the actual narrative more succinct, and in these cases the printed version will fall short. This book also makes use of color to help the reader navigate the oftentimes intertwined narrative style—a style intended to provide maximum credibility and clarity by the extensive use of quotes from numerous sources. Facts and Math unlike Myth and Opinion are not created by any one individual—and by definition facts can be verified. The beauty of modern technology is that the ebook reader can be seamlessly directed to the source.

If you purchased the print book, I want to say thank you and offer you a chance to buy the ebook at a reduced rate. Please visit StupidpartyMathvMyth.com for details.

 Rusty Red – usually links to funny or sad Videos to highlight a theme

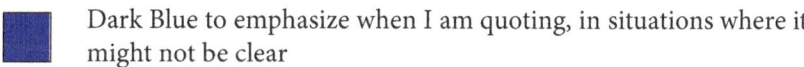 Olive Green links within the narrative paragraph as opposed to the end of the paragraph – usually to provide additional information

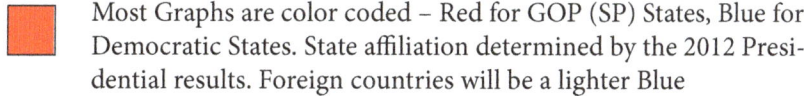 Dark Blue to emphasize when I am quoting, in situations where it might not be clear

Most Graphs are color coded – Red for GOP (SP) States, Blue for Democratic States. State affiliation determined by the 2012 Presidential results. Foreign countries will be a lighter Blue

Blue hyperlinks link to the source:
http://www.theguardian.com/commentisfree/2013/jun/15/republican-party-stupid-mistakes

Link disclaimer: Links worked at the time of publication but websites constantly change, which means a certain number will over time no longer work.

Stories evolve, progressives evolve, I evolve. I could not give all stories as much coverage as I would have liked. Also, as time passes stories develop, new angles materialize, or I learn more. Since the book reached the point of no return, much has already happened. One example is that I feel concerned that I treated George H. W. Bush (who predated Stupidparty) with kid gloves. In this day and age there is a solution—my blog. Please join me at StupidpartyMathvMyth.com.

Contents

Introduction

The title of the book might appear contentious, but it really should not surprise anyone. This terminology is not my idea. I am fully aware that people who vote for the Republican Party are not by definition stupid. The term "Stupidparty" was catapulted into the public domain by Bobby Jindal, the Republican governor of Louisiana, who not too long ago was being groomed as the modern face of the conservative movement. Jindal was giving the keynote address at the Republican National Committee's winter meeting in Charlotte January 24, 2013, where he said:

> "We've got to stop being the stupid party. It's time for a new Republican Party that talks like adults."

I bet he wishes he could take those words back. The audience must have winced. They all knew that the intellectual integrity of the Republican Party was under attack—and here was this one-time rising star of the party crystalizing what was already on many people's minds. As I illustrate in Chapter 1, many well-known prognosticators from across the political spectrum had long ago arrived at a similar conclusion.

There are many good and intelligent people who still insist on voting Republican. However upset the rest of us get with this dogged loyalty, we still recognize that the United States must have at least two parties. There will always be a place for a party primarily focused on a fiscally sound economic approach. There will always be times when cutting taxes is a good idea. There will always be times when cutting spending is a good idea. We must always be on the watch for government overreach. As for cutting waste, well, that is invariably a good idea, and all large bureaucracies are bound to find new ways to be wasteful.

This book is not about trying to destroy the Republican Party. It is about trying to save the Republican Party. I have long since decided to avoid using the term "Republican Party"—because today's Republican Party is an insult to the very essence of what the Republican Party should be. It is an insult to George Bush Sr., to Reagan, to Ford, and all the preceding Republican leaders who no doubt helped make America the model for an effective, wealth-producing capitalist country. For this reason, the book itself will avoid referring to the Republican Party—for the Republican Party in my opinion has undergone a wraithlike transformation.

By any rational interpretation, I am a conservative. I was a determined advocate for Margaret Thatcher; I gleefully crossed trade union picket lines. I wanted to conserve rural lifestyles, raged against urbanites campaigning to infringe on rural pastimes. I would of course like to pay less income tax and I have a libertarian streak in me that revolts when the government tells me how to run my life or expects me to spend time filling out complex forms or complying with cumbersome nuisance taxes that hinder my ability to run my business efficiently.

So I Decided to Help

I have always been interested in politics, and being multicultural, I tend to view issues from a more international perspective. I wanted to have some impact on elections, to do my bit and a little bit more. In 2004, I figured out that I wanted to be at ground zero for the election. Therefore, five days before the election I flew to Cleveland, camped at some motel, and pitched in to help.

But I guess Karl Rove had come to the same conclusion, and in my opinion he colluded with Ken Blackwell, then Ohio secretary of state, to execute sufficient voter-suppression strategies to effectively change the outcome and give George W. Bush a second term **(Chapters 6, 15)**. Other books have been written about the details, and these books make some extremely serious charges. Regardless of the facts, I was there and witnessed the consequences.

I was in Cleveland on the evening of November 2, 2004. It was a windy night, pouring with rain. Voters in the poorer urban neighborhoods, such as where I had been canvassing for five days, could not wait hours in lines (lines caused by the not so mysteriously insufficient number of voting machines)—these drenched, resourceless voters having a limited window of opportunity to vote before needing to hurry home to tackle the difficulties of raising, feeding, and guarding eclectic family members. Single mothers, or grandmothers, aunts, or uncles filling voids, always trying to provide hope but not knowing how in pressure-cooked neighborhoods with houses festooned with eviction notices; multiple temptations vibrantly milling around, ready to knock on the door; looking to captivate the bored, the rebellious, the depressed—picking them off one by one: the very opposite of the American Dream.

In the rain I stood and I watched these voters trying to play their part, trying to be heard—being kicked in the gut, for no one was listening. And gradually they melted away into that miserable night, and I witnessed what I came to believe was the destruction of one of the pillars of democracy—equal-opportunity voting. Even then there was hope. In spite of these lost votes, exit polls still showed that Kerry was up by a significant margin. Exit polls (because of the law of large numbers) should not have a high margin for error. But it turned out that the Ohio exit polls had a strangely high margin of error. I will leave analysis about that to other journalists and authors.

Regardless, it was enough to make the best of us despair. But defeat makes one stronger; one must "get up, dust oneself off, and start all over again." I was already getting rather uninspired by canvassing. Conventional wisdom suggests that the best strategy for a canvasser is to get "your" people out to vote. Thus, you target people who agree with you, after a while (24 hours actually) this gets a bit old.

To Tweet or Not to Tweet?

The 2008 election was pretty much a forgone conclusion. I guess, with ten seconds to go, if John McCain had aimed that fifty-yard Hail Mary pass to an actual player on his team, maybe the election would have been less predictable. His legacy will always be damaged by his not taking sixty minutes to do some Google research to prevent him from banking on an individual barely qualified to be on a school board, let alone in line as a future president.

For 2012, the Math always implied an incumbent victory—but the nonstop stream of stunningly ill equipped presidential wannabes did not allow for complacency. I could not sit idly by and allow a Gordon Gekko twin to be the U.S. conduit to humanity.

So having grown tired of canvassing, cold calling, and competing monetarily against individuals with more personal wealth than entire nations, I decided shortly before the 2012 election to take to Twitter. I tweeted away. I retweeted other people's tweets. I wanted to be retweeted, so I built up my followers and got retweeted as much as possible. I guess I rapidly got to nearly 2,000 followers by election time. I wanted to be part of a movement to drive specific news; I wanted to be the initiator of news and the initiator of themes to be driven. Was I remotely successful? I have no idea.

Unfortunately, Cataloging Stupidity Wasn't Hard

In the aftermath my tweeting activities subsided. But I began to reflect on the pros and cons. Two sentences to win an argument? Now, that is a mighty tweeter. You can tweet a theme by tweeting numerous examples to drive home the same point, and that was fun. You can tweet attachments—the winning argument—lost to 99% of your audience, even when retweeted. So as I reflected on my little tweeting eruption, I began to think it might be a good idea to organize my efforts, just for my own sanity, so that a winning argument would at least be remembered by just one person—an ever-more-forgetful me. As I undertook this exercise, a folder was created and the folder began to take the form of a presentation. It was a folder of a thousand jigsaw-like pieces, and I began to realize that if I could put the pieces into some type of logical order, a powerful picture would likely emerge. This picture evolved into a book. The book took on its own life.

As I started this undertaking, I realized that though I am always open to most reasonable arguments, what I abhor above anything else is excessive dishonesty, hypocrisy, and stupidity. As previously mentioned, in recent times and out of respect for what Republicans have traditionally stood for, I can no longer refer to the Republican Party by its historical name. This is because the prognosticators are correct. The Republican Party has now become the Stupidparty. If you google "Stupidparty," you will see the term is now synonymous with Republicans. This was not caused by me; nor was it my idea, and it is certainly not my preference.

Holding Up a Mirror to Our Follies

This book sets out to explain how this happened. I will also explain that the actual economic agenda of the Republican Party has become utter nonsense, that the so-called values it prattles on about are a travesty of reality (**Chapter 13**). I will show that the more influence the Republican Party presently has on the wealth, health, education, safety, values, and happiness of any specific region in the country, the worse off the inhabitants are in all those aspects (**Chapters 5 et al**). These same policies are also causing dramatic negative trends in the USA relative to other countries around the world.

Americans are extremely hard working; the land mass is huge and fertile with plentiful natural resources. It takes a lot to really screw everything up, to impoverish vast swaths of the nation. Few will argue that massive screw-ups are not occurring—but some confusion appears to exist as to why. These confusions will be cleared up. Running the U.S. economy should be dead easy. The pain and suffering is manufactured here in the USA.

On occasion I may use some pretty harsh language. But even that should be put in perspective. I believe that there is quite a lot of delusional logic on display in today's political discourse—but bear in mind, we all have some degree of delusion: I may be delusional in that anybody would be interested in this book. We all are possibly delusional in believing we have free will, when there is some science to the notion that we do not. Some may believe in the blood of Christ, while others may believe that same substance, albeit untransubstantiated red wine, is a preventative of heart disease. All these possible delusions are what add flavor to our life experience. During all this confusion, facts or getting as close to facts as possible becomes all the more vital.

By Any Other Measure

My multicultural background also allows me to see another dimension to one of the oddities of voter behavior that appears to be unique to the United States. It would appear that it is only in the parallel universe in which the U.S. finds itself residing that the less well off (a group which does not appear to have an economic label, since Americans rather oddly throw them into the middle class)—that these individuals (the white ones, at least) vote for the right-leaning party, when in every other country such voters tend to vote for the left-leaning parties. You know those parties, the ones that try and help the workers, protect their benefits, retrain them, find them jobs, and do all that safety-net stuff. Since there are no conclusive studies I am aware of that demonstrate that trickle-down policies work better than trickle-up (and this is an understatement), I will attempt to explain how this happened, why these large swaths of the electorate vote decisively and aggressively against their best interests **(Chapters 16-18)**. The results of this inverse logic will also be clearly illustrated.

American sensibilities can be quite charming. Americans never go to the toilet; they always go to the bathroom. But such sensibilities can have unfortunate consequences, such as in the odd furor surrounding Janet Jackson's wardrobe malfunction. Such sensibilities also prejudice debate about the people with the least-appealing financial options. I find it quite strange that apparently American culture, because of class sensibilities, seems to refuse to acknowledge the impoverished, especially those with full-time jobs and yet still in poverty. This is because apparently virtually everyone seems to be in the Middle class. If you are not in the Middle class—and you are not in the 1% (poetic license)—there appears to be no terminology for you, which might suggest that society has simply condemned this group as anonymous losers whose name can never be mentioned.

Americans, for whom class is based on wealth not bloodline, understandably will not readily accept the more standard class definitions (like Working, Middle, Upper, the Elites/Aristocracy) used in other countries. But what they might consider is a more mathematically based definition, especially as their cultural preference is accidentally more math-friendly in the first place. Why not call it something like the "Struggling" class, defined as those making, say, 50% or less of the median income? The bulk of the employees working for the ever-expanding multiple-branch companies such as Walmart, Home Depot, CVS, large clothing stores, fast-food chains, hotel chains, etc., are quite likely to fall into the "struggling" class. And one should not totally forget the unemployed or those who have lost hope—for an investment in their future, if done with care, is likely to reap longer-term dividends for the taxpayer and the stability of society (**Chapter 9**).

Many of these people had better jobs; now they find themselves at minimum wage or close to it. Income disparity trends suggest that this loss of wealth, this loss of the American Dream, has happened as a result of assets being transferred to the 1%. The productivity of all these workers has increased dramatically, but this increased productivity is not being passed on to the employees; it is going to the employers and the shareholders—the very same people who demand cuts in benefits for everyone else, in order to fund tax cuts for themselves.

It's Time to Once Again Be Rational People

This is also a call to arms to the people whom I blame for accidentally allowing this epic breakdown of sane governance to happen. I will show overwhelming evidence that the majority of Republican voters are extremely uninformed (**Chapter 3**). This lack of knowledge is not of the relatively harmless variety, like not knowing who the Speaker of the House is or not knowing the capital of France. If you are not interested enough in politics or geography to care about these type of questions, that is fine by me.

No, the ignorance I am referring to is far more insidious. This ignorance threatens my future, the future of my family, my friends, my compatriots, humanity, and the planet. The ignorance I am referring to is coming from the most politically active voters, the most reliable voters—who simply do not have the foggiest idea about the issues they are voting on—for example, the root cause of the debt. As long as the Republican Party keeps having even moderate success at the polls, these voters' minds will not change, they will not be enlightened. For reasons that this book will explain, such ignorance is not necessarily even their fault, as this ignorance is carefully nourished by the special interests that presently control the democratic process in the hopes of Asset Stripping every resource for their own personal myopic self-interest (**Chapter 16**).

Obviously, approximately 1/3 of Republican voters do have a perfectly reasonable grasp on reality. Like myself, they accept that the planet is more than 5,000 years old, that Iraq was not behind 9/11; they accept that bigotry is unproductive and usually caused by ignorance, and they prefer facts to myth. But they still vote Republican. Do they do this out of habit or bitterness or selfishness, misplaced religious beliefs? Perhaps they are simply too busy to stop and take note of what is happening under their noses and perhaps deep down some might be covertly somewhat bigoted in one or more of the numerous categories of bigotry that the old Republican Party would certainly never have allowed to take center stage (**Chapter 12**).

While I can only guess as to why rational people are in bed with irrational fundamentalists, I take great pains to avoid guessing when evaluating the end results and how we got to this place. There will be very minimal guesswork in the rest of this book. I will let the facts tell the story. I have tried to keep facts and statistics as simple as possible for two reasons: 1) I want to keep the narrative manageable, and 2) one should understand that if you torture statistics long enough, they will confess to anything. So an abiding principle herein will be the KISS principle—"keep it simple, stupid." No pun intended

Without You, the 67% Are Nothing

The objective of this book is to make a request to these 33.333% of Republican voters. I realize that you are informed, you care about the issues I will be raising in this book. On most issues we have never been far apart. So I am simply asking you to take a time-out and reconsider how best you can serve your own interests and help mankind, for I am not asking for charity, or empathy—just a reset opportunity to reevaluate the facts and how these facts should logically drive a certain course of action.

The issues that face us today go well beyond our borders. I would like to be given the opportunity to try and demonstrate that your strategy of thinking that you are a moderating voice in an ever-more-insane club has backfired. Your strategy of rationalizing your association with the unacceptable fringe has brought you to a cul-de-sac. This fringe has taken over. By voting Republican Party, you have empowered the extremists; also, you have not forced America to take responsibility for its disastrous energy policy, its absurd healthcare model, for the illegal war in Iraq.

I will argue that you have empowered the extremists into actually successfully selling the idea that greed is good and successfully selling the idea that the ever-increasing income-discrepancy issue, leading to more poverty, should be not only tolerated but encouraged in a country that had always prided itself in being a force for good. Would the end of the American Dream be on your watch?

Your strategy of tolerating the company of bigots, of tolerating torture, tolerating detention without due process, of tolerating the massive corruption and the consequent undermining of democracy itself has not worked. This tolerance has allowed the Stupidparty to destroy the foundations of the Republican Party. The mess you see today would never have happened if the 33% of Republican voters who are open to intelligent economic debate had not allowed themselves to become the junior partners in a movement to destroy the very notion of reason, of truth, of intelligence.

Without you, the 67% are nothing. They will have no fireplace to warm the prejudices carefully instilled in their hearts. The billions of dollars spent on corrupting the hearts and minds of good people would be wasted.

This book will, without difficulty, destroy what is now commonly referred to as the Stupidparty.

I am not trying to destroy the Republican Party. If there is a God, may God save the Republican Party.

Please join me in trying to save the Republican Party.

The Creationism of the Stupidparty
My personal "Birther" theory

1979 Iran Hostage Crisis
Failed Military Rescue. Egg leaving
Fallopian tube.

Carter Loses 1980 election, thus
ensuring no intelligent energy policy,
aggressive myopic foreign policy,
leading to future Wars.
Sperm hits the egg.

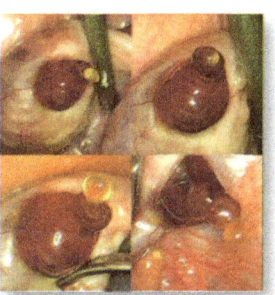

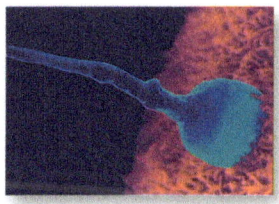

Reagan becomes very popular, leads to
1988 landslide. First signs of life.

Clinton repairs economy, but Kenneth
Starr fails to find anything of note
regarding Whitewater, stumbles on a
rather lame sex scandal—Impeached
by adulterers who had actually had
intercourse.

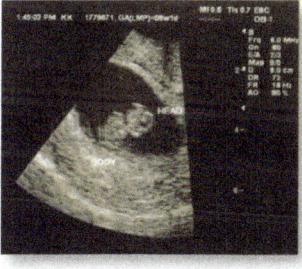

2000 Supreme Court Gives Birth
to G. W. Bush presidency.
The Stupidparty is born.

Notwithstanding the Ohio scandal,
Bush wins the popular vote in 2004;
thus, the nation sanctions an illegal
war. The Stupidparty is christened.

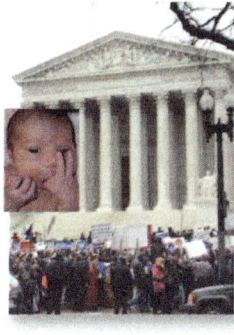

2010 Congres-
sional Elec-
tions—First
Black President
sees Stupidparty
blossom.

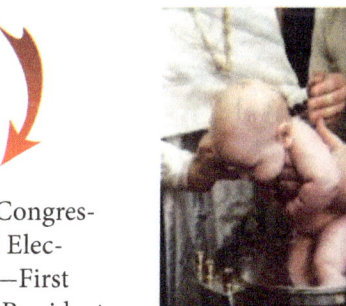

CHAPTER 1

It's not me,
it's them

Scrabble®

Suppose you were an idiot. And suppose you were a Republican. But I repeat myself.

—Harry S. Truman

It's not me, it's them

Bobby Jindal:
"'We've got to stop being the stupid party,' Louisiana Governor Bobby Jindal, one of the GOP's brightest young stars, said in a much-anticipated speech last week at the party's winter meeting. 'We've got to stop insulting the intelligence of voters. We need to trust the smarts of the American people.'"
http://www.miamiherald.com/2013/01/31/3210776/republicans-lost-in-their-own.html

Mark Mardell, North American editor for BBC News
in response to Jindal's speech:
"Are Republicans the 'stupid party'?"
His conclusion:
A for stating the obvious, C for economic plan

Rick Santorum, Stupidparty presidential contender:
"We will never have the elite smart people on our side."

Rick Moran, Stupidparty journalist from the conservative oxymoron publication *American Thinker:*
"Why the GOP really is 'The Stupid Party'"
http://www.americanthinker.com/blog/2013/06/why_the_gop_really_is_the_stupid_party.html#ixzz2cKfr4Noh

Steve Benen, Political commentator and producer for *The Rachel Maddow Show*
("So much for shedding the 'stupid party' label"):
"If the GOP intends to stop being, in Bobby Jindal's words, the 'stupid party,' they have a long way to go."

Crystal Wright, *The Guardian*
("The Grand Old Party is stuck on stupid"):
"Following two presidential election defeats in 2008 and 2012, the Republican Party is still making the same mistakes. Stupid is as stupid does and, apparently, the Republican Party didn't get Louisiana Governor Bobby Jindal's 'stupid memo' because it looks dumber by the day. After losing the 2012 presidential election the 'GOP establishment' from former Mississippi governor Haley Barbour to former GOP House Speaker Newt Gingrich and every white man in between acknowledged that the party must make 'the tent' more welcoming to minorities and women—where the votes increasingly are. So what does the GOP do? It keeps headlining white men behaving badly."
http://www.theguardian.com/commentisfree/2013/jun/15/republican-party-stupid-mistakes

Rod Dreher, *The American Conservative*
("Embracing the 'Stupid Party' Label"):
"If Michelle Obama took up the cause of literacy, Palin would recommend watching more *Honey Boo Boo.*"
http://www.theamericanconservative.com/dreher/embracing-the-stupid-party-label/

Paul Begala, CNN contributor:
"Republicans used to admire intelligence. But now they're dumbing themselves down."

Ta-Nehisi Coates, *The Atlantic* senior editor
("To Stop Being the Party of Stupid You Must Stop Being Stupid"):
"If you are not around people who will look at you like you are crazy when you make stupid claims about other people's experiences, then you tend to keep saying stupid things about other people's experiences. It is not enough to pay a political price, or even to be shamed into silence. You have to come to believe—in your heart—that sincerity itself is not the same as accurate information. It is not enough for you to not be 'the party of stupid' or to 'stop saying stupid things'[;] you must show some active commitment toward being less stupid."
http://www.theatlantic.com/politics/archive/2013/06/to-stop-being-the-party-of-stupid-you-must-stop-being-stupid/276804/

Michael Ledo, *Augusta Chronicle* (letter to)
("GOP still 'the stupid party'"):
"In looking at the last GOP primary, that is what it had in Rick Perry, Rick Santorum, Herman Cain and the poster child for stupidity, Michele Bachmann. . . . How can a party with members who [deny] global warming, evolution and rape pregnancies turn itself around when this is what so many of its voters want? . . . The language of 'stupid' is epitomized by the phrase 'socialist* agenda.' Recently the words 'nullification' and 'secession' also have entered its vocabulary."
http://chronicle.augusta.com/opinion/letters/2013-02-12/gop-still-stupid-party

Mark Shea, A Catholic author, a contributor to various publications including *The National Catholic Register.* He is also a blogger and speaker.
("Here's an Idea for the GOP: Stop Lionizing Stupidity"):
"In a related vein, when Bubba Jo Suggs and Nathan Bedford Forrest Jr. show up at your CPAC workshop on racial diversity and proceed to sing the glories of the Confederacy, crow about 'White Culture' and the threat that minorities pose to the White Race, and pine for the days when the Peculiar Institution kept all them grateful banjo-playing darkies fed and housed, you don't allow them to throw your workshop into chaos and direct most of your ire at the horrified African American lady in the house. You throw these Klan Klowns out and make clear that there is no room whatsoever for this filthy bigotry."
http://www.patheos.com/blogs/markshea/2013/03/heres-an-idea-for-the-gop-stop-lionizing-stupidity.html

Joe Scarborough, MSNBC, *Morning Joe:*
"I'm tired of Republicans being the 'Stupidparty.'"

* When an idiot says **"socialist,"** what does an idiot mean? What is the benchmark—is it North Korea or is it Sweden? Is it The UK or is it Massachusetts?

Kay Bailey Hutchison, CNN:
"Republican senator of Texas, who's retiring after this year, said Thursday the personal beliefs of some Republicans dampened her party's focus on the economy this election year. 'We had Republican candidates who got very high profile and said some very stupid things.'"
http://politicalticker.blogs.cnn.com/2012/11/08/hutchison-stupid-comments-hurt-republicans/

CHAPTER 2

Thoughts of the Founding Fathers

http://www.pinterest.com/pin/125045327127360147/

"Shouldn't we consider building something into this document just in case the people elect a moron?"

Republicans don't want to "save the world"; they want to save the country from those who would "save the world."

—Richard D. Kahlenberg, *Broken Contract*

Thoughts of the Stupidparty Founding Fathers

Whilst some of these quotes are simply humorous and anyone can say silly stuff, most display a clue to a core level of stupid or an insidious level of ignorance or ill will designed to promote fear and bigotry and thus are unique to the Stupidparty. So before assuming both sides say silly things, please be mindful of false equivalency, a topic that will dealt with in a later chapter.

Rush Limbaugh.
"Feminism was established so as to allow unattractive women easier access to the mainstream of society." ~
http://www.rushlimbaugh.com/daily/2010/10/11/feminism_and_republican_women

Jerry Falwell.
"Good Christians, like slaves and soldiers, ask no questions."
http://www.opensourcetheology.net/node/1327

Rev. John Hagee.
"How did [the Holocaust] happen? Because God allowed it to happen . . . because God said, 'My top priority for the Jewish people is to get them to come back to the land of Israel.'"
http://www.thedailybeast.com/articles/2009/09/10/18-outrageous-christian-right-quotes.html

Ronald Reagan.
"Trees cause more pollution than automobiles."
http://rationalwiki.org/wiki/Trees_cause_pollution

Ronald Reagan.
"Fascism was really the basis for the New Deal."
http://en.wikiquote.org/wiki/Ronald_Reagan

Ralph Reed.
"Gandhi: Ninny of the 20th Century": Under Ralph Reed's byline, this article on Mahatma Gandhi ran in the University of Georgia student newspaper, *Red & Black*. Reed, president of the College Republican National Committee, had plagiarized from "The Gandhi Nobody Knows" by Richard Grenier. Reed's column was dropped because of the plagiarizing. Stephen Colbert did a skit on the story that's still online.
http://www.thedailybeast.com/articles/2009/09/10/18-outrageous-christian-right-quotes.html

Mike Huckabee.
America has to import so many workers because "for the last 35 years we have aborted more than a million people who would have been in our workforce."
http://www.thedailybeast.com/articles/2009/09/10/18-outrageous-christian-right-quotes.html

Antonin Scalia. (Re: Laws banning homosexual sex)
In his dissent in the 1996 case *Romer v. Evans*:
"'Of course it is our moral heritage that one should not hate any human being or class of human beings,' Scalia wrote, in the classic prebuttal phrasing of someone about to say something ludicrous. 'But I had thought that one could consider certain conduct reprehensible—murder, for example, or polygamy, or cruelty to animals—and could exhibit even "animus" toward such conduct. Surely that is the only sort of "animus" at

issue here: moral disapproval of homosexual conduct[.]' It's true that people generally disapprove of murder, but there's more going on in laws banning murder than mere disfavor—the rights of the person being murdered, for example."
http://www.motherjones.com/politics/2013/03/scalia-worst-things-said-written-about-homosexuality-court

Ronald Reagan.

"Well, I learned a lot…. I went down [to Latin America] to find out from them and their views. You'd be surprised. They're all individual countries."
http://politicalhumor.about.com/cs/quotethis/a/reaganquotes.htm

Ronald Reagan.

"We were told four years ago that 17 million people went to bed hungry every night. Well, that was probably true. They were all on a diet."
—TV speech, October 27, 1964, cited by Mark Green, *Reagan's Reign of Error*
http://en.wikiquote.org/wiki/Ronald_Reagan

John McCain.

"We have a lot of work to do. It's a very hard struggle, particularly given the situation on the Iraq–Pakistan border." ~ (the countries share no common border)
http://crooksandliars.com/2008/07/21/foreign-policy-expert-mccain-iraq-pakistan-border-extremely-dangerous
(Note: Yes, I realize that anyone can make this type of slip, but it is included because I do not believe that John McCain's geopolitical knowledge is even close to being as impressive as John McCain believes it is. To say it lacks any nuance would be a generous description.)

John McCain.

"You know that old Beach Boys song, 'Bomb Iran'? 'Bomb bomb bomb.'"
—McCain, breaking into song after being asked at a VFW meeting about whether it was time to send a message to Iran. (Murrells Inlet, South Carolina, April 18, 2007)
http://www.youtube.com/watch?v=o-zoPgv_nYg

John McCain.

"[Sarah Palin] knows more about energy than probably anyone else in the United States of America…. And, uh, she also happens to represent, be governor of a state that's right next to Russia."
—McCain on Palin's foreign-policy experience. (Interview with WCSH-6, Portland, Oregon, Sept. 12, 2008)
http://www.youtube.com/watch?v=ObY5v_DP3Qc
(Note: "Rusty Red" Links—Link to Funny or Sad YouTube Videos)

John McCain. (Jokingly)

"I think if you're just talking about income, how about $5 million?"
—after being asked by Rev. Rick Warren to define "rich." (Lake Forest, California, Aug. 16, 2008)
http://www.huffingtonpost.com/daniel-kurtzman/mccain-and-palin-in-their_b_134730.html

John McCain.

"She's a partner and a soul-mate."
—on Palin, whom he had met only once before selecting her to be his running mate. (*Fox News Sunday* interview, Aug. 31, 2008)
http://www.huffingtonpost.com/daniel-kurtzman/mccain-and-palin-in-their_b_134730.html

Sarah Palin.
"All of 'em, any of 'em that have been in front of me over all these years."
—unable to name a single newspaper or magazine she reads. (Interview with Katie
Couric, CBS News, Sept. 30, 2008)
http://www.huffingtonpost.com/2008/09/30/sarah-palin-answers-what_n_130706.html

Sarah Palin.
"But obviously, we've got to stand with our North Korean allies."
http://www.theguardian.com/world/richard-adams-blog/2010/nov/24/sarah-palin-north-korea-allies

Sarah Palin.
"I'm the mayor, I can do whatever I
want until the courts tell me I can't."
—as quoted by former city council member Nick Carney, after
he raised objections about the
$50,000 she spent renovating the
mayor's office without approval
of the city council.
http://www.huffingtonpost.com/daniel-
kurtzman/mccain-and-palin-in-their_b_134730.
html

Sarah Palin.
"I'm very, very pleased to be cleared of any legal wrongdoing… any hint of any kind of
unethical activity there. Very pleased to be cleared of any of that."
—after an Alaska legislative report found she had broken the state's ethics law and
abused her power in the Troopergate scandal. (Conference call with Alaska reporters,
Oct. 12, 2008)
http://www.huffingtonpost.com/daniel-kurtzman/mccain-and-palin-in-their_b_134730.html

Rush Limbaugh.
"The only way to reduce the number of nuclear weapons is to use them."
http://www.addictinginfo.org/2012/03/08/35-hateful-and-stupid-rush-limbaugh-quotes/

Rush Limbaugh.
"This is no different than what happens at the Skull and Bones initiation… I'm talking
about people having a good time, these people, you ever heard of emotional release?
You ever heard of the need to blow some steam off?"
~on the Abu Ghraib prisoner-abuse scandal.
http://politicalhumor.about.com/od/rushlimbaugh/a/limbaughquotes.htm

Rush Limbaugh.
"If you feed them, if you feed the children, three square meals a day during the school
year, how can you expect them to feed themselves in the summer? Wanton little waifs
and serfs dependent on the State. Pure and simple."
~*The Rush Limbaugh Show,* Dec. 2011.
http://www.addictinginfo.org/2012/03/08/35-hateful-and-stupid-rush-limbaugh-quotes/

Rep. Virginia Foxx.
"Fool me once, shame on you. Fool me twice, shame on you."
http://www.youtube.com/watch?v=pm8a3fFM1kw

Arnold Schwarzenegger.
"I think gay marriage is something that should be between a man and a woman."
http://www.rollingstone.com/politics/news/the-10-dumbest-things-ever-said-about-same-sex-marriage-20130627

Pat Robertson.
"The feminist agenda is not about equal rights for women. It is about a socialist, anti-family political movement that encourages women to leave their husbands, kill their children, practice witchcraft, destroy capitalism and become lesbians."
http://politicalhumor.about.com/od/funnyquotes/a/patrobertson.htm

Attorney General Alberto Gonzalez.
"President Washington, President Lincoln, President Wilson, President Roosevelt have all authorized electronic surveillance on a far broader scale." (testifying before Congress)
http://en.wikiquote.org/wiki/Alberto_Gonzales

Herman Cain.
"Don't blame Wall Street, don't blame the big banks, if you don't have a job and you're not rich, blame yourself!"
http://abcnews.go.com/Politics/cain-tells-occupy-wall-street-protesters-blame/story?id=14674829

Herman Cain.
"The more toppings a man has on his pizza, I believe the more manly he is. A manly man don't want it piled high with vegetables! He would call that a sissy pizza."
http://www.cbsnews.com/8301-503544_162-57324204-503544/herman-cain-manly-men-like-more-pizza-toppings/

Rick Perry.
"From time to time there are going to be things that occur that are acts of God that cannot be prevented." (on the BP oil spill in the Gulf of Mexico in 2010)
http://www.politico.com/news/stories/0510/36691.html

Dick Cheney.
"I had other priorities in the sixties than military service." ~ on his five draft deferments
http://www.slate.com/articles/news_and_politics/chatterbox/2000/07/how_dick_cheney_is_like_dan_quayle.html

Michele Bachmann. (Politifact false)
"I will tell you that I had a mother last night come up to me here in Tampa, Florida, after the debate. She told me that her little daughter took that vaccine, that injection, and she suffered from mental retardation thereafter." ~ on the HPV vaccine. (It doesn't cause mental retardation.)
http://www.politifact.com/truth-o-meter/statements/2011/sep/16/michele-bachmann/bachmann-hpv-vaccine-cause-mental-retardation/

Michele Bachmann.
"I find it interesting that it was back in the 1970s that the swine flu broke out under another, then under another Democrat president, Jimmy Carter. I'm not blaming this on President Obama, I just think it's an interesting coincidence." ~
http://politicalhumor.about.com/od/republicans/a/michele-bachmann-quotes.htm

Michele Bachmann.
"Christians must engage in 'spiritual warfare' to combat same-sex marriage."
RS commentary: "This call-to-arms came from Representative Michele Bachmann
(R-Minnesota)—who has also claimed that a teacher who talks about the concept of
gayness with students is engaging in child abuse. This is only one of many horrifically
bigoted statements made by Bachmann, who founded the House Tea Party Caucus and
made sure her hateful beliefs were a key part of the Tea Party agenda."
http://www.rollingstone.com/politics/news/the-10-dumbest-things-ever-said-about-same-sex-marriage-20130627#ixzz2kSRonLS5

Glenn Beck.
"This president, I think, has exposed himself over and over again as a guy who has a
deep-seated hatred for white people or the white culture…. I'm not saying he doesn't
like white people, I'm saying he has a problem. This guy is, I believe, a racist." ~
http://www.newyorker.com/arts/critics/television/2009/11/23/091123crte_television_franklin

Glenn Beck.
"I don't think we came from monkeys. I think that's ridiculous. I haven't seen a
half-monkey/half-person yet."
http://en.wikiquote.org/wiki/Glenn_Beck

Glenn Beck.
"The most used phrase in my administration if I were to be President would be 'What
the hell you mean we're out of missiles?'"
http://en.wikiquote.org/wiki/Glenn_Beck

Glenn Beck.
"I know the progressives are using progressive tactics. They're not using Nazi tactics.
They're—they're—they're— The real answer is the Nazis were using early American
progressive tactics. And that's not my opinion, that's historic fact."
http://en.wikiquote.org/wiki/Glenn_Beck

George W. Bush.
"I'll be long gone before some smart person ever figures out what happened inside this
Oval Office."
http://www.cbsnews.com/8301-503544_162-4876627-503544.html

Rep. Lamar Smith.
"The greatest threat to America is not necessarily a recession or even another terrorist
attack. The greatest threat to America is a liberal media bias."
http://www.thedailybeast.com/articles/2010/01/07/the-gops-terror-wingnuts.html

Michele Bachmann.
"Carbon dioxide is portrayed as harmful. But there isn't even one study that can be produced that shows that carbon dioxide is a harmful gas."
http://www.youtube.com/watch?v=IAaDVOd2sRQ

Rick Santorum.
"Isn't that the ultimate homeland security, standing up and defending marriage?"
http://www.newrepublic.com/article/politics/99240/santorum-surge-2012-vetting-quotes

Mitt Romney.
"I should tell my story. I'm also unemployed."
http://blogs.wsj.com/washwire/2011/06/16/romneys-latest-laugh-line-im-also-unemployed/

Herman Cain.
"I'm ready for the 'gotcha' questions and they're already starting to come. And when they ask me who is the president of Ubeki-beki-beki-beki-stan-stan I'm going to say, you know, I don't know. Do you know?"
http://www.nationaljournal.com/2012-presidential-campaign/cain-says-he-s-ready-for-questions-about-ubeki-beki-beki-beki-stan-stan--20111010

Herman Cain.
"They [China] have indicated that they're trying to develop nuclear capability and they want to develop more aircraft carriers like we have. So yes, we have to consider them a military threat."
—warning that China could develop nuclear weapons. (They developed them in 1964.)
http://www.cbsnews.com/8301-503544_162-20128920-503544/
herman-cain-incorrectly-suggests-china-doesnt-have-nuclear-capability/

Orin Hatch.
"Capital punishment is our way of demonstrating the sanctity of life."
http://en.wikiquote.org/wiki/Talk:Capital_punishment

Mitt Romney.
"I went to a number of women's groups and said: 'Can you help us find folks,' and they brought us whole binders full of women." ~
http://www.theguardian.com/world/shortcuts/2012/oct/17/binders-full-of-women-romneys-four-words

Mitt Romney.
"We have a president, who I think is a nice guy, but he spent too much time at Harvard, perhaps." ~
http://abcnews.go.com/blogs/politics/2012/04/romney-not-the-best-messenger-for-harvard-attacks-on-obama/

Herman Cain.
"We need a leader, not a reader."
http://www.youtube.com/watch?v=2IgWlu_HQ6k

Newt Gingrich.
"The idea that a Congressman would be tainted by accepting money from private sources is essentially a socialist argument." (on sources of funding)
http://en.wikiquote.org/wiki/Newt_Gingrich

Michele Bachmann.
"I think it is high time that we recognize the contribution of our founding fathers who worked tirelessly—men like John Quincy Adams, who would not rest until slavery was extinguished in the country." She was unaware that the Founding Fathers did not work to end slavery and that John Quincy Adams was not one of the Founding Fathers.
http://talkingpointsmemo.com/dc/bachmann-america-was-founded-on-diversity-video

CHAPTER 3

The Disciples
and
being scared of your
own shadow

The difference between stupidity and genius is that genius has its limits.
—popularly but falsely attributed to Albert Einstein

Stupidparty Disciples.

1) 49% Believe Acorn stole 2012 election. PPP 2012. (With no funding, Acorn dissolved in 2010)
   http://www.huffingtonpost.com/2012/12/04/acorn-republican-voters_n_2239298.html

2) 65% Believe higher taxes (on people earning >$400,000) impact them. (Pew Jan. 8, '08)
   http://www.gallup.com/poll/153947/americans-split-whether-taxes-rise.aspx

3) 68% Do not believe in evolution.
   http://www.cbsnews.com/2100-250_162-2917719.htmld/

4) 58% (creationists) Believe the planet to be less than, say, 10,000 years old. (Gallup)
   http://www.huffingtonpost.com/2012/06/05/americans-believe-in-creationism_n_1571127.html

5) 69% Between 2009 and 2011 refused to believe that Global Warming had begun. (Gallup)
   http://www.gallup.com/poll/161714/republican-skepticism-global-warming-eases.aspx

6) 58% Believe Global Warming is a hoax. (PPP 2013)
   http://www.triplepundit.com/2013/04/poll-58-republicans-believe-gloabal-warming-hoax/

7) 75% Believed Iraq was providing substantial support to al Qaeda.
   http://www.worldpublicopinion.org/pipa/articles/brunitedstatescanadara/87.php Oct 21, '04 (after 9/11 Commission Report)

8) 67% Believed Saddam attacked on 9/11.
   http://www.worldpublicopinion.org/pipa/articles/brunitedstatescanadara/87.php Oct 21, '04 (after 9/11 Commission Report)

9) 63% Believed—even in 2012—that Saddam had WMDs.
   http://thinkprogress.org/security/2012/06/21/504201/poll-republicans-iraq-wmd/

10) 51% Are "birthers."
    http://www.politico.com/news/stories/0211/49554.html

11) 57% Believe Obama is a Muslim.
    http://www.thedailybeast.com/articles/2010/03/22/scary-new-gop-poll.html

12) 66% Believe Obama is a socialist.
    http://www.thedailybeast.com/articles/2010/03/22/scary-new-gop-poll.html

13) 24% Believe he may be the Antichrist.
    http://www.huffingtonpost.com/2013/04/03/americans-believe-obama-anti-christ-global-warming-hoax_n_3008558.html

14) 71% Believed in poll "skewerism" before the 2012 election.
    http://www.slate.com/blogs/the_slatest/2012/10/02/unskewed_polls_pollsters_manipulating_data_to_favor_obamaplurality_of_americans_say_.html

15) 67% Believe video games are bigger threat than guns.
    http://livewire.talkingpointsmemo.com/entry/poll-67-percent-of-republicans-think-video-games

16) 84% Approval rating for G. W. Bush. (April 2013)
    http://www.politico.com/story/2013/04/poll-george-w-bush-approval-rating-2013-90484.html?hp=r1

17) 44% Believe armed insurrection might be necessary to protect their freedoms.
    http://www.alternet.org/tea-party-and-right/44-percent-republicans-think-armed-revolution-may-be-necessary-study-finds

18) 72% Believed—as of 2004 election—that Iraq had or was developing WMDs.
    http://www.worldpublicopinion.org/pipa/articles/brunitedstatescanadara/87.php Oct 21, '04 (after 9/11 Commission Report)

19) 57% Believed the world supported G. W. Bush for reelection.
    http://www.worldpublicopinion.org/pipa/articles/brunitedstatescanadara/87.php Oct 21, '04 (after 9/11 Commission Report)

20) 69% Believed G. W. Bush supported international nuclear test-ban treaties.
    http://www.worldpublicopinion.org/pipa/articles/brunitedstatescanadara/87.php Oct 21, 2004 (after 9/11 Commission Report)

21) 87% Were unaware that Bush opposed labor & environmental standards in trade agreements.
http://www.worldpublicopinion.org/pipa/articles/brunitedstatescanadara/87.php Oct 21, 2004 (after 9/11 Commission Report)

22) 62% In Ohio (not the silliest state) do not know whether Mitt deserved equal or more credit than Obama for Bin Laden's death.
http://www.publicpolicypolling.com/pdf/2011/PPP_Release_OH_9912.pdf

23) 90% Are oblivious to the fact that 95% of population had tax cuts at time of 2012 election.
http://www.nytimes.com/2010/10/19/us/politics/19taxes.html

24) 22% In Mississippi believe in evolution. 12% believe Obama a Christian.
http://www.publicpolicypolling.com/main/2012/03/other-notes-from-alabama-and-mississippi.html

25) 73% Believe raising the debt ceiling is for future expenditures, 54% Believe the debt ceiling is no big deal.
http://www.nationaljournal.com/congressional-connection/coverage/poll-most-americans-don-t-understand-the-debt-ceiling-20131008

26) Believe Hurricane Katrina occurred after Obama became President. Who do Louisiana Republicans say was to blame for the poor handling of Katrina? 29% Obama 28% Bush 44% Do not know (PPP poll 8/21/2013).
http://www.huffingtonpost.com/2013/08/21/obama-hurricane-katrina_n_3790612.html

Key Clues to Stupidparty.
For the sake of succinctness and ironic humor this list may be somewhat oversimplified.

1) Creationism.
2) Obama a Muslim.
3) Obama born in Kenya.
4) Obama Antichrist.
5) Obama socialist dictator
6) Evolution denier.
7) Global Warming denial.
8) Iraq attacked us on 9/11.
9) Rape does not cause pregnancy.
10) Austerity during deflation.
11) Second Amendment right to bear arms not impacted by various Supreme Court decisions.
12) Mental illness a significant cause of America's "gun problem" (defined later).
13) Violence on TV a significant cause of America's gun problem.
14) Video games a significant cause of America's gun problem.
15) No new taxes of any type.
16) No new regulations of any type.
17) Illegal immigrants bad for the economy.
18) Dislike of birth control.

19) Healthcare by bartering Chickens.

20) Fox News fair and balanced.

21) Jesus disliked gays.

22) Efforts to ratchet up fear of black-on-white crime (450 interracial murders, while higher than 218 white-on-black, is a drop in the bucket relative to 40,000 auto vehicle deaths; i.e., cars are 100x more dangerous).

23) Top Stupidparty (supporting) blog bans the quoting of facts from fact-checking sites. http://www.redstate.com/2012/09/11/quote-a-factchecker-earn-a-ban/

24) Facts are not relevant.

25) God told me to run.

26) Believing election fraud is a significant issue.

27) Voter suppression good for democracy.

28) Believing that Stupidparty would win the 2012 election in the days before the election.

29) Joe the plumber, he's not.

30) Chanting "USA! USA! USA!" as solution to climate change.
http://www.huffingtonpost.com/2012/11/01/mitt-romney-heckled-climate-silence_n_2059174.html

31) Booing a gay soldier (Florida primary debate audience). See it here:
http://www.washingtonpost.com/blogs/compost/post/with-gop-debate-crowd-it-gets-worse--booing-a-gay-soldier/2011/09/23/gIQAKcN3qK_blog.html

32) Believing Romney or G. W. Bush was respected by international community.

33) Unlimited money in campaigns is good for democracy

34) Poor people are Lazy.

35) Black people are Lazy.

36) Mexicans are moochers.

37) Europeans are... are... all like Greece... all socialists . . .

38) Women are less equal.

39) Highly educated people are elitists.

40) Teachers are subversive.

41) Scientists are wrong.

42) White race is superior.

43) Red states do not need handouts.

44) The funders of the Stupidparty care about the Disciples.

45) More money in politics equals less corruption.

46) The interests of people and corporations are the same.

47) Asset Stripping is good for the taxpayer.

48) Trickle down is better than trickle Up

Religious eccentricities.

I do not want to give the impression that I have a big issue with religious eccentricities. Usually I do not. I was brought up in a religious environment, my monastic-like boarding "high school" having the largest school chapel in the world, with the largest rose window in England—all for us 500 or so kids. We went to this chapel roughly twice a week and also studied scripture from age seven to eighteen. When in other countries, I am never really bothered by religious dogma. I have a genuine admiration for "eccentric" groups like, say, the Amish. I believe that they are great "stewards of the land." I support their efforts, happy for them to expand. I have faith that they have a superior product and that they mean well and just want to be left alone to live their lives as they see fit. They do not vote; there is no ambition (that I am aware of) to install an Amish president and no efforts to preach to me and no danger of my being forced to dress in black.

If a tribe in the Amazon or in Utah wants men to have ten wives or women to have ten husbands, all wearing homemade golden silk socks on one foot from dusk to dawn— and that makes everyone happy—then I am fine with that. If they are obviously happy, I might even give it a shot myself. But them voting in a president to rule over me and represent me to the international community, then I think not.

Evangelicals, because they are such damned good voters, represent the other extreme. I am supersensitive to their eccentricities because they want me to swap rational thinking for blind faith. They have the political cohesion to take us all back to the Dark Ages. They want me to live in their matrix, a world where reality cannot be allowed to even exist. And for those evangelicals who are less strident, my rebuttal is you have chosen to align your religion with the Stupidparty; therefore, your religion is guilty of the same sins as the Stupidparty. That still leaves about 20% of evangelicals that I am perhaps criticizing unfairly.

Facts losing to Myth.

While the theory of evolution is considered both a fact and a theory, similar to the theory of gravity, it is a plain fact that there has been life on Earth for hundreds of millions of years. Dinosaurs did exist, for their fossils have been found and are on display in numerous places, and they did exist a very, very long time ago, because their bones have been carbon dated.

Before drilling down on numbers, I often like to take international statistics, in order to create a benchmark to analyse how various U.S. states hold up against both international and domestic comparisons. In this particular subject, I could not find a breakdown by U.S. state. But we do know that only about 22% of Mississipians and 26% of Alabama "folk" believe in evolution, and those numbers would no doubt shrink even further if one stripped out the lonely Democratic voters in those states.

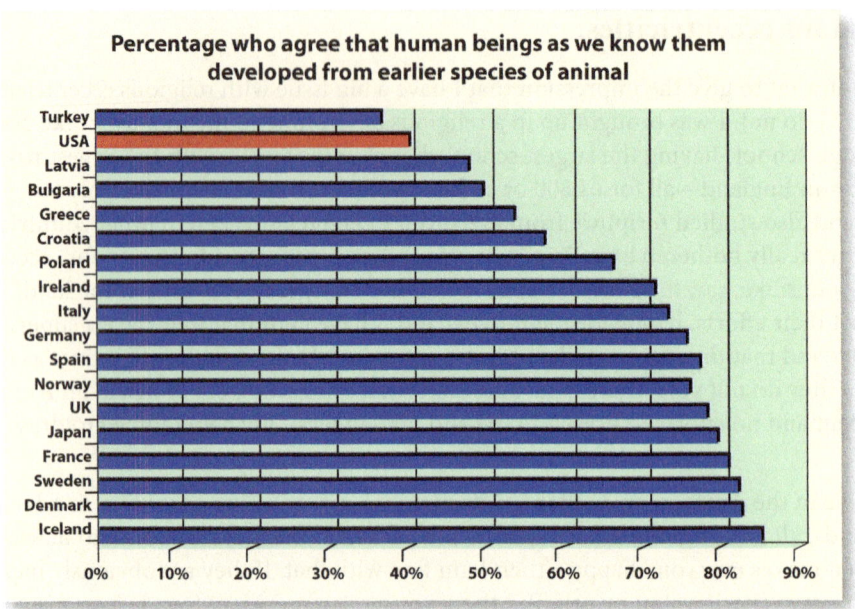

Percentage who agree that human beings as we know them developed from earlier species of animal

http://www.publicpolicypolling.com/main/2012/03/other-notes-from-alabama-and-mississippi.html

One quite well known quote on evolution comes from the author of the biology-focused book (for this is a biological question) *The Selfish Gene,* Professor Richard Dawkins:

In the chapter "Why are people?" he writes:

"Intelligent life on a planet comes of age when it first works out the reason for its own existence. If superior creatures from space ever visit earth, the first question they will ask, in order to assess the level of our civilization, is: 'Have they discovered evolution yet?'"

"Have they discovered evolution yet?"

In the USA only 40% accept evolution, half of what one would expect.

Here is the Generic Political split

Political identification	Creationist	Believe in evolution	NA
Republican	60%	11%	29%
Democrat	29%	44%	27%

http://upload.wikimedia.org/wikipedia/en/b/b5/Views_on_Evolution.jpg 2005 Pew Research Center poll

In lieu of a U.S. state breakdown, we can do a breakdown by religious affiliation, which perhaps in this instance is more revealing.

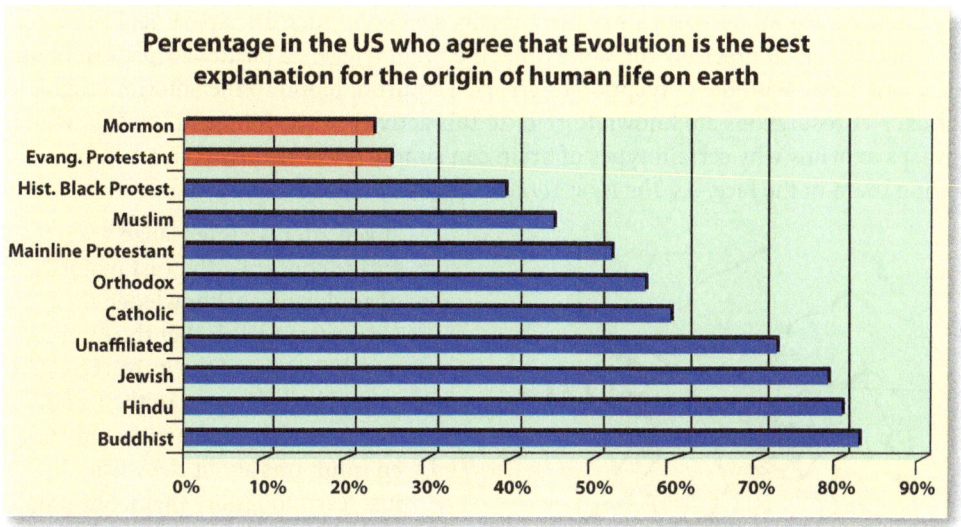

Percentage in the US who agree that Evolution is the best explanation for the origin of human life on earth

http://upload.wikimedia.org/wikipedia/en/b/b5/Views_on_Evolution.jpg
http://en.wikipedia.org/wiki/Level_of_support_for_evolution

Evangelicals appear to be in good company, and as a block they vote for Stupidparty more reliably than any other significant grouping. Taking the above charts, along with stats on Mississippi and Alabama, one can now start connecting the dots to figure out where creationists are going to be most concentrated. Probably less than 20% of Disciples who live in Red states believe in evolution—one quarter of what one would expect, all things being equal.

Less than 20% believe in evolution… truly awe-inspiring levels of… um… eccentricity.

Why is it that facts, when battling fiction, do not always come out on top?

Our gut informs us that stuff we have been erroneously taught or "brainwashed" about, possibly since birth, must simply be true. For the incurious, the story apparently ends there. However, if one's life depended on it, I suspect even the most calcified of brains could learn new tricks. But how can the brain be so "deceiving"?

Luckily, science, in the form of a study in cognition by Andrew Shtulman at Occidental College, can shed some light.

Most nonphysicists believe that if you dropped two balls of similar shapes (but one ball being obviously more massive than the other) from a great height at the same time, the heavier ball would land first. That is what our gut would tell us.

But even when nonphysicists are confronted by a video of such an experiment showing the balls landing at precisely the same time, the brain triggers a particular pattern of activity associated with the perception of errors, a squirt of blood to the anterior cingulate cortex. Neurosurgeons are known to refer to this activity as the "oh, shit!" circuit, which perhaps explains why certain types of brain can simply reject reality, even when it is staring them in the face. As *The New Yorker* reports:

"IF I COULD JUST FIGURE THIS OUT, IT'S GOODBYE NEANDERTHAL, HELLO HOMO SAPIENS."

"Even after we internalize a scientific concept—the vast majority of adults now acknowledge the Copernican truth that the earth is not the center of the universe—that primal belief lingers in the mind. We never fully unlearn our mistaken intuitions about the world. We just learn to ignore them. Shtulman and colleagues summarize their findings: 'When students learn scientific theories that conflict with earlier, naïve theories, what happens to the earlier theories? Our findings suggest that naïve theories are suppressed by scientific theories but not supplanted by them.'"

http://www.newyorker.com/online/blogs/frontal-cortex/2012/06/brain-experiments-why-we-dont-believe-science.html
Cartoons: Sydney Harris. ScienceCartoonsPlus.com

The mind of a Stupidparty Disciple

So while those of us born not blessed with the bliss of ignorance mull over issues like alleviating poverty, pollution, wars and illegal wars, bigotry, etc., the people we would so like to converse with tend to disappear into their fully Fox-equipped caves and cyber miscommunicate in a fact-devoid world of fear and paranoia. They waste countless resources on never-ending nonsense. Let's see what they come up with when thinking about just one quite talented and extraordinarily disciplined and patient Black guy:

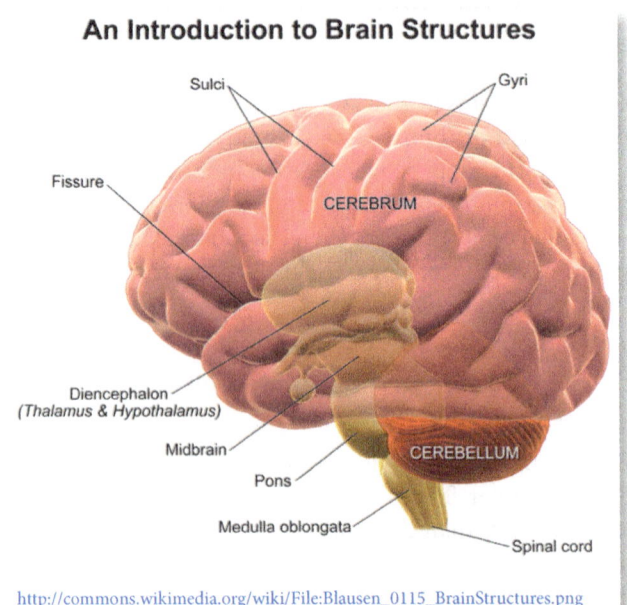

An Introduction to Brain Structures

Sulci

Gyri

Fissure

CEREBRUM

Diencephalon
(Thalamus & Hypothalamus)

Midbrain

Pons

Medulla oblongata

CEREBELLUM

Spinal cord

http://commons.wikimedia.org/wiki/File:Blausen_0115_BrainStructures.png

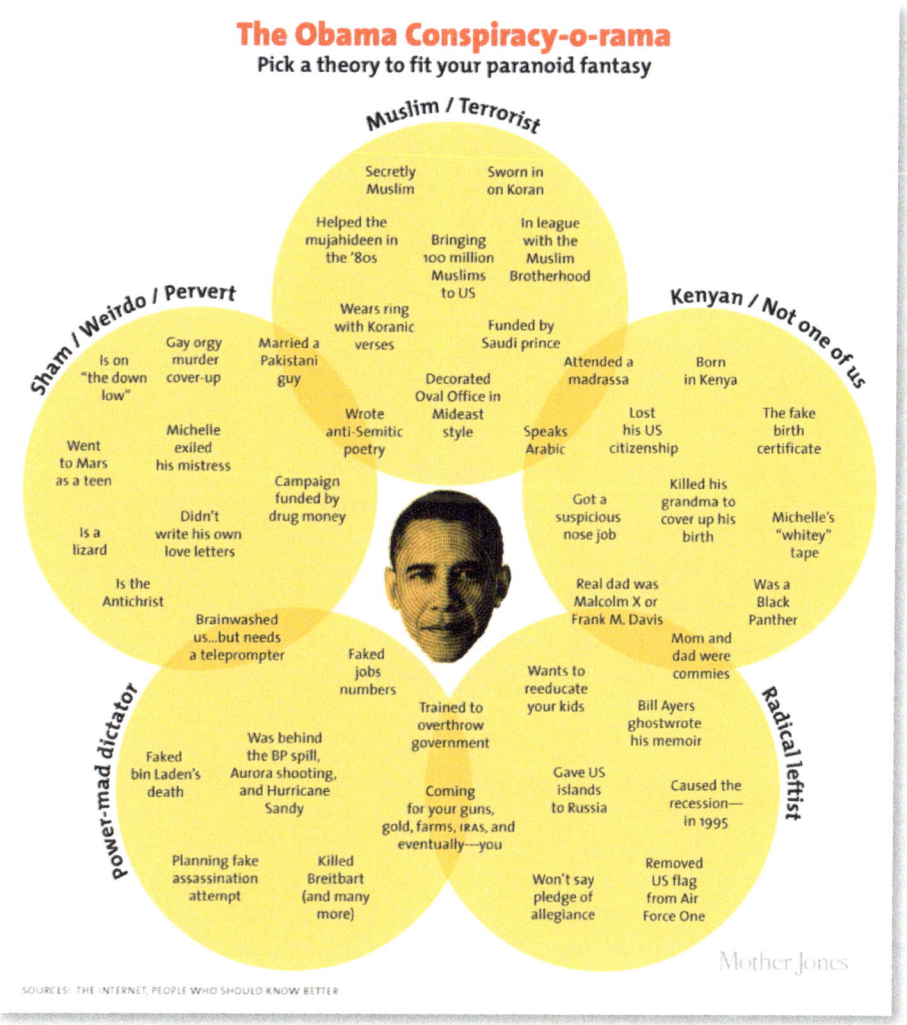

The Obama Conspiracy-o-rama
Pick a theory to fit your paranoid fantasy

Links to all these conspiracies can be found here:
http://www.motherjones.com/politics/2012/10/chart-obama-conspiracy-theories

The Stupidparty brain:

Fear makes man unwise in the three great departments of human conduct: his dealings with nature, his dealings with other men, and his dealings with himself. Until you have admitted your own fears to yourself, and have guarded yourself by a difficult effort of will against their myth-making power, you cannot hope to think truly about many matters of great importance.
—Bertrand Russell ("Outline of Intellectual Rubbish" in *Unpopular Essays*, 1950)

"Numerous political psychologists have commented on the right's 'Darwinian' dangerous-world metaphor. The Authoritarian Personality group at UC Berkeley remarked how highly ethnocentric subjects had 'a conception of a dangerous and hostile world' that resembled an 'oversimplified survival-of-the-fittest idea.' Others who have linked folk-Darwinism's dangerous-world motif to conservatism include the British psychi-

atrist Roger Money-Kyrle (1951), Princeton political psychologist Fred Greenstein (1975), and Berkeley metaphor theorist George Lakoff (2002)."
http://www.salon.com/2013/09/15/inside_the_conservative_brain_what_explains_their_wiring/

"Research suggests that conservatives are, on average, more susceptible to fear than those who identify themselves as liberals. Looking at MRIs of a large sample of young adults last year, researchers at University College London discovered that 'greater conservatism was associated with increased volume of the right amygdala.' The amygdala is an ancient brain structure that's activated during states of fear and anxiety. (The researchers also found that 'greater liberalism was associated with increased gray matter volume in the anterior cingulate cortex'—a region in the brain that is believed to help people manage complexity.)"
http://www.alternet.org/story/155210/why_is_the_conservative_brain_more_fearful_the_alternate_reality_right-wingers_inhabit_is_terrifying

"From climate change to evolution, the rejection of mainstream science among Republicans is growing, as is the denial of expert consensus on the economy, American history, foreign policy and much more. Why won't Republicans accept things that most experts agree on? Why are they constantly fighting against the facts? Science writer Chris Mooney explores brain scans, polls, and psychology experiments to explain why conservatives today believe more wrong things; appear more likely than Democrats to oppose new ideas and less likely to change their beliefs in the face of new facts; and sometimes respond to compelling evidence by doubling down on their current beliefs."
http://www.amazon.com/The-Republican-Brain-Science-Science/dp/1118094514

"ProCon.org has gathered 13 peer-reviewed studies of behavioral and neurological studies and come to the conclusion that differences between Republicans and Democrats are more than skin-deep. 'Basically, the different sides have been yelling at each other for millennia, and we're trying to figure out what could be the root cause of this,' said Steven Markoff, ProCon.org's founder. The studies looked at things like differences between groups' perception of eye movement, and aversion to threatening noises. Researchers also noted that Democrats had larger anterior cingulate cortexes, which are associated with tolerance to uncertainty, while Republicans had larger right amygdalae, which are associated with sensitivity to fear… Markoff concluded the studies combine to mean that the different groups communicate in different ways [and] psychiatrist Greg Appelbaum said the studies point toward conservatives' tendency to avoid something called self-harm, while liberals avoid collective group harm."
http://abcnews.go.com/blogs/health/2012/09/03/conservatives-and-liberals-have-different-brains-studies-show/

"There's no gentle way to put it: People who give in to racism and prejudice may simply be dumb, according to a new study that is bound to stir public controversy. The research finds that children with low intelligence are more likely to hold prejudiced attitudes as adults. These findings point to a vicious cycle, according to lead researcher Gordon Hodson, a psychologist at Brock University in Ontario. Low-intelligence adults tend to gravitate toward socially conservative ideologies, the study found. Those ideologies, in turn, stress hierarchy and resistance to change, attitudes that can contribute to prejudice, Hodson wrote in an email to LiveScience."
http://www.livescience.com/18132-intelligence-social-conservatism-racism.html

"In a study that is bound to incite controversy, Canadian researchers at Brock University in Ontario have published the results of a research project in the academic journal

Psychological Science, that they say demonstrates that people with lower intelligence are more likely to be conservative in their political views than are those that are more liberal."

http://voices.yahoo.com/controversial-canadian-study-says-conservative-people-10924582.html
http://www.huffingtonpost.com/2012/01/27/intelligence-study-links-prejudice_n_1237796.html

Evolutionary psychologist Satoshi Kanazawa at the London School of Economics and Political Science correlated data on these behaviors with IQ from a large national U.S. sample and found that, on average, people who identified as liberal and atheist had higher IQs.

http://www.cnn.com/2010/HEALTH/02/26/liberals.atheists.sex.intelligence

Undoubtedly, there are legitimate studies from groups not sponsored by the Koch brothers that might point to different types of weaknesses in a "liberal" brain—evidently conservative college students have tidier, better-organized rooms with more calendars and ironing boards—but less books and travel memorabilia. The scientists who publish these studies seemed to have arrived at a consensus; however, they are very careful in how they present their results, more careful than the sensationalist media tends to be. For what is a conservative brain? Many people would argue that they are fiscally conservative; I argue that I am fiscally conservative. Just by "self-identifying" as a conservative does not make it so. The concept is also relative: one may have a conservative brain in Europe that morphs into a communist one as it breaches U.S. air space. But I am not overly sympathetic to all these nuances, when proffered as a sometimes-legitimate fig leaf, because by being both a fiscal conservative and a Stupidparty disciple, such individuals are an existential threat through the agenda they (unwittingly?) help to drive. So it is not simply genes that determine how one "self-identifies"; there are uniquely powerful cultural factors that drive this determination—factors that will be explained later in the book.

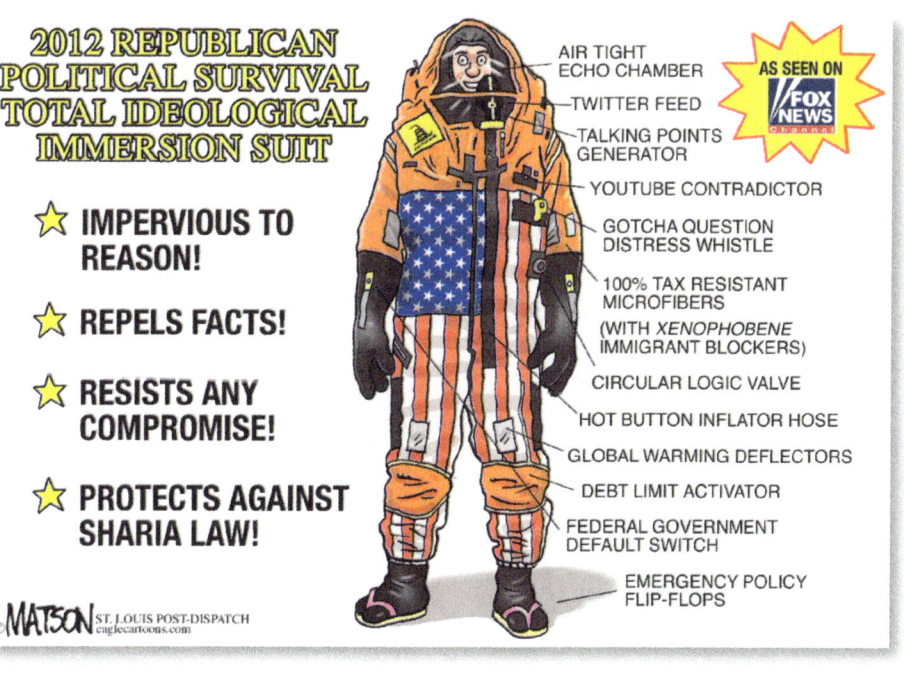

So all brains are fallible and liable, if left unchecked, to keep us in the dark. Then on top of that, the conservative brain has its own set of baggage. With its heightened sense of fear, it can become more susceptible to demagoguery, leading to a reflexive and uncontrollable urge to reach for the pitchfork. Think about that conservative brain, living in the old Confederate South or more accurately in some regions trying to re-create the old Confederate South, when confronted with the generally accepted science that we have all evolved from a primate, perhaps from Africa. I do not think one would need a CAT scan to actually see that "oh, shit!" circuit kicking into overdrive.

Religion in itself does not have to add fuel to the fire—but when only the demagogues get to use the bully pulpit, one needs to start asking why. How can such an alternate myth-driven reality occur? Why are so many people determined to live in history rather than learn from it? Who is really behind all the nonsense? Who is pulling the strings, and why do so many people fall for it? Because we are in an escalating vicious circle of ignorance, always tending to fall further behind the benchmarks—a society finding it more and more difficult to tackle relatively easy problems in a rational manner. Gradually, I hope that the answer will take shape, as all the pieces to the puzzle begin to come together.

The base,
where they are
strong & weak

"I think you should be more
explicit here in step two."

There are two political truisms: Old people vote and Republicans eat their young.

—Eddie Whitlock

Stupidparty, where they dominate—and where they are weak.

Stupidparty Wins by >10%		Stupidparty losses by >10%	
1 Utah	73%	1 DC	91%
2 Wyoming	69%	2 Hawaii	71%
3 Oklahoma	67%	3 Vermont	67%
4 Idaho	65%	4 New York	63%
5 West Virginia	62%	5 Rhode Island	63%
6 Arkansas	61%	6 Maryland	62%
7 Alabama	61%	7 Massachusetts	61%
8 Kentucky	60%	8 California	60%
9 Nebraska	60%	9 Delaware	59%
10 Kansas	60%	10 New Jersey	58%
11 Tennessee	59%	11 Connecticut	58%
12 North Dakota	58%	12 Illinois	58%
13 South Dakota	58%	13 Maine	56%
14 Louisiana	58%	14 Washington	56%
15 Texas	57%		
16 Montana	55%		
17 Mississippi	55%		
18 Alaska	55%		

Source Wiki 2012 Presidential election

I tend to avoid including Washington DC on the various lists, as the people of DC for some obscure reason are largely and inequitably disenfranchised, having no congressional representation.

Utah comes with its own unique set of issues, being that they are over 50% Mormon. So while normal explanations of behavior may not apply, Utah does create an additional layer of nuance, when trying to analyze why so many people are oblivious to introspection, determinedly in denial of facts, science, and critical thinking—virtues that are vital in a healthy democracy.

Some basic understanding of Mormonism would certainly help illustrate how easy it is for charismatic charlatans (Hitler, Mao, Ron Hubbard, Jim Jones, various expired doomsday cults, Roger Ailes,* and of course Joseph Smith*) to mislead very large groups of people and can serve as cautionary tales of how gullible people can be.
* These individuals will be discussed later.

Shrinking Stupidparty base. As the number of older white males shrinks, the core remnants must scream louder and cheat ever more creatively

1) Higher Levels of Education.
Stupidparty has become quite hostile to higher education. Let's figure out why.

Before the Stupidparty was born, going back to 1984, people who had advanced degrees made up about 35% of the electorate. Back then Reagan performed extremely well amongst the college educated. People who attended college and those who secured advanced degrees voted for Reagan by about 63% to 37%.

But since 1984 the trend has been moving to the Democrats. A McClatchy-Marist poll, conducted in March 2012, indicated that Obama now had a 51–42 advantage with this group.

Compounding the problem for the Stupidparty is the fact that these higher-educated groups are becoming a larger segment of the electorate. According to this, people without college degrees go for Romney over Obama 49–40.

Historically, repressive regimes targeted the "elites," eradicated them before all else. Regimes such as of Stalin, Mao, or Pol Pot (who would kill people who wore glasses) and Hitler *(Mein Kampf)* were all anti-intellectual. Same with religious revolutionaries like Khomeini, and we all know how centuries ago the Christian religious establishment feared Galileo or Charles Darwin. This group, these "elites," had to be silenced before such dictators could be free to execute their agenda. These oppressors were terrified, are terrified, of the highly educated, the artists, the writers, the teachers, the filmmakers— the so-called elites (for that is the label most likely to resonate amongst those who get their hands dirty for a living, the hardworking and often highly skilled struggling class). Because it is these "elites" who are most able to scratch below the surface, read between the lines, bear witness, record, and empathize with the oppressed. It is these elites that most understand the human condition and are the most likely people to take on, to mock, to expose the oppressors—in this case, as we will soon unmask, better described as the Benefactors.

So now one can begin to understand why the Stupidparty disdains higher education. One begins to understand why Rick Santorum, who appears to disdain secular education, labels the more highly educated as the Elite, and people trying to assist qualified aspirants to further their education as Snobs. God forbid that we are to learn that the Crusaders were not primarily populated by people with a good Christian heart—but more likely by sons of noblemen who had no inheritance (by virtue of the fact that they had an elder brother) and thus headed off to the Middle East searching for fame and fortune. Somewhat akin to Dick Cheney and his Big Oil Industry brethren.

Note: This book does not attempt to discuss education policy in the USA, as it was never a topic that I have spent much time considering. However, I do suspect that the charter school solution may become a stalking horse for the Benefactors (and even worse groups*), taking direct aim at the public schools and threatening democracy. Charter schools are probably not outperforming public schools. None of the countries with a vibrant educational system have gone down this road. The Asset Strippers, when they get involved, do not understand or care about education. I suspect charter schools should return to their original mission—to focus on underachieving children. The motivation should be to strengthen, not to destroy public education. I have not read *Reign of Terror* by Diane Ravitch yet—but before presuming that charter schools are the solution, I suspect that this should be a must read. This book questions "the sincerity of conservative foundations [SP] backing the movement in an effort to dismantle public education." * The Gulen charter schools are the largest charter chain in the country. Ironically, I suspect that people like Rick Santorum and people like me might be equally perturbed at the powers that control these schools.

2) Same Pattern for Professionals.

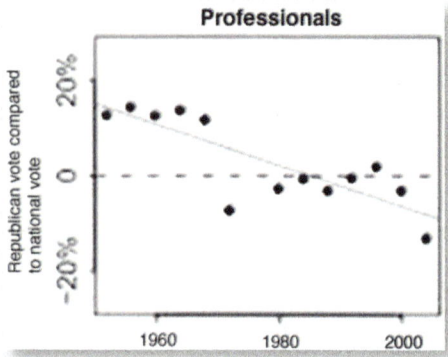

http://campaignstops.blogs.nytimes.com/2012/04/01/the-politics-of-going-to-college/?_r=0

3) Stupidparty and Religion.

Nearly eight-in-ten white evangelical Protestants voted for Romney (79%), compared with 20% who backed Obama. As in other recent elections, those who attend religious services most often exhibited the strongest support for the Republican presidential candidate. Nearly six-in-ten voters who say they attend religious services at least once a week voted for Romney (59%), while 39% backed Obama.

http://www.pewforum.org/2012/11/07/how-the-faithful-voted-2012-preliminary-exit-poll-analysis/

4) Stupidparty Rural v. Urban.

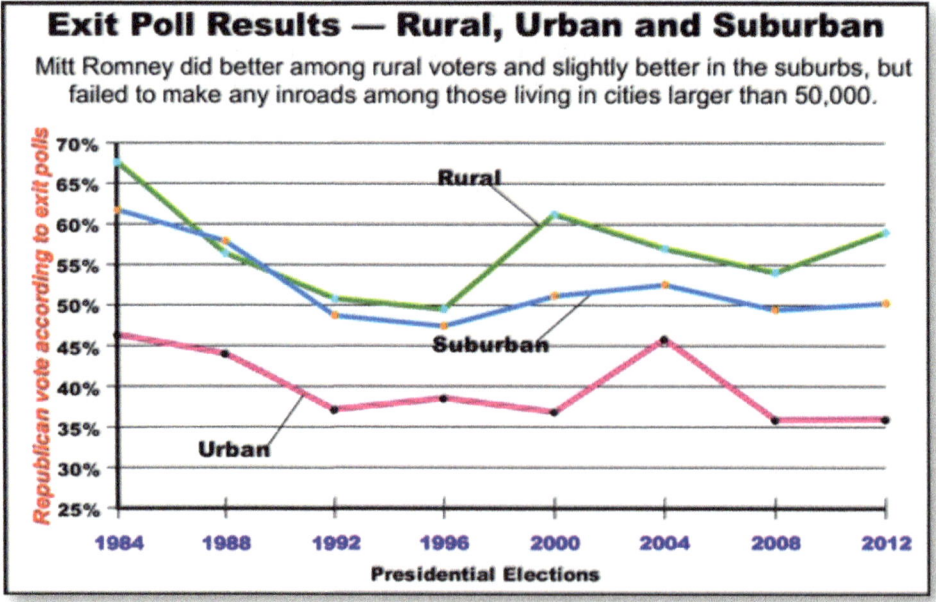

http://www.dailyyonder.com/exit-polls-romney-improves-rural/2012/11/07/4912

5) Aging White Men.

Age by race	Total	Obama	Romney
White 18–29	11%	44%	51%
White 30–44	18%	38%	59%
White 45–64	29%	38%	61%
White 65+	14%	39%	61%

	Total	Obama	Romney
All White Men.	34%	35%	62%

I am confident that there would be an even larger gap for white men over 65.
http://www.foxnews.com/politics/elections/2012-exit-poll

6) Why Does Stupidparty have to live in the past?

Before 1870, only white men could vote. Here's how the 2012 election would have looked before that pesky Fifteenth Amendment.

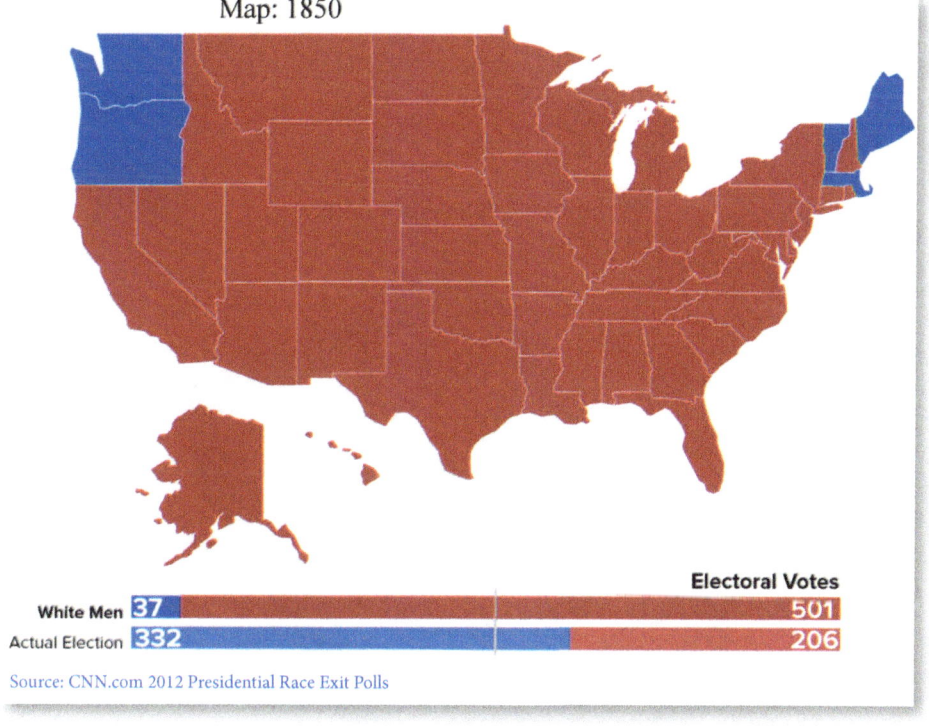

Map: 1850

	Electoral Votes	
White Men	37	501
Actual Election	332	206

Source: CNN.com 2012 Presidential Race Exit Polls

http://www.buzzfeed.com/buzzfeedpolitics/what-the-2012-election-would-have-looked-like-with

Why does Stupidparty fear democracy in the USA?

The above maps changes as

a) 1870—Black Men can vote.

b) 1920—Women can vote.

While women's suffrage passed in 1920, there were still huge impediments to minority vote during that period, for instance, in the form of poll taxes (only finally outlawed by the Twenty-Fourth Amendment, in 1964).

c) 1970—Voting age lowered to 18.

Debt is a big driver for Stupidparty.

One would think that the state of the economy would be more important than the debt, as a healthy economy would be better able to handle any debt fears; also, economic numbers such as inflation or unemployment rates are easier to quantify than any specific debt number—an issue that can be quite obscure and easily misunderstood. (Further, by looking at the numbers below, one has to wonder, Why does Stupidparty keep focusing on repealing Obamacare?)

Which ONE of these four issues is the most important facing the country? (CHECK ONLY ONE)

	Total	Obama	Romney
Foreign policy	5%	56%	33%
Federal budget deficit	5%	32%	66%
The economy	59%	47%	51%
Healthcare	18%	75%	24%

Sample: 10,798 respondents

http://www.foxnews.com/politics/elections/2012-exit-poll

While Stupidparty is stuck in the past, even the smartest technology will backfire.

CHAPTER 5

How is it working out for ya?

For an entire wing of the G.O.P., a dysfunctional government, whose only visible activity is mismanaging crises, is not an embarrassment but the vindication of a worldview.

—Amy Davidson

How is the Stupidparty helping out its most fervent Disciples?
(Healthcare will be discussed in Chapter 7)

A) Poverty.

Comparing poverty amongst different nations is quite complex, but however you slice the numbers (the World Bank, the CIA—take your pick), the USA ranking is quite pitiful. Stupidparty thinking simply stops at the closest boundary and if you throw out a country like Norway then they simply yell "socialist." What is wrong with poverty anyway?—moochers deserve poverty—I guess Children deserve the same level of empathy, the same lack of introspection.

Child Poverty Rank	Av ranking, All Criteria See below*	Relative Child Poverty	Child Poverty Gaps
Netherlands	4.2	2	3
Sweden	5.0	7	8
Denmark	7.2	3	21
Finland	7.5	1	5
Spain	8.0	26	29
Switzerland	8.3	10	12
Norway	8.1	5	7
Italy	10.0	24	25
Ireland	10.2	9	26
Belgium	10.7	16	16
Germany	11.2	11	9
Canada	11.8	21	13
Greece	11.8	n/a	18
Poland	12.3	20	17
Czech Republic	12.5	13	15
France	13.0	12	6
Portugal	13.7	22	19
Austria	13.8	8	4
Hungary	14.5	15	2
United States	18.0	28	28
United Kingdom	18.2	14	14

The first column is a combination of various criteria including material, health and safety, and educational wellbeing. (http://en.wikipedia.org/wiki/List_of_U.S._states_by_poverty_rate)

Highest rates of Poverty By Household Income	%	Numbers '''000,s
#1 Mississippi	20.1%	571
2 Louisiana	18.3%	748
3 New Mexico	17.9%	347
4 Alabama	16.7%	750
5 Texas	16.2%	3,681
6 Arkansas	15.9%	509
7 Oklahoma	15.6%	543
8 West Virginia	15.4%	276
9 Arizona	15.2%	917
10 South Carolina	15.0%	626
Total		8,968

Lowest rates of Poverty By Household Income	%	Numbers '''000,s
#1 New Hampshire	5.6%	73
2 New Jersey	6.8%	592
3 Vermont	7.6%	47
4 Minnesota	8.1%	412
5 Hawaii	8.6%	110
6 Delaware	9.2%	78
7 Utah	9.2%	231
8 Virginia	9.2%	684
9 Connecticut	9.7%	326
10 Nebraska	9.5%	167
Total		2,720

B) Education. The Organization for Economic Co-operation and Development (OECD) school league tables, published Dec. 2013, compare 15-year-olds' abilities in core academic subjects across 65 countries.

COMPARISON COUNTRY / ECONOMY	Mean Score Reading Rank	Math Rank	Science Rank
1 Shanghai-China	570		
2 Hong Kong-China	545		
3 Singapore	542		
4 Japan	538		
5 Korea	536		
6 Finland	524		
7 Ireland	523		
8 Chinese Taipei	523		
9 Canada	523		
10 Poland	518		
11 Estonia	516		
12 Liechtenstein	516		
13 New Zealand	512		
14 Australia	512		
15 Netherlands	511		
16 Belgium	509		
17 Switzerland	509		
18 Macao-China	509		
19 Vietnam	508		
20 Germany	508		
21 France	505		
22 Norway	504		
23 United Kingdom	499		
24 United States	498	36	28
25 Denmark	496		

http://www.telegraph.co.uk/education/leaguetables/10488555/OECD-education-report-subject-results-in-full.html

Education Top States by Undergraduate degree	
1 Massachusetts	38.2%
2 Colorado	35.9%
3 Maryland	35.7%
4 Connecticut	35.6%
5 New Jersey	34.5%
6 Virginia	34.0%
7 Vermont	33.1%
8 New York	32.4%
9 New Hampshire	32.0%
10 Minnesota	31.5%
11 Washington	31.0%
12 Illinois	30.6%
13 Rhode Island	30.5%
14 California	29.9%
15 Hawaii	29.6%

Education Worst States by Undergraduate degree	
1 Arkansas	18.9%
2 Mississippi	19.6%
3 Kentucky	21.0%
4 Louisiana	21.4%
5 Nevada	21.8%
6 Alabama	22.0%
7 Indiana	22.5%
8 Oklahoma	22.7%
9 Tennessee	23.0%
10 Wyoming	23.8%

http://en.wikipedia.org/wiki/List_of_U.S._states_by_educational_attainment
http://commons.wikimedia.org/wiki/File:Olivehurst,_Yuba_County,_California._Child_of_parents_who_were_migratory_workers,_now_settling_in_Ol_._._._-_NARA_-_521604.jpg

C) Quality of life.

Rank	Country or Territory	Quality of Life Score		Rank	Happiest State	Unhappiest
1	Ireland	8.333		1	Hawaii	W. Virginia
2	Switzerland	8.068		2	Colorado	Kentucky
3	Norway	8.051		3	Minnesota	Mississippi
4	Luxembourg	8.015		4	Utah	Tennessee
5	Sweden	7.937		5	Vermont	Arkansas
6	Australia	7.925		6	Montana	Alabama
7	Iceland	7.911		7	Nebraska	Ohio
8	Italy	7.810		8	New Hampshire	Louisiana
9	Denmark	7.797		9	Iowa	Indiana
10	Spain	7.727		10	Massachusetts	Oklahoma
11	Singapore	7.719				
12	Finland	7.618				
13	United States	7.615				
14	Canada	7.599				
15	New Zealand	7.436				
16	Netherlands	7.433				

Wiki International Table http://www.businessinsider.com/happiest-states-2013-2?op=1
http://www.nydailynews.com/life-style/hawaii-happiest-state-west-virginia-unhappiest-article-1.1280936

As the *International Business Times* reported May 2011:

Some states are depressive because of the economic instability and the inadequate access to healthcare. Here are the top 10 most depressing states in the U.S.

1. Arkansas

This is one of the rural southern states that ranked low because of several concerns on mental health, especially among young adults. Suicidal rate is high. As a result, many families are affected by mental illness.

2. Indiana

This Rust Belt state has constantly struggled with economic instability, high unemployment rate, and enormous budget downfalls. The financial trouble directly affects the mental-health care. As a result of budget problems, a lot of community health centers closed down or downsized. There is even a shortage of psychiatrists.

3. Kentucky

Poor mental health is one of the biggest social problem concerns of the government. This is brought about by the unemployment and drug abuse. Without good and sustainable jobs, they won't be able to support families. As a result, more would get depressed and anxious making them turn to drug abuse.

4. Michigan

Residents are feeling more distressed because of the high unemployment rate in this place. The state misfortunes have resulted to psychological fallout for many individuals.

5. Mississippi

Sad to say, Mississippi is the poorest state in the U.S. There are so many concerns to focus on in this area, like obesity, heart disease, and mental-health disorders. It even has the highest depression rate as rated by the Center for Disease Control and Prevention.

6. Missouri

Serious psychological distressed is at 13%. However, the Show-Me State has taken action and is now preventing and treating mental-health illnesses. They have integrated a primary mental-health care much like a Mental Health First Aid. It is a program that trains teachers, policemen, and the like to identify symptoms of mental illness.

7. Nevada

Nevada is always linked to partying, gambling, and having a carefree life. But it is opposite in reality. One in eleven residents has suffered a major depression. Such problems worsen before they get cured. Because of the financial crisis, many have lost their jobs and suffered huge emotional distress.

8. Oklahoma

Even the official state rock song can attest to the depressive state of this place. Because it's always stricken with a calamity brought about by severe weather, they never seem to overcome the poverty rate.

9. Tennessee

When you hear the word Tennessee, you can then picture out Memphis and Nashville. These are two of the famous areas known for the country and blues music. Sad to say, it is the unhappiest state to be in. 10% of residents suffered major depression. Not only that, there are high rates of obesity and diabetes that further lead to depression.

10. West Virginia

West Virginia is a mountain state [that] ranked last in the mental-health category. They have high rates of unhappy people wherein 15% suffer mental and emotional distress every single day. Because the state has two-thirds of Virginians living in rural areas, access to mental-health care is limited. Also, in 2000, a study found out that one in three residents had high episodes of depression.

http://www.ibtimes.com/10-most-depressing-states-live-283529

D) Unhealthiest States. Ranking by Issue

Unhealthiest States							
	Obesity	Air Pollution	Lack of Health Ins	Immu-nisation	Primary Care Physicians	Cardio Deaths	Cancer Deaths
Louisiana	47	35	47	39	20	45	49
Mississippi	50	29	46	34	48	50	46
South Carolina	44	37	34	17	34	36	38
Tennessee	47	41	27	22	17	47	47
Texas	39	33	50	38	42	30	15
Florida	10	13	48	10	33	15	14
Oklahoma	43	23	42	25	49	49	36
Arkansas	45	32	40	46	41	43	45
Nevada	13	14	43	50	46	38	32
Georgia	40	50	41	19	38	40	26

Healthiest States	Obesity	Air Pollution	Lack of Health Ins	Immu-nisation	Primary Care Physicians	Cardio Deaths	Cancer Deaths
Vermont	6	10	10	29	5	10	13
Hawaii	2	2	2	4	7	2	1
New Hampshire	14	10	11	1	16	19	28
Minnesota	24	17	4	7	9	1	11
Utah	7	25	32	37	45	3	1
Massachusetts	2	19	1	8	1	9	25
Connecticut	2	26	6	3	6	11	19
Idaho	14	7	31	45	50	21	8
Maine	17	16	5	40	12	18	49
Washington	23	18	16	48	13	13	17

http://www.forbes.com/2008/12/04/healthy-unhealthy-obesity-forbeslife-cx_ds_1205health_slide1.html

How are Stupidparty values—in good old small town USA?

Greed—see obesity above.
Crime—discussed later.
Rape—discussed later.

E) Divorce Rates.

Worst Divorce Rates per 1,000 Wiki		Best Divorce Rates per 1,000	
1 Louisiana	8.2	Georgia	2.5
2 Indiana	7.8	Massachusetts	2.5
3 Nevada	7.1	Illinois	2.9
4 Oklahoma	6.6	North Dakota	3.0
5 Arkansas	6.2	Iowa	3.1
6 Alabama	5.4	Minnesota	3.1
7 Wyoming	5.4	Pennsylvania	3.1
8 Idaho	5.3	Rhode Island	3.2
9 Kentucky	5.2	Wisconsin	3.2
10 West Virginia	5.2	Connecticut	3.3
11 Florida	5.1	South Dakota	3.3
12 Tennessee	5.1	Maryland	3.4
13 Mississippi	4.9	New Jersey	3.4
14 Arizona	4.7	New York	3.4
15 Colorado	4.7	South Carolina	3.4

http://en.wikipedia.org/wiki/Divorce_in_the_United_States

F) Sloth.

Stupidparty Disciples are the laziest.

States where residents get less physical exercise tend to vote Republican. (Figure 10d in Appendix.) The relationship is highly significant statistically. Figure 3 combines physical exercise and lack of obesity into a single index of physical fitness.

Least Physical Exercise		Most Physical Exercise	
1	Mississippi	1	Minnesota
2	Kentucky	2	Utah
3	Louisiana	3	Oregon
4	Tennessee	4	Washington
5	Alabama	5	Vermont
6	Oklahoma	6	Wisconsin
7	New York	7	New Hampshire
8	Arkansas	8	Colorado
9	Texas	9	Montana
10	Georgia	10	Connecticut

http://www.statemaster.com/graph/hea_phy_exe-health-physical-exercise

Driving you Mad?

Do the facts drive you nuts, as one just begins to realize the Mad Hatter environment that has been created? This might be a good time to look at driver safety skills, first by international comparison and then by drilling down by state.

Ranked By Country Fatalities per 100,000		
4	United Kingdom	2.8
5	Iceland	2.8
10	Netherlands	3.9
11	Norway	4.3
12	Switzerland	4.3
13	Germany	4.4
19	Japan	5.2
20	Spain	5.4
23	Australia	6.6
26	France	6.4
31	Canada	6.8
45	Slovakia	9.4
51	Croatia	10.4
52	USA	10.4
53	Bahrain	10.5

http://en.wikipedia.org/wiki/List_of_countries_by_traffic-related_death_rate

Worst Drivers		Best Drivers	
1	Louisiana	1	Vermont
2	South Carolina	2	Utah
3	Mississippi	3	New Hamp
4	Texas	4	Minnesota
5	Alabama	5	Oregon
6	Florida	6	Maine
7	Missouri	7	Connecticut
8	North Carolina	8	Iowa
9	Montana	9	Mass
10	North Dakota	10	Alaska
11	Oklahoma	11	Rhode Island
12	Nevada	12	Washington

http://www.usatoday.com/story/news/nation/2013/12/15/worst-drivers-states/4025109/

For the U.S.-state breakdown a different methodology was used.

The categories are the following: fatality rates per 100 million vehicle-miles traveled, failure to obey traffic signals and seatbelt laws, drunk driving, tickets issued for speeding and careless driving.

In his recent book, *Coming Apart,* **Charles Murray** argues that those who live in the "super-zip codes"—the areas with high education levels, like Belmont, Massachusetts—have maintained traditional American values of hard work, while those who live else-where show "crashing" rates of industriousness. He writes that those who live in areas with less education have been leaving the labor force for years, often falsely claiming disability. They "goof off," "sleeping and watching television" (p. 180–181). Those that remain employed have reduced the length of their work-week and their dedication to their jobs, at the same time that those living in the super-zip codes have increased theirs (p. 176–77). Some academic researchers and news media fear accusations of liberal bias if they talk about such things. AEI scholar Murray may be immune from this fear: he is well-known as a conservative/libertarian whose earlier book *The Bell Curve* dealt with black-white differences in test achievement.

http://content.ksg.harvard.edu/blog/jeff_frankels_weblog/2012/10/04/sinners-red-states-blue-states/

G) Porn. Guess who likes their porn:

	Most Porn		Least Porn
1	Mississippi	1	Rhode Island
2	Hawaii	2	Vermont
3	Arkansas	3	New Hampshire
4	Alabama	4	Massachusetts
5	Louisiana	5	Connecticut
6	Georgia	6	New Jersey
7	Maryland	7	Washington
8	Oklahoma	8	New York
9	South Carolina	9	Maine
10	California	10	Utah

http://gizmodo.com/heres-all-the-dirty-details-on-americas-thriving-porn-1208587525

Stupidparty (SP) takes over the House

The facts are coming! The facts are coming!

http://www.ucsusa.org/
http://www.narellecartoons.com/

Republicans are taking the defeat over Healthcare as well as Tiger Woods took to marriage.

—Bill Maher

Let's Google "Congress" to see what pops up:

The Stupidparty took over Congress in 2010. The outgoing Congress was one of the most productive in history. But if you had googled the following question (Nov. 2013), "What has Congress achieved since 2010?"…this is what appears:

THIS IS A SCREEN SHOT OFF A GOOGLE SEARCH

●●●○○ Verizon 🛜   6:29 PM   🛜 93% ▮▮▮

🔒 google.com

| Welcome to… | rotten tomat… | Movies | Mo… | Brick Testa… | mentalist se… | cogress ach… | ⊗ congress… ••• |

952 Days Since Congress Passed Major Law - Outside The Beltway
www.outsidethebeltway.com/952-days-**since-congress**-passed-majo…
by James Joyner - in 924 Google+ circles
Feb 21, 2013 - In other words, the Senate **has done** big stuff, bipartisan stuff, and …
cleared the Senate on December 18, **2010** — it's still been 795 days.).

What has the Tea Party **Congress done since 2010** ? - SodaHead
www.sodahead.com/…**has**…**congress-done-since-2010**/question-2522039/
Mar 16, 2012 - Now I already asked what President Obama **has done** in his time so far in
office and you can read and respond to that here: …

This **Congress** could be least productive **since** 1947 - USA Today
www.usatoday.com/news/washington/story/2012-08-14/…**congress**…/1
Aug 14, 2012 - **2012**: 61; 2011: 90; **2010**: 258; 2009: 125; 2008: 280; 2007: 180; 2006: 313; …
Issues on which the divided **Congress has** not found consensus include the Dec. … The lazy,
useless, con-artist GOP **Congress has got** to go!

The least productive **Congress** ever - Washington Post
www.washingtonpost.com/…/the-least-productive-**congress**-ever/
by Chris Cillizza - in 324 Google+ circles
Jul 17, 2013 - Passing legislation equals productivity? **Have** you noticed that **since**
we **got** a divided **Congress** in the **2010** elections we **have had** economic …

As Gridlock Consumes **Congress**, Boehner Says House '**Has Done** …
abcnews.go.com › ABC News Blogs › Politics › Political Punch
by Jake Tapper - in 36,824 Google+ circles
Jan 29, 2012 - Despite the bitterly divided political environment in Washington, House
Speaker John Boehner said that the House "**has done** its job" to work …

> For this last story – we will now activate the link (see below) and see where it takes us

Congress: Same hours, half the work - CNN.com
www.cnn.com/2012/06/19/politics/**congress**-productivity/
by Allison Brennan - in 106 Google+ circles
Jun 19, 2012 - The current **Congress has** worked just as many days as its legislative
predecessors. … It was also a time of political unity **after** the 9/11 attacks. …
Republican freshman and gave the GOP control of the 112th House in **2010**.

Following up on that last CNN story:

What has Congress achieved or tried to achieve? According to a CNN analysis of congressional records…

http://www.cnn.com/2012/06/19/politics/congress-productivity/

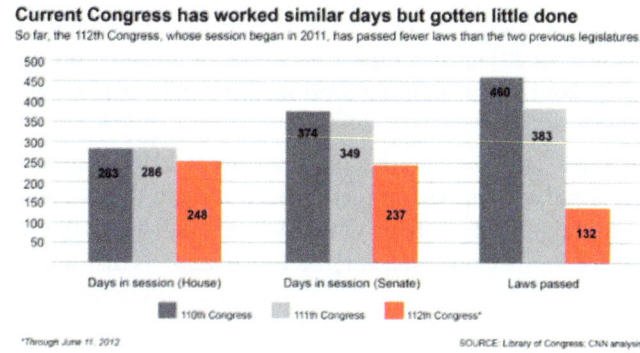

Current Congress has worked similar days but gotten little done
So far, the 112th Congress, whose session began in 2011, has passed fewer laws than the two previous legislatures.

But the reality is far worse.

Did someone say to keep making the same mistake repeatedly and expect a different outcome is the definition of insanity, or stupidity?

Well, by that definition we are evidently dealing with hitherto-unknown levels of Stupidparty. The Affordable Care Act has been passed, and to undo it, both chambers of Congress would have to vote to override a presidential veto. Nobody has suggested that this is possible while Obama is president. But such realities do not trouble the Stupidparty.

$55m of taxpayer money wasted on stupid.
Note: Most of the time throughout the book I will indicate quotations clearly. However at times, I will use blue font for longer quoted passages, or to help clarify when I am quoting someone else.

Stupidparty had voted over 40 times to repeal what they call "Obamacare" (by Sept. 2013). Last year, CBS News calculated that the number of hours spent on 33 repeal votes—then roughly 80 hours, or two full work weeks—cost taxpayers an estimated $48 million. Since then, Congress has held three more votes (another $4.5 million) and will add another $1.5 million with their latest.
http://thinkprogress.org/health/2013/05/15/2016821/affordable-care-act-repeal-taxpayer-money/ (May 2013)

55 Anti-Women Bills.
In the Congress of 2012–2014—the Stupidparty House has 20 women, compared to 62 female Democrats. (**In my narrative the 113th Congress is 2012–2014, not 2013–15…**)

A report (PDF) released Wednesday by Democrats on the House Energy & Commerce Committee counts 55 "anti-women" bills House Republicans have passed since they took over in 2011. They range from restricting abortion rights and de-funding women's health programs to slashing food security and weakening domestic violence protections.
http://tpmdc.talkingpointsmemo.com/2012/09/dems-house-gop-passed-55-anti-women-bills.php (Sept. 2012)

The much-criticized 112th Congress—from 2010 to 2012—was the least productive and least popular Congress on record, according to the available statistics. Now six months in—highlighted by a string of legislative stalemates—the 113th Congress (2012–2014) is on track to match or even surpass those dubious distinctions
http://firstread.nbcnews.com/_news/2013/06/30/19206400-unproductive-congress-how-stalemates-became-the-norm-in-washington-dc?lite
(I have clarified the dates in the quote, to comply with a more standard definition of Congressional terms)

Environmental protection and climate change.

On a largely party-line vote, the House voted to strip the Environmental Protection Agency of the authority to enact any regulations "concerning, taking action relating to, or taking into consideration the emission of a greenhouse gas to address climate change." They called this proposal the "Energy Tax Prevention Act of 2011." A year later, they also voted to eliminate green energy funding—a bill they termed the "No More Solyndras Act."
http://thinkprogress.org/politics/2013/07/22/2336171/by-his-own-measure-john-boehners-congress-is-still-the-most-counterproductive-in-histroy/

Attacking Democracy.

After Watergate a public-financing law was enacted to encourage politicians to accept public funds at the expense of special-interest funds. Fewer and fewer politicians accept these funds, so instead of updating and repairing the law, Stupidparty votes repeatedly to eliminate the system altogether. They also voted to eliminate the Election Assistance Commission, the bipartisan group created after the 2000 election to help local officials ensure smooth and fair elections.
http://www.huffingtonpost.com/rep-steny-hoyer/the-abandonment-of-the-el_b_1890793.html

As will be discussed later, the corrupting power of money is the key explanation why critical thinking has been impaired to the point where "citizens" are voting against their own interests.

From Reuters:
The framers were clearly concerned about institutional corruption. They wrote into the Constitution specific structural safeguards—ranging from bans on foreign gifts to requirements for regular elections. Subsequent constitutional amendments added anti-corruption protections—ensuring that senators were elected by the people, not state legislatures, and expanding the pool of voters with women and African Americans to make democracy even more inclusive.

When Congress passed the campaign finance law now being challenged in the Supreme Court, it used the broad anti-corruption rationale that was at the heart of these efforts—and of central concern to the Constitution's framers.
http://blogs.reuters.com/great-debate/2013/07/29/the-framers-on-campaign-finance-law-via-tumblr/

Ban any new Regulation.

Stupidparty actually passed a bill last year that would have effectively stopped all new regulations…taking away the administration's power to protect safety, public health, and a level playing field.
http://thinkprogress.org/politics/2013/07/22/2336171/by-his-own-measure-john-boehners-congress-is-still-the-most-counterproductive-in-histroy/

Violence against Women.

"On January 2, 2013, the United States 112th Congress officially ran out its term and allowed reauthorization of the Violence Against Women Act to die without a vote."
http://www.takepart.com/article/2013/01/03/america-drops-its-law-against-violence-against-women

Treating female war heroes and other women with Contempt.

Joe Walsh, former StupidParty (SP) Rep. Illinois: Earlier this year he said of Tammy Duckworth, the woman running against him for his congressional seat, "Female, wounded veteran…ehhh." After that he attacked women's health advocate Sandra Fluke, joining a long list of Republicans in denigrating Fluke after her speech at the Democratic National Convention. Over the weekend, Walsh complained that Fluke should "get a job"—by making this statement he and his peer group

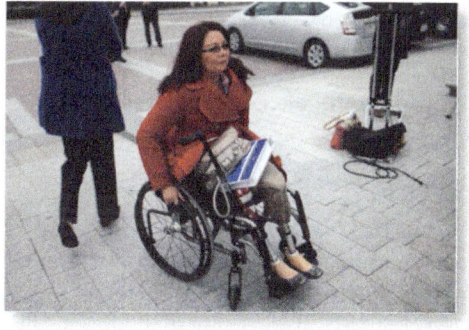

are basically agreeing with Rush Limbaugh that if you are advocating for contraceptives and you happen to be a woman, you must therefore be a slut.
http://thinkprogress.org/politics/2012/09/10/818281/joe-walsh-sandra-fluke/

Sex Education.

Louie Gohmert, SP Rep. Texas: "Human Beings Don't Need Sex Ed"
"Actually, mankind has existed for a pretty long time without anyone ever having to give a sex ed lesson to anybody. And now we feel like, oh gosh people are too stupid unless we force them to sit and listen to instructions. It is just incredible," Gohmert said. "For heaven's sake, let the kids be innocent."
http://www.outsidethebeltway.com/gop-congressman-human-beings-dont-need-sex-ed/

Plan for the poor.

Stephen Fincher, SP Rep. Tennessee, wants to cut $4 billion from the SNAP food subsidy program for the poor…He thinks God does, too, and backs up that assertion by quoting 2 Thessalonians 3:10: "For even when we were with you, we gave you this command: Anyone unwilling to work should not eat." Also the 2nd most heavily subsidized farmer in Congress—and one of the largest subsidy recipients in Tennessee history—

said Washington should not "steal" from taxpayers to support food assistance like the Supplemental Nutrition Assistance Program (SNAP)—better known as food stamps. While Fincher interprets food assistance for the needy as "stealing," he has not similarly condemned the Farm Bill's massive agricultural subsidies. In fact, he supported a

proposal to expand crop insurance by $9 billion over the next 10 years. Fincher has a great personal stake in maintaining these particular government handouts, as the second most heavily subsidized farmer in Congress and one of the largest subsidy recipients in Tennessee history.

(above quotes mingled from sources below)
http://notionscapital.wordpress.com/2013/05/24/gop-congressman-god-wants-the-poor-to-starve/
http://www.ewg.org/agmag/2013/05/fincher-stole-food-stamps#.UZuNCBIGM-M.twitter

Rape.

Roger Rivard, SP State Rep. Wisconsin: "Some girls, they rape so easy."

House Intelligence Committee.

Bachmann appointed to House Intelligence Committee.

Liberals hating America and God.

Robin Hayes, SP Chairman, North Carolina, warming up a [Stupidparty] crowd in North Carolina on Saturday…offered the diagnosis that "liberals hate real Americans that work and achieve and believe in God." His remarks came shortly after he had said he would "make sure we don't say something stupid, make sure we don't say something we don't mean." Hayes had followed [SP] Rep. Patrick McHenry, also a North Carolina Republican, who laid out the choice between McCain and Obama.

"It's like black and white," yelled someone from the crowd.

(**Robin Hayes** denied making the remark believing that national journalists, who had been delayed, had not heard the remark—but he forgot that local journalists were present.)

Gun Control after Newton Child Massacre.
Not a single Obama suggestion regarding gun control is even considered.

No deals are allowable (July 2013). "In the wake of the tax-cut deal, Republican leaders in both houses had to pledge that they would not engage in any— to quote the ubiquitous buzzword—'backroom deals.' Since all deals get made in back rooms (there is no such thing as a front room, and leaders in Western cultures like the United States habitually transact their business in rooms), this means no negotiation at all…

"'The idea of Boehner's negotiating with Pelosi over how to proceed is implausible,' a recent story by Jonathan Strong, a National Review reporter, noted as an aside. 'It would telegraph weakness.'"
http://nymag.com/news/features/republican-congress-2013-7/index2.html

Stupidparty Women's outreach:
Marsha Blackburn, SP Rep. Tennessee 7th.
When the House Judiciary Committee passes a late-term abortion ban, which many deem to be anti-women legislation, they find that trying to explain themselves to women is complicated by the fact that not a single Stupidparty woman sits on the twenty-three-member House Judiciary Committee. So they send out Tennessee Rep. Marsha Blackburn to reach out to women. But this plan gets further complicated by Blackburn's actual track record on women's issues: she opposes Pay Equity Laws because women "Don't Want the Decisions made in Washington."

She voted against the Lily Ledbetter Fair Pay Act of 2009, which gives women more latitude to sue companies for workplace discrimination.

She voted against the Paycheck Fairness Act of 2009, which bars employers from arbitrarily paying employees less on the basis of gender and forces them to use legitimate reasons such as education or past experience.…

Blackburn also voted against reauthorizing the Violence against Women Act, citing concerns that the law would protect "different groups" such as Native American women and LGBT Americans from domestic violence alongside straight, white women.

She falsely claimed that science supports Stupidparty views on fetus pain at 20 weeks: "What we're saying is science is on our side on this; public opinion is on our side on this," said Republican Rep. Marsha Blackburn of Tennessee in an interview Tuesday on MSNBC.

Evidently, her anti-abortion bill will rid society of rapists…Perhaps she really believes that the House GOP's anti-abortion bill is meant to help women, too. Even though it includes an exception for victims of rape and incest, it will only apply to women who have reported those crimes to police. It would appear that Blackburn is oblivious to the fact that most survivors do not report these crimes to police.

(June 2013) On MSNBC Tuesday morning, Blackburn tried to explain to an incredulous Craig Melvin that the measure is designed to help women, because it will "rid our society of these perpetrators who carry out these crimes, many times repeatedly."

Clearly, she will not be able to give much comfort on abortion or contraception, or speak truthfully about Planned Parenthood—issues which even the Pope has indicated the Catholic Church must stop droning on about. So when it comes to women, Stupidparty is now even more outmoded than the Catholic Church. (Various Sources)

DARRELL ISSA
Chairman of House oversight Committee

CROOK?

http://www.nationaljournal.com/politics/
republicans-confront-lady-problems-in-congress-20130806
http://thinkprogress.org/economy/2013/06/02/2089701/
gop-congresswoman-opposes-pay-equity-mtp/
http://tv.msnbc.com/2013/06/18/republicans-claim-science-on-their-side-in-abortion-wars/
http://www.salon.com/2013/06/18/gops_war_on_women_has_a_new_face_marsha_blackburn/

A Stupidparty Crook and his endless witch hunts:

"The only thing that makes Rep. Darrell Issa remotely qualified to chair the House Oversight Committee is his personal familiarity with the investigative process—on the receiving end. The man Republican House Speaker John Boehner put in charge of investigating government wrongdoing was himself indicted for stealing a car, accused of stealing at least one other car, arrested for carrying a concealed weapon, and twice suspected of insurance fraud—and once extensively investigated by authorities for arson, because his former business associates accused him, on the record, of burning down a building to collect the insurance payout."
http://www.salon.com/2013/06/04/the_farce_that_is_darrell_issa/

Is Darrell Issa a Crook? Clearly this question must be asked. It must be asked because of the role the Stupidparty decided to hand to him. You really would hope that an individual in charge of investigating the president should have a great deal of ethical credibility. So before listening to anything this man has to say, should you not evaluate the source?

Never Interested in facts.

"Even before he took over the House Oversight and Government Reform Committee, with zero evidence in hand, Issa called Obama 'one of the most corrupt presidents in modern times.' In his relentless search for evidence (and headlines) since, he has found nothing to back up that statement, making him look like a buffoon. (Even the Solyndra scandal turned out to be a question of incompetence, not corruption, as Issa himself has admitted.)"
http://www.theatlantic.com/politics/archive/2012/06/darrell-issa-and-house-republicans-permanent-witch-hunt/258847/

Benghazi Witch Hunt (Treason).

Stupidparty does not care about treason, and Issa clearly is not worried about Cheney/Scooter Libby-like disclosures of CIA assets.

House Oversight Committee Chairman Darrell Issa (R-Calif.) has come under fire after posting 166 pages of "sensitive but unclassified" State Department cables online Friday afternoon. The documents relate to the Sept. 11 attack on the U.S. consulate in Benghazi, which killed Ambassador Christopher Stevens and four others. Administration officials, speaking with *Foreign Policy* magazine, accused Issa of endangering the safety of Libyans working with the U.S. government, whose names were not redacted from the report:

"Administration officials Administration officials told *Foreign Policy* magazine the leak, along with Issa's failure to redact the names of Libyan civilians and local leaders mentioned in the cables, could have 'unintended consequences.'

"This does damage to the individuals because they are named, danger to security cooperation because these are militias and groups that we work with and that is now well known, and danger to the investigation, because these people could help us down the road," an administration official said.

http://www.huffingtonpost.com/2012/10/20/darrell-issa-libya_n_1991064.html

Fast and Furious Witch Hunt. (Breaks the Law*)

"In the course of his partisan witch hunt to hold the Attorney General in contempt, Rep. Darrell Issa knowingly broke disclosure laws. During floor debate over a motion to hold Attorney General Eric Holder in contempt over the Fast and Furious operation, the California Republican inserted information from a sealed wiretap application into the Congressional Record. Disclosing material from a sealed wiretap application without a judge's permission violates federal law. Rep. Issa knew that he could shield himself from prosecution by including the information in the Congressional Record, which would be protected under the Constitution's Speech or Debate Clause."

http://www.crewsmostcorrupt.org/mostcorrupt/entry/darrell-issa

*Citizens for Responsibility and Ethics in Washington (CREW) is a nonprofit 501(c)(3) dedicated to promoting ethics and accountability in government and public life by targeting government officials who sacrifice the common good to special interests.

The IRS Witch Hunt.

By releasing the full transcript of interviews with the IRS Screening Group manager, Rep. Elijah Cummings has proven that Rep. Darrell Issa lied about Obama's involvement in the IRS scandal. Rep. Cummings absolutely destroyed Issa's conspiratorial claims that Obama was masterminding the IRS scandal:

This interview transcript provides a detailed firsthand account of how these practices first originated, and it debunks conspiracy theories about how the IRS first started reviewing these cases. Answering questions from committee staff for more than five hours, this official—who identified himself as a "conservative Republican"—denied that he or anyone on his team was directed by the White House to take these actions or that they were politically motivated.

http://www.politicususa.com/2013/06/18/full-transcript-reveals-darrell-issa-lied-obama-involvement-irs-scandal.html

Darrell Issa's bluff on the IRS investigation is being called in a big way by top Democrats on Issa's House Oversight Committee. In a letter sent today to Issa, they are demanding he explain in more detail why he continues to refuse to release full transcripts of witness testimony on the IRS scandal—and they are giving him until Monday to do so....

Issa has already been pilloried by news organizations for failing to substantiate his more lurid charges of White House involvement in the IRS targeting, and his answer to this challenge will likely be seen by news orgs as another test of his credibility. If Cummings is right, and the transcripts dramatically undercut Issa's claims, it's unclear what Issa's endgame is here.

http://www.washingtonpost.com/blogs/plum-line/wp/2013/06/13/calling-darrell-issas-bluff/

No Jobs Bills:

Back in 2010, John Boehner, Stupidparty Speaker of the House, claimed Jobs were his number-one priority, but Senate Minority Leader McConnell was perhaps being more honest when he admitted that the number-one priority would be to derail Obama. Hence, no job bills, just job bill filibusters. Stupidparty House and Senate have since blocked jobs bills, such as incentives to bring back outsourced jobs—using the warped logic that they cannot support such legislation unless it includes legislation to repeal "Obamacare"…

According to *The Hill*, "Republicans were expected to support the 'insourcing' bill until Senate Majority Leader Harry Reid (D-Nev.) said he was unlikely to include any Republican amendments." Specifically, Republicans wanted to include an amendment repealing the Affordable Care Act.
http://www.dailykos.com/story/2012/07/19/1111774/-Republicans-block-Bring-Jobs-Home-Act-protecting-companies-that-outsource-jobs#

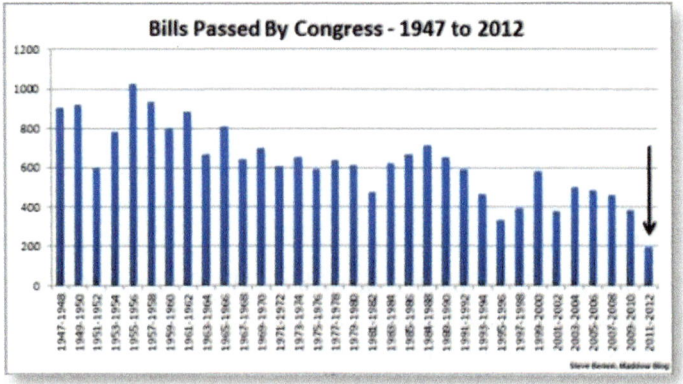

http://republicanjobcreation.com/

If they are so Stupidparty how come they are in the majority?

Since they cannot win an argument, they win by other means.

a) Gerrymandering:

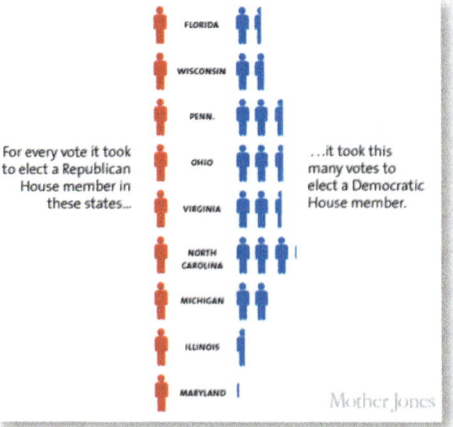

http://www.motherjones.com/politics/2012/11/republicans-gerrymandering-house-representatives-election-chart

Some examples:

Florida has been deemed by my approach herein a Blue state, since it went for Obama in the 2012 elections—thus, it would be inconsistent to call it a Stupidparty state, even though a great deal of silly and dangerous stuff comes out of it. It also contains the most distressing hub of Stupidparty solidarity on the entire planet, in Palm Beach (which will be discussed later).

But when it comes to the U.S. House of Representatives, Stupidparty wins this "Blue state" hands down, 17 seats to 10. So how come? Well, study how the districts below have been cunningly created to corral as many Democratic voters into one district as possible.

Florida—20

How to condense Democratic votes into one congressional district

In 2012 The Democrats won this seat with 88% of the vote.

North Carolina 2012 Congressional Election.
In 2008 North Carolina was not a Stupidparty state, but it took a step back in 2012. However, even though Obama did not win the state, the Stupidparty got less votes in the congressional elections.

In North Carolina, where the two-party House vote was 51% Democratic, 49% Republican, it would have been logical for seven Democrats and six Stupidparty reps to be selected. But the Stupidparty got 9 seats to the Democratic 4. If districts were drawn fairly, this lopsided discrepancy would hardly ever occur. How does this inequity happen?

North Carolina—12

Democrat wins with 80% of the vote

North Carolina—1

Democrat wins with 75% of the vote

But all is not lost: A ray of California sunshine.

By understanding what has transpired in California since the
recall events of 2003, perhaps we can hope to start reversing
some of the carnage presently being done to democracy. Until
recently, California and its runaway deficits had been a total
gridlocked mess—a mess overseen by a Stupidparty governor
and a strong Stupidparty presence. Ironically this Stupidparty
state of affairs came to pass, at least in part, as a result of unfet-

tered capitalism in the form of the Enron crisis (see the 2004 documentary *The Smartest
Guys in the Room*—Rotten Tomatoes 97%), that led to instability, helping to create an
environment that allowed for an absurd recall election (forcing a competent governor
out of office) and various voter initiatives that have since played havoc with the ability to
execute sound governance.

But in the last couple of years we have seen a Democratic governor (Jerry Brown)
installed, and now in 2014, Democrats hold a massive majority in the Assembly and the
Senate. The Stupidparty is presently pretty much irrelevant at the local level; it might
even be dead, thus allowing for a rebirth of something that used to be referred to as
Republicans—a general description that is still allowed to be used, for reasons I do not
really have much sympathy for.

There has been dynamic electoral reform.
1) Lawmakers have been voted in from districts drawn up by a nonpartisan commission. Yea!
2) In the new nonpartisan system, the two top primary finishers run against each other. Yea!!
3) Last year voters eased the stringent term limits that forced out seasoned legislators. Yea!!!

***The New York Times* reports (Oct 19, 2013):**

In the past month, California has been the stage for a series
of celebrations of unlikely legislative success—a parade of
bill signings that offered a contrast between the shutdown in
Washington and an acrimony-free California Legislature that
enacted laws dealing with subjects including school financing,
immigration, gun control and abortion...The new atmosphere

in Sacramento also offers the first evidence that three major changes (listed above)
in California's governance system intended to leach some of the partisanship out of
politics—championed by reform advocates—may also be having their desired effect in a
state that has long offered itself as the legislative laboratory for the nation.

As *The New York Times* goes on to report, Stupidparty representatives in more logically
drawn up districts have to contend with a less-partisan base. Now such representatives
(not having been selected from a partisan primary) have to deal with the realities of an
election where the outcome is not preordained; they have to be more responsive to their
constituents and be sensitive to the changing demographics. Stupidparty reps have to
listen to minorities, immigrants, etc., and they can begin to morph back into Republicans, back into being in touch with humanity.

Republican Rep. Anthony Cannella (for he is no longer Stupidparty) is quoted as saying,
"It's given more courage to my Republican colleagues...They were afraid of getting primaries. Now, it's not just their base they have to appeal to."

Another Republican: "It gives Republicans the chance to break from their caucus on certain issues…It is very different than it was four or five years ago."
http://www.nytimes.com/2013/10/19/us/california-upends-its-image-of-legislative-dysfunction.html?_r=0

b) Voter Suppression:

Voter-suppression strategies are openly admitted by Stupidparty operatives.
But before discussing voter suppression, I need to spend a moment dispelling the Myth of Voter Fraud.

Voter Fraud, a vital Myth.

Voter Fraud is a miniscule problem. To substantiate this statement, I must first explain that while certain paid political operatives may try to commit fraud in counting votes, it is rare/almost nonexistent that actual voters attempt fraud. In numerous investigations, nothing material ever shows up. We will see

And why is this so scary? Why are they pretending this is scary?

Link for actual screen grab

that the full wealth and might of the Benefactors (a group that I'll gradually unmask) is behind voter-suppression efforts, because to prove a pattern of fraud would massively help their goals. The fact this even has to be discussed is evidence of the haplessness of the media in general and the institutionalized and intentional dishonesty inherent within Fox News, a subject that I will cover in some detail in a later chapter. Let me allow the Brennan Center for Justice to explain why it is a fact that voter fraud is insignificant.

Fraud by individual voters is both irrational and extremely rare. Most citizens who take the time to vote offer their legitimate signatures and sworn oaths with the gravitas that this hard-won civic right deserves. Even for the few who view voting merely as a means to an end, however, voter fraud is a singularly foolish way to attempt to win an election. Each act of voter fraud risks five years in prison and a $10,000 fine—but yields at most one incremental vote. The single vote is simply not worth the price.

Because voter fraud is essentially irrational, it is not surprising that no credible evidence suggests a voter fraud epidemic. There is no documented wave or trend of individuals voting multiple times, voting as someone else, or voting despite knowing that they are ineligible. Indeed, evidence from the microscopically scrutinized 2004 gubernatorial

election in Washington State actually reveals just the opposite: though voter fraud does happen, it happens approximately 0.0009% of the time. The similarly closely-analyzed 2004 election in Ohio revealed a voter fraud rate of 0.00004%. National Weather Service data shows that Americans are struck and killed by lightning about as often.
http://www.brennancenter.org/analysis/policy-brief-truth-about-voter-fraud

So a miniscule amount—but it is actually far less than miniscule because what the Brennan Center fails to point out is that there is no suggestion that one group of voters is more inclined to commit fraud; thus, even if it does occur, the probability is that one would cancel out the other. So it is not simply miniscule; the impact is more likely zero.

Acorn.

Voting is an important civil right, and many argue it is a civic duty. In Australia you must vote. In Belgium you must show up at the polls, but having shown up, you do not have to vote. Over twenty countries have some form of mandatory voting.

Acorn was an organization devoted to adding voters to the rolls. Acorn often paid homeless people to collect signatures. Thus, it was providing a double public service.

So while on occasion such workers did try and rip off Acorn (using fake signatures to invent nonexistent people) for a few extra dollars, the Acorn organization never created any voter fraud. This may come as a shock to the paranoid conservative brain, but the fact is that nonexistent people cannot vote, not of course unless Jesus decides

to rise from the dead (for a second time) in order to vote. Ironically, if one understands anything about Jesus, his likely abhorrence of the Stupidparty and their antics, this must surely be a very tempting option. But like Kerry, Acorn was swiftboated by the Benefactors, i.e., Big Money devoted to an insidi-ous and widespread deception. Big Money wins; the public and its treasured democracy lose. Even after Acorn was hounded out of business, 49% of Stupidparty voters believed that Acorn stole the 2012 election.
(Poll data from source below.)
http://www.theblaze.com/stories/2012/12/05/poll-half-of-republicans-believe-2012-election-was-stolen-but-was-the

Voter Suppression—a real issue.

Stupidparty reps and Disciples carry on about voter fraud. But there is no material voter fraud. All this noise and deception was just tapping into Stupidparty Disciple ignorance and energy in order to create a rationale for ever-increasing voter-suppression efforts. While both parties might be tempted by fraud, only one party pursues voter-suppression strategies.

Misinformation is spread to create an environment where even good people will believe strategies amounting to suppression might be warranted. Many Stupidparty strategists make no secret of the importance of making it more difficult for urban minorities to vote. This was a crucial component of Karl Rove's strategy; by successfully repressing minority voters in Cleveland, Ohio, on election night 2004, he handed a second term to George Bush.

At the urgings of key strategists like Rove and the party bosses, Stupidparty officials have instituted various forms of voter suppression aimed at preventing Democratic-leaning blocs from voting. The Brennan Center for Justice notes:

> * Restrictive voter identification policies—especially those that require state-issued photo ID cards—threaten to exclude millions of eligible voters.
> * As many as 10% of eligible voters do not have, and will not get, the documents required by strict voter ID laws. For some groups, the percentage is much higher.
> * ID requirements fall hardest on people who have traditionally faced barriers at the polls.
> * ID requirements are not justified by any serious or widespread problem.
> * There is no reason for states to implement burdensome ID requirements.
> * States that do require proof of identity at the polls should permit an expansive range of proof.
> http://www.brennancenter.org/analysis/policy-brief-voter-identification

The Brennan Center for Justice adds:

… The impact of ID requirements is even greater for the elderly, students, people with disabilities, low-income individuals, and people of color…African Americans have driver's licenses at half the rate of whites, and the disparity increases among younger voters; only 22% of black men aged 18–24 had a valid driver's license. Not only are minority voters less likely to possess photo ID, but they are also more likely than white voters to be selectively asked for ID at the polls.

Bloomberg reported:

First we saw the efforts during the George W. Bush Administration by Karl Rove and Justice Department officials to get rid of U.S. attorneys who refused to pursue bogus voter fraud cases. When Republican prosecutors complained, Rove and company ran for cover.

Then came *Crawford v. Marion County,* the 2008 case in which the U.S. Supreme Court ruled that mandatory photo-identification laws were constitutional on the basis of ballot protection. The evidence presented included not a single case of in-person impersonation fraud—the only fraud that photo ID laws can prevent. And the millions of Americans—mostly less-affluent seniors—without driver's licenses? Good luck.

The big Republican victory in the 2010 election was essential to the Voter Suppression Project. With the help of ALEC—a conservative lobbying outfit that spreads cookie-cutter bills to state legislatures—Republicans moved with lightning speed to implement their scheme. Since 2011, 18 states have enacted voter-suppression bills, with similar ones pending in 12 more.
http://www.bloomberg.com/news/2012-06-21/republicans-voter-suppression-project-grinds-on.html

There are many forms of voter suppression. It is particularly easy to target poor minorities, especially in urban areas—those without driving licenses, who have had run-ins with the law or changed their home address or people not good with forms. Reducing voter turnout, voter disenfranchisement—these are vital Stupidparty tools. Here are some tricks:

Driving up Incarceration rates and the number of criminal records (47–65m Americans have records)
Cutting back voting hours.
Putting voting centers in obscure, hard-to-find locations.
Reducing the number of precincts, thus increasing traveling distance.
Reducing resources at precincts, thus increasing wait times.
Designing Voter Fraud campaigns to intimidate specific populations.
Intimidation, with heightened police presence.

Increasing wait times is particularly effective. People have to work all day and get home to their kids. They simply cannot stand in line for one to five hours after work—and if it starts raining, such waits become intolerable.

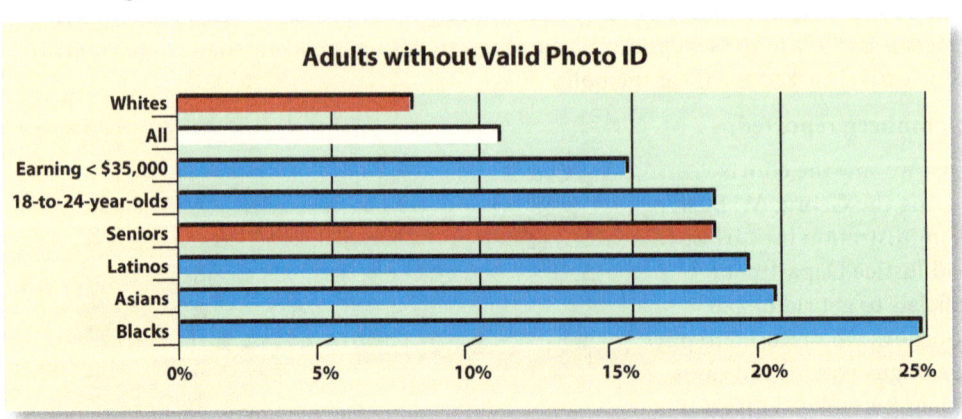

http://www.motherjones.com/kevin-drum/2012/07/no-taxation-without-representation-field-guide-voter-suppression

Increasing Incarceration rates also is a wonderful tool for Stupidparty, as it is not only a profit maker, with handy kickbacks to politicians, but also, being tough on crime and yelling "three strikes and you are out" is always a great sound bite. And it is clearly working, for Stupidparty at least. With *47,000,000 Americans having criminal records, 5,300,000 (now updated to 5,850,000**) can definitely not vote, because of various state disenfranchisement laws—and boy, can you have fun trying to find creative ways to discourage the other 40,000,000 or so from voting. And then, when these people cannot get a job (yes, society always has a price to pay for stupidity), well then, they become moochers. More self-inflicted nonsense.

*Others put the number at 65,000,000, or one in four adults.

**http://www.huffingtonpost.com/2012/07/12/felon-voting-laws-disenfranchise-sentencing-project_n_1665860.html

https://www.aclu.org/racial-justice-voting-rights/voting-criminal-record-executive-summary

http://thinkprogress.org/justice/2012/11/08/1165531/poll-finds-minorities-democrats-faced-longer-voting-lines/

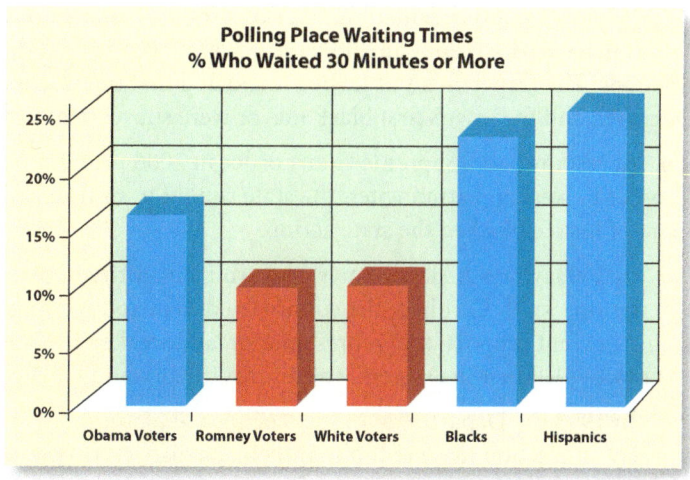

The Supreme Court recently ruled that Congress needs to update the rules designed to prevent racially driven voter suppression. The court chose to take the case at a time they knew Congress was under the control of Stupidparty and thus dysfunctional—and with the House controlled by the Stupidparty, it has zero interest in discussing and legislating against discriminatory practices. The goal of partisan voter suppression is clear-cut; it is to cheat, to cheat the targeted voter group. To cheat democracy.

If the Supreme Court had acted in good faith, they would have waited for the death of Stupidparty. But the aging white male judges tend to have a warped concept of racism, and as for Clarence Thomas, he is a fully paid up member of the Stupidparty; his wife is an activist and they both (along with Chief Justice Scalia) attend functions organized by the financiers of the Tea Party (the stunningly stupid wing of the Stupidparty).The Supreme Court's highly questionable logic was that the country had evolved since the Voting Rights Act was enacted. This questionable logic, however, has been properly addressed by their colleague:

Justice Ruth Bader Ginsburg's—Supreme opinion:

By reviewing her examples, one can fully understand how easy, insidious, and ubiquitous voter suppression is and the cultural history it is rooted in.

According to Justice Ginsburg's dissenting opinion, between 1982 and 2006 the Department of Justice "blocked over 700 voting changes based on a determination that the changes were discriminatory." She cites the following examples, as reported by the Feminist Majority Foundation (below). I took the liberty to conform a few things to the original.

   1. In 1995 Mississippi tried to revive a dual voter system, in which voters were required to register separately for federal and state elections. The law was first enacted in 1892 to disenfranchise black voters. The Department of Justice struck down the law on the grounds that it discriminated against minority voters.

   2. In 2000 the Department of Justice rejected a redistricting scheme in the city of Albany, Georgia, because it deliberately weakened the black vote.

3. When an unprecedented number of African-Americans decided to run for office in Kilmichael, Mississippi, in 2001, the all-white Board of Aldermen canceled local elections. The Department of Justice mandated that the elections occur, and three black aldermen and the town's first black mayor were subsequently elected.

4. In response to a Supreme Court order in 2006 prohibiting Texas from redistricting in order to weaken Latino votes, the state sought to restrict early voting. The Department of Justice blocked the state action.

5. In 2003, when African-Americans won a majority of seats on the school board in Charleston, South Carolina, the county tried to introduce an at-large voting system that would prevent proportional representation and weaken the black vote. The Department of Justice ruled that the system was discriminatory and violated the Voting Rights Act.

6. In 1993 the Department of Justice blocked a motion by the city of Millen, Georgia, to delay an election in a predominantly black district by two years, leaving it without representation.

7. In 2004, Waller County, Texas, attempted to curtail early voting at polling places near a historically black university.

8. In 1990, Dallas County, Alabama, sought to disenfranchise voters who did not return a voter update form. The Department of Justice ruled that the action was discriminatory and unnecessary.

9. In 2011, eight states—Alabama, Georgia, Indiana, Kansas, Missouri, Pennsylvania, Tennessee, Texas, and Wisconsin—passed voter identification laws. With one tenth of the population without identification, the law would discourage the votes of minorities, students, seniors, and people in rural areas. 24 other states introduced voter identification laws that year.

10. In 2011 Florida and Texas passed restrictions on non-profit voter registration drives. These non-profits, such as the League of Women Voters, have proved incredibly effective at helping eligible citizen register to vote, especially on college campuses and in areas with low voter turnout.

11. In 2011 Florida passed a law reducing the early voting period by nearly half and effectively limiting black, Latino and Democratic votes, as those groups constitute the majority of early voters. Ohio, West Virginia, Tennessee, Georgia, and Wisconsin also reduced their early voting periods.

12. Partly as a result of reduced early voting, lines at the polls proved unbearable for some 201,000 Florida voters who left before casting their ballots in the 2012 Presidential Election.

13. In 2012, billboards erected in predominantly black neighborhoods in Cincinnati threatened that VOTER FRAUD IS A FELONY!

14. Last week the Supreme Court struck down Arizona's law requiring proof of citizenship at the polls. The law would have targeted and suppressed minority, and in particular Latino, votes. 17 other states introduced similar legislation in 2011, and proof of citizenship laws passed in Alabama, Kansas and Tennessee. A study by the Black Youth

Project predicted that these kinds of laws will disenfranchise approximately 700,000 young minority voters.

15. In a recent Los Angeles mayoral race, candidates confused Latino voters by releasing misinformation about the opponents' immigration and labor policies.

16. In a 2010 gubernatorial election in Maryland, one candidate's campaign manager authorized misleading robocalls to predominantly black counties that encouraged voters to "stay home" rather than go to the polls.

The Feminist Majority Blog explains why this is so important:

> Just like racial discrimination, voter suppression isn't all in the past. Hours after the Supreme Court released its decision, Texas Attorney General Greg Abbott announced that the state's voter identification law, perhaps the most stringent in the country, would go into effect immediately. Last year under the Section 5 pre-clearance provision a group of federal judges struck down the law, claiming that it imposed "strict, unforgiving burdens on the poor," and in particular on racial minority groups. Texas lawmakers wasted no time.

> It's easy to remove ourselves from the past, to underscore how we've changed rather than acknowledge historical continuities. But the overwhelming evidence of suppression aimed at minority groups whose votes could affect the status quo shows, if nothing else, that the systems of racism that disenfranchised citizens in 1965 still exist—that we've inherited and in many ways actively perpetuated them. Underlying the majority opinion is a frustratingly elementary notion of racism: so long as we don't physically obstruct individuals from voting, minority disenfranchisement is a vaporous claim.

> In her statement of dissent Justice Ginsburg refers to contemporary acts of voter suppression as "second-generation barriers." Her language is apt: the racial discrimination we see now may not look exactly like the "flagrant" racism of the 1960s, but it is no doubt a close relative. Our voter identification and proof of citizenship laws are not far removed from literacy tests and "grandfather clauses." These 16 examples and more affirm that the Voting Rights Act is still relevant, and still necessary—in full.
>
> http://feminist.org/blog/index.php/2013/06/26/why-the-voting-rights-act-still-matters-16-recent-examples-of-voter-suppression-and-discrimination/

And just in case you were not paying attention:

House Intelligence Committee.

Bachmann appointed to House Intelligence Committee

Just bear in mind, if she had been the SP nominee, I suspect 45-47% of the electorate would have voted for her.

Trying the impossible?—Keeping them honest

CHAPTER 7

Consequences
of being misled
+ Healthcare case study

Across

2. …Rules
3. Recreational group radicalized by a coup
6. Romney owns, Bush plays, evangelicals await
8. Profiting off the labor of struggling people
10. …Is peace
12. …Is Slavery
13. Removed on entry into Stupidparty
15. House committee meeting room
16. Nonexistent in Stupidparty land
17. Supreme Court was its midwife
21. Supreme Court's wet
    dream to facilitate them
22. …United against the interests of the people
24. Feeling superior based on tribal birth
26. The food fed to Disciples to trigger allegiance
28. No child, adult or animal is left behind
29. 280 million in the USA

Down

1. Helped the poor, the sick and admonished the rich
2. Foundation of facts
4. Watch in order to see less
5. The puppetmasters
7. Salivating over your Assets
9. Disciples' wet dream
11. Dislike born out of Ignorance
14. Mental condition of "cutting" and self-harm
18. Supremely safe ancient Mythical horse
19. Freedom fighters for Willy,
    Watergate for Dick, Disciples for …
20. True believer of Benefactor Mythical claptrap
23. …Up might be better than down
25. Like Garlic to a vampire,
    these are to a Disciple
27. Foundation of Stupidparty

There is a President Obama that only Republicans can see. —Jon Stewart

Consequences of supporting Stupidparty
Artist http://www.mattrotasart.com/

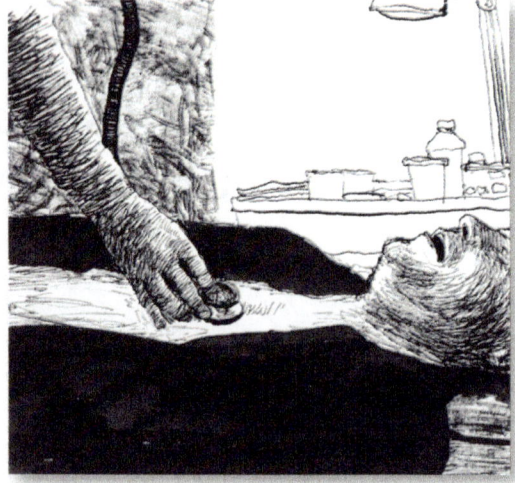

Most of these consequences will be evaluated in more detail.

a) Lack of intelligent energy policy since 1980 leads to three Gulf wars, the rise of militant Islam, additional Global Warming. Trillions wasted.

b) Lack of intelligent health-care discussions leads to 50 million without medical coverage, with this number projected to massively increase (67m) if not for the Affordable Care Act. (See discussion below)

c) Lack of concern or actions regarding income discrepancy leads to 40% of the population living in poverty or one crisis away from poverty.

d) Adopting Gordon Gekko-like mantra of "greed is good" leads to the deregulation of Wall Street and the financial meltdown of 2008.

e) Inability to learn from history: Gordon Gekko carbon copy selected as Stupidparty presidential candidate in 2012.

f) Cost cutting during a deflationary period stalls economic recovery.

g) Adoption of economic policies that allow the top 1% to Asset Strip the resources of the planet in unsustainable ways, undermine the financial security of the majority, and dismantle the "American Dream."

h) Invented family values—not based on the Bible, or anything else for that matter—trump intelligent debate about the risks facing humanity and the needs of the people around the world.

i) The Supreme Court, now favoring Stupidparty tendencies, has unleashed corporate money onto an already massively corrupted political system.

j) The Supreme Court deemed that racist voter-suppression efforts now must be tackled by the very same Stupidparty House that actively needs such voter-suppression efforts to maintain its gerrymandered majority.

k) SP support allows religious dogma, racism, homophobia, sexism, anti-foreigner, all-round ignorance, and bigotry to trump facts, science, math, objective expertise, tolerance, and consensus-seeking middle ground that would otherwise lead to problem-solving solutions.

l) Ever-increasing incarceration rates, torture, and systematic inhumane activities overseas and at home in the prison system and the factory-farm system.

m) USA loses moral authority (impacting ability to lead).

n) Voters lose critical-thinking abilities; ability to discern fact from fiction, sane from insane, Math from Myth, and accept notion of "both sides have a credible point, deserve equal time."

o) USA Constitution,* by failing to evolve, becomes ever more backward relative to other countries' constitutions. As reported by *The New York Times:* "Among the world's democracies," Professors [David S.] Law [of Washington University] and [Mila] Versteeg [of the University of Virginia] concluded, "constitutional similarity to the United States has clearly gone into free fall. There are lots of possible reasons. The United States Constitution is terse and old, and it guarantees relatively few rights. The commitment of some members of the Supreme Court to interpreting the Constitution according to its original meaning in the 18th century may send the signal that it is of little current use to, say, a new African nation. And the Constitution's waning influence may be part of a general decline in American power and prestige."

* http://www.nytimes.com/2012/02/07/us/we-the-people-loses-appeal-with-people-around-the- world.html?pagewanted=all&_r=0

p) As a result of the toleration, rationalization, and encouragement of stupidity, this is who ends up running for the highest office:

These were the main Stupidparty candidates for the 2008 Presidential election:

Believe in	Evolution	Global Warming	Other odd Stuff
Brownback	No	No	Runs on God Power
Tom Tancredo	No	No	Obama = al-Qaeda
Ron Paul	No	No	Ayn Rand
McCain	a nervous yes	Yes	Palin
Huckabee	No	No	Sandy Hook massacre happened because of lack of religious expression in schools

These were the main Stupidparty candidates for the 2012 Presidential election:

Huntsman	Yes	Yes ("call me crazy")	Quite Sane
Romney	Pandering	Pandering	Lost tribe in USA
Santorum	No	No	College for snobs
Gingrich	Pandering	Does not know	Family Values
Cain	Unknown	No	All for sexual harassment
Backman	Has doubts	No	Intelligence Committee
Ron Paul	No	No	Zero bailout 2008
Perry	Just a theory	No	God has a grand plan for Texas

Thus, in 2012 the Stupidparty had only one individual equipped intellectually to be president. Yes, he is a Mormon but not apparently a fundamentalist. He was the only person feared by the president's reelection advisers. That is why (many believed) Obama sent him off to China. Huntsman was relatively smart, decent, and honest. Therefore, he managed to secure only about 2% of the Stupidparty Disciples' vote. He was the one major candidate who never had a surge; no Stupidparty Disciple gave him a chance to shine.

1+1=2   1+1=3

Now, there is this competing theory...

If math was taught like science.

Stupidparty Myth #1—USA has the best healthcare system; thus, why reform?

This is what Stupidparty does not want to reform—USA #46 out of #48:

Rank	Country	Efficiency score	Life expectancy	Health-care cost as a percentage of GDP per capita	Health-care cost per capita
1	Hong Kong	92.6	83.4	0.0	$1,409
2	Singapore	81.9	81.9	4.4	2,286
3	Japan	74.1	82.6	8.5	3,958
4	Israel	68.7	81.8	7.8	2,426
5	Spain	68.3	82.3	10.4	3,027
6	Italy	66.1	82.1	10.4	3,436
7	Australia	66.0	81.8	8.9	5,939
8	South Korea	65.1	80.9	7.2	1,616
9	Switzerland	63.1	82.7	11.5	9,121
10	Sweden	62.6	81.8	9.6	5,331
11	Libya	56.8	75.0	3.8	398
12	United Arab E…	56.6	76.7	4.1	1,640
13	Chile	56.2	79.0	7.0	1,075
14	United Kingdom	55.7	80.8	9.4	3,609
15	Mexico	54.9	76.9	6.4	620
16	Austria	54.4	81.0	11.2	5,280
17	Canada	53.4	80.9	10.8	5,630
18	Malaysia	52.8	74.3	3.3	346
19	France	52.3	81.7	12.5	4,952
20	Ecuador	51.7	75.6	6.1	332
21	Poland	50.6	76.7	7.1	899
22	Thailand	50.2	74.1	3.7	202
23	Finland	49.5	80.5	9.4	4,325
24	Czech Republic	48.9	77.9	8.1	1,507
25	Netherlands	48.5	81.2	13.0	5,995
26	Venezuela	48.3	74.3	4.3	555
27	Portugal	47.2	80.7	11.4	2,311
28	Cuba	46.8	79.1	11.3	606
29	Saudi Arabia	46.0	74.1	3.6	758
30	Germany	45.5	80.7	11.7	4,875
30	Greece	45.5	80.7	13.0	2,864
32	Argentina	45.1	75.8	7.7	892
33	Romania	44.9	74.5	6.3	500
34	Belgium	44.5	80.5	11.4	4,962
35	Peru	43.2	74.0	4.4	289
36	Slovakia	41.1	76.0	9.1	1,534
37	China	38.3	73.5	4.6	278
38	Denmark	38.1	79.8	11.8	6,648
38	Hungary	38.1	74.9	8.6	1,085
40	Algeria	37.2	73.1	4.2	225
41	Bulgaria	37.0	74.2	7.5	522
42	Colombia	36.2	73.6	5.6	432
43	Dominican Rep	35.3	73.4	5.2	296
44	Turkey	33.4	73.9	6.5	696
45	Iran	31.5	73.0	5.1	346
46	United States	30.8	78.6	17.2	8,608
47	Serbia	27.2	74.6	12.0	622
48	Brazil	17.4	73.4	9.9	1,121

http://www.bloomberg.com/visual-data/best-and-worst/most-efficient-health-care-countries

As you can see, not only is the system lousy; it is far more expensive—with the only exception being Switzerland, which comes in at #9. In terms of percentage of GDP, the USA is in a class of its own.

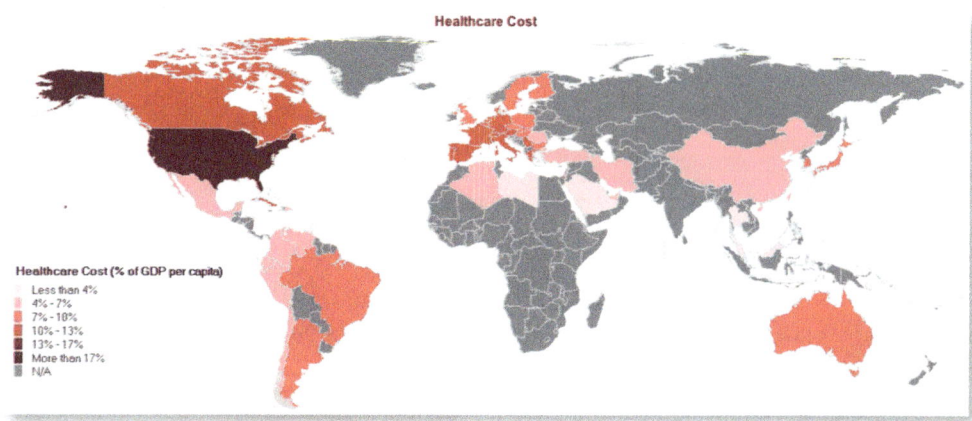

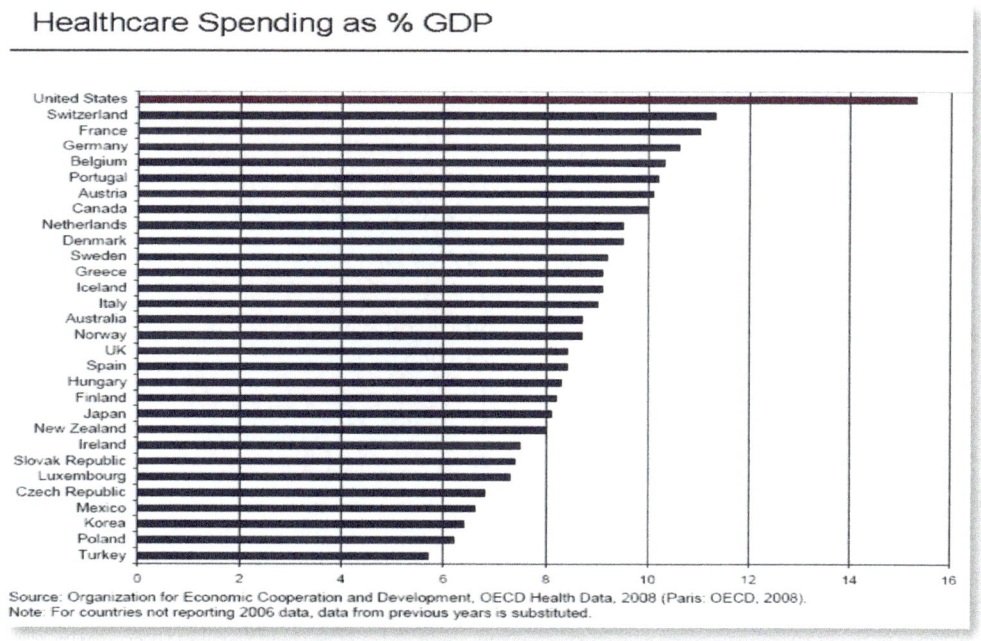

There are several key problems with the U.S. healthcare system, one being that even though 49.9m Americans (in 2010) did not have coverage, the rest of us still pay about 50% more than we should.

Absent reform (i.e., Stupidparty plan), the number of Americans without insurance was projected to grow to 67m by 2020 as premiums doubled. This number a) assumes that Stupidparty states stop their attacks on public workers (i.e., no more Stupidparty) and

b) does not factor in the ever-decreasing coverage actually provided by most employer-sponsored plans.

http://www.cnn.com/2012/06/27/politics/btn-health-care/index.html
http://www.urban.org/UploadedPDF/412049_cost_of_failure.pdf

Stupidparty states relative to Blue States in % uninsured.

Stupidparty States relative to Blue States in % Uninsured Before reform implementation:				
Best 25 States		**Worst 25 States**		
1 Massachusetts	3.4	50 Texas	23.8	
2 Hawaii	7.8	49 Nevada	22.6	
3 Connecticut	8.6	48 Louisiana	20.8	
4 Vermont	8.6	47 Florida	19.8	
5 North Dakota	9.1	46 California	19.7	
6 Minnesota	9.2	45 New Mexico	19.6	
7 Delaware	10.0	44 Georgia	19.2	
8 Iowa	10.0	43 South Carolina	19.0	
9 Maine	10.0	42 Montana	18.3	
10 Wisconsin	10.4	41 Alaska	18.2	
11 Pennsylvania	10.8	40 Wyoming	17.8	
12 Indiana	12.0	39 Arkansas	17.5	
13 Rhode Island	12.0	38 Arizona	17.3	
14 New York	12.2	37 Idaho	16.9	
15 Nebraska	12.3	36 Oklahoma	16.9	
16 Michigan	12.5	35 North Carolina	16.3	
17 New Hampshire	12.5	34 Mississippi	16.2	
18 Alabama	13.0	33 Colorado	15.7	
19 South Dakota	13.0	32 New Jersey	15.4	
20 Tennessee	13.3	31 Missouri	14.9	
21 Virginia	13.4	30 West Virginia	14.9	
22 Kansas	13.5	29 Illinois	14.7	
23 Ohio	13.7	28 Utah	14.6	
24 Maryland	13.8	27 Washington	14.5	
25 Oregon	13.8	26 Kentucky	14.4	

State Color based upon 2012 Presidential Election

http://en.wikipedia.org/wiki/Health_insurance_coverage_in_the_United_States#Estimates_of_the_number_uninsured

The rest of us still pay about 50% more for healthcare than we should.

So how did the U.S. end up being 50% more expensive than necessary—in addition to ignoring the needs of the people who cannot afford such usurious pricing? It is all in the History and the Myth.

The History.

Winning the Second World War opened up a Pandora's box for the Allies. Europe went broke fighting the Nazis, and the biggest concern was social unrest, leading to more and more countries falling under the spine-tingling shadow of Stalin. The American economy was in better shape, having benefitted from Keynesian medicine during a deflationary environment—i.e., the investment in the war effort, on top of the New Deal, put America ahead, and Americans were willing to provide loans (the Marshall Plan) to Europe (debt for Europe) to help mitigate unrest.

Churchill dreaded the implication of millions of people who had put their lives on the line coming home to no jobs, no hope. Stupidparty philosophy would say people without jobs should starve (even veterans), but Churchill had never heard of Stupidparty and was in fact destined to die about thirty years before its birth. So he had another idea. Winston Churchill, a Conservative icon in the USA and Britain, initiated what is now called the welfare state. This included the national health system. The prime motivation was simply to help people who needed help get people back on their feet, and create social stability.

The birth of healthcare in the USA was somewhat different. Its birth has been captured on audiotape. You can hear it here: http://www.youtube.com/watch?v=RmHTte8jRLk. When policy advisers introduced the concept to President Richard Nixon, he was initially aghast. But when it was explained that insurance would provide the coverage and that plenty of profits could be made, well, he was immediately on board.

The USA started on a more suspect foundation, but how does it remain so far behind the other developed nations? Because of various Myths.

Myth #1.
The USA is the best. See charts above.

Myth #2 Obamacare.
Actually, it is the Affordable Care Act—built on old GOP philosophy and enacted by Romney as governor of Massachusetts, the state that now has the lowest number of uninsured and ranks at the top or near the top in various categories of health, as will be illustrated.

Myth #3 Europeans have to pay higher Taxes.
Even when the U.S. mainstream media attempts to do objective analysis, they fall into this trap. When Dr. Sanjay Gupta of CNN did his earnest and heartfelt analysis comparing the USA to other countries, all his efforts came crumbling down—because he said

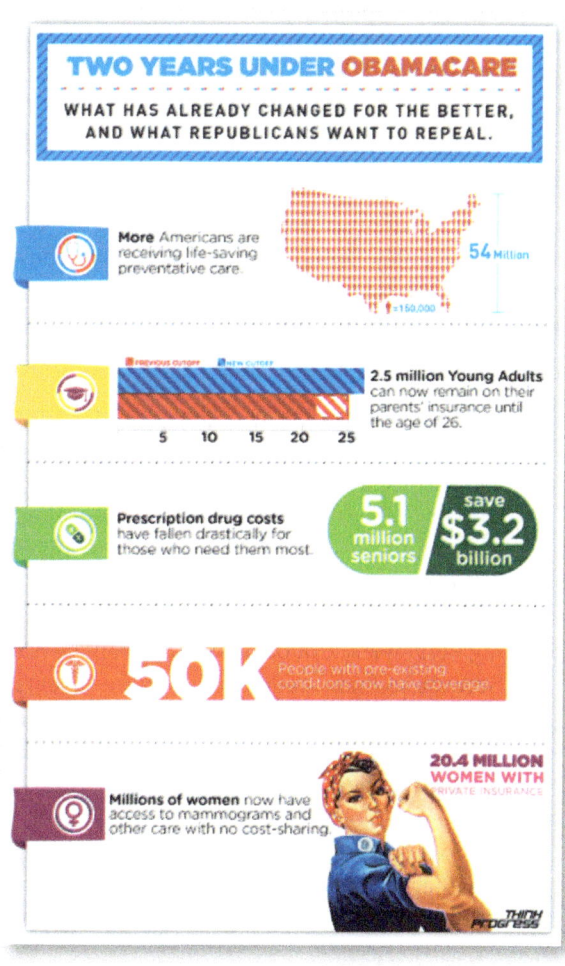

Europeans pay more taxes, a point you can only make if you put it into perspective. This tax argument implies that Americans are getting healthcare free (since it is often part of a person's benefit package). At the end of the day, an American is paying 50% more—so calling the European system a tax is just playing with words. If an American company were not responsible for your healthcare and the associated administrative costs, these fees (taxes), that they would no longer have to pay could simply go back into the employee's paycheck.

Myth #4 Obamacare is a government takeover.
No, it is not.

Myth #5 The public option is a government takeover.
Since the Stupidparty failed to change the title in an Orwellian fashion, to the "public death panel option" (as they tried to!!!!!! with the Affordable Care Act), it is really a mystery how Stupidparty Disciples can get so confused. Well, maybe not such a mystery when one considers the massive amount of misinformation put out by lobbyists, Stupidparty reps, and their Benefactors.

The public option is in fact remarkably simple. You would merely have the option of buying insurance from the government. Nobody is forcing you to opt out of your current plans. The Stupidparty feared the public option because they realized that mathematical logic would over time drive consumers eagerly to reevaluating the single-payer approach (an approach that could still allow people to buy healthcare from the private market). The reform we ended up with, while vital, is far less satisfactory and far more complex—all in order to keep Benefactors well fed. Math was mainly overpowered by Myth.

Sometimes I hear businessmen complaining about Obamacare. But unless they advocated for the public option or the single payer, these businessmen deserve no sympathy, this is their fault. However Business should not be forced to do this task. It is a tremendous waste of their resources.

So why is the U.S. system so inefficient?

1) Insurance companies can only pay out about $65 for every $100 in premium.
2) Individual insurance companies have less clout to bring down costs of medicine and medical care.
3) Doctors' offices employ an array of people and systems to figure out coverage and co-insurance issues, chase down the disputes, the nonpayers, liaising with multiple insurance companies, each with its own rules, etc.
4) Hospitals likewise devote massive resources to coverage issues, disputes and chasing nonpayers, and dealing with people with no resources.
5) Because so many people do not have coverage, they cannot get preventive measures; thus, by the time they're up in the emergency room, their condition is more severe, making more it difficult to get back to work, to look after kids or other family members or save their own business.
6) The U.S. health system has another major drawback, which hurts not only people without coverage but also those with coverage or those who may be owed money by others......

Bankruptcy—barely an issue in Europe.

2007. As many as 62% of bankruptcies were caused by medical costs, according to a Harvard study. Close to three out of four health-cost related bankruptcies are filed by people who had insurance—just not good enough insurance enough to cover the high costs of modern medical care. "I may see a $100,000 bill covered by insurance—but it comes with a $20,000 co-pay," Rose said.

http://www.washingtonpost.com/wp-srv/politics/documents/american_journal_of_medicine_09.pdf

Myth #6. Bankruptcy no big deal, only 1% a year.

Actually, 1% is a big deal when you put this number in its proper perspective, Assume someone has a working career of thirty-five years; this would mean that person has a 35% chance of going bankrupt. Are you happy with those odds?

Myth #? (no number, as it is not an obvious myth): **cancer-survivor rates.**

So now Stupidparty Disciples fall back onto one rather dubious argument, that U.S. cancer-survival rates are better. But this is highly dubious.

While it appears that U.S. rates are generally better than in Europe (only if you are insured), Dr. Otis Brawley, the chief medical officer and executive vice president at the American Cancer Society (in commenting on a paper written by Tomas Philipson, of the University of Chicago, with others), said that it "has a huge fatal flaw in it…. When you look at survival from time of diagnosis to time of death and you have a screened population that has a lot of diagnoses, you're filling that population with people who don't need treatment and because they are over-diagnosed, they have very long survival," he added.

http://health.usnews.com/health-news/news/articles/2012/04/09/cancer-care-costs-higher-in-us-than-europe-but-survival-longer

But even with that caution in mind, survival rates in Canada, Japan, Australia, and Cuba were all comparable to or higher than U.S. rates on all types of cancer except for prostate. The prostrate-cancer exception is also likely due to aggressive screening picking up cases that actually never need to be treated (and unnecessary treatment comes with its own problems)—thus, one is not comparing apples to apples.

Dr. Marie Diener-West, a professor of biostatistics at Johns Hopkins University Bloomberg School of Public Health, told us that it would be a stretch to draw too many conclusions from comparing survival rates. "Part of the problem with the comparison is that it might not actually be comparable populations," she said. "It could be [one is] an older population, it could be they have more comorbidities [other conditions] that are affecting their survival in addition to cancer, there could be occupational differences. There are many different factors that could be playing a role."

http://www.factcheck.org/2009/08/cancer-rates-and-unjustified-conclusions/

How does one explain such massive levels of confusion? The Stupidparty strategically just wants to destroy Obama. They do not really care how. The method is misrepresentation; the driving force is the money from the Benefactors, and the conduits are Fox "news," non-sport talk radio (what many people refer to as hate radio), and paid-off congressmen. All of this will be properly illustrated in later chapters.

Personally, and outside of satellite radio and NPR, I have yet to come across, on a regular basis, any talk radio that actually benignly cultivates the mind. From my experience, it invariably cultivates fear, zero objectivity, questionable information—creating fertile ground for increased fundamentalism and bigotry. Obviously there are other exceptions in other regions. But because of this, I rarely listen to terrestrial talk radio anymore. This may explain why there will no chapter devoted to the characters that dominate that media.

CHAPTER 8

Who are the 47% Moochers?

When widely followed public figures feel free to say anything, without any fact-checking, it becomes impossible for a democracy to think intelligently about big issues.

—Thomas L. Friedman

47% Moochers

A uniting factor of Stupidparty Disciples is their dislike of government. (We will put aside that such energetic efforts apparently dissipate significantly under a Stupidparty administration, conversely achieving a rabid fever pitch when confronted by a black president.) We will also put aside that this movement thrived as the result of funding by billionaires looking for ever-cheaper labor, promoted by the News Corp empire, whose American cable news outlet is run and staffed by Stupidparty leaders—who report to Rupert Murdoch, an Australian media mogul with a history of editorial interference—as explained, rather ironically, by *The Wall Street Journal.*

Having a debate about the size and power of the government is totally rational. No taxpayer wants to see waste, or individuals gaming the system, or laziness being rewarded. But when the debate is based upon misinformation, prejudice, or one section of society hoodwinking the other, such debate needs to be put into perspective. Stupidparty Disciples apparently agree that people who do not pay federal income taxes are moochers and such people evidently represent 47% of society.

But these attitudes on government and moochers patently belong in the dunce's corner on so many levels.

Problem #1.

Stupidparty advocates touting this argument appear unaware of the following:

They are mainly attacking Stupidparty Disciples/Beneficiaries, like zombies eating their own flesh. The states that contain the highest percentage of Stupidparty Disciples clearly receive the most government handouts:

	States that get most back	$1 in gets back		States that get least back	$1 in gets back
1	New Mexico	$ 2.03	1	New Jersey	$ 0.61
2	Mississippi	$ 2.02	2	Nevada	$ 0.65
3	Alaska	$ 1.84	3	Connecticut	$ 0.69
4	Louisiana	$ 1.78	4	New Hampshire	$ 0.71
5	West Virginia	$ 1.76	5	Minnesota	$ 0.72
6	North Dakota	$ 1.68	6	Illinois	$ 0.76
7	Alabama	$ 1.66	7	Delaware	$ 0.77
8	South Dakota	$ 1.53	8	California	$ 0.78
9	Kentucky	$ 1.51	9	New York	$ 0.79
10	Virginia	$ 1.51	10	Colorado	$ 0.81
11	Montana	$ 1.47	11	Massachusetts	$ .82
12	Hawaii	$ 1.44	12	Wisconsin	$ 0.86
13	Maine	$ 1.41	13	Washington	$ 0.88
14	Arkansas	$ 1.41	14	Michigan	$ 0.92
15	Oklahoma	$ 1.36	15	Oregon	$ 0.93

http://taxfoundation.org/article/federal-spending-received-dollar-taxes-paid-state-2005

Problem #2.

The number of moochers is nowhere close to 47%, for the following reasons:

1) Only 18% of tax filers paid Zero Federal Income Tax or payroll tax. Of these

    a) 10.3% were elderly

    b) 6.9% earn less than $20,000

    c) Combat Military pay is not taxable

    d) 13,000 filers earning >$533,000 pay Zero Federal income Tax

2) Virtually everyone is on the hook for Sales, Property, State Income, Gas, Alcohol, and Cigarette Taxes.

Source: ABC—September 18, 2012.
(http://abcnews.go.com/Politics/OTUS/mitt-romneys-47-percent-pay-income-taxes/story?id=17263629)

Also, bear in mind that poor people buy lottery tickets in a disproportionately high number. The lottery is a decidedly regressive tax.

A more rational estimate of moochers might be around *4% of the population—and yes, the government should try to reduce that number.
* It must be reasonable to assume that a good chunk of the Unemployed would work if they could find a job.

Problem #3.

The people who theoretically actually need the most help (the less well educated, the less healthy, those with less healthcare, those living in poverty)—well, those individuals are the most likely to benefit from progressive government largesse. While a Stupidparty government would look to cut education, "profitize" (i.e., put at risk and siphon off margins) Social Security, restrict Medicare and programs for the needy—leaving it to corporations like McDonald's to train workers, insurance companies to determine coverage, and Supreme Court justices like Scalia and Alito to protect worker safeguards.

Problem #4.

Stupidparty Disciples (voters) actually love big governments.

They love having a bloated military.
They are happy with Social Security.
They are happy with Medicaid.
I have also established that Stupidparty states benefit disproportionately from federal spending.

Problem #5.

Stupidparty leaders dare not explain their plan. What did the last Stupidparty presidential contender (Mitt) say? Yes, he would cut such (discretionary spending), but he steadfastly refused to say what. He knew that any effort to be to be honest could only backfire because his Stupidparty Disciple voters would immediately recognize that they would be the ones suffering.

Problem #6.

Stupidparty Disciples simply cannot fathom how little scope there is for cutting, especially if they do not want to cut their own throats. So how does one cut down the government in a way that actually helps Stupidparty Disciples? Let's look at the options, bearing in mind that only 30% of the federal budget is discretionary. Here is the pie chart for that 30%.

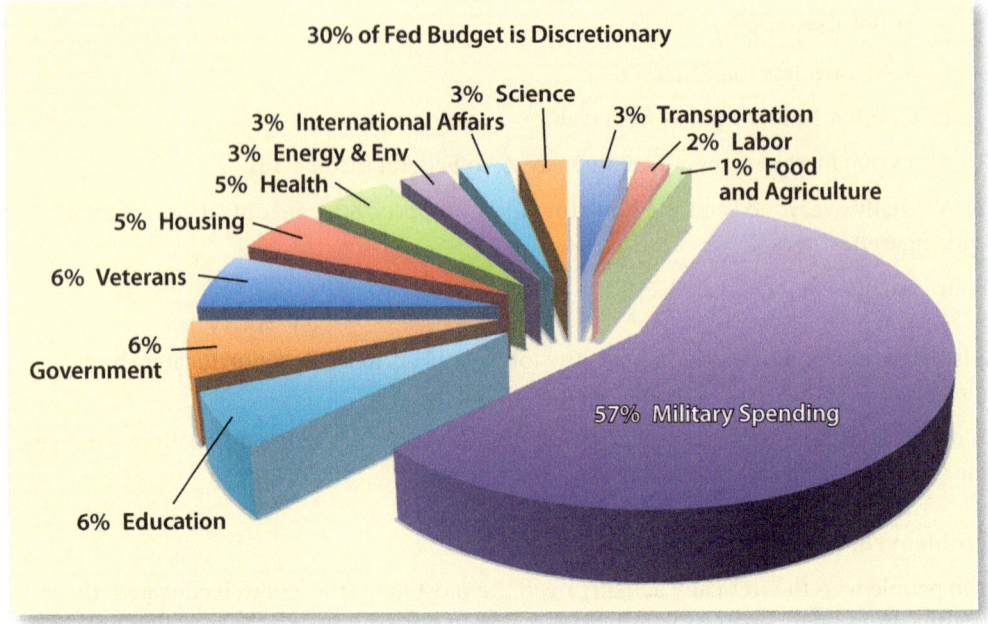

Who is really against the Military's 57% of 30% (we will get back to this), Public Education's 6% of 30%, and the Veterans' 6% of 30%. Now we are left with about 30% of 30% = i.e., about 10%.

But what do we get from the governments for this?

a. Clean air, clean water, safe food
b. Housing to keep people off the streets.
c. Public transportation, easing congestion, mobilizing workers, & job seekers
d. Business regulations that prevent insurance companies from reckless investments and profiteering—so that your claims can be paid. Or bank regulations to prevent people from walking away with all your assets, or job-retraining programs, etc.
e. Investments in scientific research

Putting investments in science aside for the moment, that leaves the favorite Stupidparty targets:

a) Foreign aid? 3%.
    Okay, let's cut that. Let China bribe themselves into the hearts and minds, furthering their trade and security interests. Or let's start by cutting security of overseas representatives; you can always blame someone else for Benghazi.

b) The post office.

It should be noted that the finances of the post office are misrepresented and generally misunderstood: 1) reforms are hampered by Congress, 2) losses are in fact being reduced, and before even thinking about closing down the service, 3) retirees should be shifted to Medicare and 4) other healthcare economies made.

The post office now has to prefund its retiree health costs, maybe up to 75 years. Darrell Issa is investigating, but we have already established Issa's credentials. His opinion is not worth the dust sitting under the paper it is written on. According to Josh Barro in a Bloomberg article, 75% of private firms do not prefund their retiree healthcare obligations. Until 2006 the post office did not prefund its retiree healthcare benefits. In 2006 Congress forced the post office to prefund (some lawmen suggested up to 75 years, including liabilities for people not even born yet) these benefits to the tune of $8 billion a year—when their actual annual costs are less than $3 billion. Consequently, they are taking an accounting hit of $5 billion a year—a remarkably similar amount to what the post office is actually unable to pay; thus, the calls for closing it down.

http://www.bloomberg.com/news/2012-08-02/understanding-the-post-office-s-benefits-mess.html

But regardless, those debts have to be paid and the taxpayer is on the hook. Therefore, when analyzing the viability of the post office today and going forward, one should assign that additional $5 billion to paying off past debts; it should be put to one side.

The post office recently reported (November 2013) that they had reduced losses by about 67%, down to around that magic $5 billion number, and had actually increased revenue.

The post office is an easy target, whose demise can only help its competitors increase their monopoly and margins. Closing down post offices—who gets hurt? Think about rural communities that lack easy access to alternatives. The post office provides local jobs; it is a fabric of the community, a staple of a diminishing High Street. The postman, a person we might see on a day-to-day basis, can act as a friendly local watchdog over a barely visited neighbor.

Who lives in rural communities? Yes, these communities are disproportionately represented within the Stupidparty power base, another clear example of Stupidparty Disciples acting against their best interests. Virtually all rural districts are Red.

Problem #7.

The best way of cutting discretionary spending would be to ask: Does the USA need an army larger than the rest of the World's combined? Do we really have to start another illegal war? Or attack Iran, bomb Assad's Syria . . . ?

Perhaps we could cut discretionary spending if we lowered the crime rate by changing gun culture, or reduced the absurd incarceration rates, closed tax loopholes; reduced subsidies to factory farms, subsidies to Oil Companies; had cheaper access to birth control (which leads to reduced poverty); and, yes, went after those 4% of moochers in a bipartisan fashion.

But suggest any of this to Stupidparty Disciples—they would then revert to one of their favorite slogans: U-S-A! U-S-A! U-S-A!

Problem #8.

The debt, which is the uniting theme of the Stupidparty (as it has the appearance of being a rational and unbigoted topic), was actually created by the Stupidparty.

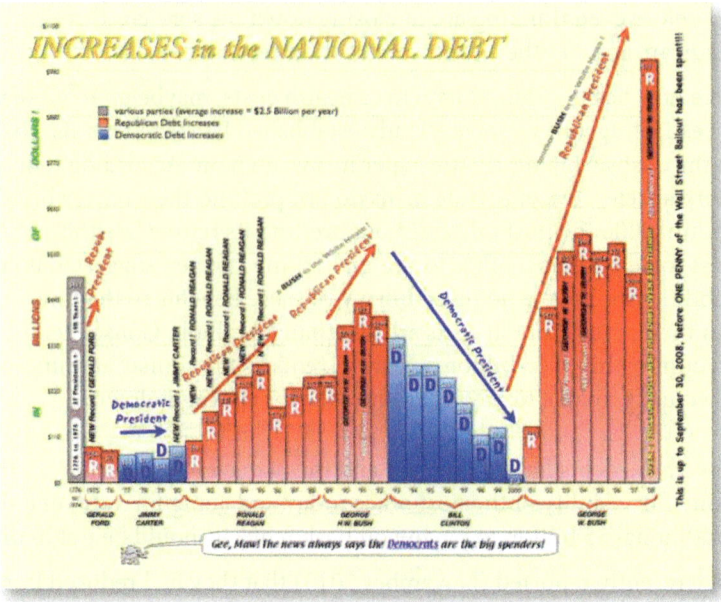

Government helping Capitalism flourish.

a) Keynesian Economics

How could capitalism ever need government assistance in creating economic growth? First, one should bear in mind that up through the Second World War, the capitalist system had had pretty mixed results. In the sixty-year period 1880 to 1940, the economy grew by 100%, or about 1.15% a year. In the next sixty-year period, the economy grew by about 400%, or almost 2.5% a year.

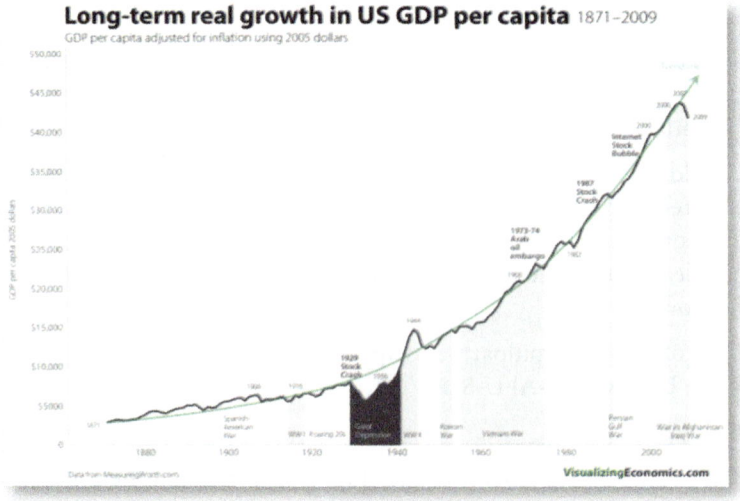

http://visualizingeconomics.com/blog/2011/03/08/long-term-real-growth-in-us-gdp-per-capita-1871-2009

Bear in mind the 1880–1940 period included the so-called Gilded Era: a time when the few, the Robber Barons, pillaged society—gaining staggering wealth—while evidently the rest of society progressed very slowly. A period that Stupidparty now harkens back to. There are perhaps two huge factors for this improvement of the capitalistic economic report card, both of which Stupidparty and Disciples cannot fathom.

1) In the 1930s, Keynes spearheaded a revolution in economic thinking, overturning the older ideas of neoclassical economics that held that free markets would, in the short to medium term, automatically provide full employment, as long as workers were flexible in their wage demands. Keynes instead argued that aggregate demand determined the overall level of economic activity, and that inadequate aggregate demand could lead to prolonged periods of high unemployment. According to Keynesian economics, state intervention was necessary to moderate "boom and bust" cycles of economic activity. (Wiki)

In short, this means that when the free market leads us into a swamp, it is at these junctures that governments can pull us out of that swamp. They can invest in those big ideas (such as a space program, medical research, or national defense), which are too expensive, too indirect, or too risky for the private sector. The private sector needs to be confident of a high likelihood of a profitable return within a fairly short window. Venture capital is similarly averse. Also, it is clear (to everyone but Stupidparty) that profit should not be the motivating factor behind war, crime prevention, incarceration, deadly disease, education, basic safety, etc. This may appear to be a damning statement, but any confusion, which clearly exists, is subliminally exacerbated by the Benefactors—playing into the lack of clarity as to what caused the debt and how serious the issue is, and the methodology and timing for debt reduction.

Investments in Scientific Research:

Back to those Investments is Scientific Research. I am sure the very notion of the government creating anything is beyond the scope of Stupidparty Disciples.

2) **Hardly anyone, of any party,** appears to understand one of the key aspects of what lies behind economic growth. When one asks a person, "Who is responsible for the technological advances that have fueled improved productivity leading to economic growth?" everyone will come up with Bill Gates or Stephen Jobs or Google, and so on.

Steve Jobs was obviously a remarkable innovator—especially in designing very appealing consumer products. Look at the technologies in the iPhone. These smart phones tap into a number of things: a) the Internet, b) the GPS, c) touch screen technology, d) the HTML common language, and e) many other ideas coming out of Silicon Valley. Before taking a closer at why Steve Jobs could be so successful, I just need to insert some brief historical context.

The U.S. government—yes, that same consistently denigrated entity—has additional if somewhat indirect tools at its disposal to stimulate private-sector growth. There are massive side benefits (ripple effects) to simply keeping the nation safe. When the Second World War began in earnest, on September 1, 1939, with the German invasion of Poland, the U.S. Army ranked seventeenth in size and combat power. This ranking placed the U.S. just behind Romania. http://www.fpri.org/footnotes/1415.200905.atkinson.usarmywwii.html

It was not the private sector or capitalism that stepped in. With extraordinary speed the government turned that situation around. Having secured military preeminence, it then also realized that to ensure the U.S. remained strong and secure, it had to keep investing in ideas. To win, the government had to take risks. It had to run risks in ways the private sector is not capable of. A rule of thumb is that the greater the risk, the greater the potential reward. The government had to invest in what with hindsight may have been some pretty crazy ideas. Most failed, but that was not the point. The point was not about making profits for investors but about ensuring that the United States could not be beaten by Russia or China—or today by radicalized Islamists. Since the stakes are higher, there must be a greater tolerance for risk. Armed Forces personnel and CIA operatives routinely put their lives at stake.

So within this context, let's now go back to Steve Jobs. Before Apple even went public, it received a $500,000 loan from an obscure government agency. Let's take another look at that ever-so-smart iPhone:

a) The Internet.
The Internet was created by a slew of government agencies and a wide range of academic research organizations, freely collaborating and sharing the fruits. The Internet was perhaps born in 1962:

"In October 1962, [J. C. R.] Licklider was hired by Jack Ruina as Director of the newly established IPTO within DARPA, with a mandate to interconnect the United States Department of Defense's main computers at Cheyenne Mountain, the Pentagon, and SAC HQ. There he formed an informal group within DARPA to further computer research."
http://schools-wikipedia.org/wp/h/History_of_the_Internet.htm

b) GPS.
The U.S. Congress during the Cold War—fearing for the very existence of the United States as a consequence of nuclear proliferation—authorized the funding of GPS:

"GPS was created and realized by the U.S. Department of Defense (DOD) and was originally run with 24 satellites. It became fully operational in 1995. Bradford Parkinson, Roger L. Easton, and Ivan A. Getting are credited with inventing it."
http://en.wikipedia.org/wiki/Global_Positioning_System

c) Touch screen technology.
Academic scientists in publicly funded universities and labs developed the touch screen and the HTML language.
http://www.emergingmarketsoutlook.com/?p=2174

d) The HTML common language.
See a) and d) above.

e) Voice-activated "virtual assistants."
This technology was created by government funds for the armed forces:

"Speech recognition technology made major strides in the 1970s, thanks to interest and funding from the U.S. Department of Defense. The DOD's DARPA Speech Understanding Research (SUR) program, from 1971 to 1976, was one of the largest of its kind in the history of speech recognition."
http://www.techhive.com/article/243060/speech_recognition_through_the_decades_how_we_ended_up_with_siri.html

f) Many other ideas coming out of Silicon Valley.

The government provided much of the early funding for Silicon Valley:

"The entity that built the Valley and gave birth to its culture of collaboration and experimentation was none other than Uncle Sam. In other words, the creation of the hub of American entrepreneurship and innovation was a federal project."
http://www.inc.com/eric-schurenberg/inconvenient-history-of-silicon-valley.html

So Steve Jobs came into a world of government-created inventions, of government-supported business. So why do the founders and the shareholders of Apple get all the profits—and do everything they can to mitigate their taxes?

Likewise, the research that produced Google's search algorithm, the fount of its wealth, was financed by a grant from the National Science Foundation.
http://www.economist.com/news/business/21584307-new-book-points-out-big-role-governments-play-creating-innovative-businesses

As for pharmaceutical companies, they are even bigger beneficiaries of state research than Internet and electronics firms. America's National Institutes of Health, with an annual budget of more than $30 billion, finances studies that lead to many of the most revolutionary new drugs.
http://www.economist.com/news/business/21584307-new-book-points-out-big-role-governments-play-creating-innovative-businesses

Economists have long recognized that the state has a role in promoting innovation. It can correct market failures by investing directly in public goods, such as research, or by using the tax system to nudge businesses towards doing so.
http://www.economist.com/news/business/21584307-new-book-points-out-big-role-governments-play-creating-innovative-businesses

The Entrepreneurial State: Debunking Public vs. Private Sector Myths (Mariana Mazzucato) argues:

The entrepreneurial state does far more than just make up for the private sector's shortcomings: through the big bets it makes on new technologies, such as aircraft or the Internet, it creates and shapes the markets of the future. At its best the state is nothing less than the ultimate Schumpeterian innovator—generating the gales of creative destruction that provide strong tailwinds for private firms like Apple.
http://www.economist.com/news/business/21584307-new-book-points-out-big-role-governments-play-creating-innovative-businesses

Stuff That Came from the Space Program | NASA.

Better, smaller digital cameras; flexible, insulating aerogels; environmentally friendly lubricants; medical-exam LED lights.
http://www.consumerreports.org/cro/news/2011/07/5-consumer-innovations-that-came-from-the-space-shuttle-program/index.htm

Or what about scratch-resistant glasses, comfy sneaker insoles, enriched baby foods, ear thermometers, smoke detectors, protective paint, better cardiac pacemakers?
http://www.cnn.com/2007/LIVING/worklife/10/04/nasa.everyday/

The Large Hadron Collider | CERN.

One realizes that Stupidparty Disciples are happy to think that Jesus rode around on dinosaurs—but the rest of us have a thirst for knowledge, a thirst for answers, for solutions. It is not just us: Ancient Greeks, Egyptians, Persians, Romans, et al., created better education, literacy, medicines, irrigation, etc.

These cultures also created or promoted Philosophy, History, Theater, the Olympics, and of course Democracy. They were asking, "Where do we come from? What is our place in the universe?" It turns out that even though many questions have been answered, many tough questions remain. Not even the Asset Strippers can afford the time and money to help humanity understand its existential place—and once again, the government steps into the abyss. And as they explore, they discover. A side benefit of all this additional

knowledge will be new potential products that consumers will demand, presenting opportunities for the private sector.

So next time Stupidparty moans about nonscandals such as Solyndra (a government investment that did not lead to profit), you might just want to ask why they do not appreciate the many ways they have profited from government investments or actions, including not having been invaded by Germany or Japan in 1940—a time when the USA was extremely vulnerable—or Russia since 1940. Or on the other hand, ask them about Tesla—a car company built on the back of government assistance—because the government can be a lot smarter than Stupidparty Disciples, in that it clearly has a better understanding of the importance of the technologies behind Tesla (zero gas) or Solyndra, for that matter (solar panels).

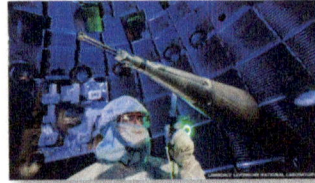

Next Big idea?

It could be anything. It might be extremely cheap energy from nuclear fusion, a decades-old project, with a recent breakthrough that many governments are working on (see link below).

http://www.bbc.co.uk/news/science-environment-24429621

It is also clear that the U.S. infrastructure is somewhat suspect when it comes to international comparisons. One way to leapfrog over everyone else might be the proposed Hyperloop. If venture capital finds the logistics too complicated, perhaps this is a potential job for the government. I do not know how feasible it is. I am certainly no engineer. But if anyone says that this is daft, you only need to evaluate one thing: how does that person (the cynic)'s résumé compare to the résumé of the person proposing the idea, a man by the name of Elon Musk? Ignorance of such matters is ever more inexcusable because of that government invention—the Internet.

The Hyperloop. San Francisco to LA in 30 minutes.

CHAPTER 9

Jobs & the economy, is it so difficult?

Republicans don't like people to talk about depressions. You can hardly blame them for that. You remember the old saying: Don't talk about rope in the house where somebody has been hanged.

—Harry S. Truman

Stupidparty Learning Curve.

One studies history to learn from it—evidently a pointless exercise if you have a
brain that cannot adapt from 1760 or (in
terms of economics) learn from 1929.
Putting Stupidparty Economics into
perspective might be slightly tedious, but
vital—because if Stupidparty Economics
is nonsense, then the Stupidparty is totally
worthless.

www.mywebface.com

The Great Depression began with a stock
market crash in 1929 after a period of
easy money and ever-increasing risk taking. Stocks plummeted, bankruptcies erupted;
banks closed, leading people to panic, to withdraw their savings; leading to more banks
folding, and so on. Business laid off workers; consumers stopped spending. President
Hoover made it worse by listening to American industrialists and signing into law the
Hawley-Smoot Tariff to protect industry from overseas competition. This disastrous
move was followed by a desire to balance the budget, leading in 1931 to austerity, which
ended up making it far more difficult to spur the
economy. Then came Roosevelt and the New Deal—
bringing reflationary spending (i.e., spending boosts,
or reflates, economic activity)—followed eventually
by the Second World War, which forced even more
spending, all of which combined to eventually end the
Great Depression.

Even though the Republicans were in charge through
1931, they were not the Stupidparty back then. Even
though they cut taxes, they did not simply focus
cutting the tax burden on the few while stiffing the
many, and since the collapse was unprecedented,
they did not have an economic roadmap (history) to show them the path. It might be
unfair to blame Hoover for the actual collapse, since he had only been president for a
few months, but his actions after the crash
simple added fuel to the flames.

The conditions that led to the Great Recession in 2008 were similar to the conditions
that led to the Great Depression. Luckily,
economists had a pretty good idea how to
prevent the Great Depression from recurring and such economists succeeded in conducting an intervention on the Stupidparty
in late 2008. Most people understood,
everyone except the Stupidparty, that is,
and specifically people like the greatest non

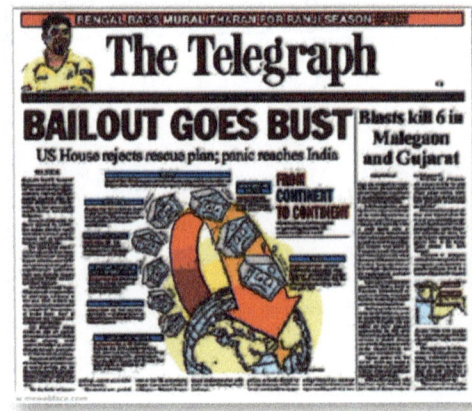

guru and Ayn Rand fan boy,* Ron Paul. These people in Congress fought the incorrectly titled Auto and Bank bailouts. Opportunistic and extremely dangerous op-eds from Mitt Romney did not help either. These were not bailouts; they were extremely penal loans wherein the taxpayers took equity and eventually walked out with handsome profits. (The taxpayers did not get all their money back on General Motors, but numerous direct and indirect jobs were saved.)

http://www.slideshare.net/hanksjunk/2008-recession-pics-and-headlines
*See end of Chapter for an explanation.

Stupidparty Economic Plan:

Mitt Romney had an opportunity to put the best possible spin on his economic plan during his speech at the Stupidparty 2012 presidential convention. It is a speech that would be overseen by the very best talent available to Stupidparty. This is a speech that a candidate would pour his heart into—assuming, of course, that he has a heart. This is his chance to explain why we should overcome our collective doubts as a nation about what really motivates him. At

www.mywebface.com

the time, everyone was asking of this Asset Stripper, yes we understand that you (like everyone else) plan to reduce the debt (the only supposedly rational raison d'être for even considering the Stupidparty), but please explain how. This was the answer every reporter, every informed voter really needed to hear.

www.mywebface.com
The very best talent available to the stupidparty

This is the time when everyone was watching, everyone paying attention, ready to be informed, waiting for answers. Romney gives us his best shot; he enumerates the Stupidparty plan in the best possible light.

The following is an exact transcript of the part of his speech that deals with his actual economic plan:

First, by 2020, North America will be energy independent by taking full advantage of our oil and coal and gas and nuclear and renewables.

Second, we will give our fellow citizens the skills they need for the jobs of today and the careers of tomorrow. When it comes to the school your child will attend, every parent should have a choice, and every child should have a chance.

Third, we will make trade work for America by forging new trade agreements. And when nations cheat in trade, there will be unmistakable consequences.

Fourth, to assure every entrepreneur and every job creator that their investments in America will not vanish as have those in Greece, we will cut the deficit and put America on track to a balanced budget.

And fifth, we will champion SMALL businesses, America's engine of job growth. That means reducing taxes on business, not raising them. It means simplifying and modernizing the regulations that hurt small business the most. And it means that we must rein in the skyrocketing cost of healthcare by repealing and replacing Obamacare.

Today, women are more likely than men to start a business. They need a president who respects and understands what they do.

And let me make this very clear, unlike President Obama, I will not raise taxes on the middle class.

Sounds all good? Now hold on to your horses Mr. Romney……

Putting Romney's 5-point plan under a Microscope.
(Or was it a 7-point plan?):

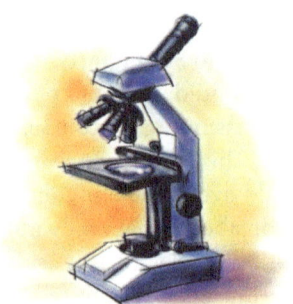

First—Energy Independence.
Looks like Obama will achieve that by 2018.
U.S. oil and gas production is evolving so rapidly—and demand is dropping so quickly—that in just five years the U.S. could no longer need to buy oil from any source but Canada, according to Citigroup's global head of commodities research.
http://www.cnbc.com/id/100450133

Second—Job skills.
All presidents talk about Job retraining; they usually care enough and are excited enough to proudly provide some details. But for Romney these plans are highly dubious—especially since Paul Ryan (his VP choice) and the House of Representatives keep trying to slash such programs (as discussed elsewhere).

Third—Trade Agreements.
Mitt Romney convention comments build upon his campaign's assertion that Barack Obama didn't expand U.S. trade deals.

Politifact rates this statement false

After lengthy negotiations, Obama signed trade agreements with three separate nations on Oct. 21, 2011—South Korea, Colombia, and Panama. These were not trivial deals. The one with South Korea, in particular, was "the largest trade deal since 1994," when the U.S. approved the North American Free Trade Agreement, Bloomberg News reported at the time, citing administration data. The South Korea deal was poised to increase U.S. export access "for everything from cars to farm goods," Bloomberg wrote.
http://www.politifact.com/truth-o-meter/statements/2012/jan/08/mitt-romney/
mitt-romney-says-barack-obama-didnt-expand-us-trad/

Fourth—cutting the deficit.
Yes, but please, please, please tell us how.

Fifth—cutting taxes on Businesses.

Yes, but how will you pay for those tax cuts?

Sixth—respecting Women.

I don't think so; just look at the actions of the House, of "binders full of women," the history of the Mormon Church, and the advice he dispensed as a Mormon priest: he respects and understands that women should stay at home and raise the kids.

Seventh—"And let me make this very clear—unlike President Obama, I will not raise taxes on the middle class."

Actually, virtually every taxpayer ended up with at least $1,000 in tax cuts in the prior three years. The only exceptions being the unemployed smokers and unemployed (sun) tanners.

http://firstread.nbcnews.com/_news/2012/10/02/14181546-romney-did-obama-raise-taxes?lite

So it was not only that Romney had zero substance, but also that even the nebulous assertions he made were utter nonsense. However, that Stupidparty audience did not care; they lapped up every vacuous word, every falsehood. Fox did not care. The supposedly biased mainstream media did not care. The CNN panel of experts were nowhere close to pointing out how absurd the speech was. They must appear neutral and that means not bursting into laughter when Stupidparty does Stupidparty stuff. But the mainstream media needs to grow a pair and laugh at these clowns, these emperors with no clothes.

Romney's tax cuts.

Everyone loves to hear about tax cuts (how could they not be popular?). But how can you be allowed to get credit for the easy stuff (which would likely increase the deficit) unless you explain the central pillar of your economic values, i.e., cutting the deficit? But these guys are so Stupidparty that even the good stuff is actually nothing but garbage (i.e., Stupidparty economics), therefore easy to destroy. So here is all the good stuff.

www.mywebface.com

Romney's tax plan pledged to cut income tax rates by 20% across the board, get rid of the estate tax and the Alternative Minimum Tax, maintain progressivity, and pay for these rate cuts by eliminating tax loopholes but not ones that provide incentives for savings and investment. While Romney has been very specific about which taxes to cut, he and Ryan have roundly refused to specify which loopholes they would eliminate.

Sounds great, except for the fact that the nonpartisan Tax Policy Center said the plan cannot work mathematically, and while it might help the wealthy, everyone else would suffer.

To rebut this, Romney and Ryan tout five (or six) studies that support their math. These guys appear to have a unique understanding of the concept of "study." Their studies are actually blog posts or *Wall Street Journal* editorials. But it is worse than that.

In addition, as PolitiFact notes, the, ahem, studies "come from people or groups with ties to Romney." Two come from a Romney campaign adviser, while "three come from conservative think tanks, the Heritage Foundation and the American Enterprise Institute, which have analysts who advise the Romney campaign." The Tax Policy Center, on the other hand, not only doesn't have similar ties to the Obama campaign, but one of the lead authors of its study was a senior staff economist on President George H. W. Bush's Council of Economic Advisers.
http://www.usnews.com/opinion/blogs/robert-schlesinger/2012/10/17/
romneys-six-studies-dont-actually-support-his-tax-plan-math

Regardless, numerous organizations still studied these studies, and all concluded that the Romney-Ryan cited studies did not prove that Romney's plan added up.

The Atlantic's Matthew O'Brien published an assessment under the headline THE 6 STUDIES PAUL RYAN CITED PROVE MITT ROMNEY'S TAX PLAN IS IMPOSSIBLE.

The Washington Post's Ezra Klein neatly summarized the giant and very relevant question this raises about how the Romney campaign operates. He wrote, "It's worth pointing out the brazenness of the Romney campaign's talking point. They know four of their six studies aren't, even in the loosest definition of the term, 'studies.' They know two of the four are duplicates."

Separate and apart from all the massive dishonesty of the Romney campaign and their faux studies, conservative austerity hawks had been excited by having what they believed was a credible study from Harvard professors Reinhart and Rogoff in 2010, showing that austerity in the USA would work. But this study, as a result of "coding" issues, had too many errors.

Massachusetts professors Thomas Herndon, Michael Ash, and Robert Pollin criticized Reinhart and Rogoff's findings in a study of their own. In an attempt to duplicate R and R's results, they discovered what Reinhart and Rogoff are calling a coding error that omitted several countries from an Excel spreadsheet of historical data used in the calculations. Another found the Harvard calculations selectively excluded data that would have produced different results, had they been included. The correct results, calculated by the Massachusetts team, canceled out Reinhart and Rogoff's conclusion.

As part of the effort to rehabilitate their image, Reinhart and Rogoff's have since been distancing themselves from austerity, stating in a 2013 *Financial Times* piece:

"A higher borrowing trajectory is warranted, given weak demand and low interest rates, where governments can identify high-return infrastructure projects. Borrowing to finance productive infrastructure raises long-run potential growth, ultimately pulling debt ratios lower. We have argued this consistently since the outset of the crisis."
http://www.huffingtonpost.com/2013/05/02/reinhart-rogoff-austerity_n_3201453.html

Ryan's Austerity.

So while the Romney campaign adamantly refused to detail how it would reduce the debt, we are in luck—since Romney chose the Stupidparty debt guru as his VP, Paul Ryan (chairman of the House Budget Committee). Ryan already had a detailed austerity plan rapturously approved by the Stupidparty House.

1) Massive tax cuts for the wealthy.
2) Repeal of the Affordable Care Act.
3) Privatization of Medicaid and Medicare. Granny would have try and secure insurance.
4) Cuts for food stamps, other welfare, and federal employee pensions.

Taken together, Ryan would cut spending on such programs by $5.3 trillion, much of which currently goes to the have-nots. He would then give that money to America's haves: some $4.3 trillion in tax cuts, compared with current policies, according to Citizens for Tax Justice. Ryan's justification was straight out of Dickens. He wants to improve the moral fiber of the poor. Ryan warned that a generous safety net "lulls able-bodied people into lives of complacency and dependency, which drains them of their very will and incentive to make the most of their lives. It's demeaning."

http://articles.washingtonpost.com/2012-03-20/opinions/35448553_1_paul-ryan-complacency-and-dependency-ryan-plan

How does the Stupidparty sell this?—by using Orwellian techniques. His plan would "repair the safety net," helping "those who need it most." Financial aid for college would be slashed "to put us on a sustainable path," and job training slashed as well (see point 2 of Romney's 7-point economic "plan"), which would evidently give workers "the tools to thrive in the twenty-first century."

So this (the Romney-Ryan plan) is actually nothing other than Asset Stripping, all so Romney and his chums can pay even less tax and glob off additional billions for their own bank accounts—mooching off the backs of the American people. This of course dovetails with Romney's longstanding expertise in Asset Stripping, and hardly paying any taxes, deferring taxes, and possibly paying Zero taxes for ten years, all by using numerous loopholes.

Job Retraining.

Earlier this year [2011], House Republicans voted to cut $3.8 billion from job training programs [those types of programs Romney so disingenuously indicated were part of his 5-point plan]—a particularly harsh cut given that the House GOP budget would make food and housing assistance for struggling families dependent upon participation in training programs.

http://politicalcorrection.org/blog/201105100015

From the Committee on Appropriations, 2011.

DEPARTMENT OF LABOR—The bill provides $10.4 billion in new discretionary budget authority for the Department of Labor, which is $2.6 billion (-20%) below last year's level and $2.4 billion (-19%) below the president's request. The legislation also reforms the funding structure of several DOL programs, to make them more transparent and accountable to the taxpayer by eliminating advance funding for future years and transitioning agency budgets to correspond with the regular fiscal year.

Employment Training Administration (ETA)—The legislation provides the ETA with $7.5 billion in new discretionary budget authority: $2.2 billion (-23%) below last year's level and $2.1 billion (-22%) below the president's request. Much of this reduction is due to the transition of employment and training programs to a federal fiscal year and the elimination of $2.4 billion in advance appropriations for the 2013 fiscal year.
http://appropriations.house.gov/news/documentsingle.aspx?DocumentID=262231

Income discrepancy (look, then try and imagine trends under a Romney presidency):

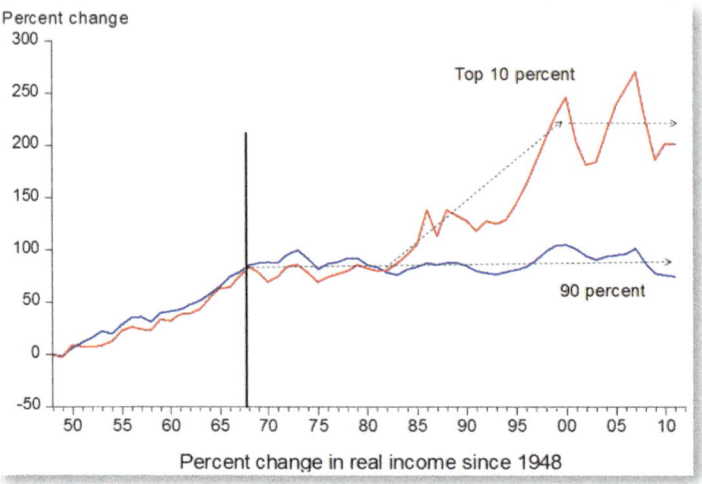

http://www.forbes.com/sites/louiswoodhill/2013/03/28/the-mystery-of-income-inequality-broken-down-to-one-simple-chart/

But Forbes is a pretty conservative publication, and I thought that the 10%/90% was likely to gloss over what Romney and his paymasters are really up to. So let's also look at the graph from *The Economist*, which focuses on the top 1%.

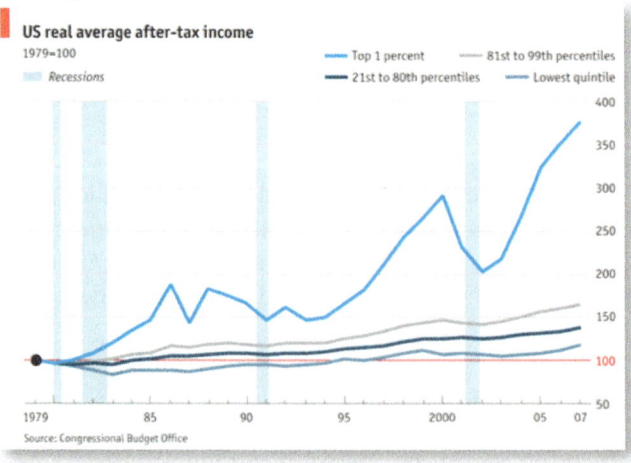

http://www.economist.com/blogs/dailychart/2011/10/income-inequality-america

Top 1% and their Tax Burden. (Wiki)

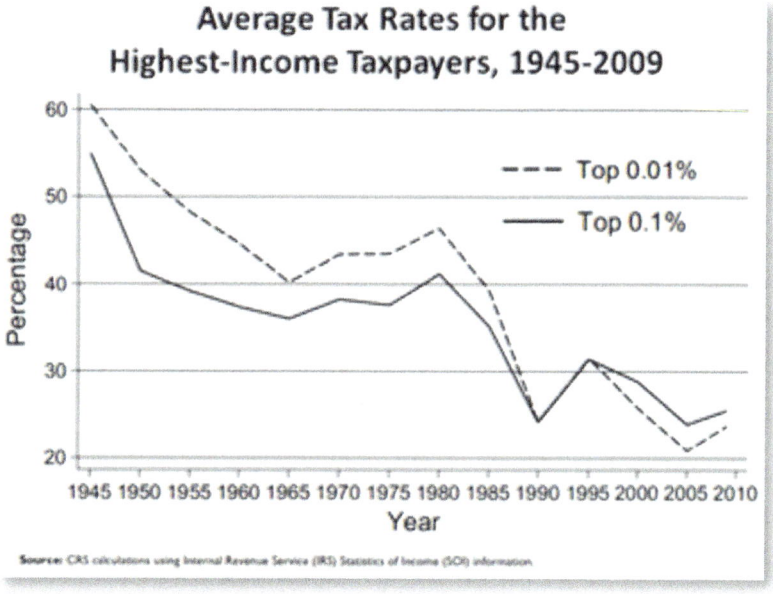

How have those CEOs performed?

In 1978, CEOs took home 26.5 times more than the average worker. They now make roughly 206 times more than workers, EPI found. **The pay isn't always tied to the performance** of their businesses—as *ThinkProgress* has noted, CEOs at companies like Bank of America often pocket huge pay increases, even as the company's stock price plummets and jobs are cut.

SOURCE: Adapted from Lawrence Mishel and Josh Bivens, *Occupy Wall Streeters are right about skewed economic rewa* *in the United States,* Economic Policy Institute Briefing Paper #331, 2011.

Workers' wages aren't tied to productivity either. Yet virtually all productivity benefits trickle up. Despite substantial gains in productivity since the 1970s, worker pay has remained flat. According to Labor Department data cited by *The Huffington Post*, inflation-adjusted wages fell 2 percent in 2011.

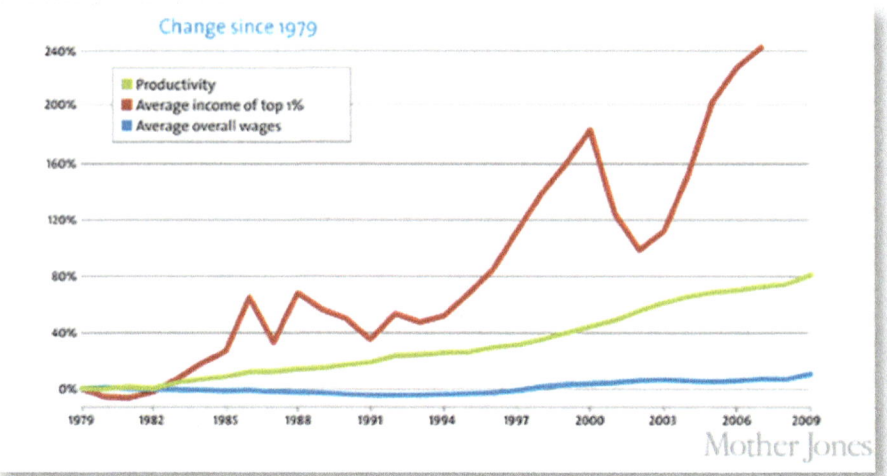

As a result, American income inequality has skyrocketed, growing worse than it is in countries like Pakistan and Ivory Coast. Wealth inequality is worse than it was even in Ancient Rome. And as pay skyrockets and tax rates fall for the richest Americans, the rising inequality has left the bottom 95 percent of Americans saddled with more debt than ever before.

http://thinkprogress.org/economy/2012/05/03/475952/ceo-pay-faster-worker-pay/

In order to keep more, pay less and less and less benefits.

So the Romney plan just wants to keep stripping away, pay less and less, and work harder and harder. In order to Asset Strip, you need to emasculate the unions:

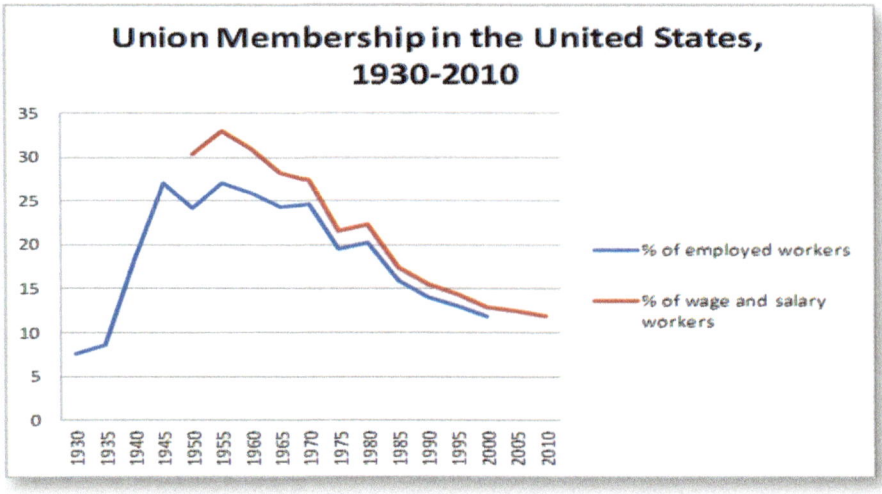

http://en.wikipedia.org/wiki/Labor_unions_in_the_United_States (graph)

Income Discrepancy statistics.

1) One family has the same wealth as 40% of America combined.

"'The wealthiest family in this country is the Walton family. They are worth about a hundred billion dollars. That's more wealth than the bottom 40 percent of the American people. One of the reasons that the Walton family, the owners of Walmart, is so wealthy is that they receive huge subsidies from the taxpayers of this country,' [Sen. Bernie Sanders] said. 'When you pay, at Walmart, starvation wages, you don't provide benefits to your workers, who picks up the difference? The answer is that many of the workers in Walmart end up getting Medicaid, they get food stamps, and they get affordable housing paid for by the taxpayers of this country.'"

http://www.rawstory.com/rs/2013/08/03/bernie-sanders-walmart-familys-obscene-wealth-subsidized-by-taxpayers/

2) 43% of Americans live in poverty or are one crisis away from poverty.

"According to the report, 43 percent of households in America—some 127.5 million people—are liquid-asset poor. If one of these households experiences a sudden loss of income, caused, for example, by a layoff or a medical emergency, it will fall below the poverty line within three months. People in these households simply don't have enough cash to make it for very long in a crisis."

http://assetsandopportunity.org/scorecard/about/main_findings/

3) 42% of Americans have household income less than $25,000.

4) 87% of Americans earn less than $100,000.

5) As for all that Joe the Plumber outrage, all that horror over the expiration of the Bush tax cuts—i.e., the top rate going up 3%...

0.17% of Americans earn more than $500,000—thereby being possibly impacted by higher tax rate. (Those earning, say, $450,000, should find it quite easy to bring taxable income down to $400,000. There are numerous ways of bringing down one's taxable income, via deductions, expenses, charity, IRAs. The Defined Benefit Plan alone allows higher earners to defer $2,000,000 per person or $4,000,000 for a married couple. Thus, only about 50% of 0.17% of tax filers will be significantly impacted—by paying a little bit more. But the Stupidparty and Romney will do anything to protect these people.)

Data from http://www.lazymanandmoney.com/how-many-people-make-more-than-250000-per-year/Aug 2011.

Joe the not quite a Plumber soars to fame as a result of Stupidparty strategy of not laughing themselves silly over his upside-down concerns about the lifestyles of the top 0.1%. Down on his luck, Joe is tortured by the fact that Limbaugh will now have to a pay a bit more tax on top of his $500,000 annual property tax on his Palm Beach property, with its five homes. He sold his Manhattan apartment, as New York is no longer his type of place, but he can always come back on his Gulfstream.

USA and the Rest of the World.

In terms of time off, annual leave, and maternity leave, how does the USA compare to the rest of the world:

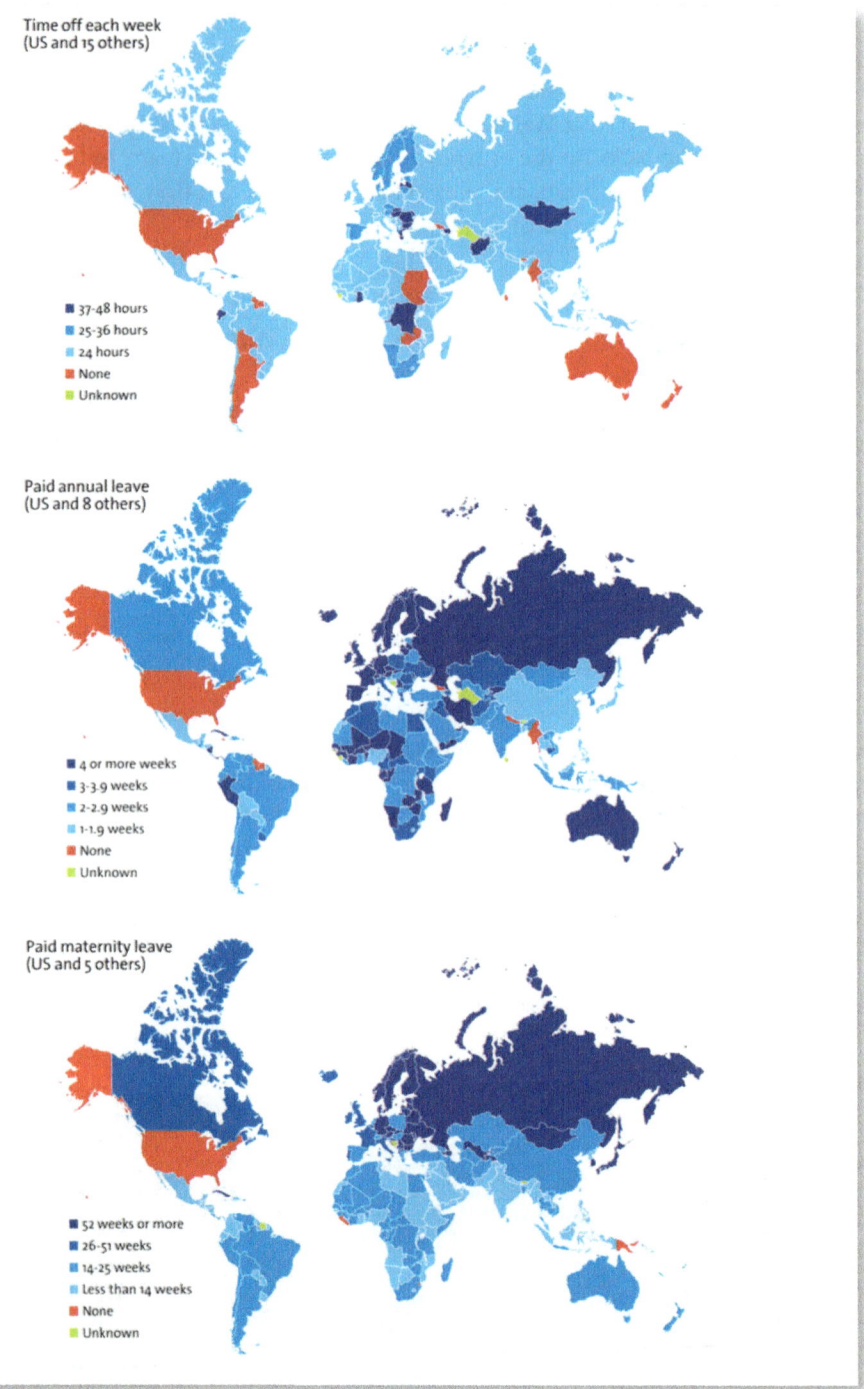

Stupidparty v. the Democrats
Or Stupidparty Myth # whatever*—Trickle-down economics works.
*I think we can stop counting the countless myths; I believe the pattern is now established.

So apart from the Great Depression, the Great Recession, the efforts to make both events far worse, and the massive debt created by Oil-induced wars (inflamed by corporate donations) and the uncalled-for Bush Jr. tax cuts, what evidence is there that mental-midget trickle-down economic claptrap ever works?

http://www.nytimes.com/interactive/2008/10/14/opinion/20081014_OPCHART.html?_r=0

The Stock Market.
2008—thus, excluding the Obama boom.

Or according to *Forbes*:
Average annual compound return on the stock market has been 18 times greater under Democratic presidents (If you invested $100k for 40 years of Republican administrations, you had $126k at the end; if you invested $100k for 40 years of Democrat administrations, you had $3.9M at the end.)

***Forbes* had some other tidbits:**
Personal disposable income has grown nearly 6 times more under Democratic presidents. Gross Domestic Product (GDP) has grown 7 times more under Democratic presidents. Corporate profits have grown over 16% more per year under Democratic presidents (they actually declined under Republicans by an average of 4.53%/ year).

Republican presidents added 2.5 times more to the national debt than Democratic presidents.

The two times the economy steered into

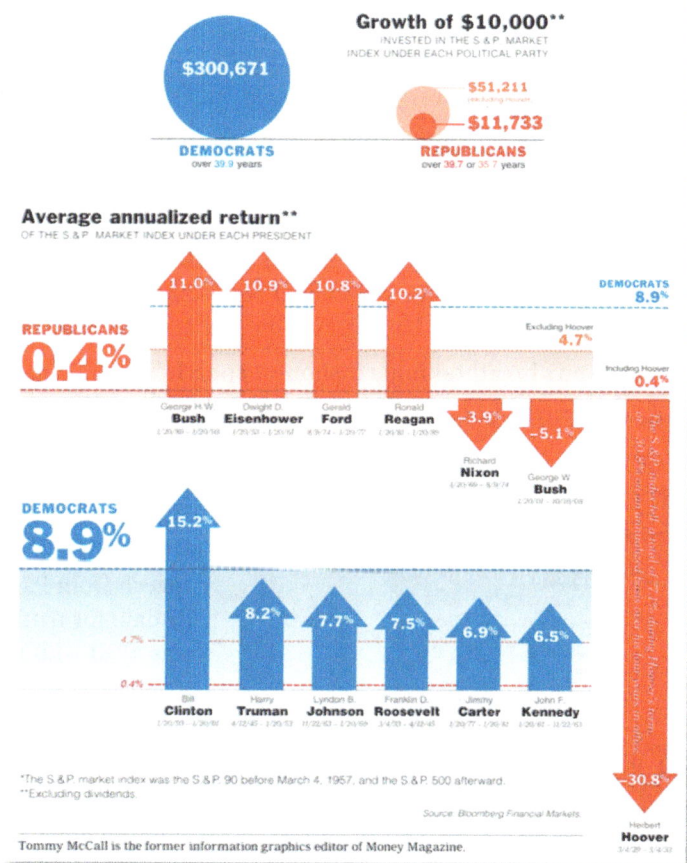

Growth of $10,000
INVESTED IN THE S&P. MARKET INDEX UNDER EACH POLITICAL PARTY

$300,671
DEMOCRATS
over 39.9 years

$51,211
$11,733
REPUBLICANS
over 39.7 or 35.7 years

Average annualized return
OF THE S&P. MARKET INDEX UNDER EACH PRESIDENT

REPUBLICANS
0.4%

11.0% George H.W **Bush**
10.9% Dwight D. **Eisenhower**
10.8% Gerald **Ford**
10.2% Ronald **Reagan**

DEMOCRATS 8.9%
Excluding Hoover 4.7%
Including Hoover 0.4%

–3.9% Richard **Nixon**
–5.1% George W **Bush**

DEMOCRATS
8.9%

15.2% Bill **Clinton**
8.2% Harry **Truman**
7.7% Lyndon B. **Johnson**
7.5% Franklin D. **Roosevelt**
6.9% Jimmy **Carter**
6.5% John F. **Kennedy**

*The S&P. market index was the S&P. 90 before March 4, 1957, and the S&P. 500 afterward.
**Excluding dividends.

Source: Bloomberg Financial Markets

–30.8% Herbert **Hoover**

Tommy McCall is the former information graphics editor of Money Magazine.

the ditch (Great Depression and Great Recession) were during Republican, laissez-faire administrations.

And another one, another Myth bites the dust... (audience participation welcome)

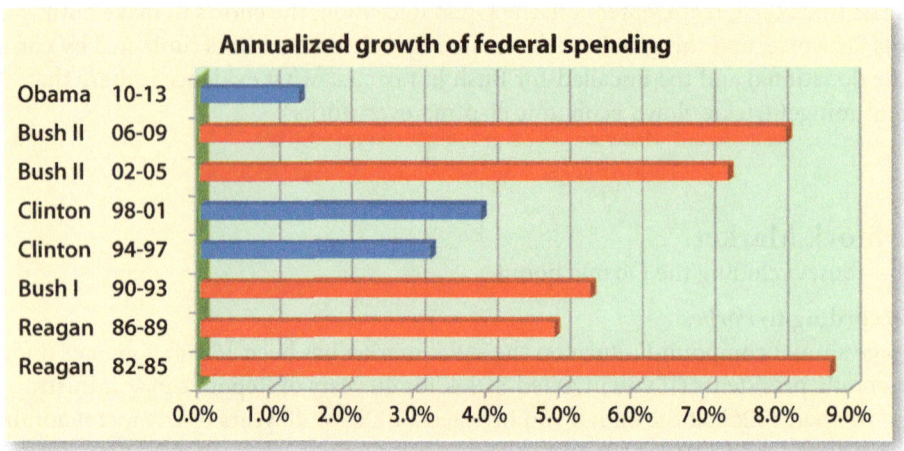

http://www.forbes.com/sites/adamhartung/2012/10/10/want-a-better-economy-history-says-vote-democrat/

Truth v. Lies & Substance v. Emptiness:

The Romney campaign took lying to new levels, calculating that the confusion caused would be beneficial—especially with a media terrified of being seen to take a side.

So how can you tell what is true? Well, that is quite easy since the truth to Stupidparty is like garlic to a vampire.

While discussing false equivalency in a later chapter, I will establish that the Stupidparty told 500% more lies than Democrats during their convention. Romney's speech had zero content. Ryan's speech was riddled with lies. As *The Washington Post* and everyone else (except Fox) agreed:

* **"Paul Ryan's breathtakingly dishonest speech."**

During the 2012 Campaign, at an ABC News panel, Mitt Romney pollster Neil Newhouse said, "We're not going to let our campaign be dictated by fact-checkers." *Washington Post* digital opinions editor, James Downie, continued, "Wednesday's speech from Paul Ryan certainly took that disdain for truth to heart, as his address was filled with falsehoods from start to finish."

*http://www.washingtonpost.com/blogs/post-partisan/post/paul-ryans-dishonest-speech/2012/08/30/16bb62d8-f24f-11e1-adc6-87dfa8eff430_blog.html

www.mywebface.com

Therefore, it is important to spend some time and take in what Bill Clinton was saying during his highly praised 2012 convention speech. None of his facts can be tolerated by Stupidparty and their Disciples. Clinton was simply trying to give a straightforward economics lesson—something that all voters who value democracy are responsible for trying to understand. If one can absorb and remember this, then the billions spent by the Benefactors supporting the Stupidparty out of pure self-interest would become ineffective.

The following is a condensed version of a report from *The Washington Post* "Wonk Blog" with some added images:

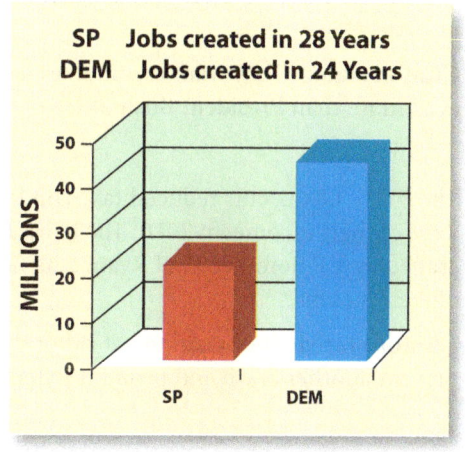

Clinton stated: As the Senate Republican leader (**Mitch McConnell**) said, in a remarkable moment of candor, two full years before the election, their number-one priority was not to put America back to work. It was to put the president out of work.

TRUE

The Washington Post supplies the video (see link below).

Clinton stated: Well, since 1961, for 52 years now, the Republicans have held the White House 28 years, the Democrats 24. In those 52 years our private economy has produced 66 million private-sector jobs. So what's the job score? Republicans: 24 million. Democrats: 42.

TRUE WITH A BUT

If you look at total private-sector employment, this checks out. But nonfarm payrolls are the preferred measure. There, the Democratic record is actually more impressive, with 43.8 million nonfarm payrolls added. But Republicans added 35.3 million. More generally, these numbers would benefit from being compared to population growth. As it turns out, very rarely do any presidents manage growth that outpaces the growth in the size of the civilian population older than 16.

Clinton stated: Just in the last couple of elections, they [Stupidparty] defeated two distinguished Republican senators because they dared to cooperate with Democrats on issues important to the future of the country, even national security.

TRUE

Dick Lugar and Bob Bennett lost to primary challengers in 2012 and 2010 respectively, Richard Mourdock, who defeated Lugar in a primary this year, attacked him as "Obama's Favorite Republican," and Bennett's defeat is often attributed to his sponsorship of a universal healthcare bill with an individual mandate, along with Democrat Ron Wyden.

Clinton stated: They beat a Republican congressman with almost 100% voting record on every conservative score because he said he realized he did not have to hate the president to disagree with him.

TRUE

Clinton is talking about Rep. Bob Inglis, who had a 93% American Conservative Union rating but voted to censure fellow South Carolina Republican Joe Wilson for shouting "you lie!" during the State of the Union. Inglis then lost re nomination in 2010, 71% to 29%.

Clinton stated: They want to cut taxes for high-income Americans even more than President Bush did.

TRUE

The 2001–'08 tax cuts reduced taxes on the top 1% by an average of 7.3% of their income, in 2010. The latest House Republican budget, crafted by VP nominee Paul Ryan, cuts taxes on the top 1% by 11.7% of their income.

Clinton stated: They want to get rid of those pesky financial regulations designed to prevent another crash and prohibit federal bailouts.

TRUE

House Republicans voted to end all of Dodd–Frank last year as part of Ryan's budget plan, and just this year pushed for repeal of the "resolution authority" provisions meant to wind down failing banks without bailouts.

Clinton stated: They want to actually increase defense spending over a decade $2 trillion more than the Pentagon has requested, without saying what they'll spend it on.

TRUE

The 2013 Republican budget funds defense at $6.2 trillion over the next decade, whereas the Pentagon request funds it at $5.6 trillion over a decade. That's $600 billion, not $2 trillion. But Mitt Romney's defense plan does increase spending by $2.1 trillion over the Pentagon baseline. So Clinton's statement checks out there.

Clinton stated: In 2010, as the president's recovery program kicked in, the job losses stopped, and things began to turn around. The Recovery Act saved or created millions of jobs

TRUE

As I've explained, most studies suggest the stimulus created millions of jobs.

Clinton stated:… and cut taxes—let me say this again—cut taxes for 95% of the American people.

TRUE

The "Make Work Pay" tax credit in the stimulus helped 94.3% of Americans.

Clinton stated: And in the last 29 months, our economy has produced about 4.5 million private-sector jobs.

TRUE

Dead-on: Private-sector employment went up by 4.544 million over the past 29 months, according to BLS (the U.S. Bureau of Labor Statistics).

Clinton stated: More than 500,000 manufacturing jobs have been created under President Obama. That's the first time manufacturing jobs have increased since the 1990s.

TRUE

Measuring from manufacturing's trough in January 2010, jobs have increased by 532,000. But many manufacturing jobs were lost between January 2009 and January 2010—which means they were also lost under Obama. Whether you want to blame Obama for that first year is up to you.

Clinton stated: It saved more than a million jobs, and not just at GM, Chrysler, and their dealerships, but in auto parts manufacturing all over the country.

TRUE

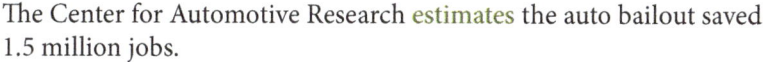

The Center for Automotive Research estimates the auto bailout saved 1.5 million jobs.

Clinton stated: So what's happened? There are now 250,000 more people working in the auto industry than on the day the companies were restructured.

TRUE

The companies were formally restructured in July 2009, with GM, for example, being reorganized on July 10. Since then, auto industry employment is up by 233,800 workers, according to BLS.

Clinton stated: Now, the agreement the administration made with the management, labor, and environmental groups to double car mileage, that was a good deal, too. It will cut your gas prices in half, your gas bill… according to several analyses, over the next 20 years, it will bring us another 500,000 good, new jobs into the American economy.

TRUE

The new mileage standards will double fuel efficiency which, in principle, should halve fuel costs. A study by the Blue Green Alliance, a joint Labor–Environmental group, estimates the standards will create 570,000 new jobs. That's hardly an independent source, but it shows Clinton's not pulling the number out of thin air.

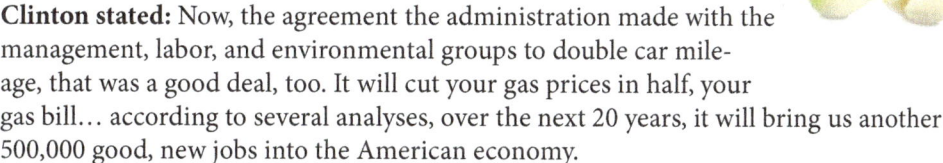

Clinton stated: So the president's student loan reform is more important than ever. Here's what it does. Here's what it does. You need to tell every voter where you live about this. It lowers the cost of federal student loans. And even more important, it gives students the right to repay those loans as a clear, fixed, low percentage of their income for up to 20 years.

TRUE

It's true. Obama has **lowered interest rates** on student loans, and the reforms passed as part of the healthcare reconciliation package allow you to **pay back as a percentage of income**, rather than based on the principal. Then again, the latter policy was already in place, but Obama lowered the cap from 15% of income to 10%. He also saved money by having the Department of Education loan directly rather than using private companies, and **used the proceeds** to increase Pell Grant funding.

Clinton stated: When some Republican governors asked if they could have waivers to try new ways to put people on welfare back to work, the Obama Administration listened.

TRUE

Republican governors did request waivers for welfare on the same lines as those the Obama Administration is implementing.
http://www.washingtonpost.com/blogs/wonkblog/wp/2012/09/06/fact-checking-bill-clinton-on-the-economy/

Stupidparty Myth #.......

The stimulus did not create Jobs.

Obama was inaugurated president on Jan 20, 2009. The country, the world was in crisis, facing an imminent financial meltdown. On Jan. 29, the American Recovery and Reinvestment Act passed the House—this without a single Stupidparty congressman's vote. This was an $831 billion stimulus package. It was a pretty orthodox Keynesian effort to create demand and put a stop to the deflation-ary death spiral. Notwithstanding all eternal vitriolic bluster about every breath Obama takes, history has a habit of shedding light on who the heroes and villains really are. The nonpartisan Congressional Budget Office estimated (early 2012) that this act had already contributed 1.6m jobs. Other sources at later dates have higher numbers. As *The New Times* reported: "This month, the Booth School of Business at the University of **Chicago surveyed** a panel of economic experts of different political persuasions about the impact of the president's stimulus package: 8 out of 10 said it had contributed to lower unemployment by the end of 2010. There was less consensus on whether its benefits would exceed its long-term costs, including high-er taxes to pay for the spending. Still, when asked if the policy was worth it, four times as many economists agreed as disagreed."
http://www.nytimes.com/2012/02/29/business/economy/republicans-malign-a-stimulus-but-the-plausible-options-were-few-economic-scene.html

I would add that in spite of every effort by Stupidparty to do absolutely nothing—for they have displayed zero interest in Job creation—that as of November 2013 the econ-omy has added private-sector jobs for 44 straight months. During this time, almost 8,000,000 private-sector jobs have been added.

Stupidparty Myth #.......
Workers are crap.

Multi-millionaire John Boehner demonstrates trickle down economics for the growing crowds of homeless people in the street below.

© 2010 C.W.Cunningham   www.ChrisWeigant.com

Dave Joyce, SP Rep. Ohio 14th:
"And the trouble is, it's because they either can't find people to come to work sober, daily, drug-free and want to learn the necessary skills going forward to be able to do those jobs," he added.

Rick Scott, SP Gov. Florida, did not save money when he mandated drug-testing for welfare recipients. In fact, 2.5 percent of beneficiaries flunked—far lower than the percentage of people in the general population who use drugs.

Michael Evangelist is a policy analyst with the National Employment Law Project, which advocates for low-wage workers. He said the substance-abusing unemployed person is a "bogeyman" that occasionally leads to drug-testing. "Most states ended up not doing it," said Evangelist. "One reason was the cost—it just costs too much. You don't find enough people that failed the drug test to make it worthwhile to save you the money."

The National Federation of Independent Business.

A conservative group representing small businesses published a 2012 report, "Small Business Problems and Priorities," that ranked "finding and keeping skilled employees" as the 39th most pressing problem for small businesses and "locating qualified employees" as the 32nd problem.

Tom Corbett, SP Gov. Pennsylvania, recently faced criticism when he said, "there are many employers who say, 'look, we're looking for people but we can't find anybody that has passed a drug test,' a lot of them."

Nikki Haley, SP Gov. South Carolina, in 2011 "found herself in hot water when she claimed that 'half' of the job applicants at a nuclear reservation site failed a drug test. In reality, fewer than 1 percent of the applicants flunked."

http://www.huffingtonpost.com/2013/08/23/dave-joyce-workers-drug-free_n_3804552.html?ref=topbar

Myth #..... Defaulting on the Debt, no big deal.

Ted Yoho, SP Rep. Florida, told constituents the nation's credit rating would actually be better if the United States defaulted on its debt: "I think the creditors that we owe money to around the world would say, 'you know what, they're getting their house in order.' And I think our credit rating would do better."

http://www.addictinginfo.org/2013/08/09/ted-yoho-government-shutdown/#ixzz2dfhtv17F

Pat Toomey... Steve Scalise... Daniel Webster, SP lawmakers.

"The looming debt-ceiling fight may look like a classic 'who will blink first' Washington debate, with a ticking time bomb waiting at the end.

"But for lawmakers like Pat Toomey, Steve Scalise, and Daniel Webster, there's no reason for Republicans to blink—because the time bomb is a dud."
http://www.politico.com/story/2013/01/default-deniers-pooh-pooh-debt-ceiling-apocalypse-86253.html#ixzz2dfx1vWzd

More than 50% of Stupidparty congressmen okay with default.

Politico reports:

"House Republicans are seriously entertaining dramatic steps, including default or shutting down the government, to force President Barack Obama to finally cut spending by the end of March (2013).

"The idea of allowing the country to default by refusing to increase the debt limit is getting more widespread and serious traction among House Republicans than people realize…

"Republican leadership officials, in a series of private meetings and conversations this past week, warned that the White House, much less the broader public, doesn't understand how hard it will be to talk restive conservatives off the fiscal ledge. To the vast majority of House Republicans, it is far riskier long term to pile up new debt than it is to test the market and economic reaction of default or closing down the government.

"GOP officials said MORE THAN HALF OF THEIR MEMBERS ARE PREPARED TO ALLOW DEFAULT unless Obama agrees to dramatic cuts he has repeatedly said he opposes." (my emphasis)
http://www.politico.com/story/2013/01/behind-the-curtain-house-gop-eyes-default-shutdown-86116.html

Stupidparty Myth # …… The Debt must be so deadly as to induce Economic suicide—right?

Bloomberg Report Aug. 2013:

As congressional Republicans prepare to risk a government shutdown or U.S. debt default over the budget, one economic indicator undercuts the urgency for a showdown: The deficit is steadily shrinking.

The federal budget deficit narrowed from more than 10 percent of the gross domestic product at the end of 2009 to 5.7 percent of GDP for the 12 months ended March 31 [2013]—the smallest gap in four years, according to data compiled by Bloomberg.

With tax collections rising and spending growth slowing down, the deficit is on track to drop to 4 percent of the $16 trillion U.S. GDP for the fiscal year ending Sept. 30, according to a May forecast by the Congressional Budget Office. It will shrink to 3.4 percent of GDP next year, the CBO says, close to the 3.3 percent average over the past 30 years, according to Bloomberg data.

"When you look at the 10-year projections for the deficit and debt as a percentage of GDP, it's not an issue," said Jim O'Sullivan, chief U.S. economist for High Frequency Economics in Valhalla, New York.

At the same time, should House Republicans carry out a threat to default on U.S. debt, even if only for a day or two, "you'd never be able to reverse that," O'Sullivan said. "You'd probably always have a little bit of an extra premium" that investors would demand on U.S. obligations.
http://www.bloomberg.com/news/2013-08-06/deficit-shrinks-to-5-7-of-gdp-as-debt-ceiling-no-vote-risks-all.html

Stupidparty Myth # ...... does not matter how one cuts spending

Tom Price, SP Rep. Georgia 6th,

made a startling admission on CNN's *Starting Point* on Wednesday morning, telling host Soledad O'Brien that Republicans are not concerned about how they cut spending—or the millions of people who suffer as a result—so long as they achieve a balanced budget.

O'BRIEN: [The President] said he doesn't want balance for the sake of balance, that actually the wrong kinds of cuts that would be hurtful to people would be a problem. What do make of what he told George Stephanopoulos?

REP. PRICE: We believe it's important to balance not the how of "how you balance," but the "why," why is it important to balance. Well, it's important to get our budget in balance, so that means that Washington doesn't spend more money than it takes in, just like families can't, just like businesses across this country can't.

This is an infantile view of family or business finances, since business and families take on debt/ loans all the time. How many homes are bought without a mortgage?
http://thinkprogress.org/economy/2013/03/13/1710571/gop-congressman-admits-republicans-dont-care-what-gets-cut-in-the-budget/

Note:

The names "Ayn Rand," "Ron Paul," "John Galt" crop up at various times during this book. Here is a very brief contextual explanation.

Ayn Rand: Having been born into a bourgeois family in Russia in 1905, she and her family suffered under the antibourgeois purges of Lenin that began in 1917. Against and amongst this background, she did, against all odds, get to study philosophy. This led her to have an understandable hatred of communism and God but did not qualify her to write utopian fantasies with any grounding in economic theory and even philosophical rants (monologues) that bore objectivity rather than being born out of bitterness. Ayn Rand does ask perfectly valid questions:

Why is it moral to serve the happiness of others, but not your own? If enjoyment is a value, why is it moral when experienced by others, but immoral when experienced by you?

But the question is also revealing and seems to lack middle ground. Because of Rand's formative years, she apparently overreacted, as a child might overcompensate for the perceived imperfections of her parent(s). To a person inclined to be somewhat self-centered, Ayn Rand offers wonderful rationalizations; the same applies to any prejudices one might have. In short, her philosophy allows a sort of "be prejudiced, be happy" vibe. Obviously, we only want government if it is good and efficient, and deep down most people are more likely to help others if they see some benefit for themselves. To live "free," as will be discussed, is a double-edged sword; it has the potential for better or worse, depending on innumerable ever-moving factors. But by studying the goals of the Ayn Rand fundamentalists, we can see why Stupidparty is so vested in bad government.

John Galt was perhaps Ayn Rand's most famous character—a man in search freedom from government intervention. Now, this is all fine in parable form—but reality can be a bit more inconvenient, as what we are really talking about is unfettered capitalism, unfettered prejudice, and unfettered power. H. G. Wells, who, it seems to me, proved to be an awesomely prophetic writer, peering ahead of his time in his 1895 book *The Time Machine,* envisioned a distant future in which humanity had devolved into two species—the subterranean masters (the Morlocks), whose food was the innocent and naïve aboveground agrarian (Eloi). Here we have the logical end game of John Galt's "paradise."

But populist authors like Ayn Rand, Joseph Smith, or Ron Hubbard (inventor of scientology) apparently can hit a populist nerve, at any time, and attract cult like followings. At the time, Ayn Rand's books were not well received, and she went into depression.

But Rand did gain a few notable disciples (one being a now rather chagrined Alan Greenspan, a tarnished ex-chairman of the Federal Reserve; another being Ron Paul, as this philosophy allows him to rationalize many of his more unsavory prejudices, now swept under the carpet, under the guise of being an "honest politician"). And of course, those hordes of adolescent fans, who are sometimes unable to move on from her rather childlike and remarkably self-centered visions of an ideal society.

So sadly, her ramblings live on. But you would think that before the world's largest economy ever turns to Ayn Rand for inspiration, an experiment should be carried out on a smaller scale—like a small nation state. I say this because if we had listened to Ron Paul during the 2008–09 economic meltdown, we would have lost our homes. The Great Recession would have become the Greatest Depression—making the events of 1931 look like child's play. That and of course civil rights would have been overturned, and even the 1% would have had to turn on themselves.

Unfortunately, familiarizing oneself with this topic will become quite important, as we can expect to see another Rand nincompoop running for the highest office in 2016—another tragically wasteful distraction, when one considers the weighty issues facing humanity.

CHAPTER 10

Do you get to have an opinion on the climate? or

Can Joe Barton be really that Stupidparty?
or
is something else going on?

It isn't pollution that's harming the environment. It's the impurities in our air and water that are doing it.

—Dan Quayle

When I was a teenager, and sometime prior to 1980, a scientific consensus had emerged that certain products were most likely very harmful to the ozone layer. I quickly learned why the ozone layer was so important. Evidently, this was a relatively simple problem to fix. Apparently, one company, DuPont, was the primary culprit, and I guess regulations were eventually necessary to prevent DuPont from initiating a worldwide catastrophe. At the time, I immediately did what I could. Instead of using aerosol deodorant, I switched to roll-on. Hardly a big sacrifice.

Sometime in the late '70s, I became aware that scientists (in this case, climatologists) had reached an overwhelming consensus that increasing levels of various greenhouse gasses were leading to Global Warming, which would eventually lead to awful consequences for all living creatures. Many if not most of these actual and projected increases in such gasses were being produced as a result of human activity.

At the time, Jimmy Carter, being a president with an impressive intellect, tried to get this issue some traction. He also realized that U.S. growing dependence on Middle Eastern Oil would pose serious long-term problems for the U.S. economy. (The Oil Cartel nations had already experimented with holding the world economy hostage.) But now tragedy strikes, a tragedy that would doom the American economy to suffer from various wars (which would be a catalyst for the ever-increasing radicalization of Islam), and trillions of dollars of U.S. taxpayer dollars being diverted away from important needs such Education, Healthcare, and basic Infrastructure.

The tragedy in question was the Iran Hostage Crisis. Jimmy Carter did eventually resolve the crisis, the hostages being released safely and without a war. Their release came politically too late for Carter. He was blamed for the military's botched rescue effort. I am not a military man, but as I understand it, helicopters can be quite unreliable, especially under stressful conditions. Evidently, the mission failed as result of several helicopters failing under stressful conditions. Carter was always taking a huge risk. This was a lesson that the military (or the presidency) had learned by the time of the Bin Laden takedown. The military had screwed up or Carter's brave gamble had backfired; regardless, Carter lost the election, so setting off a chain of catastrophic Economic and Climate Warming events.

If the United States had adopted an intelligent energy policy, then all such wars would have been unnecessary, the U.S. taxpayer would not have had to fund the very parties that would seek to terrorize America. America would not have needed a military presence in Saudi Arabia, which eventually turned Bin Laden from an ally of U.S. foreign policy to a sworn enemy. After Jimmy Carter, it was the Oil Companies that were in charge of energy policy—to such an extreme that when George Bush Jr. tasked Dick Cheney (an Oil executive) to revamp an energy policy, the committee met in secret and only Oil executives were invited to the table. Putting the Oil Industry in charge of energy policy would be the equivalent of putting DuPont in charge of ozone oversight.

Of course, this is all fine with the Stupidparty. They see no problem. Stupidparty doesn't care. So before analyzing the Stupidparty (non)thinking on this, by spending some time looking at Congressman Joe Barton, let's just look at some very simple facts:

First, let's go back to the comments about heat trapping gasses that cause Global Warming:

Now, remember that decades ago climatologists predicted this would happen and also that it would cause global temperatures to rise.

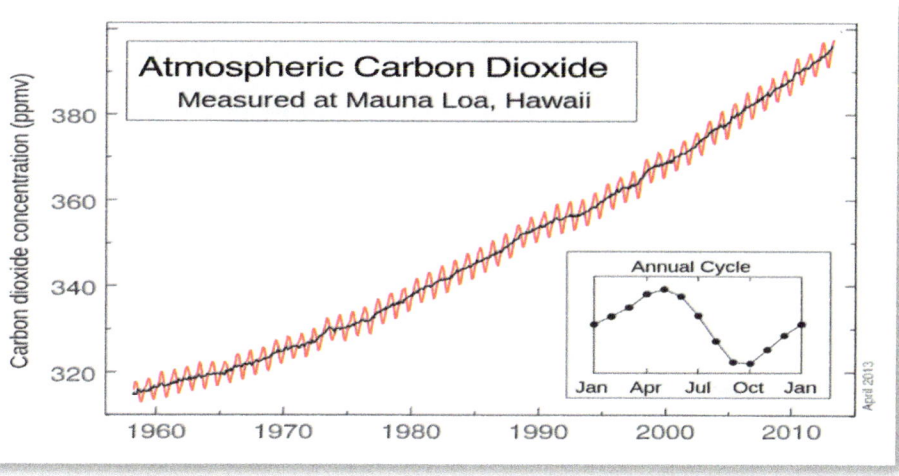

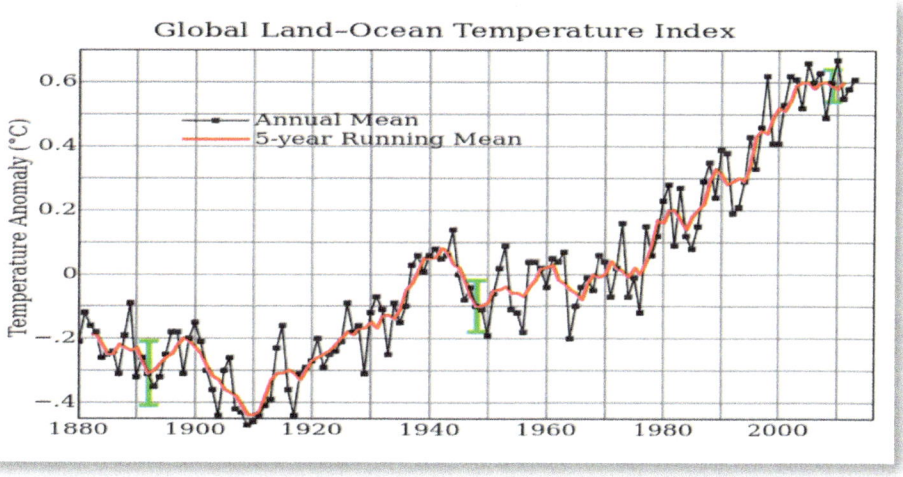

So what happens next? These are the predictions using various scenarios; the scenarios are dependent on the level of Stupidparty we are all willing to tolerate.

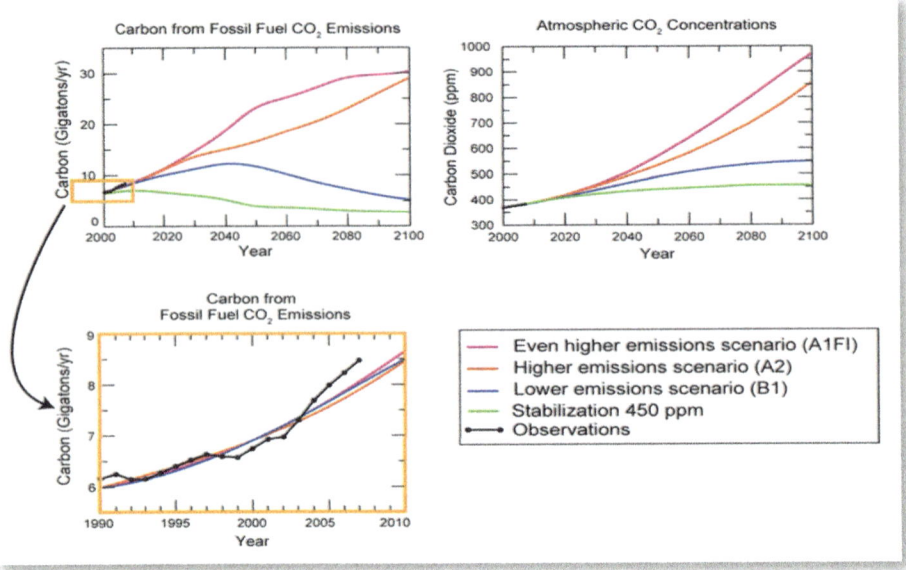

So how will our planet change?

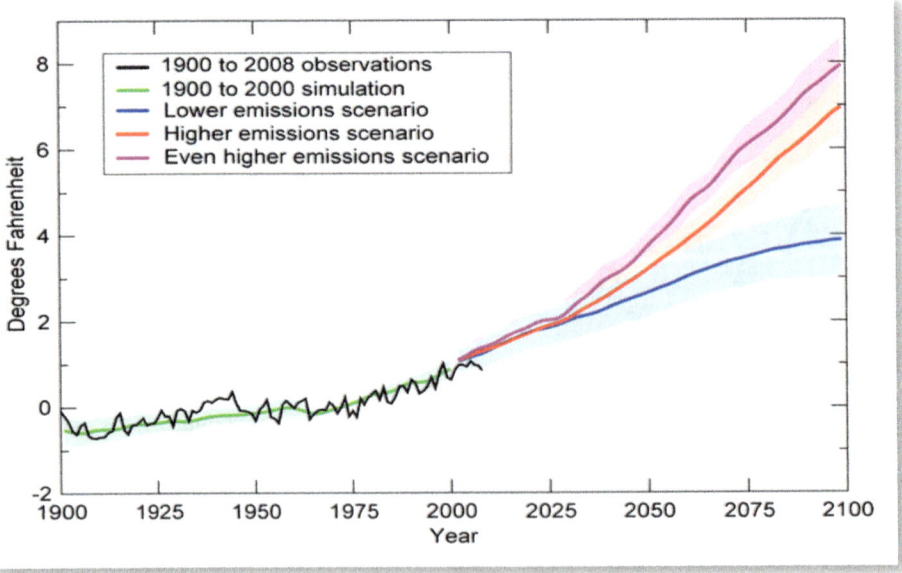

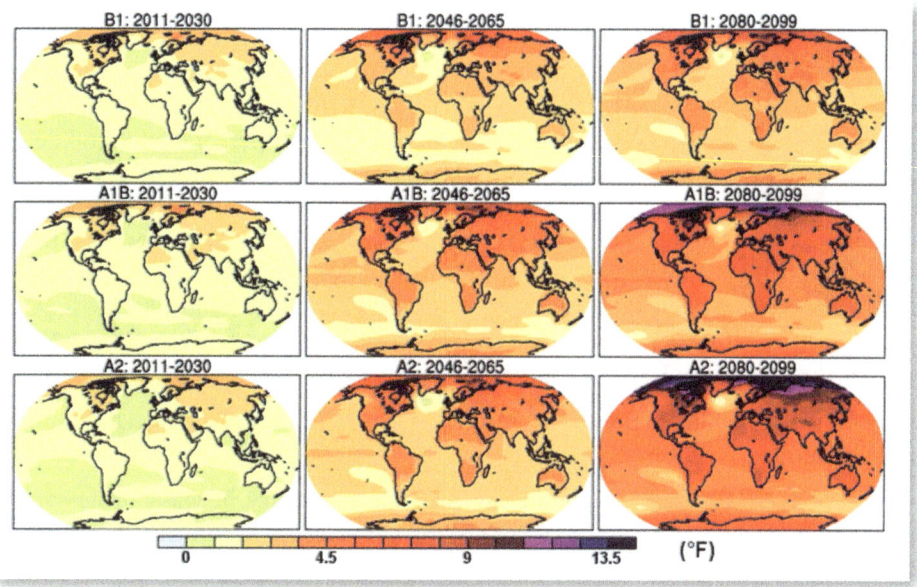

Projected changes in global average temperatures under three emissions scenarios (rows) for three different time periods (columns). Changes in temperatures are relative to 1961–1990 averages. The scenarios come from the IPCC Special Report on Emissions Scenarios: B1 is a low-emissions scenario, A1B is a medium-high-emissions scenario, and A2 is a high-emissions scenario. Source: NRC (2010)
http://www.epa.gov/climatechange/science/future.html

Articles supporting Global Warming v. Articles Rejecting Global Warming

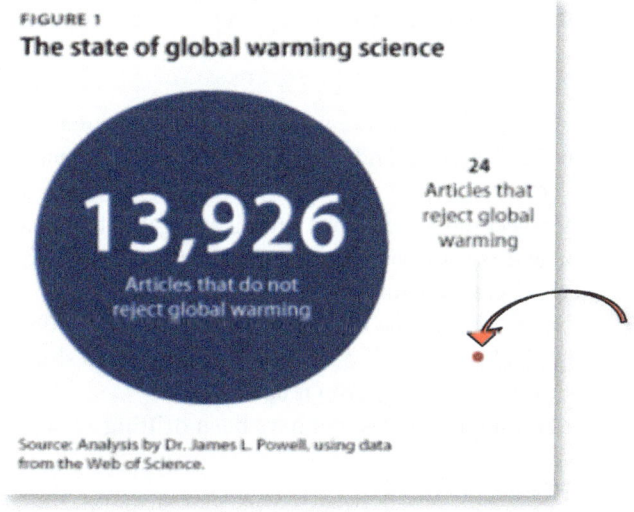

FIGURE 1
The state of global warming science

13,926
Articles that do not reject global warming

24
Articles that reject global warming

Source: Analysis by Dr. James L. Powell, using data from the Web of Science.

Joe Barton, SP Rep. Texas 6th,

is the longstanding congressman for the Sixth Congressional District. In 2012, 144,892 residents of this district once again decided that Joe was their man. Of passing interest is that fact that this district was going to be the site for the superconductor collider, the world largest particle accelerator, to look for stuff such as black holes. The project was canceled in 1993 as a result of budgetary problems (deficits) created by eight years of Reaganomics—the Stupidparty godfather of fiscal discipline. Either that or why spend $12,000,000,000 (having already spent $2,000,000,000) to look for objects that some might argue can **be found right in Texas**? Now Geneva is the host of the Hadron collider.

Joe Barton is the ranking member and former chairman of the House Energy and Commerce Committee.

Steven Chu. At the time of his appointment as energy secretary, he was a professor of physics and molecular and cellular biology at the University of California, Berkeley, and the director of the Lawrence Berkeley National Laboratory, where his research was concerned primarily with the study of biological systems at the single-molecule level. Previously, he had been a professor of physics at Stanford University. He is a vocal advocate for more research into renewable energy and nuclear power, arguing that a shift away from fossil fuels is essential to combating climate change.

While it is highly unlikely that anyone in Congress is quite as smart as Steven Chu, this was never going to daunt Barton, who has a staff of researchers at his disposal. Joe Barton is desperate to please his Stupidparty Disciples and his Oil Industry paymasters. It is worth noting at this point that Barton has received $1.7m for Oil and gas plus $1.5m from Electric Utilities.* So Joe and his people must have been so excited when they came up with their dream gotcha question for public-enemy number one, a supremely smart Nobel Prize– winning scientist occupying a key cabinet seat in the Obama Administration.

*http://www.opensecrets.org/politicians/industries.php?cid=N00005656&cycle=Career

BARTON: Dr. Chu, I don't want to leave you out. You're our scientist. I have one simple question for you in the last six seconds. How did all the oil and gas get to Alaska and under the Arctic Ocean?

CHU (Laughs): This is a complicated story, but oil and gas is the result of hundreds of millions of years of geology and in that time also the plates have moved around. And so, it's a combination of where the sources of the oil and gas . . .

BARTON: Isn't it obvious that at one time it was a lot warmer in Alaska and on the North Pole? It wasn't a big pipeline that we've created from Texas and shipped it up there and put it underground so we can now pump it up?

CHU: No, there are continental plates that have been drifting around throughout the geological ages.

BARTON: So it just drifted up there.

CHU: Uh… That's certainly what happened. It's a result of things like that.

CHAIRMAN: The gentleman's time has expired.

http://scienceblogs.com/authority/2009/04/22/rep-joe-barton-not-smarter-tha/

Remember that Chu had six seconds to explain tectonic plates to someone who had no interest in listening. But he did actually manage to fit in the answer, immediately and gracefully. Does this answer help Joe Barton and his team? Evidently not, as he later tweeted the following: "I seem to have baffled the Energy Sec with basic question— Where does oil come from?" So oblivious did Joe Barton remain that the YouTube video of the exchange was proudly headlined on his webpage. This of course makes sense if you are seeking the votes of Stupidparty Disciples.

But do not think that such intellectual prowess is a mere flash in the pan.

At a 2007 House hearing, Barton explained to Al Gore that global warming increased greenhouse gases, not the other way around. He added: "You're not just a little off. You're totally wrong." At a hearing in 2009, Barton dismissed Gore's warnings about climate change as "alarmist predictions."

At a hearing last year, as *Time's* Jay Newton-Small and Katy Steinmetz remind us, Barton suggested that wind is a "finite resource" and that trying to harness it could "slow the winds down" and in turn "cause the temperature to go up." (On an extremely localized basis—maybe.)

http://grist.org/article/2010-06-24-gop-has-forgiven-joe-barton-six-reasons-not-to-forget-him/

Why Congress does not Speak Norwegian.
As reported by Aaron Wiener, of *The Washington Independent,*
"Here's his solid evidence that adaptation has worked in the past: 'During the Little Ice Age, both the Vikings and the British adapted to the cold by changing. I suppose that one possible adaptation response of Viking retrenchment and British expansion is that we're conducting the hearing today in English instead of Norwegian.'"
http://washingtonindependent.com/35892/rep-joe-barton-global-warming-no-problem-well-adapt

"Barton is the person behind a political action committee called the Texas Freedom Fund that funnels campaign contributions from oil execs and lobbyists to candidates who'd rather not be seen taking money from Big Oil. One recent recipient of Texas Freedom cash is a Republican named Tim Griffin, who's running for Congress in Arkansas. Howie Klein, writing for *The Huffington Post,* provides some background."
http://grist.org/article/2010-06-24-gop-has-forgiven-joe-barton-six-reasons-not-to-forget-him/

"Most of us became familiar with Griffin around the time of the 2000 election when he worked as an opposition research director for Bush. His job, to smear Al Gore, was covered in Peter Marshall's BBC documentary *Digging the Dirt,* and viewers got the impression, which over the years has proven correct, that he is one of the slimiest and least trustworthy rogues to mount the political stage in our lifetime."
http://www.huffingtonpost.com/howie-klein/joe-barton-sticking-his-o_b_622889.html

Elsewhere, I argue that places that are heavily religious tend to be less fact driven. The following is a good example of why this correlation probably exists.

Barton cited the biblical Great Flood as an example of climate change not caused by man. (Maybe Barton should spend more time pondering how Noah and his family crew of seven would have had time to feed, clean out the pooh, and water all those animals every day, animals who must have been living in quite cramped conditions.)

And, of course, once you start talking gibberish and start getting plaudits from Stupidparty Disciples, then there is no stopping ever more absurd analogies.

"So if you put 20,000 marathoners into a confined area, you could consider that a single source of pollution, and you could regulate it," Barton says. "The key would be whether the EPA said that 20,000 people running the same route was one source or not."
http://www.youtube.com/watch?v=v2j-atUgGBw

Fred Upton, SP Rep. Michigan 6th:

In 2010, Fred Upton is the chairman of the House Committee on Energy and Commerce. What is notable about Fred Upton is how is views on the climate had suddenly changed.

Even though he is from Michigan and receives significant funds from the auto industry, he always appeared to have a reasonable position on climate and energy. His website once stated, "I strongly believe that everything must be on the table as we seek to reduce carbon emissions." In April 2009, he maintained that "climate change is a serious problem that necessitates serious solutions. Everything must be on the table."

In 2007 he co-sponsored the Energy Independence and Security Act of 2007. This act mandated phased-in energy efficiency standards for most light bulbs. This act was signed into Law by George Bush. Fred Upton said that that the legislation, would "help preserve energy resources and reduce harmful emissions, all while saving American families billions of dollars on their electric bills." (Hard to bicker about that.)
http://en.wikipedia.org/wiki/Fred_Upton (other info also from Wiki)

But by 2010 he was quickly becoming a full-fledged loyalist to the Stupidparty. By late 2010 he had co-authored a *Wall Street Journal* editorial. Evidently, he no longer accepts that carbon needs to be regulated. He starts trying to weaken EPA regarding the Clean Air Act. Also co-sponsors, the Energy Tax Prevention Act of 2011 (H. R. 910). This tectonic shift in his views on the environment leads the *Los Angeles Times* to write in 2011 that Upton "represents one of the biggest threats to planet Earth on planet Earth."
http://opinion.latimes.com/opinionla/2011/12/republicans-environment.html

So what could explain this? Perhaps the following:

1) The further you sink into the belly of the Stupidparty, the less light you see.

2) "Hate Radio," etc. Upton has been criticized for not being conservative enough by Rush Limbaugh, Glenn Beck, FreedomWorks, Right to Life of Michigan, and the Southwest Michigan Tea Party Patriots.

3) Political pressure from the really silly arm of the Stupidparty. In 2011, Jacob "Jack" Hoogendyk met with the Club for Growth, a fiscally conservative 501(c)4 organization, about running against Upton in a rematch in 2012. (Wiki)

4) The corrupting power of money.

Follow the money Fred Upton received from Oil and Gas. By 2010 he is persuaded.

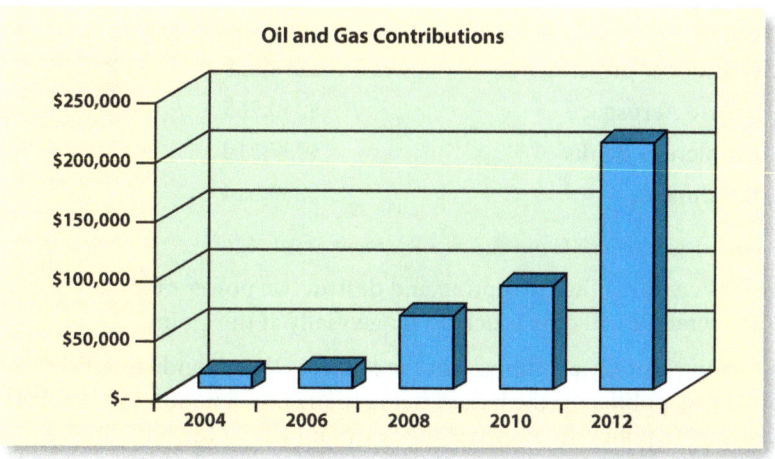

http://www.opensecrets.org/politicians/industries.php?cycle=2014&type=I&cid=N00004133&newMem=N&recs=20

This might be a good time to temporarily remove tongue from cheek. It is only fair to point out that people like Joe Barton might not be quite so stupid—even if that label does give them an ethical escape clause. You see, before Joe Barton's stint consulting for Atlantic Richfield Oil and Gas, he had actually earned a B.S. in industrial engineering, which would indicate that he can put $2 + $2 together. As hinted at, the real reasons may simply be more related to the corrupting power of money, without which he cannot win elections. So if Joe Barton is indeed quite smart, let's look at the most likely $mo-tive$$$$ for his actions.

Joe Barton's total career contributions exceed $20,000,000. The following list shows how much importance various industries place on Barton being elected:

Industry	Total
Oil & Gas	$1,734,255
Electric Utilities	$1,552,385
Health Professionals	$1,265,321
Pharmaceuticals/Health Products	$895,938
Lawyers/Law Firms	$638,065
TV/Movies/Music	$566,849
Chemical & Related Manufacturing	$389,490
Lobbyists	$387,992
Automotive	$372,250
Misc Manufacturing & Distributing	$337,090
Telephone Utilities	$336,720
Insurance	$327,099
Real Estate	$299,400
Retail Sales	$283,180
Hospitals/Nursing Homes	$263,834

Retired	$261,072
Securities & Investment	$254,858
Defense Aerospace	$240,765
Commercial Banks	$237,210
Misc Finance	$233,514

http://www.opensecrets.org/politicians/industries.php?cycle=Career&cid=N00005656&type=I

The discussion regarding the corrupting and destructive power of money and its ability to negate democracy, I will only touch on tangentially at this point.

But perhaps being morally corrupt about the planet is the second largest sin that can be committed by a politician (the largest being to mislead a nation into war). The costs of an absurd energy policy are massive; the key point is that the Stupidparty is caught in a circular argument: "Well, we want our Freedoms to rape and pillage the planet, but we want to be free to not pay the consequences—thus, we must deny that there are consequences."

2010 Stupidparty Congress and the Environment

Database of Anti-Environment Votes in the 112th Congress
Committee on Energy and Commerce, Democratic Staff

In the 112th Congress, the House of Representatives voted 317 times to block action to address climate change, to halt efforts to reduce air and water pollution, to undermine protections for public lands and coastal areas, and to weaken the protection of the environment in other ways.

Total Anti-Environment Votes under GOP House Majority in the 112th Congress:

317

Votes targeted at the Environmental Protection Agency: 145
Votes to block actions that prevent pollution: 137
Votes targeted at the Department of Energy: 55
Votes to defund or repeal clean energy initiatives: 57
Votes to promote offshore drilling: 47
Votes to dismantle the Clean Air Act: 95
Votes targeted at the Department of the Interior: 81
Votes to undermine protections for public lands and wilderness: 67

Votes to block actions that address climate change: 53
Votes to dismantle the Clean Water Act: 38
http://democrats.energycommerce.house.gov/index.php?q=legislative-database-anti-environment&legislation=All&topic=All&statute=All&agency=All
Last Updated November 14, 2012

97% of Climatologists believe in human-caused Global Warming.

"As if the backing of NASA, 18 independent American scientific societies, and the intergovernmental panel established under the United Nations weren't enough to quell the protests popping up in comment sections across the Internet, a new study published in the journal Environmental Research Letters confirms—once again—that climatologists almost unanimously believe that climate change is directly related to human-made carbon emissions.

"Researchers pored over nearly 12,000 peer-reviewed scientific papers from 1991 to 2011. These papers, according to Michael Todd at Pacific Standard, represented the work of 29,083 authors and 1,980 journals. The conclusion could hardly be stronger: 97 percent of scientists agree that anthropogenic, or human-caused, global warming exists."
http://theweek.com/article/index/244345/scientists-climate-change-is-real

Before voicing an opinion against Global Warming, one should consider what it takes to become a Climatologist.

"Climatologists typically need at least a bachelor degree in climatology or other related field. Some employers prefer applicants with a master or doctorate degree and extensive experience. Prospective climatologists often complete courses in climatology, atmospheric science, meteorology, physics, mathematics, astronomy, and oceanography. Many aspiring climatologists complete internships while pursuing their education to gain practical experience in the field. Most employers provide some on the job training to enable new climatologists to learn the policies and procedures. Climatologists must complete continuing education throughout their careers to keep their skills current and stay up to date with advancements in the field."
http://www.degreefinders.com/jobs/how-to-become-a-climatologist.html

No Climate Change here.

But Joe Barton on behalf of the Oil Industry and the 148,000 people who voted for him; they say no. Fred Upton, the chairman of the House Committee on Energy, he says no, as do a large majority of Stupidparty Disciples. Even Stupidparty Disciples who accept science, who vote for the Stupidparty—well, by allowing the Stupidparty to exercise power on a national level, they are also a threat to humanity.

Ed Orcutt, SP Rep. Washington 18th:

Washington Representative Ed Orcutt responded to an email in order to support a new tax on cyclists, stating that bicycling is not environmentally friendly because

http://www.sangrea.net/free-cartoons

the activity causes cyclists to have "an increased heart rate and respiration." The email exchange between owner of BikeTech in Tacoma and Orcutt is perplexing:

"Carbon dioxide is portrayed as harmful. But there isn't even one study that can be produced that shows that carbon dioxide is a harmful gas."
http://freakoutnation.com/2013/03/04/gop-genius-says-bicycles-are-worse-for-the-environment-than-cars/

Michele Bachmann, SP Rep. Minnesota 6th,
is on the House Intelligence Committee. (I am just going to keep repeating that.)

"[Pelosi] is committed to her global warming fanaticism to the point where she has said that she's just trying to save the planet. We all know that someone did that over 2,000 years ago, they saved the planet—we didn't need Nancy Pelosi to do that."

Dana Rohrabacher, SP Rep. California 48th:
"We don't know what those other cycles were caused by in the past.
Could be dinosaur flatulence, you know, or who knows?"

& one big Stupidparty….

Thirty-one Republicans on the House Energy and Commerce Committee—the entire Republican contingent on the panel—declined to vote in support of the very idea that climate change exists.

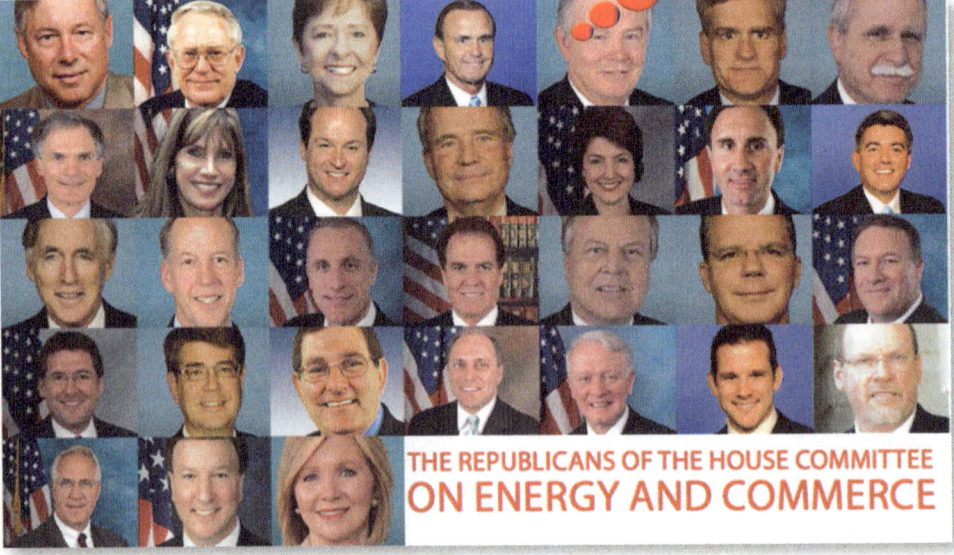

http://gawker.com/5782364/not-one-republican-on-energy-committee-will-admit-climate-change-is-real 3/5/11

CHAPTER 11

Environmental stewardship = better capitalism

Expect poison from the standing water.

—William Blake, The Marriage of Heaven and Hell

Rural Voters and the Environment.

Why would rural voters not care about the environment? In other countries they do and for good reason. And in the USA of course they do too. Hunting is perhaps America's favorite pastime. Hunters need open space and healthy targets in order to either live off the land, free of government dependency, or simply for sport. "Ducks Unlimited" (duck hunters) cares deeply about maintaining the necessary woodlands and wetlands, lakes and rivers, that allow migrating birds to do what they must do. Breed and migrate.

Family farmers understand the land, know how to keep the earth fertile, livestock healthy and productive; know how to make a living, again free from government dependence. They are rightly proud of the lives they try to live.

They appreciate the outdoors, the fresh air, and clean water. They understand simple stuff like how to stop soil degradation; that fields need to lie fallow or to have a buffer of woodland to prevent run off into the rivers. They can use the waste from their own fields or neighboring farms to fertilize their own farm.

Out West, America is unusual in that vast amounts of land are owned by the government. This land is leased to farmers at exceptionally low costs. One would think that should earn the government some respect. The government creates and maintains parks and monuments that attract tourists, who inject vibrancy into local economies. Farmers get massive taxpayer subsidies. One would think all that should earn the government some respect.

But the problem is that family farmers do not contribute enough money to their congressmen's coffers, so their congressmen are actually acting against the interests of all these individuals. Hunters may contribute to the NRA, but the NRA is only interested in the bottom line of the Gun Manufacturers (to be established in a later chapter), and they make no effort to represent gun owners—who do not object to background checks, and given a less polarized atmosphere probably would have no overwhelming desire to hunt with semi-automatics—they know that such hunting is uncouth.

Congressmen get financed by property developers, by the large agriculture firms, by the fertilizer manufacturers, by the NRA, by the factory farms and the large corporations like McDonald's that pretty much dictate the price of beef.

Congressmen thus must figure out how to satisfy their Benefactors, whilst at the same time distracting the farmers by raising all sorts of basically irrelevant issues. They get the voter worked up about false or non-issues

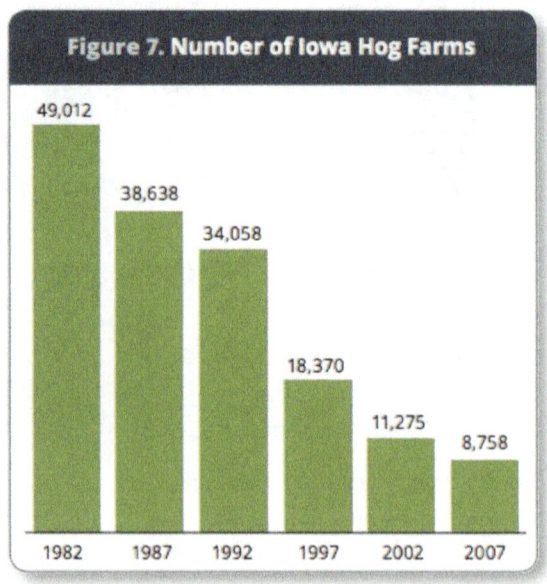

Figure 7. Number of Iowa Hog Farms

1982	1987	1992	1997	2002	2007
49,012	38,638	34,058	18,370	11,275	8,758

SOURCE: USDA Census of Agriculture

such as patriotism, foreigners, the lazy minorities, and various other pieces of nonsense. As small farms goes out of business, blame the immigrant. They fail to advise the small farmer of the real reasons he went bankrupt, which was more likely caused by allowing the following:

The factory farm is allowed to employ illegal immigrants.

The factory farm monopolies dictate the price of the product.

The factory farms get more subsidies from the taxpayer.

The factory farms are allowed to skirt pollution, irrigation, and run-off issues.

The factory farms are allowed to treat workers so poorly that neighborhoods of crime and poverty emerge.

The factory farmers lack affordable health coverage, exposing themselves to bankruptcy.

Congressmen must creatively distract; invent faux Christian values of greed, intolerance, and bigotry, displacing the real core Christian values of humanity, love, empathy, and caring.

The Mega-Hog Farms (Source: Tom Philpott, *Mother Jones*).

Large farms buy about a third less per hog worth of goods from local businesses than small farms, the report shows. And that's a third less money circulating through local economies, building wealth and creating jobs.

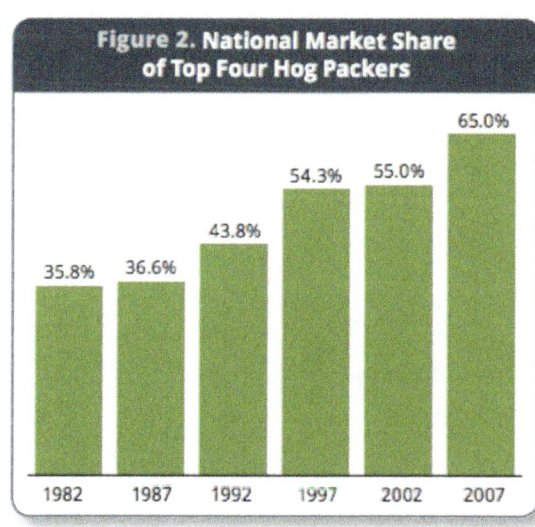

Figure 2. National Market Share of Top Four Hog Packers

1982	1987	1992	1997	2002	2007
35.8%	36.6%	43.8%	54.3%	55.0%	65.0%

SOURCE: USDA GIPSA

A study by the University of Tennessee's Agricultural Policy Analysis Center, working with the Food and Water Watch (FWW), found that for the average Iowa County, the average number of nonfarm local businesses grew by about 30 percent between 1982 and 2007. For the hog-heavy counties, though, the average number of such establishments fell by more than 10 percent [i.e., large hog farms have reduced other local businesses by 40%]. Not surprisingly, while the average Iowa County saw robust growth in total jobs over that period, for hog-heavy counties, total jobs dropped.

Now, in their defense, the meatpacking giants often counter that the changes described here are necessary for the provision of cheap food. To deliver you a bountiful supply of pork chops, farmers and workers must be squeezed. But here, too, FWW brings a cold slap of reality. The report finds that when hog prices rise, the pork packers tend to pass on the increase to consumers "completely and immediately"; but when they fall, as they have for much of the past 25 years, the companies tend to pocket

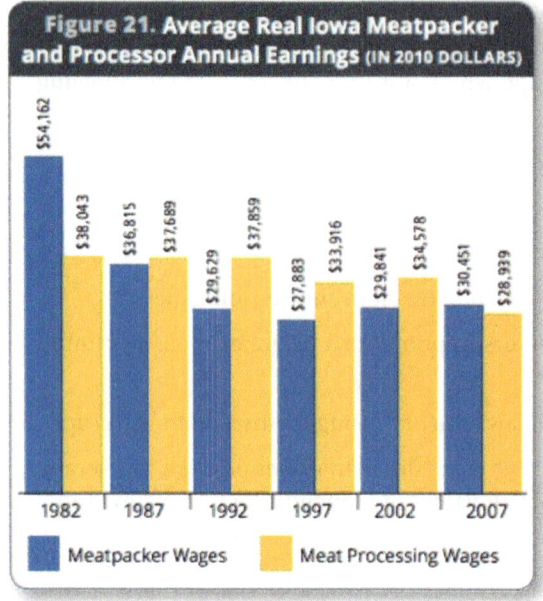

Figure 21. Average Real Iowa Meatpacker and Processor Annual Earnings (IN 2010 DOLLARS)

$54,162
$38,043
$36,815 $37,689
$29,629 $37,859
$27,883 $33,916
$29,841 $34,578
$30,451 $28,939

1982   1987   1992   1997   2002   2007

■ Meatpacker Wages   ■ Meat Processing Wages

SOURCE: U.S. Census Bureau

much of the difference as profit, passing only some on to consumers.

So, in addition to all the **environmental damage associated with factory-scale hog farming,** it's an economic disaster, too—unless you happen to be a shareholder in one of the Big Four pork packers.

http://www.motherjones.com/tom-philpott/2012/11/industrial-scale-hog-farming-screws-small-towns

So it is the shareholders, "the 1%," the few owners—they benefit. The taxpayer must pick up the tab for the poverty, unemployment, crime, health, and pollution issues that ensue. The 1% who knowingly invest in monopolies pillaging the very soul of humanity—they get their dividend.

I would acknowledge that participating in funds and 401(k)s and pension plans, etc., has the potential to benefit many people—but socially aware investing becomes virtually impossible, once you become vested in such investment strategies.

Beef Ranchers and Poultry Farms.

Where is John Wayne when we need him?

Many ranchers have sold their cattle and land and those still in the business tend to be merely hanging on. Only four meatpacking plants dominate the industry; they slaughter 84% of the nation's cattle and use unfair tactics to drive down the price of cattle in an increasingly less competitive market. Poultry growers (being

abused franchisees are) similarly powerless and debt-ridden: About one-half of the nation's chicken growers leave the business after just three years. In recent years, both the ranchers' and the poultry growers' share of the retail dollar has drastically decreased and both industries are riddled with corruption. Their plight is so severe that the suicide rate of ranchers and farmers is three times the national average.

http://www.lagcc.cuny.edu/fastfoodnation/chapters/chapter6.htm

Pollution and threats to local community.

Small, diversified farms that raise animals as well as other crops have always used manure as fertilizer without polluting water. The difference with factory farms is scale. They produce so much waste in one place that it must be applied to land in quantities that exceed the soil's ability to incorporate it. The vast quantities of manure can—and do—make their way into the local environment where they pollute the air and water. Manure contains nitrogen, phosphorus and often bacteria that can endanger the environment and human health. Manure lagoons leak, and farmers over-apply manure to their fields, which allows manure and other wastes to seep into local streams and groundwater. Residential drinking wells can be contaminated with dangerous bacteria that can sicken neighbors and the runoff can damage the ecological balance of streams and rivers. In some cases, manure spills that reach waterways can kill aquatic life. These factory farms techniques lead to overuse of antibiotic and represent cruel torture to the livestock.

http://www.factoryfarmmap.org/problems/

Family-farm Jobs replaced with miserable Jobs.

Nor do most farmers benefit from the shift to factory farming. The number of dairy, hog and beef cattle producers in America has declined sharply over the last twenty years as the meat packing, processing and dairy industries have pressed farmers to increase in

scale. Most farmers barely break even. In 2007, more than half of family farmers lost money on their farming operation. The tiny handful of companies that dominate each livestock sector exert tremendous control over the prices farmers receive, and they micromanage the day-to-day operations of many farms. The real price that farmers receive for livestock has fallen steadily for the last two decades.

The rapid transformation of livestock production from hundreds of thousands of independent farmers with reasonably sized operations to a few thousand mega-farms did not evolve naturally. Factory farming was facilitated by three policy changes pushed by the largest agribusinesses: A series of farm bills artificially lowered the cost of crops destined for livestock feed; the Environmental Protection Agency (EPA) ignored factory farm pollution; and the Department of Justice allowed the largest meatpackers to merge into a virtual monopoly.

http://www.factoryfarmmap.org/problems/

Small farmers are often absorbed into factory farm operations, acting as contract growers for the industrial facilities. In the case of poultry contract growers, farmers are required to make costly investments in construction of sheds to house the birds, buy required feed and drugs—often settling for slim profit margins, or even losses. Factory farm workers also cite the repetitive actions and high line speeds that are features of the

**Would a family farm do this?
Unwanted male Chicks.**

**Would a rural voter want this?
Chickens still alive waiting for slaughter.**

large-scale slaughtering and processing facilities that characterize the factory farming poultry sectors, as causing injuries and illness to workers.
http://en.wikipedia.org/wiki/Factory_farming

The U.S. Office of Technology Assessment studied 200 communities and learned that as farm size increases so does poverty, and the faster that farm size increases, the faster poverty increases. And a University of California at Davis study concluded that as farm size and absentee ownership increase, social conditions in the local community deteriorate. Empty storefronts. Poverty. Crime. Social breakdown. So please, let's not speak of efficiency where such costs are not included.

But ignore these external costs for the moment. Are large industrial farms efficient even in their own terms? Do they produce a greater output per unit of input? They don't. The most efficient farms are not big farms, but "small to medium-sized," just large enough for a family to work fully, while using small scale technology. A recent study also shows that small farms (27 acres or less) are more than ten times as productive (in terms of dollar output per acre) than large farms (6,000+acres), and extremely small farms (4 acres or less) can be over one hundred times as productive.

When farms do get larger, the costs of production per unit often go up. Larger acreage may require more expensive machinery and more chemicals to protect crops. So, why do many farms choose to get larger? For absentee owners, the goal is not efficiency, it's profit. Even if per unit costs go up, as long as prices are above cost, each unit sold adds to profit.
http://journeytoforever.org/farm_eff.html

Soil erosion.

The Huffington Post
Reports:

The Environmental Working Group (EWG) working with Iowa State University

The organization blames irresponsible farming practices for putting America's land and water at risk. As the video says, pesticides, fertilizers, and manure run into water, which "renders our water undrinkable, our beaches unfit to swim in, and has created an area in the Gulf so contaminated that aquatic life has to flee or die."

There is little incentive for farmers to stop erosion, and EWG places part of the blame on Washington. According to *The New York Times,* "Enforcement is needed more than ever, environmentalists say, because high crop prices provide a strong incentive for farmers to plant as much ground as possible and to take fewer protective measures like grass buffer strips." As EWG states, while wealthy landowners receive taxpayer money, "the rest of us, and the environment, pay the price."

According to the report, $51 billion is spent on boosting all-out production in farm states. Meanwhile, 97% of soil loss could be prevented with simple conservation measures. Effective practices include placing strips of grass or trees near the edge of crop fields, and creating grass waterways to both prevent gullies from forming and filter out pollutants. It's time to stop destroying this land, and start embracing conservation practices.

http://www.huffingtonpost.com/2011/04/12/soil-erosion-ewg-losing-ground-report_n_848096.html

Banning Photos.

Separate movements are afoot across the United States to ban the taking of food photos, whether it's haute cuisine at five-star restaurants or animals being abused on factory farms.

To date, lawmakers in six states have adopted so-called "Ag-Gag" laws that make it a crime to take videos or still photos on industrial farms that reveal illegal or unethical practices towards livestock.

http://www.allgov.com/news/top-stories/banning-food-photosfrom-factory-farming-to-expensive-restaurants-130129?news=846898

How did we get from this…   **…to this?**

Notice in above photo:

a) Woodlands protecting from runoff.
b) Fallowed field being naturally fertilized.
c) Crops (background) require no or few chemicals.
d) Land can be used by other wildlife, recreation, hunting.
e) No crime, no time to Watch Fox.

The Strippable Assets:

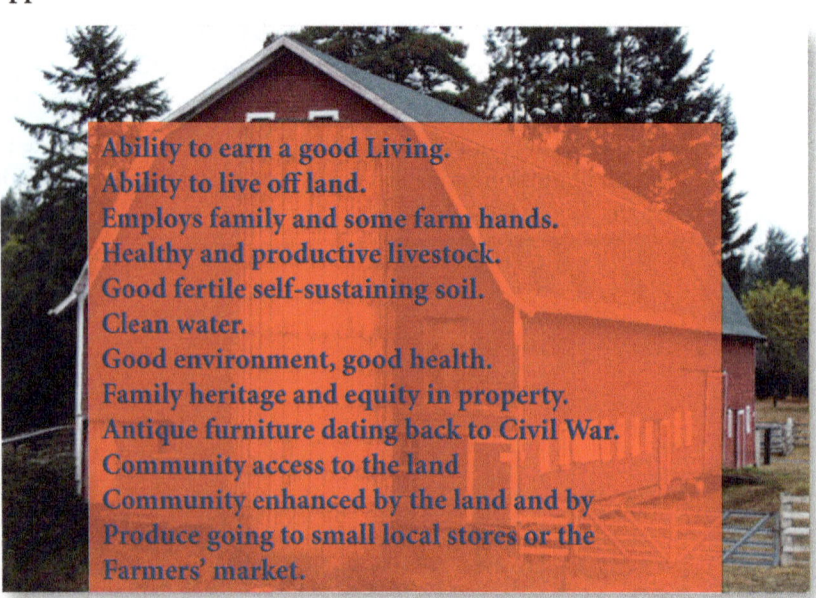

Ability to earn a good Living.
Ability to live off land.
Employs family and some farm hands.
Healthy and productive livestock.
Good fertile self-sustaining soil.
Clean water.
Good environment, good health.
Family heritage and equity in property.
Antique furniture dating back to Civil War.
Community access to the land
Community enhanced by the land and by
Produce going to small local stores or the
Farmers' market.

The Asset Strippers*

Bain, etc.   Looking to reduce pay, benefits, and pensions
(Romney & Co)   Looking at short-term livestock, land values—

Will Invest in any group that can strip these values

* Asset Stripper is taking Company funds or assets of value, while leaving debts behind

The Beneficiaries

Walmart family & others...... Force ex-Farmers into low-income Consumers

McDonald's & others............ Force ex-Farmers into extra-large, obesity lifestyles

Big Pharma........................... Idle and unhealthy lifestyles = reliance on medicine

Chemical Industries .... Mass-farming degradation = fertilizers, pesticides

Agra Business....................... Merge farms, mini-housing for livestock, sell land

Property Developers............. Turn rural into Suburban, cheap homes for displaced or immigrant farm workers

Wall Street and the 1% .... Margins, transaction fees, dividends, & capital gains

Murdoch, "hate radio," etc. ... Unemployed farmers relearn whom to blame, and ratingsincrease with idle, embittered minds

Funds ....

Stupidparty Congressmen	Stupidparty Think Tanks	Stupidparty PAC	Stupidparty Judges	Chamber of Commerce	Lobbyists in Washington

The Losers	Before being stripped.	After being saddled with the debts
The Farmer's Wife	Cooked, etc., for the family	Is cashier at Rite Aid $7 hour

Grandpa	Helped around the Farm Ate with family	Packs groceries at $7 hour Eats alone
Head of Farm	Oversaw and worked all day	Is unemployed—Listens to Rush Blames the immigrant labor
Farmer's Son	Was being groomed to take over	Works at Burger King, $7.50 an hour Watches Fox, blames gov.
Farmhand 1	Helped where needed Ate with family, lived in cottage	Listens to Religious leaders Blames decline in morality, gays, single mums, etc.
Farmhand 2	Helped where needed Lived with parents	Becomes bitter, listens to farmhand 1; both buy guns
The Planet	Cleaned stuff	Taints stuff
The Taxpayers	Pay for higher crimes rates, pollution cleanup, sickness, poverty, welfare, falling property values, worse schools, less services, plus all the other consequences of voting Stupidparty	

The Unseen Asset Strippers:

The consequences of overfishing and soil erosion are easy to understand, and solutions in a properly functioning democracy should be dead simple. Solutions if not undertaken create a massive economic burden for society by driving up the cost of the product in the not-so-distant future. This is the essence of good government, managing a healthy economy, promoting abundance, health and safety for all.

So if one looks at a somewhat more obscure issue—an issue that primarily occurs in Stupidparty locations—one can understand how such an issue does not get much attention and is easily cast aside, since you might be able to lead a Stupidparty mind to the water but you cannot make it drink.

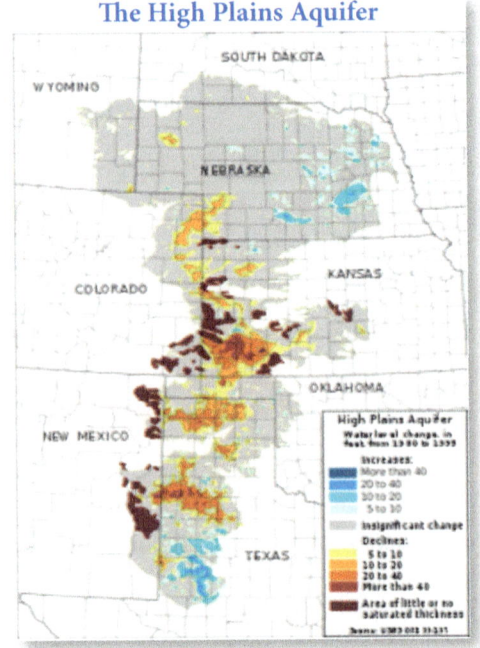

The High Plains Aquifer

Let us look at that water, or the lack of it. For abundant food, you need abundant water. The Midwest has effectively become the bread basket of the country. Kansas is the leading producer of beef in the country, with 19% of the production. Because of this niche, they have also had to massively increase corn crops to feed the cattle.

A Beef with Kansas.

Kansas, for the time being, is one of the better-performing Stupidparty (antigovernment and debt) states. Kansas, even though it only has a population of less than 3,000,000 (10% of California), has racked up over $16b in farm subsidies in the period 1995 through 2012. "Little old Kansas" is in the top five states in handouts.

Data: http://farm.ewg.org/regionsummary.php?fips=20000

Kansas has another national resource. Kansas is one of the states that sits on top of "The High Plains Aquifer," which supplies 30% of the nation's irrigated groundwater.

Good for Kansas. Well (no pun intended), the problem is that Kansas is drawing down water from The High Plains Aquifer at more than six times the natural rate of recharge.

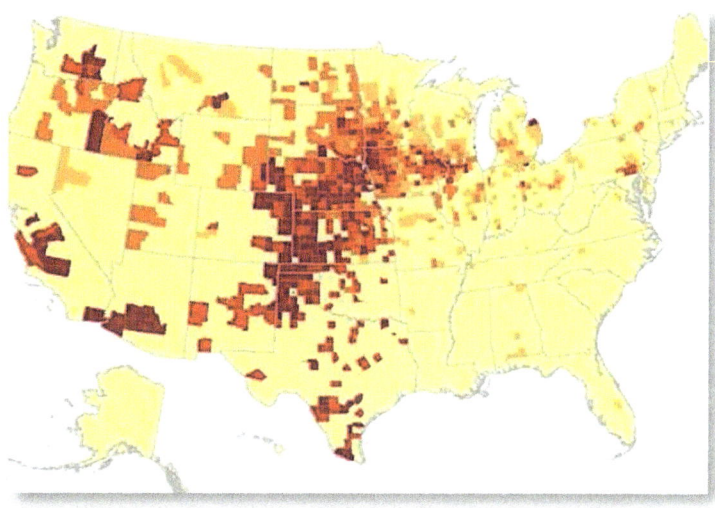

Map of Concentration of Factory farms. Note how they sit on top of the **High Plains Aquifer**

Michael Wines of *The New York Times* reports: "This is in many ways a slow-motion crisis—decades in the making, imminent for some, years or decades away for others, hitting one farm but leaving an adjacent one untouched. But across the rolling plains and tarmac-flat farmland near the Kansas–Colorado border, the effects of depletion are evident everywhere. Highway bridges span arid stream beds. Most of the creeks and rivers that once veined the land have dried up as 60 years of pumping have pulled groundwater levels down by scores and even hundreds of feet."

This rate of water reduction is directly magnified by the heavily subsidized beef industry, because beef is very different from any other

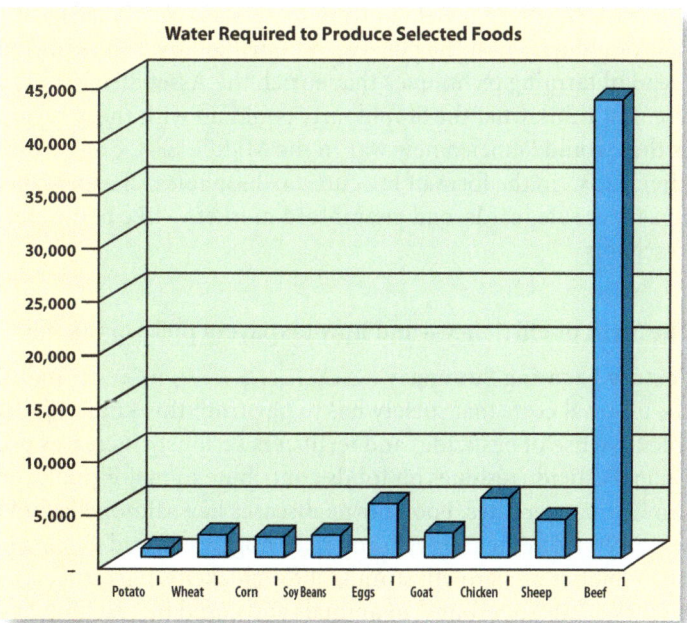

http://www.worldwater.org/data20082009/Table19.pdf
(when a range was provided, I took the midpoint of that range)

food when it comes to the amount of water required per unit of food. The below chart is liters of water required per kilo of product.

The Asset Strippers are looking at a resource, the high plains aquifer, and are literally stripping its asset (water) at everyone else's expense, as fast as possible and will eventually leave the debt (a huge dustbowl and abandoned small farms) enveloping the newly minted poverty-stricken communities.

Clearly, the Asset Strippers and their corporate colleagues only care about immediate profits, and do not care about stewardship of the land. They control the congressmen, since money has corrupted the system (see Chapter 16 on Stupidparty funding) and the media. Can you imagine Fox News reporting on any form of Asset Stripping or about clean air, clean water, farm-animal welfare? For them to rationalize their alternate reality, the poor must be lazy moochers.

Stupidparty Disciples are thus kept in the dark. In Kansas they teach creationism, which is not an academic subject but a nonsensical myth that destroys critical thinking. They complain about the government and the debt and their children's impacted future—but an inability to think critically leads them to fail to understand that they are the very moochers they complain about and they are wantonly creating the very debts they supposedly abhor. They will lose their assets to the very people who trick them into voting for the Stupidparty.

The taxpayer subsidizes the raising of cattle in arid areas; the taxpayer subsidizes the propaganda of the Beef Industry (a diet of which creates disproportionate burdens on the healthcare system), and the debt that they will leave their kids would be property in a wasteland and a diet without any meat at all—as beef will become very expensive in a water-starved food-production system.

If every U.S. citizen benefited from these Kansas-style farm subsidies proportionately, it would have cost the taxpayer $1.6 trillion over the same period—all to subsidize dreadful farming techniques that enrich the Asset Strippers at the expense of everyone else. Just think what the Stupidparty could do with those savings. Actually nothing, as they would launch a new war in the Middle East, or give their Benefactors various "dividends," in the form of tax cuts, tax loopholes, cheaper labor, less worker safety, less consumer safeguards, and guaranteed markets—like being allowed to sell suspect meat to schools.

The Myth of efficiency—and how taxpayers pick up the tab.

Factory Farming Summary (passage from *Journey to Wherever*): Industrial farms don't count the external costs that society has to pay from this kind of production. For example, intensive use of pesticides and fertilizers seriously increases pollution of air, soil, and water. Pesticide residues on foods contribute to major public health problems, like growing cancer rates. Food borne diseases like salmonella and E. coli have dramatically increased from the factory farming of hogs, beef, and chickens. Use of massive amounts of antibiotics as a growth stimulant for chickens, pigs and cattle may be causing antibiotic resistant "superbugs" in animals and could be reaching humans through the food chain. With that come fears of a global pandemic.

Use of machinery to replace hands-on farmers means a major increase in oil consumption, with associated pollution. The overuse of chemicals and machines combine to produce a massive loss of topsoil. The U.S. has lost half of its topsoil in the last four decades; fertile farmlands are turning to dust.

The emphasis on export trade, rather than local use, means tremendous public investment in transport infrastructure: new ports, airports, roads; subsidized by taxpayers. Meanwhile, shipping foods across oceans, rather than growing for local consumption, increases greenhouse gases and ocean pollution from the cargo ships and oil tankers.

Can we really call it "efficient" that the average plate of food on American tables is transported thousands of miles by ship and plane, when it could be grown a few miles away?

Then there are the external costs of the exodus of small farmers from their lands and communities. One such cost is welfare and other government payments to ex-farmers and farm workers, driven into poverty. Even worse is what happens to the communities they leave.

http://journeytoforever.org/farm_eff.html

Stupidparty House of Representatives & the Environment.
Report by Rebecca Leber at *Thinkprogess,* September 2012, describing typical Stupidparty efforts to help their Benefactors:

Republican package of pro-coal bills, which dismantle essential water, air, and climate protections:
Backed by a pile of corporate polluter cash, House Republicans and the Romney campaign have rallied around the myth that the administration is waging a "war on coal." Instead of focusing on the slew of bills needing action, the GOP has waged a messaging campaign to oppose safeguards for public health against air pollution.

The GOP's campaign is a giveaway to big polluters. It's a plan that does nothing to moving energy policy forward—only threatening public health:

It undermines clean air, clean-water protections:

The package blocks EPA greenhouse gas regulation, prevents the EPA from regulating mercury, arsenic, smog, and coal ash from power plants. One bill repeals mercury standards that prevent up to 11,000 premature deaths, 5,000 heart attacks, 130,000 asthma attacks, and 5,700 hospital visits annually. The legislation also threatens water quality by stripping the Department of Interior's and EPA's strip mining regulation and protections in the Clean Water Act.

Selectively edits out health concerns, science:

Ignoring overwhelming scientific consensus, H.R. 910 declares that carbon pollution is not a danger to health and the climate. In the latest version of legislation blocking EPA carbon pollution standards, the House Energy and Power Subcommittee deleted a mild climate change mention, which said the U.S. plays a role "in resolving global climate change matters on an international basis." On Thursday, the Energy and Commerce Committee heard from a hearing witness that carbon pollution is good for the environment, because it is "plant food."

Public health standards will create jobs:

A spokesman for House Majority Leader Eric Cantor (R) calls the package "jobs legisla-tion." But the same health standards Republicans oppose create tens of thousands more jobs in the manufacturing, installation, and maintenance of modern pollution reduction equipment.

EPA protections against mercury would create a net 84,500 jobs by 2015, according to the Econom-ic Policy Institute. Meanwhile, coal mining jobs in West Virginia reached a two-decade record in 2011. In Pennsylvania and Virginia, data shows a 2.3 percent increase and 6.7 percent increase in coal mining employment from 2009 to 2010.

The GOP's effort could end up hurting the coal industry more by opposing technology that reduce the industry's carbon pollution so it complies with the Clean Air Act. For

Cartoon: http://www.jklossner.com/

instance, McKinley's bill would prevent the EPA from reducing carbon pollution from power plants—the largest uncontrolled source—until the pollution control technology is economical. But that will never happen without a market for it, which requires some sort of pollution reduction regime.

Makes U.S. more dependent on foreign Oil:

H.R. 3409 blocks new fuel economy standards that will save the U.S. 3 million barrels of oil daily and creates hundreds of thousands of jobs. These standards will reduce U.S. oil use, so blocking them will maintain our demand for foreign oil. The standards would also save the average driver a net of $4,400 on lower gasoline purchases over the life of a 2025 car. With this package, House Republicans will add to their 302 votes against the environment, including 87 efforts to dismantle the Clean Air Act, 34 against the Clean Water Act, and 128 against pollution measures.

http://thinkprogress.org/climate/2012/09/20/873851/the-gops-war-on-coal-myth-brought-to-you-by-millions-in-coal-cash/

Rural voters supporting Stupidparty?

How can this be? Wantonly destroying their own environment, something that they require to make a living? Biting the hand that feeds it? In a rational universe such voters might be conservative, and the conservative parties that represent them would be strong advocates for the environment, for their constituents. But I will show quite clearly why congressmen do not represent their constituents.

To understand this Mad Hatter environment, one needs to investigate in more detail. How do the Stupidparty Benefactors (the money) manipulate otherwise-decent people into making insane choices? Here are the tools they use:

a) Lies, as exemplified by the Ryan-Romney campaign.

b) Employing debating techniques (Gish Galloping) that involves rapidly spewing multiple lies and half-truths that cannot be rebutted without sounding long winded (that was how Romney "won" the first 2012 presidential debate).

c) Mocking facts, science, education, and knowledge.

d) A deconstruction of Christianity.

e) Fear mongering, leading to:

f) Creating and pandering to bigotry.

g) Deflecting blame onto people without resources to defend themselves.

h) Intimidating the media—thus, creating an environment of false equivalency; thus, neutralizing the media.

If any of this sounds harsh, then please bear with me—since most of the following chapters will illustrate quite clearly (I hope) how this is achieved.

CHAPTER 12

In the company
of racism

Images www.mywebface.com

Latinos for Republicans—it's like roaches for Raid.

—John Leguizamo

Racism—it is still all around.

MOST RACIST STATES Twitter Location Quotient LQ 1 = average		
1	Alabama	8.1
2	Mississippi	7.4
3	Georgia	3.6
4	North Dakota	3.5
5	Utah	3.5
6	Louisiana	3.3
7	Tennessee	3.1
8	Missouri	2.7
9	W. Virginia	2.8
10	Minnesota	1.9
11	Kansas	1.9
12	Kentucky	1.9
13	Arkansas	1.9
24	S. Carolina*	1.4

http://www.zdnet.com/mapping-racist-tweets-where-post-election-hate-came-from-7000007202/

The above list really focuses on overt (hateful tweets) but barely touches on the more common, yet not-very-subtle forms of racism that dominate the Stupidparty Disciples. On the above list, South Carolina appears to be fairly average, being the twenty-fourth-ranked state. So let us take a closer look at this "average" state, which also means that it is one of the better Stupidparty states

*Newt Gingrich and South Carolina.

The South Carolina Stupidparty presidential primary was held on January 21, 2012. Gingrich won quite easily over Mitt Romney 40% to 28%. This was quite a turnaround from the polls just a few days before the primary, which showed Mitt Romney with a lead of 37% to 22%.

So what happened? No one appears to question that Newt Gingrich's debate performance was a resounding success. Newt, being the pro that he is, had a pretty simple strategy. While he was successful in attacking Mitt Romney's credentials (not a tough job), such attacks could hardly have been new—unless, of course, you get your news from Fox. No, Newt had a more devious plan: to tap into the energy and lifeblood of the Stupidparty audience attendees and the watching Disciples.

Newt Gingrich did not simply go after Mitt Romney; he went after the black debate monitor, Juan Williams. And he electrified the debate audience, an audience that became highly excited and raucous:

There were two standing ovations for Gingrich in the hall, where 3,000 Republicans roared, cheered and booed [including when it was mentioned that Romney's father was born in Mexico] and he was so pleased with his performance that he came into the press spin room to discuss it afterwards.

He told me that he felt the most important single moment was his exchange with Juan Williams, a black, liberal-leaning Fox News commentator, who accused him of racial insensitivity for calling President Barack Obama "the food stamp president."

The crowd rose up when he responded: "Well, first of all, Juan, the fact is that more people have been put on food stamps by Barack Obama than any president in American history. Now, I know among the politically correct you're not supposed to use facts that are uncomfortable."

http://harndenblog.dailymail.co.uk/2012/01/did-newt-just-grab-a-south-carolina-lifeline-gingrich-wins-debate-as-mitt-romney-stumbles-and-tries-.html

Food stamps.

Newt Gingrich, by having a high-voltage exchange with the moderator about food stamps, knew exactly was he was doing—tapping into the Stupidparty core belief system: "Blacks are lazy single-parent lay-about criminals, who just mooch off the taxpayer."

It should be noted that food-stamp utilization has increased not simply as a result of the 2001 and 2008 recessions; utilization has increased under both parties by design, the philosophy being to get nutrition to people (mainly children) before families become destitute. Destitution, of course, becoming more likely as the 1% takes an ever-increasing share of the wealth and as the number of people without medical insurance soars. (A trend that is now reversing.)

Stupidparty Disciples cannot fathom that economic conditions set in motion before Obama came to office were bound to lead to a greater use of food stamps. The greater the recession, the more important food stamps become.

But there is a far more dramatic response to this racial stereotype born out of racism. These Stupidparty Disciples will perhaps never understand that once again, the "food stamp president" is actually trying to help them disproportionately.

Among the 254 counties where food stamp recipients doubled between 2007 and 2011, Republican Mitt Romney won 213 of them in the 2012 presidential election, according to U.S. Department of Agriculture data compiled by Bloomberg. Kentucky's Owsley

County, which backed Romney with 81 percent of its vote, has the largest proportion of food stamp recipients among those that he carried.
http://www.bloomberg.com/news/2013-08-14/food-stamp-cut-backed-by-republicans-with-voters-on-rolls.html

That South Carolina Stupidparty primary audience is not an exception to the rule. In everyday events, the culture of racism rears its head.

Wild Wing Café Kicks Out 25 African Americans.
After White Customer Felt "Threatened":

The owners responded to complaints only after the story took off on Facebook. This is was management's apology, which confirms that the incident occurred as charged:

"We had a conversation," says Stokes. "It was a really good conversation. He and many of his family and friends were there about a month ago, and they are regular customers of ours. So, they were having a going away party, and they just didn't receive the experience that they have come to know and love."
http://www.live5news.com/story/23235524/complaint-of-racial-discrimination-at-n-chs-restaurant-taken-to-facebook

History of Slavery.

Of course, all countries have some degree of racism. But what makes parts of the South such a hotbed? It appears that the Confederacy history with slavery might be a key indicator.

Map Showing Concentration of Slaves in 1860

These deep-Stupidparty states account for 133 out of the 212 electoral votes Romney secured in the 2012 Presidential election

Examining data from nearly all of the 1,344 Southern counties in the Cotton Belt, researchers found that a 20% increase in the percentage of slaves in a county's pre-Civil War population is associated with a 3% decrease in whites who identify as Democrats today and a 2.4% decrease in the number of whites who support affirmative action… Residents of those counties are much more likely today to express more negative attitudes toward blacks than their fellow Southerners who live in nearby areas that had few slaves…

"In political circles, the South's political conservatism is often credited to 'Southern exceptionalism,' but the data shows that such modern-day political differences primarily rise from the historical presence of many slaves," said Matthew Blackwell, one of the study authors, expanding on the report's conclusion that without slavery, the South today might look fairly similar politically to the North.
http://www.huffingtonpost.com/2013/09/20/slavery-strongholds-harbor-nations-racists-infographic_n_3962959.html

Evidently, some on the Supreme Court believe that we live in a post-racial society. So now we must watch as various Stupidparty states move to restrict voting rights, targeting the poorer urban dwellers in general, and nonwhites is particular. Racism, like all forms of bigotry, is rooted in ignorance, which is the lifeblood of the Stupidparty. Rarely can a politician be openly racist, so they tap into an underworld of coded symbolism. Here are some of the ways they tap into this massive racist element in virtually all Stupidparty states.

Birtherism.

Q64: Which of the following statements best describes your views on whether Barack Obama was born in the United States or another country?					
	All	Democrat	Republican	Independent	Other/ Not Sure
I used to think President Obama was born in another country, but ow I think he was born in the United States.	3.1%	4.2%	2.8%	2.7%	1.0%
I used to think President Obama was born in the United States, but now I think he was born in another country.	5.7%	4.3%	8.0%	5.6%	5.2%
I have always believed President Obama was born in the United States.	47.2%	74.9%	19.1%	45.5%	14.3%
I have always believed President Obama was born in another country.	25.5%	5.3%	55.6%	24.6%	24.4%
Don't know	18.5%	11.3%	14.7%	20.6%	55.1%

http://www.dartmouth.edu/~benv/files/poll%20responses%20by%20party%20ID.pdf

This survey, administered by YouGov (formerly Polimetrix) from April 26–May 2, 2012, examines public attitudes on U.S. foreign policy.

Evidently, only 19.1% of Stupidparty Disciples have always believed that Obama was born in the United States.

You really have to be either remarkably uninformed or a racist to be so concerned about Obama's birthplace. Thus, this problem—we will call it ignorance—is not simply rooted in the South, the Confederate South, but crosses all such boundaries. McCain was not even born on American soil, yet there were no "birthers"; no serious-minded person went after him on a technicality.

Donald Trump's Birth Certificate—is it real?

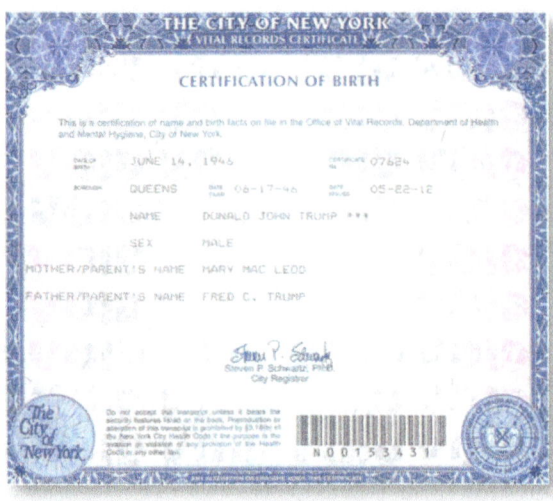

In my opinion Donald Trump has proven himself to be such a questionable human being that anyone who chooses to do business with him should not be allowed to complain when Trump reneges on a deal (not an unheard-of charge). Trump Atlantic City hotels and casinos have filed for bankruptcy protection three times. In 2002 the SEC issued a cease-and-desist proceedings against Trump Hotels & Casino Resorts, Inc., claiming misleading statements in financials. More recently Donald Trump's epic nonquest (sending teams of investigators to Hawaii), while simply seeking the limelight, highlights the total nonsense that passes as discourse. Various journalists have caught him on so much nonsense. While being interviewed on CNN, when Trump cited a (mis)quote from the president's grandmother that said Obama was born in Kenya. In fact, the recording to which he refers shows Sarah Obama repeatedly saying through a translator, "He was born in America." You can listen to the actual tape yourself—something that this sorry excuse for a … (controlling myself) … clearly refused to do.

CNN pointed out that they had the actual tape, with the correct translation. Donald Trump refused to listen, had zero interest in the facts, and just ploughed on spewing his bile. But Stupidparty Disciples don't care.
http://www.factcheck.org/2011/04/donald-youre-fired/

Combine his business etiquette, his political commentary, his offensive and unfounded accusations, and add a dash of egomania, a splash of self-aggrandizement, and you get more than a whiff of a toxic brew, enough to pollute a whole franchise. Why even do business with such a man? If you get screwed, I would have zero sympathy. As for me, his character flaws are so glaringly transparent, I would not touch this guy with a barge-pole. I do not get close to understanding how anyone can give this character the time of day. Every time you see this guy on TV (outside of Fox), you must surely be witnessing money (ratings) "Trumping" journalism. For me, you are guilty by association.

But I digress, and there are many reasons for this continuance of imagined 1760s values. "Hate radio" is just one of them.

Rush the Not-Racist.

Rush Limbaugh is crucial to the Stupidparty. If you vote Stupidparty, you are (whether you like it or not) voting to enable Limbaugh. Talk radio is dominated by "hate radio," and Rush Limbaugh is the undisputed king of "hate radio." There are worse hate jocks than Rush, but we will bypass these rather odious fringe characters. Every now and again, an elected Stupidparty representative will dare to criticize Limbaugh but will invariably rue the day and recant any such criticism. Therefore, various Stupidparty leaders totally understand that Limbaugh is underpinning racism and underpinning other insidious types of "isms." More Rush, courtesy of News One for Black America:

THAT'S RIGHT, FOLKS! EVERY VINDICTIVE, JEALOUS, SMALL-MINDED, SHORT-SIGHTED AND NAIVE THOUGHT YOU EVER HAD HAS BEEN ABSOLUTELY CORRECT!

Talkback radio
http://www.sangrea.net/freecartoons/polit_guns-for-liberty.jp

a) "Have you ever noticed how all composite pictures of wanted criminals resemble Jesse Jackson?"

b) "The NAACP should have riot rehearsal. They should get a liquor store and practice robberies."

c) "They're 12% of the population. Who the hell cares?"

d) [To an African American female caller]: "Take that bone out of your nose and call me back."

e) "Obama's entire economic program is reparations."

f) Obama is "more African in his roots than he is American" and is "behaving like an African colonial despot."

g) People also didn't like "paying millions of dollars" for Obama's vacations. "They understand it's a little bit of a waste," Rush said. "They understand it's a little bit of uppity-ism."

h) After Michelle Obama was booed at a NASCAR event, Limbaugh defended the booers, saying that they booed her because she's "uppity."

h) "You're a foreigner. You shut your mouth or you get out."

i) "Let the unskilled jobs that take absolutely no knowledge whatsoever to do—let stupid and unskilled Mexicans do that work."

j) "A bunch of white people who thought electing a black president would assuage all of their guilt and erase our racial past, voted for Obama. They couldn't have cared less what he thought, what he said. They didn't think of him as uppity; they were being selfish! They didn't like feeling guilty over our racist past, slavery, and so they thought pulling the lever for Obama would absolve them."

http://newsone.com/16051/top-10-racist-limbaugh-quotes/
http://www.examiner.com/article/rush-limbaugh-calls-president-obama-uppity (final quote)

Rush again.
"The problem is, and dare I say this, it doesn't look like Michelle Obama follows her own nutritionary, dietary advice … I'm trying to say that our First Lady does not project the image of women that you might see on the cover of the *Sports Illustrated Swimsuit Issue* or of a woman Alex Rodriguez might date every six months or what have you."

To the eye of the beholder, I guess, but I was always under the impression that most people find Michelle Obama quite attractive. But clearly some people see the world in a different light. Regardless, holding up a First Lady to supermodel status for the purpose of tearing her down illustrates desperation. I speculate that the light that hits the prism inside of Rush's mind would lead him to thirstily ogle Barbara Bush clad in a two piece, strutting around like Jane Fonda in *Barbarella*.

But of course, Stupidparty racism runs so much deeper than just Rush and his "hate radio" colleagues.

Leon Acton "Lynn" Westmoreland (born April 2, 1950) is the U.S. representative for Georgia's Third Congressional District:

"Just from what little I've seen of her and Mr. Obama, Senator Obama, they're a member of an elitist-class individual that thinks that they're uppity," Westmoreland said.

When a reporter sought clarification on the racially loaded word, Westmoreland replied, "Uppity, yeah."

Jennifer Olsen, chairwoman of the Yellowstone County Republicans and co-founder of the Montana Shrugged Tea Party.

Todd Kincannon, former executive director of the South Carolina Republican Party, kicks off 2013 with some of his world-class Twitter humor:

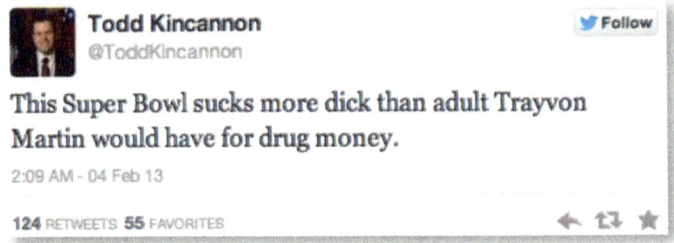

And then there's **Ron Paul,** who would like to repeal civil rights legislation and who once claimed that "order was only restored in LA [after the Rodney King riots] when it came time for the blacks to pick up their welfare checks." Or at least newsletters bearing his name did—newsletters he paid for and once defended. Ron Paul now disavows any connection.

Doug Lamborn, SP Rep. Colorado 5th, said that working with President Obama on the debt ceiling was like "touching a tar baby." Perhaps he was not familiar with the fact that "tar baby" is a racial slur.
http://www.youtube.com/watch?v=qUgVT56Li7E

Sally Kern, SP State Sen. Oklahoma, said the reason African American males are in prison is because they don't want to study in school.
http://newsone.com/1755255/top-10-racist-quotes-of-2011/

Jim Gile, SP Saline County Commissioner, used the term "nigger-rigging" during a commission discussion about hiring an architect to work on a county building.
http://republicansareracists.com/

Don Young, SP Rep. Alaska at Large, "used to hire 50 to 60 wetbacks to pick tomatoes."

Here's a conversation at a CPAC convention, where Stupidparty reps discuss reaching out to minorities:

K. Carl Smith, the moderator of the CPAC session, calls himself a "Frederick Douglass Republican." While he was speaking, the following exchange took place. Smith, speaking of Frederick Douglass, said, "When Douglass came through slavery ... he [wrote] a letter to his former slave master and said, 'I forgive you for all the things you did to me."

From the floor, Scott Terry (Republican and self-proclaimed direct descendant of former Confederate president Jefferson Davis) spoke up, saying, "For giving him shelter and food for all those years?"
http://www.theguardian.com/world/2013/mar/15/race-debate-cpac-slavery-slur

Reince Priebus, SP National Committee Chair:
Aug. 2013. In damage-control mode, fearing for Stupidparty's outreach to Latino voters—that this effort was being undermined by an environment created by people like Iowa Rep. Steve King and his visions of "cantaloupe-calved drug-mules"—Priebus had strong words:

"Using the word 'self-deportation'—it's a horrific comment to make," Priebus said, in a forceful rebuke. "I don't think it has anything to do with our party. When someone makes those comments, obviously, it hurts us."

Well, that is all fine except for the fact that he is "dissing" his party's most recent presidential nominee. But self-deportation is not just Mitt Romney's immigration policy. It's in the Stupidparty platform:

"We will create humane procedures to encourage illegal aliens to return home voluntarily, while enforcing the law against those who overstay their visas." In addition, the current GOP platform declares that "state efforts to reduce illegal immigration must be encouraged, not attacked." Here, they are referring to laws like Arizona's SB 1070, which are at the core of the "self-deportation" concept, as they're designed to make life for undocumented immigrants so miserable they leave on their own accord.

As *The Guardian* reports:

Jeff Flake, SP Senator, had to apologize for his fifteen-year-old son's Twitter comments. According to Buzzfeed, Tanner Flake in addition to homophobic tweets, also posted screenshots of his scores from an online game "Fun Run," where he used the handle "niggerkiller." Buzzfeed also reported that Tanner's now-locked Twitter account revealed his repeated use of the racial slurs. Tanner made equally offensive comments on You-Tube, including "nigger" and "faggot," along with calling Mexicans "scum of the Earth."

The question is, Where did Tanner hear this kind of "unacceptable" language? The fact that Tanner Flake used these words with impunity across various social media platforms for months suggests he's quite at ease with bigoted thinking.
http://www.buzzfeed.com/johnstanton/arizona-senators-son-used-homophobic-anti-semetic-language-o

Alan Clemmons, SP State Rep., South Carolina (2012): A supporter named Ed Koziol wrote to the representative first, saying that he was glad of the voter-suppression laws that Clemmons had drafted. He then commented that the government shouldn't offer a reward for people to obtain voter ID cards because, in his words, "It would be like a swarm of bees going after a watermelon." Alan Clemmons's response? "Amen, Ed."

Meanwhile, Clemmons's voter-suppression law was recently declared discriminatory by the Supreme Court. And now the law's opponents have the email exchange to prove it.
http://www.alternet.org/hot-news-views/another-stupid-racist-comment-republicans-say-it-aint-so

Two attendees at the SP National Convention were removed from the grounds after tossing nuts at a black camera operator for CNN and saying, "This is how we feed animals," the network said.
http://www.truthdig.com/eartotheground/item/ejection_after_racist_taunts_at_rnc_20120829/

Reverse Racism.

Stupidparty people keep referring to reverse racism. By so raising this issue, they are rationalizing their racist feelings. This (dishonest) concern about reverse racism might be warranted in a balanced scenario where the Black population is as empowered as the White population and there had been no history of slavery, disenfranchisement, the KKK, voter suppression, profiling, and continued significant racism, especially in the Confederate States. Once you accept that we have a racism problem, and that such problems need to be tackled and that you can show respect to other races, genders, orientations, and cultures—if you have established such a track record, then you might be qualified to talk objectively about reverse racism. But in the meantime, the Stupidparty is doomed to talk gibberish on the subject:

The Sun God must be racist??
How a hate radio host suffers: "And the pain of racism"???
—we need to go back to this ever-so-oppressive sun-tanning tax …
The Sun-Tanning Tax.

Ted Yoho, SP Rep. Florida 3rd: In the recording, the congressman goes on to explain that, when asked if he'd ever visited a tanning booth, an Indian doctor in his office with "very dark skin" responded that he hadn't, as he had no need to do so.

"So therefore it's a racist tax," Yoho explained. "And I thought I might need to get to a sun-tanning booth so I can come out and say I've been disenfranchised, because I got taxed because of the color of my skin. As crazy as that sounds, that's what the left does right. By God, if it works for them, it'll work for us."

http://www.huffingtonpost.com/2013/08/05/ted-yoho-tanning-tax-racist_n_3709155.html

Allen West, former SP Rep Florida 22nd: The claim that such a measure is discriminatory against white Americans is not original to Yoho. Allen West an African American said, "You want to talk about something that's really racist? They have a tanning tax. I'm not tanning."

Doc Thompson: In 2010, conservative radio host voiced a similar complaint while standing in for Glenn Beck on his Fox News radio show. "I now too feel the pain of racism. Racism has been dropped at my front door and the front door of all lighter-skinned Americans," Thompson said. "Why would the President of the United States of America—a man who says he understands racism, a man who has been confronted with racism—why would he sign such a racist law?"

Remember that Obama had only introduced two new taxes, one for smokers and this Sun Tanning tax. The tax in question was initially proposed to deter Americans from frequenting tanning beds, which one study found causes roughly 170,000 cases of skin cancer each year.

Earlier this year, the FDA proposed a warning label requirement for all materials promoting tanning beds, and completely barring bed use by customers under 18. According to the Skin Cancer Foundation, skin cancer is the most common form of cancer in the U.S.

http://www.huffingtonpost.com/2013/08/05/ted-yoho-tanning-tax-racist_n_3709155.html

Voter Suppression.

As discussed already, and illustrated by Supreme Court Justice Ginsburg's examples, voter suppression is either by design or by coincidence connected to racism, as after black emancipation in 1870, Stupidparty states were always looking for ways to turn back the clock.

Birtherism is Racism.

One has to be either ignorant or a racist to keep harping on about President Obama's birth certificate. If it had ever been a valid issue (which it was not), then the time to deal with it was during 2008 election. That is when the Stupidparty had the leadership (McCain) and the resources to raise the question—since if it had any validity, McCain would have known that he would have become the president. McCain did not pursue the issue, because it was infantile crap, based in an alternate racist reality.

Ted Yoho, SP Rep. Florida 3rd: Right Wing Watch posted audio of Yoho's comments from a Saturday town hall, in which the Florida republican said he called his colleague … **Rep. Steve Stockman** (SP Texas) to pledge his support for a potential bill that would launch an investigation into whether the president's birth certificate is fake.
http://www.huffingtonpost.com/2013/08/05/ted-yoho-tanning-tax-racist_n_3709155.html

The Racism behind Immigration issues.

Let's face it, immigrants (unless they are from Eastern Europe or Cuba) do not vote Stupidparty. Hence, the 11 million illegal immigrants in the USA represent a huge electoral problem for Stupidparty. This is also a real conundrum for the Benefactors of the Stupidparty—since on the one hand they love the cheap labor associated with illegal immigration; thus, you will never see the House tackle immigration by going after the employers (which would be the logical approach). So what do the Benefactors do? Well, they want to keep the cheap labor, while having the taxpayer pick up the tab for any of the negative consequences of immigration policy. At the same time denigrating the very same immigrants they employ. Thus, they created the ultrastupid wing of the Stupidparty—the Tea Party—and use their stooges at Fox to help promote the Tea Party and get its bigoted message across.

The Benefactors also fund various thinkless-thinking think tanks.

The **Heritage Foundation** is perhaps the most powerful Stupidparty "think tank." They want to undermine immigration reform—because they are funded by the Benefactors.

Their report "predicts a $6.3 trillion economic loss for the nation if immigration reform is passed." Jason Richwine, a co-author of this report, "who received his doctorate in public policy from Harvard in 2009, wrote in his dissertation, 'IQ and Immigration Policy,' that immigrants in the U.S. have lower IQs than native white Americans …" He wrote:

> The average IQ of immigrants in the United States is substantially lower than that of the white native population, and the difference is likely to persist over several generations. The consequences are a lack of socioeconomic assimilation among low-IQ immigrant groups, more underclass behavior, less social trust, and an increase in the proportion of unskilled workers in the American labor market … No one knows whether Hispanics will ever reach

IQ parity with whites, but the prediction that new Hispanic immigrants will have low-IQ children and grandchildren is difficult to argue against.
http://republicansareracists.com/

Well, I guess unleashing 11,000,000 zombies into the economy might well be a disaster—and we have some precedent for fearing those consequences by simply analyzing the devastating damage done by the unleashing of the Stupidparty Disciples.

Immigration Reform would be a boon to the Economy.
Ssshhh … don't tell the Stupidparty Disciples this.

It is quite ironic that a country built upon the backs of immigrants needs to be reminded about the economics of immigration.

When reform was first introduced in 2007, the Congressional Budget Office analyzed President George W. Bush's proposed immigration overhaul. The CBO, as Ezra Klein notes, found that modernizing the system would increase federal revenue by $48 billion while costing only $23 billion in increased public services—before even considering the broader economic benefits. There is general consensus across the ideological spectrum that the economic benefits to immigration reform will be a boon for the U.S. economy.

Factoring in broader economic benefits, research from the left-leaning Center for American Progress finds reform would add $109 billion additional tax revenue, create 121,000 jobs due to increased consumer spending, and add $832 billion in U.S. GDP over 10 years. Further, an analysis from the right-leaning American Action Forum illustrates that benchmark immigration reform would raise the pace of economic growth by nearly a percentage point over the near term, raise GDP per capita by over $1,500 and reduce the cumulative federal deficit by over $2.5 trillion.

Think tanks compete with numbers and ideas. Finding two as far on the opposite side of the spectrum as Center for American Progress and American Action Forum in agreement on an issue is a rare occurrence. The data and facts supporting immigration reform simply do not lie.
http://www.policymic.com/articles/38717/immigration-reform-2013-a-huge-opportunity-to-grow-the-economy

Not only that, but the libertarian Cato Institute also chimes in. U.S. gross domestic product (GDP) would increase by at least .84% each year after the reform is implemented. The study also estimated net personal income would increase $30 to $36 billion in the first three years following earned legalization, as a result of the higher earning power of newly legalized workers.

In addition, in a recent survey of a group of eminent economists 85% agreed that undocumented immigrants have impacted the U.S. economy in a positive (74%) or neutral (11%) manner. Moreover, a report by the Immigration Policy Center estimated that each immigrant pays in taxes an average of between $20,000 and $80,000 more than he or she consumes in public benefits.

But immigration reform is a political, not an economic issue. All of the studies referenced above point to the fact that passing comprehensive immigration reform increases the nation's GDP and net personal income.

Read more, http://thehill.com/blogs/congress-blog/foreign-policy/306597-immigration-reform-good-for-america-and-our-economy#ixzz2gCc6yyTT

Aug 2013. Quite a week for the President as he meets Stupidparty Disciples
Joan Walsh is Salon's editor at large, and she writes:

It's been quite a week for anti-Obama racism. At the Missouri State Fair Sunday, rodeo fans cheered to see a "clown" in an Obama mask get run down by a bull. On Friday in Florida the president faced a gaggle of protesters on the way to address a disabled veterans' group; one carried a sign reading "Kenyan Go Home." Three days earlier, Arizonans protested Obama's visit by singing "Bye Bye Black Sheep." One man mocked him by calling him "47 percent Negro"; another held a sign that read, "Impeach the Half-White Muslim!" ... Fairgoer Perry Beam told the Associated Press that "everybody screamed" and "just went wild" when an announcer asked if they'd like to see "Obama run down by a bull."

"It was at that point I began to feel a sense of fear. It was that level of enthusiasm," the 48-year-old white musician said. Another clown approached and began to play with the lips of the Obama mask. "There would have been no reason to play with his lips if he were a white president," Beam said. "They mentioned the president's name, I don't know, 100 times. It as sickening. It was feeling like some kind of Klan rally you'd see on TV. I've never seen anything so blatantly racist in my life," he added. "If an old country boy picks up on something like that, imagine what a person of color would think."

Meanwhile, John Boehner golfs with birther-in-chief Trump, while he headlines ABC's respected Sunday news show. The GOP seems content to live on the fumes of Obama-hatred. It's not a strategy for a post-Obama politics, but they seem to reckon there are enough rodeo clowns out there to get them through 2014.

http://www.salon.com/2013/08/12/gop%E2%80%99s_rodeo_of_racism_blows_up/

Confused about religion

Mark my word, if and when these preachers get control of the [Republican] party, and they're sure trying to do so, it's going to be a terrible damn problem. Frankly, these people frighten me. Politics and governing demand compromise. But these Christians believe they are acting in the name of God, so they can't and won't compromise. I know, I've tried to deal with them.

—Barry M. Goldwater

Stupidparty and Religion.

Definitions of religion (being religious) can be as nebulous or as diverse as how we individually might imagine God or interpret the Bible or the Koran—but for the purposes hereunder and generally speaking, let us go with this: "Is Religion important in your daily life?"

This book leaves aside the circular debate about whether God exists or not. Also, this is not about trying to establish whether religion causes poverty or conversely whether poverty leads to more religious fervor. Religion tends to initiate early, to assuage one's childhood fear of death. But beyond that, people who can see few rational options to their earthly problems are more inclined to default to prayer, and prayer can at the very least have a meditative, Zenlike ability to reorder and calm one's thoughts.

Many countries or peoples have encountered untold misery as a result of godless tyrants. There was China under Mao, Russia under Stalin, or the Jews under Hitler.* These tyrants demanded total obedience, but total obedience would not be enough to save you.

*I tend to accept that Hitler was not a Christian—but I also question the Christianity of many supposed Christians.

But it is not only ungodly tyrants who have the potential to create misery. Religions seeking money and power have an extremely questionable history—whether it be the Crusades, inquisitions, witch hunts, Bible/Koran-bashing rabble-rousing fundamentalist bigots, suppression of science… well, in the wrong hands or minds, it can be a force for dreadful activities.

If only Stupidparty Disciples understood this aspect of history, if only their historical insight could range beyond the Second Amendment, they could at least understand the direction they are headed in.

As a general rule, the more religious a country is, the more backward or impoverished it is.

Let's look at the world's least religious countries, and their relative educational ranking:

Least Religious Countries	Religion Unimportant to	Education Ranking
1 Sweden	83.0%	18
2 Denmark	80.5%	3
4 Norway	78.0%	7
5 Hong Kong	75.5%	N/A
6 Japan	75.0%	35
8 UK	73.0%	31
9 Finland	70.0%	2
10 France	69.5%	21
11 Vietnam	69.5%	115
12 Australia	67.5%	4
14 New Zealand	66.0%	1
42 USA	34.5%	13

Most Religious Countries and their Educational Rank:

Religion > 95% Importance

	Country	Yes, important	Education Ranking
1	Bangladesh	100%	165
2	Niger	100%	181
3	Indonesia	99%	104
4	Morocco	99%	155
5	Sri Lanka	99%	108
6	Congo	99%	130
7	Djibouti	98%	158
8	Malawi	99%	138
9	Mauritania	98%	160
10	Sierra Leone	98%	174
11	Somaliland	99%	N/A
12	Egypt	98%	136
13	Burundi	98%	157
14	Comoros	96%	N/A
15	Laos	97%	139
16	Nigeria	96%	145
17	Pakistan	97%	150
18	Afghanistan	97%	177
19	Guinea	97%	121
20	Myanmar	97%	121
21	Zambia	97%	140
22	Bahrain	96%	63
23	Cambodia	96%	134
24	Jordan	97%	93
25	Malaysia	96%	98
26	Saudi Arabia	95%	110
27	Senegal	97%	173
28	Tanzania	97%	143
29	Yemen	96%	153
30	Philippines	96%	71
31	Cameroon	96%	148
32	Qatar	95%	151
33	Rwanda	95%	148
34	Ghana	95%	125
35	Tunisia	95%	125
36	Kuwait	95%	91
37	Mali	95%	179

Now, the USA does not fair too badly on either count. But we are not discussing the relative merits of America versus other countries. We are really analyzing America's Achilles' heel: the Stupidparty and its Disciples. So having established a clear correlation between religious countries and their education, let's now apply the same test within the United States.

Most and Least Religious States and their Educational Rank:

	Most Religious	Percentage Religious	Education Rank
1	Mississippi	58%	48
2	Utah	56%	19
3	Alabama	56%	44
4	Louisiana	53%	46
5	Arkansas	52%	49
6	South Carolina	52%	35
7	Tennessee	50%	41
8	North Carolina	50%	25
9	Georgia	48%	20
10	Oklahoma	48%	42
	Average Education rank		37

	Least Religious		
1	Vermont	19%	7
2	New Hampshire	23%	9
3	Maine	24%	23
4	Massachusetts	27%	1
5	Rhode Island	29%	13
6	Oregon	29%	17
7	Nevada	31%	45
8	Alaska	31%	24
9	Hawaii	31%	15
10	Connecticut	31%	4
	Average Education rank		16

International Religion Wiki / States Religion: Gallup 2013 / Education, Undergraduate degree Wiki.

Religion can be a constructive source of community or personal bonding, solace, hope, and charitable acts. This does not mean that giving to the church is the same as giving to charity. Most such donations are as charitable as paying dues to your club. Organized religion hardly has a pristine history. The real Founding Fathers of the United States clearly understood the dangers of any one religion playing too big a role in society. The early settlers came to America to escape religious persecution, not to enact it. The writers of the Constitution went to great lengths to try and mitigate the chances of religion becoming a highly destructive force.

It is a terrible idea for a country to be run by an all-powerful Religion. It is also very silly for a religious group to be too closely identified with any one particular party—because however good the philosophy of such a religious group, this philosophy will be hijacked by the philosophy of the political party it has allied itself to.

Take the Christians in the United States, most especially the evangelicals, who are a powerful political force. Surely, a Christian should primarily follow the teachings of Jesus Christ. But Jesus Christ is the polar opposite of the Stupidparty, and thus any such political association massively undermines the very notion of Christianity in the USA, and the very integrity of supposedly practicing Christians.

Ann Coulter: "We should invade their countries, kill their leaders and convert them to Christianity."
http://www.washingtonmonthly.com/features/2001/0111.coulterwisdom.html

Jesus Christ: Lived in a land under occupation and at the time many believed that he was of a line of kings and was thus destined to overthrow the Roman occupiers. But Jesus had a different agenda, an agenda the polar opposite of Stupidparty:

1) He was not interested in waging war or rebellion.
2) He never needed to be carrying a weapon.
3) He was unusually welcoming to foreigners (gentiles).
4) He treated women, even prostitutes, with utmost respect.
5) He wanted help the sick.
6) He wanted to help the poor.
7) He never advocated for the death penalty.
8) He never disrespected the land (environment).
9) He never raised funds from the wealthy.
10) He lost his temper once, railing against the "money changers" (Wall Street).
11) He was not an eye-for-an-eye guy—rather, turn the other cheek.
12) His teachings were brilliant (not hateful gibberish) and stand the test of time.
13) Had no interest in wealth or material possessions.
14) Thus, he would have no interest in Asset Stripping the planet.
15) He was certainly not homophobic.
16) Never preached antifact, antiscience, fear mongering, or conspiracy-theory claptrap.
17) And, oh yes, he was probably Black.

Jesus also never discussed abortion issues, or contraception—so any such modern dogmatic policy is an invention by lesser beings.

Jesus Christ is as close philosophically to the Stupidparty as Nelson Mandela is to Pat Robertson. Can such a disconnect be explained? Perhaps the constitutional separation of church and state creates a contextual vacuum. Perhaps homeschooling or heretofore-unknown state madrasas shape views. But the disconnect between these Christians and the reality of Jesus is wide:

Evangelicals fear a Christian Obama so much that they would rather vote for a Mormon (they voted for Mitt 78–21).

I must own up to having a bit of a pet peeve about Mormonism—in that, with one exception, I have

Jesus meets Bain Capital

never heard a debate or read an article on the subject that has not left me feeling "Are you kidding? Is that it?" I seem to remember *Time* magazine doing an "in depth" exposé a few years ago, and I was just left scratching my head in bemused confusion. The one exception to this debate vacuum being rather oddly an episode by the ever-so-creative *South Park* cartoon series on Comedy TV. South Park Studios later went on to create the Broadway sensation *Book of Mormon,* a kindly crafted musical tale—considering the source material.)

Mitt Romney is a Mormon. Romney is actually no average Mormon; he was a Mormon priest, and his family line is akin to Mormon royalty. As such, for Mitt Romney his go-to prophet would be Joseph Smith. Unfortunately for such proudly Christian supporters of Mitt Romney, Joseph Smith is not quite in the same league as Jesus.

It should be noted that Mormons also believe that the Bible is the word of God, but when they do their outreach (missionary work), they place greater emphasis on the Book of Mormon. It would seem to me that by apparently being so easily taken in by Joseph Smith, this would undermine their credibility when evangelizing about Jesus.

Joseph Smith:

Mormons believe in the Book of Mormon. They believe that in around 1826, Joseph Smith received a vision and visitation from two angels, who left him golden tablets, which Joseph Smith translated—directly from God's words. Later these angels came back to repossess the tablets. Well, the translation made some interesting reading—the core contention being that Holy Land prophets came to the USA around 500 BC and started a massive civilization that was destroyed around 400 AD.

Well, there are some problems with this whole history:
1) Joseph Smith had a number of visions between 1820 and 1830. But in 1826 Joseph Smith was convicted of fraud. Fraudulently getting money by claiming that he could find hidden treasures, lost goods, etc., by using a seer's stone.
2) This Book of Mormon civilization used Steel, Chariots, Horses, pigs, sheep, Ox, Goats, Cattle, Barley, figs, grapes, Wheat, Swords, Engravings, Glass, Carriages, Wheels, etc. Well, none of this existed in the New World until after being introduced by Europeans. Some items were used by the Mayan civilization—but that all occurred after 400 AD.
3) 2,000,000 die in the battle of Cumorah in 500 BC. In New York. There is no archeological evidence of such a battle. Another 230,000 die in 400 AD. Not one item has ever been dug up.

4) Joseph Smith (and his followers), in their endless futile efforts to discover architectural support for his nonsense, quickly began to realize that there were perhaps no appropriate ruins in North America. So they were forced to reach ever-further afield at a time when archeologists were unearthing Mayan ruins. They glob onto the ruins at Palenque, stating that Palenque, not far from Belize, was a Nephite city. But today it is apparent that Palenque was a Mayan city, only becoming impressive when it was rebuilt around 600 AD (200 years after the Nephites were destroyed). Of course, nobody would have known this in 1820.

5) Joseph Smith claimed that the great Guatemalan ruins tied in with the Book of Mormon, but these ruins were built after the end of the Book of Mormon.

6) According to Smith, papyri he translated were of the Book of Abraham. These papyri were lost and later rediscovered, in November 1967—and by this time scholars knew how to translate hieroglyphics. The papyri had absolutely no connection to Abraham but were about Osiris and Isis.

7) Joseph Smith incorrectly pointed out that Mayan tablets read left to right like ancient Hebrew.

8) There is now also strong evidence that the Book of Mormon was not simply inspired nonsense but that there was plagiarism involved. In 1823 a book, *View of the Hebrews,* had similar themes. It was written by Ethan Smith, a congregational minister in Vermont. Joseph Smith's assistant (scriber), Mr. Chowdrey, attended these services, and his family had close ties with Ethan Smith (no relation to Joseph Smith).

9) DNA analysis proves there is no connection between the Jewish people and the various Indian tribes in the Americas.

10) If the Book of Mormon is the word of God, why would it need around 4000 corrections?

Sample of Items that the Book of Mormon describes in the narrative, but that we now know did not exist in North America at that time:

Animals	Metals	Weapons, etc.	Plants
Ass	Brass	Swords	Barley
Cows/Cattle	Breastplates	Wheels	Figs
Goats	Chains	Carriages	Grapes
Horses	Copper	Chariots	Wheat
Sheep	Gold	Glass	
Swine	Iron		
Elephants	Steel		
	Silver		

Evidently, some church leaders have the ability to get visions from God in the middle of the night, inspiring them to change the Book of Mormon, thus allowing them to cover up racism and less-odious forms of the absurd. Odd, since the Book of Mormon came from those angels, who provided those vanishing golden tablets, sent directly from God (an infallible God, no doubt).

Oh, yes, and let's not forget that stunning sex drive and that whole "lost tribe of Israel, king of your own planet" stuff. Let's not forget the need for those massive buildings, housing such an impressive civilization, and the huge battles that took place in North America at a time when America was actually inhabited by a few horseless hunter gatherers. Archeologists would have no trouble unearthing some of this vivid history, if any of it had actually happened.

The White Horse Prophecy:
(Wiki)

Based upon the family's heritage, going back to the first Mormon generation, and to their modern-day prominence in business, politics, and as part of The Church of Jesus Christ of Latter-day Saints, authors Richard and Joan Ostling have written variously that the Romneys are "an LDS political dynasty" and that "The Romneys are LDS royalty." The family is linked by marriage to the Smith family.

The prophecy is purported to have been made in 1843 by Joseph Smith, Jr., founder of the Latter Day Saint movement, regarding the future of the Latter Day Saints (Mormons) and the United States of America. The Latter Day Saints, according to the prophecy, would "go to the Rocky Mountains and… be a great and mighty people," identified figuratively with the White Horse described in the Revelation of John. The prophecy further predicts that the United States Constitution will one day "hang like a thread" and will be saved "by the efforts of the White Horse."

Some have speculated, on the basis of the White Horse Prophecy, that Mormons expect the United States to eventually become a theocracy dominated by The Church of Jesus Christ of Latter-day Saints (LDS Church). The authenticity of the prophecy as a whole, which was not made public until long after Smith's death, is debated, and the leadership of the LDS Church has stated that "the so-called 'White Horse Prophecy'… is not embraced as Church doctrine." However, the belief that members of the LDS Church will one day need to take action to save the imperiled US Constitution has been attributed to Smith in several sources and has been discussed in an approving fashion by Brigham Young and other LDS leaders.

Several famous Mormons have made statements related to the White Horse Prophecy. For instance, former US presidential candidate Mitt Romney has said he considers the White Horse Prophecy to be a matter of "speculation and discussion by [LDS] church members" and "not official [LDS] church doctrine."

George W. Romney In 1967, the U.S. presidential candidate said the following regarding the White Horse Prophecy: "I have always felt that they meant that sometime the question of whether we are going to proceed on the basis of the Constitution would arise and **at this point government leaders who were Mormons would be involved in answering that question.**"

Mitt Romney In 2007, the U.S. presidential candidate told the *Salt Lake Tribune*: "I haven't heard my name associated with [the White Horse Prophecy] or anything of that nature. That's not official church doctrine… I don't put that at the heart of my religious belief."

http://en.wikipedia.org/wiki/White_Horse_Prophecy

There is no Saint for insane greed

Of course, you cannot take Mitt Romney's word on anything. Of course, he would deny his belief that his presidency was preordained (explaining why he was so convinced he was about to win the election—when mathematically inclined critical thinkers knew otherwise). Is it so incredible?—of course not; he already believes in a faith that is provable gibberish. Therefore, it is my opinion that Mitt Romney truly believed that he was destined to be president and perhaps even destined to eventually turn us all into Mormons, because that is a core goal of the Latter-day Saints. So it is reasonable to suggest taking a moment out of your day to understand what they believe and the implications of having the president of the U.S., our representative on the international stage, having such an outlandish belief system. Not simply amusing but embarrassing. Also, consider that it was having a president with an outlandish belief system that caused the second Iraq war. That president was not simply amusing or embarrassing, as history might well eventually judge him a war criminal.

This is why, when we vet political candidates, their belief system is vitally relevant and should be discussed. There was no sensible discussion about this. There were some evangelicals who questioned whether Mormons were Christians or a cult—but that was like the pot calling the kettle black.

In order to understand what a serious issue Stupidparty religious dogma really is, let us look more closely at some of the most overtly religious Stupidparty leaders who have had serious opportunities to fulfill their presidential ambitions. And there by the grace of God, we have so far been spared the worst consequences of this odious zest.

Pat Robertson:

To best understand what monstrous Frankensteins are invariably conceived as the result of merging religion with Stupidparty, one should take a moment to look at Pat Robertson in some detail. Call this exercise due diligence in the name of strengthening democracy (diligence that would have been useful in vetting G. W. Bush). Since he is a leading light, one of the key pillars of the Stupidparty, hosting his own longstanding TV show, on his own TV network, it is relatively easy to get into the true hearts of people like Pat Robertson.

Marion Gordon "Pat" Robertson (born March 22, 1930) is an American media mogul, executive chairman, and a former Southern Baptist minister. He presently serves as chancellor of Regent University and chairman of the Christian Broadcasting Network. (Wiki)

In 1988 he made a serious effort to be the Stupidparty presidential nominee.

Pat Robertson evidently has regular conversations with God and is thus naturally able to predict the future.

1981—Robertson predicted global economic collapse, and that the USSR would invade Israel, control all the oil in the Middle East, and foul up the world economy.
1988—Robertson said God told him to run for President. Apparently God did not tell him to win.

1996—God told Robertson that Bill Clinton would not be elected for a second term. He also said that a terrorist with a nuclear weapon would strike within the United States. 1998—Robertson said God would strike the United States with tsunamis, hurricanes, earthquakes, and "maybe even a meteor" due to Orlando, Florida's city council voting to fly rainbow flags during a Gay Pride celebration. Orlando was never hit, though Virginia Beach, Robertson's home, was. 2005—Robertson said God told him that George W. Bush would pass Social Security reform, tax reform, and that the Supreme Court would end up packed with conservative judges. He also said there would be a wide scale conversion of Muslims to Christianity. 2006—Robertson said God told him that tsunamis would ravage the coasts of the United States. 2007—Robertson predicted that there would be a massive terrorist event aimed at the United States that would result in "mass killing" during the second half of the year. "The Lord didn't say nuclear, but I do believe it'll be something like that—that'll be a mass killing, possibly millions of people, major cities injured," Robertson said. 2012—Robertson said God told him who would win the Presidential election that year, but he would not tell. However he later said, "I won't get into great detail about elections but I sure did miss it." Robertson also said that 2012 would bring about a collapse of the American economy. This information came only after a question and answer session with God that included Robertson asking if the disaster would be the result of an "EMP blast" or a "Mayan galaxy alignment," all of which God took a pass on.

http://www.webpronews.com/pat-robertsons-annual-predictions-greatest-flops-2013-07

If a politician believing his own paranoid subconscious is the voice of God is not unsettling enough, we have only just touched the surface of Pat Robertson's Christian perversions:

Faith healing.
1970s and 1980s, whilst a faith healer, attempted to cure AIDS, proclaiming it cured after prayer.

On Homosexuality.
"Many of those people involved in Adolf Hitler were Satanists. Many were homosexuals. The two things seem to go together."

http://www.cnn.com/2013/07/09/us/pat-robertson-facebook-remark/

"A lot of people are into this homosexual thing because they've been abused by a parent, abused by a coach, abused by a sibling, abused by a friend, they're little boys and little girls and they don't know any better and then they somehow think, 'well I must be gay,' they aren't they are heterosexual and they just need to come out of that," said the *not* anti-gay Robertson.

http://www.towleroad.com/2013/07/pat-robertson-were-not-anti-gaygays-are-simply-confused-or-sick-video.html

"The June 8, 1998, edition of his TV show, where Robertson denounced Orlando, Florida, and Disney World for allowing a privately sponsored 'Gay Days' weekend: Robertson stated that the acceptance of homosexuality could result hurricanes, earthquakes, tornadoes, terrorist bombings and 'possibly a meteor'... The first hurricane of the 1998 Atlantic hurricane season, Hurricane Bonnie, actually turned away from Florida and instead damaged the rest of the east coast.... The area hardest hit by the hurricane was the Hampton Roads region, which includes Virginia Beach, where the Robertson's

The 700 Club originates. While other hurricanes did hit Florida, none of them hit Disney World."
http://en.wikipedia.org/wiki/Pat_Robertson_controversies

In 1999 Robertson said Scotland was "a dark land" overrun by gays. (He was upset by the Bank of Scotland declining to do business with Pat Robertson.)
http://en.wikipedia.org/wiki/Pat_Robertson_controversies

More on Natural Disasters.

Robertson prayed to God to steer hurricanes away from his company's Virginia Beach headquarters. He credited his prayers for steering the course of Hurricane Gloria in 1985, which caused billions of dollars of destruction in many states along the U.S. East Coast.
http://en.wikipedia.org/wiki/Pat_Robertson_controversies

View of Non-Christians: Termites.

In an August 1986 *New York* magazine article Robertson is quoted saying, "It is interesting, that termites don't build things, and the great builders of our nation almost to a man have been Christians, because Christians have the desire to build something. He is motivated by love of man and God, so he builds. The people who have come into [our] institutions [today] are primarily termites. They are into destroying institutions that have been built by Christians, whether it is universities, governments, our own traditions, that we have… The termites are in charge now, and that is not the way it ought to be, and the time has arrived for a godly fumigation."
http://en.wikipedia.org/wiki/Pat_Robertson_controversies

On January 14, 1991, on *The 700 Club,* Pat Robertson attacked a number of Protestant denominations when he declared: "You say you're supposed to be nice to the Episcopalians and the Presbyterians and the Methodists and this, that, and the other thing. Nonsense. I don't have to be nice to the spirit of the Antichrist."
http://en.wikipedia.org/wiki/Pat_Robertson_controversies

Pot calling the kettle black: On the September 25, 2006, broadcast of *The 700 Club* Robertson stated, "It's amazing how the Muslims deal with history and the truth with violence. They don't understand what reasoned dialogue is…"
http://en.wikipedia.org/wiki/Pat_Robertson_controversies

Views on Women.

He has described feminism as a "socialist, anti-family political movement that encourages women to leave their husbands, kill their children, practice witchcraft, destroy capitalism and become lesbians."
http://www.cnn.com/2013/07/09/us/pat-robertson-facebook-remark/

On a broadcast of Robertson's television show, *The 700 Club,* he answered a question from a viewer named Michael about how to repair his marriage to a woman who "has no respect for me as the head of the house."

Robertson's response: "Well, you could become a Muslim and you could beat her… I don't think we condone wife-beating these days but something has got to be done."

"I know this is painful for the ladies to hear, but if you get married, you have accepted the headship of a man, your husband. Christ is the head of the household and the husband is the head of the wife, and that's the way it is, period"—Pat Robertson
http://www.cnn.com/2013/07/09/us/pat-robertson-facebook-remark/

What caused 9/11?

Pat Robertson and Stupidparty twin Jerry Falwell agree. He agreed with Falwell when Falwell stated that the September 11, 2001, terrorist attacks were caused by "pagans, abortionists, feminists, gays, lesbians, the American Civil Liberties Union and the People for the American Way."
http://en.wikipedia.org/wiki/Pat_Robertson_controversies

Abortion fine for foreigners.

In a 2001 interview with CNN's Wolf Blitzer, he said that the Chinese were "doing what they have to do," regarding China's one-child policy, sometimes enforced with compulsory abortions.
http://en.wikipedia.org/wiki/Pat_Robertson_controversies

Foreign Policy.

Robertson repeatedly supported former president of Liberia, Charles Taylor, in various episodes of his *The 700 Club* TV program during the United States' involvement in the Second Liberian Civil War in June and July 2003. Robertson accuses the U.S. State Department of giving President Bush bad advice in supporting Taylor's ouster as president, and of trying "as hard as they can to destabilize Liberia." Robertson was criticized for failing to mention in his broadcasts his $8,000,000 (USD) investment in a Liberian gold mine. Taylor had been indicted by the United Nations for war crimes at the time of Robertson's support.
http://en.wikipedia.org/wiki/Pat_Robertson_controversies

In an October 2003 interview with author Joel Mowbray about his book *Dangerous Diplomacy*, a book critical of the United States Department of State, Robertson made suggestions that the explosion of a nuclear weapon at State Department headquarters would be good for the country, and repeated those comments on the air: "What we need is for somebody to place a small nuke at Foggy Bottom."
http://en.wikipedia.org/wiki/Pat_Robertson_controversies

On the August 22, 2005 broadcast of *The 700 Club*, Robertson said of Venezuelan President Hugo Chávez: "I don't know about this doctrine of assassination, but if he thinks we're trying to assassinate him, I think that we really ought to go ahead and do it. It's a whole lot cheaper than starting a war, and I don't think any oil shipments will stop."
http://mediamatters.org/video/2005/08/22/robertson-called-for-the-assassination-of-venez/133694

On why Israeli Prime Minister Ariel Sharon suffered a massive stroke: "God considers this land to be his. You read the Bible and he says 'This is my land,' and for any prime minister of Israel who decides he is going to carve it up and give it away, God says, 'No, this is mine'... He was dividing God's land. And I would say, 'Woe unto any prime minister of Israel who takes a similar course to appease the E.U., the United Nations, or the United States of America.' God says, 'This land belongs to me. You better leave it alone.'"
http://thehjellejar.com/Writings/Christianity,%20Culture,%20and%20Current%20Events/15%20Israel.html

On the earthquake in Haiti that destroyed the capital and killed tens of thousands of people, Jan. 13, 2010: "It may be a blessing in disguise… Something happened a long time ago in Haiti, and people might not want to talk about it. Haitians were originally under the heel of the French. You know, Napoleon the third, or whatever. And they got together and swore a pact to the devil. They said, we will serve you if you will get us free from the French. True story. And so, the devil said, okay it's a deal. Ever since they have been cursed by one thing after the other."
http://www.theliberalcurmudgeon.com/2010/01/pat-robertson-haitian-earthquake-caused.html

There is just endless material on Pat Robertson. If anything in the above is out of context, well, I just really do not care. Trying to cover his utterly hateful nonsense is like tackling Hydra's head: cut one off and a new bunch come screaming at you. It is just overwhelming. If you have a direct line to God, you need to be pitch perfect; one might be tempted to say infallible.

Rick Santorum:

Not only is Santorum a concern for his religious dogma, but he is a poster boy for the whole concept of misunderstanding freedom. His Freedoms would be intellectual and real slavery for those people on the other side of the aisle. He is aiming right for your bedroom. Santorum believes in homeschooling—so that everyone can end up with the same world view that he preaches. All Stupidparty Disciples, plus everyone else, can be just like Rick.
Art http://commons.wikimedia.org/wiki/File:%C5%9Aw._Alojzy.jpeg

But at least he understands the basics:

On Smart People.
Rick Santorum: "The Elite Smart People Will Never Be On Our Side."
http://www.nydailynews.com/news/politics/rick-santorum-tells-audience-smart-people-side-article-1.1161335
I cannot resist pointing out the following leading lights of the Stupidparty set to speak at the same convention: Rep. Michele Bachmann, Glenn Beck, Kirk Cameron, Gov. Jan Brewer, Sen. Rand Paul, Rep. Steve King.

On Rape.
"I think the right approach is to accept this horribly created—in the sense of rape—but nevertheless a gift in a very broken way, the gift of human life, and accept what God has given to you… rape victims should make the best of a bad situation."
http://www.dailymail.co.uk/news/article-2091170/Rick-Santorum-Rape-victims-gift-baby-pregnant.html

Contraception a big *no no*.
"One of the things I will talk about, that no president has talked about before, is I think the dangers of contraception in this country… Many of the Christian faith have said, well, that's okay, contraception is okay. It's not okay. It's a license to do things in a sexual realm that is counter to how things are supposed to be"—Rick Santorum, interview with Caffeinated Thoughts blog (October 2011).
http://www.cnn.com/2012/02/14/opinion/coontz-santorum/

I think we can leave it to the imagination as to how some basic and usually rather fun Freedoms are under threat. Santorum would no doubt suggest only the "missionary position," no more than once a year, before Lent, maybe using a sheet with a hole in it.

Yes, the Catholic Church has always been against contraception, yet 99% of Catholic women ignore this doddering old white-male, prehistoric utter claptrap, which never had anything to do with the teachings of Christ. In the real world, linking public policy or charitable assistance with abstinence is a death sentence. It is nothing short of manslaughter.

Suffice to say, contraception is an absolutely vital tool in combating overpopulation, poverty, and disease. But almost as importantly, the repression of sexual activity is simply not acceptable under the constitution, or in any sane society. So the Catholic orthodoxy of every sperm being sacred (as Monty Python so beautifully and poignantly sang about) is perhaps the single most damaging piece of dogma that I can imagine, within the context of the problems facing humanity in the twenty-first century.

The Constitution.

"Earlier in my political career, I had the opportunity to read the speech, and I almost threw up"—Rick Santorum, on JFK's 1960 speech about the importance of separation of church and state (October 2011)

http://www.washingtonpost.com/blogs/post-politics/post/santorum-says-he-almost-threw-up-after-reading-jfk-speech-on-separation-of-church-and-state/2012/02/26/gIQA91hubR_blog.html

Education Policy (Stupid comment plus Obama never said it. Can God's messengers lie?)

"President Obama wants everybody in America to go to college. What a snob… Oh, I understand why he wants you to go to college. He wants to remake you in his image"—speaking to a Tea Party group in Michigan (February 2012)

http://www.politifact.com/truth-o-meter/statements/2012/feb/27/rick-santorum/rick-santorum-calls-barack-obama-snob-wanting-ever/

For the first 150 years, most presidents homeschooled their children at the White House, he said. "Where did they come up that public education and bigger education bureaucracies was the rule in America? Parents educated their children, because it's their responsibility to educate their children."

http://www.nytimes.com/2012/02/19/us/politics/santorum-criticizes-education-system-and-obama.html?_r=0

Inflaming Racism.

"I think the Democrats are actually worried he (Obama) may go to Indonesia and bow to more Muslims"—Rick Santorum, Fox News interview (May 2010)

http://politicalhumor.about.com/od/republicans/a/Rick-Santorum-Quotes.htm

Homophobia.

"Is anyone saying same-sex couples can't love each other? I love my children. I love my friends, my brother. Heck, I even love my mother-in-law. Should we call these relationships marriage, too?"—Rick Santorum, in a *Philadelphia Inquirer* column (May 2008)
http://thinkprogress.org/politics/2008/05/22/23672/santorum-gay/

Homeschooling leads to this historical expertise and Christian foreign policy.

"The idea that the Crusades and the fight of Christendom against Islam is somehow an aggression on our part is absolutely anti-historical. And that is what the perception is by the American Left who hates Christendom… What I'm talking about is onward American soldiers. What we're talking about are core American values"—campaigning for president in South Carolina (February 2011)
http://archives.politicususa.com/2011/02/26/rick-santorum-says-dont-hate-on-the-crusades.html

"Satan has his sights on the United States of America… If you were Satan, who would you attack in this day and age? There is no one else to go after other than the United States and that has been the case now for almost 200 years, once America's preeminence was sown by our great Founding Fathers."
http://www.cbsnews.com/8301-503544_162-57382008-503544/santorum-in-08-satan-is-attacking-america/

"You know, Mitt, I don't want to go to a trade war, I want to beat China," he said. "I want to go to war with China and make America the most attractive place in the world to do business."

"All the people that live in the West Bank are Israelis, they're not Palestinians," he says. "There is no 'Palestinian.'"
http://thinkprogress.org/security/2011/11/21/373985/santorum-west-bank-israelis/

He should perhaps do some fact-checking before conferring Israeli citizenship on 4 million Palestinians.

Solution to Social Security concerns.

"The reason Social Security is in big trouble is we don't have enough workers to support the retirees. Well, a third of all the young people in America are not in America today because of abortion"—Rick Santorum, during a Republican presidential debate (May 2011)
http://politicalhumor.about.com/od/republicans/a/Rick-Santorum-Quotes.htm

Healthcare Expertise.

"Shortly before the Missouri primary, Santorum—arguing against Barack Obama's healthcare law—made some rather startling claims about the medical system in the Netherlands, claiming that 1 in 20 deaths in the country were caused by forced euthanasia, and that elderly Dutch wear bracelets that say 'do not euthanize me' and 'don't go to the hospital, they go to another country, because they're afraid because of budget purposes that they will not come out of that hospital if they go into it with sickness.'

"When asked by a Dutch reporter where the candidate had gotten these alarming facts, a campaign spokeswoman would only say, 'It's a matter of what's in his heart.'"
http://blog.foreignpolicy.com/posts/2012/04/10/our_favorite_rick_santorum_moments

Energy and Environmental Policy.

"Drill everywhere… There is no such thing as global warming."
http://www.theguardian.com/environment/2012/jan/04/santorum-romney-climate-change

The Science Guy.
"What we should be teaching are the problems and holes and I think there are legitimate problems and holes in the theory of evolution."
http://www.brainyquote.com/quotes/quotes/r/ricksantor414852.html

Mike Huckabee:

At one point in 2008, it looked like he was going to beat out McCain to be the Stupidparty nominee for president.

The Role of Women.
"A wife is to submit graciously to the servant leadership of her husband even as the church willingly submits to the headship of Christ."
http://crooksandliars.com/2007/12/11/
mike-huckabee-women-should-submit-to-their-husbands

Creationist (Most Christian religions accept science—hence, their willingness to take medicines, etc.; the creationist stuff is somewhat peculiar to evangelicals and their ilk.)
"It doesn't embarrass me one bit to let you know that I believe Adam and Eve were real people."
http://www.motherjones.com/politics/2007/12/huckabee-hides-his-full-gospel

The Birther (although he denies it).
HUCKABEE: I would love to know more. What I know is troubling enough. And one thing that I do know is his having grown up in Kenya, his view of the Brits, for example, very different than the average American. When he gave the bust back to the Brits—

MALZBERG: Of Winston Churchill.

HUCKABEE: The bust of Winston Churchill, a great insult to the British. But then if you think about it, his perspective as growing up in Kenya with a Kenyan father and grandfather, their view of the Mau Mau Revolution in Kenya is very different than ours because he probably grew up hearing that the British were a bunch of imperialists who persecuted his grandfather.
Mike Huckabee has claimed that he "simply misspoke when I alluded to President Obama growing up in 'Kenya' and meant to say Indonesia." Numerous media figures have noted that Huckabee's defense is implausible: he made the false assertion twice, said Obama grew up "with a Kenyan father and grandfather," and claimed that learning about Kenya's Mau Mau Rebellion led Obama to develop a deep-seated hatred of the British.
http://mediamatters.org/research/2011/03/02/media-criticize-huckabees-gibberish-defense-for/177090

Sinners must be punished—even if they are 5 years old.
When asked about how God could allow the Newtown massacre, Huckabee mused: "It's an interesting thing. We ask why there's violence in our schools but we've systematically removed God from our schools. Should we be so surprised that schools would become a place of carnage? Because we've made it a place where we do not want to talk about eternity, life, what responsibility means, accountability. That we're not just going to have to be accountable to the police, if they catch us, but we stand one day before a holy God in judgment… Maybe we ought to let [God] in on the front end and we would not have to call him to show up when it's all said and done at the back end."
http://talkingpointsmemo.com/livewire/huckabee-schools-a-place-of-carnage-because-we-systematically-removed-god

Sinners must be punished.

"According to a recent guest on Fox & Friends, Christians are unfairly accused of being stupid. One has to look no further than Fox News to see why rational people might have this opinion. As part of their advocacy for the religious right, Fox News provides a platform for the discredited theory of 'intelligent design' (Bill O'Reilly), revisionist religiously based history curriculums (*Fox & Friends*) and outright hatred of atheists (Eric Bolling). And while Fox's Mike Huckabee doesn't appear to lack cognitive process-es, those processes can result in amazingly, extraordinarily, and stupendously STUPID statements such as those he made regarding the horrific massacre in Aurora, Colorado. While the motivation for the shooting is not known, it is probable that the shooter was exhibiting ideation related to mental-health issues. In linking the behavior to other soci-etal problems (including, he believes, abortion), Mike Huckabee attributes it to—ready for it—sin! Yup, you heard it right."

http://www.newshounds.us/20120722_mike_huckabee_aurora_shooting_caused_by_sin_godlessness_in_
schools#oF0Xp3tcjdyaTxLg.99

Public Education Agenda.

"I almost wish that there would be, like, a simultaneous telecast, and all Americans would be forced—forced at gunpoint, no less—to listen to every David Barton message, and I think our country would be better for it. I wish it'd happen."

"David Barton is an Evangelical Christian who tries to spread a warped version of American history where our founding is based entirely on Christian values, and separation of church and state doesn't exist."
http://www.patheos.com/blogs/friendlyatheist/2011/03/31/mike-huckabee-wants-to-indoctrinate-you-at-gunpoint/

More expertise in U.S. history—*The Right Field* (blog).

"During the Republican debate, Mike Huckabee said he believes one of the defining issues facing the country is the sanctity of human life. Arguing that the issue is of his-torical importance, he invoked the Declaration of Independence's rights of life, liberty and the pursuit of happiness and said that most of the signers of the declaration were clergymen.

"Not even close.

"Only one of the 56 was an active clergyman, and that was John Witherspoon."
http://fivebeforechaos.com/2007/10/22/dumb-all-over-mike-huckabee/

Expert on the pivotal point of the Constitution.

"It's a lot easier to change the Constitution than it would be to change the word of the living God. And that's what we need to do is to amend the Constitution so it's in God's standards rather than trying to change God's standards so it lines up with some contem-porary view of how we treat each other and how we treat the family."
http://www.politicalruminations.com/mike-huckabee-quotes/#sthash.LZ9nhrL0.dpuf

Capital Punishment fine for nonbelievers.

When Huckabee was in Arkansas, managing death row and others seeking parole, inmates soon discovered that being reborn again was the way to the governor's heart, even serial rapists like Wayne Dumond—who, against the pleadings of the victims, gets released only to kill again.

Huckabee had a lot of other reasons to keep Dumond in prison, too. Another woman wrote him that Dumond had raped her mother, when she was 3 years old and sleeping in bed with her—and threatened the mother that he would rape and kill the 3 year old if the mom did not cooperate. A third woman wrote Huckabee that Dumond raped her at knifepoint, and added, "I feel that if he is released it is only a matter of time before he commits another crime and fear that he will not leave a witness to testify against him the next time."

So why was he so determined that Dumond be released? How could he ignore all of these heartfelt pleas? Well, a preacher friend of his ministered to Dumond in prison, and believed his claim that he was born-again. Huckabee commuted or pardoned over 669 prisoners, including 12 murderers—10 times as many as Bill Clinton did over 9 years, and more than all of the larger states surrounding Arkansas put together –as long as they claimed to be born-again Christians, or worked at the governor's mansion, or played in the prison band.
http://realchange.org/huckabee.htm

Expert in raising a family.
"Back in 1998, when Huckabee was Arkansas governor, his son David and David's friend Clayton Frady were fired from jobs at a Boy Scout camp. Why? Because they hung a stray dog by its neck, slit its throat, and stoned it to death. (This same son was convicted in 2007 for bringing a loaded .40 Glock handgun and a 9-round clip through airport security. He was also Homecoming King at Arkansas State.)"
http://realchange.org/huckabee.htm
http://en.wikipedia.org/wiki/David_Huckabee

Expert on Jesus's values.
"He was investigated 16 times and cited five times by the Arkansas Ethics Commission for violating ethics rules. Two of those citations were for cash that the governor or his wife accepted but did not report. Huckabee's gifts peaked at $112,000 in 1999, including $23,000 worth of clothing; over half of that was given by one businessman, whom Huckabee appointed to a state board."
http://www.realchange.org/huckabee.htm

Jesus says cover up your sins and all will be forgiven.
"And shortly before leaving office, Huckabee took all of the money in the governor's emergency fund and spent it destroying the hard drives of over 100 computers in the governor's office, to protect what he called 'the privacy' of the contents. (Since he was planning a race for president, and many of his other scandals were documented by memos and emails, many observers considered it to be a preemptive cover-up.) The new governor literally had to find and spend $335,000 just to replace the destroyed hard drives and computers. And then there was not a penny left in the emergency fund— designed to pay for extra expenses during hurricanes, tornados, etc.—for the last six months of the fiscal year."
http://www.realchange.org/huckabee.htm

Jesus says preaching bigotry in my name is great.
"He now claims that years of his sermons were destroyed in a church remodeling, and he had 100 computer hard drives destroyed—literally crushed—when he left the governor's office.

Even so, we know some of his radical views. He said in 1992 that AIDS victims should be 'isolated,' and the government shouldn't fund research; instead, he wanted Madonna and Elizabeth Taylor to pay for the studies. He does not believe in evolution, thinks

Adam and Eve were actual people, and refuses to say whether women should be allowed to be preachers."

Links to these stories and many more be found here, http://www.realchange.org/huckabee.htm

A Sociopathic Liar for Jesus.

"Huckabee has taken to repeating the lie that President Obama is a God-hating God-hater, who refuses to say the word 'Creator' when quoting from the Declaration of Independence."

What sort of person lies when he must know that we keep records of virtually everything the president says?

http://www.patheos.com/blogs/slacktivist/2012/09/05/mike-huckabee-is-lying-again/

Jesus looked upon his young single male disciples and wept.

"My thoughts on the SCOTUS ruling that determined that same sex marriage is okay: 'Jesus wept.'"

http://www.nationaljournal.com/politics/mike-huckabee-is-not-a-fan-of-the-doma-decision-jesus-wept-20130626

But can Jesus forgive Huckabee for being an ignorant, ethically challenged hypocrite?

"Five people in robes said they are bigger than the voters of CA and Congress combined. And bigger than God. May He forgive us all."

http://www.nationaljournal.com/politics/mike-huckabee-is-not-a-fan-of-the-doma-decision-jesus-wept-20130626

Why do we only hear from the faux Christians?

Does it not strike you as odd that the type of people we see lecturing us about Christianity are the very last people who should be lecturing us about Christianity: Pat Robertson, Rick Santorum, Mike Huckabee, Alan Keyes, Billy Graham's son, Glenn Beck (Mormon), the Stupidparty-loving evangelicals, various misogynist old white fart Roman Catholic bishops.

Where are the Catholic nuns, where is Nelson Mandela, Gandhi, Desmond Tutu? How about the archbishop of Canterbury, head of the Episcopalian Church? Why do we never hear from the good guys, the good Christians, Christians who can actually identify with Jesus Christ, speak his words, and live his actions?

It is all down to money. Money wants you to listen to the first category, to the bigot Christians—because these "Christians" help drive the agenda of the Benefactors. War and Arms and Guns. Asset Stripping the Citizens. Asset Stripping natural resources. Enriching those that control the political process, that control "democracy." Christianity in America has become nothing but an embarrassment, because Christians that actually give a damn have virtually no voice in the public domain.

The End of Times

Religion in the wrong hands can be really dangerous. Religion in the hands of Stupidparty becomes stupidly dangerous. Progressives tend to feel that it is tough to get into the hearts and minds of people—but when it comes to certain Stupidparty leaders, I am not so convinced, because really if you had to wade through their deepest thoughts, you would barely get your ankles wet.

In addition to this, they leave just too many clues, and these clues leave us with no choice but to connect the dots. Take House Intelligence Committee member Michele Bachmann, who simply cannot contain her outbursts of verbal diarrhea. But these people have power, and thus it is no laughing matter. Many scientists and mathematicians agree that humanity will be quite lucky to survive the next hundred years. We have the technology to blow

ourselves up. We are also indulging in behaviors that increase our exposure to global pandemics. But our biggest threat is our own stupidity, and ironically Stupidparty religious thinking could become a self-fulfilling prophecy. So let's roll the tape—Michele Bachmann:

Rep. Michele Bachmann (R-MN) claims the end of days is near, and as proof the former Republican presidential candidate cited President Barack Obama's decision last month to support Syrian rebels, which she calls al-Qaeda terrorists, with anti-chemical weapons gear and limited arms.

"This happened and as of today the United States is willingly, knowingly, intentionally sending arms to terrorists, now what this says to me, I'm a believer in Jesus Christ, as I look at the End Times scripture, this says to me that the leaf is on the fig tree and we are to understand the signs of the times, which is your ministry, we are to understand where we are in God's end times history," Bachmann told Jan Markell, radio host of "Understanding the Times," on Saturday.

"Rather than seeing this as a negative, we need to rejoice, Maranatha Come Lord Jesus, His day is at hand," Bachmann added later. "And so when we see up is down and right is called wrong, when this is happening, we were told this; that these days would be as the days of Noah. We are seeing that in our time. Yes it gives us fear in some respects because we want the retirement that our parents enjoyed. Well they will, if they know Jesus Christ."

http://talkingpointsmemo.com/livewire/bachmann-end-times-are-coming-because-obama-is-supporting-al-qaeda

Yes, we are at risk; we are threatened by Religious fundamentalists gaining the levers of powers, voting at elections, threatening the planet by myopic Asset Stripping; uncontrolled populations living unsustainable lives and deciding foreign policy based on myth. As George Bush Jr. would say, when asked if he should seek the advice of his dad before invading Iraq, I do not need to, "There is a higher father that I appeal to." If you vote Stupidparty, you own this.

Perhaps we need to demand more from Fundamentalists:

At the very least, it is not just the end of times that should concern them. Let Deuteronomy separate the fundamentalist wheat from the chaff.

Deuteronomy (23:1–2). God declared that any man with damaged or missing genitals, as well as any man who doesn't know the names of his ancestors going back ten generations, cannot enter into religious congregations.

Farming Tips.
Deuteronomy (22:10). God also doesn't want you to plow a field with an ox and a donkey on the same yoke

Help in the Kitchen.
Deuteronomy (14:21). If you're planning to boil a young goat in milk, please note that God doesn't want anyone to boil a young goat in its mother's milk

Fashion Tips.
(Leviticus 19:19). We are told to wear a piece of clothing made of more than one fabric. (Exodus 28:31–35). God will kill Aaron if he goes to minister without wearing a golden bell and blue pomegranates.

Genesis says *no* to those Carnivorous Dinosaurs of 5000 BC.
(Genesis 1:30). In the beginning, when God allegedly created the animals, they were designed to consume plants rather than meat.

Beware while hiking the Appalachian Trail.
(Isaiah 14:29). The prophet Isaiah informs us that a cockatrice, a mythical creature able to kill its victim with a casual glance, will arise from a serpent.

Dr. Doolittle.
(Numbers 22:27–30). Man has full-blown conversation with his talking donkey—as they debate why he keeps flogging the donkey.

Better get circumcised.
(Exodus 4:24–26). God has intentions to murder Moses' son because he wasn't circumcised,

The Cure for Leprosy.
(Leviticus 14). God says that we can cure leprosy by killing a bird, putting the bird's blood on another bird, killing a lamb, wiping the lamb blood on the leper, and killing two doves.

It is perhaps best not to spend too much time on Mormon polygamy, as it is just too easy and a bit of a red herring—in that polygamy is not provably nonsense—but this graphic was just too much fun to ignore.

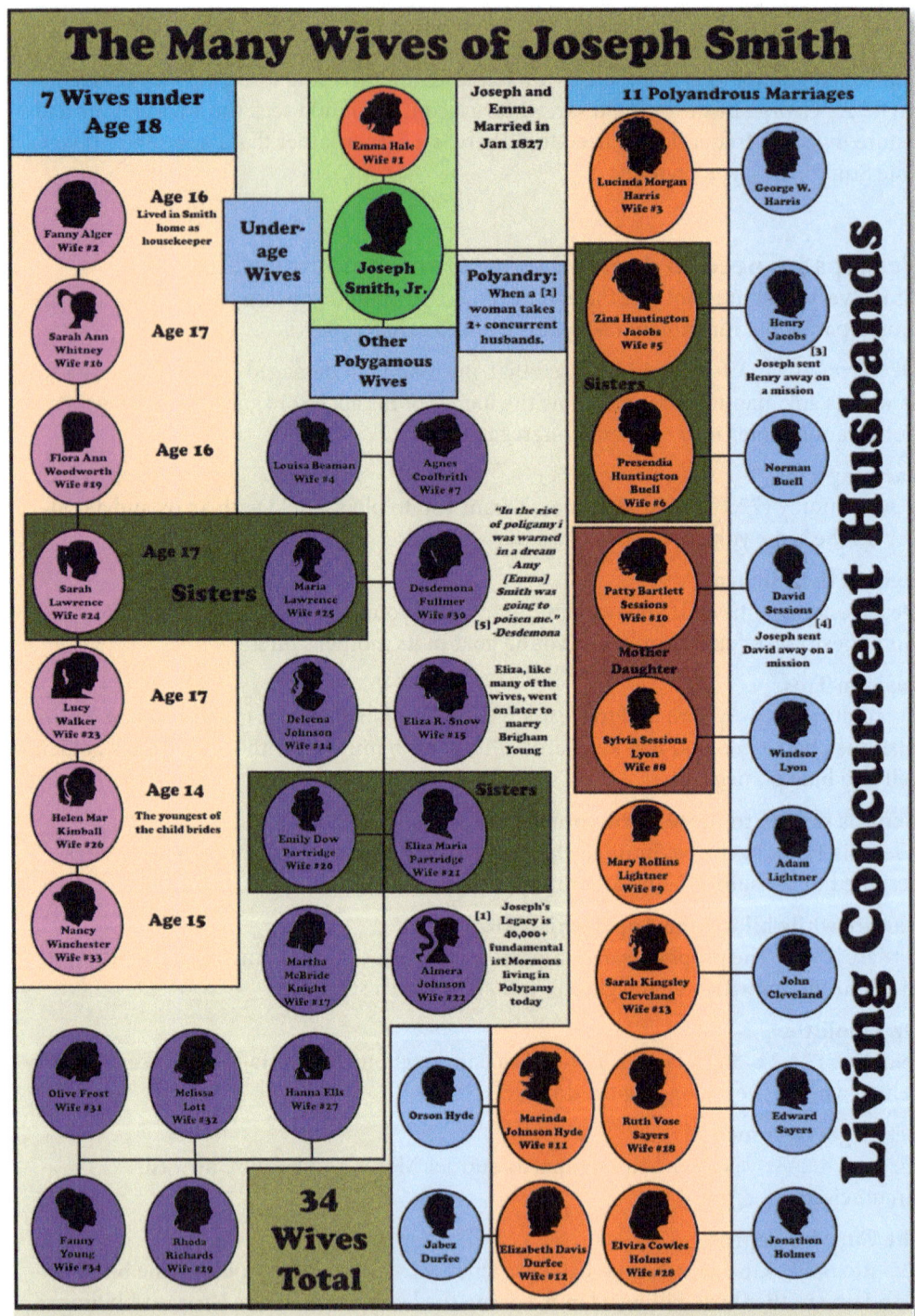

The Many Wives of Joseph Smith

7 Wives under Age 18

11 Polyandrous Marriages

Emma Hale Wife #1

Joseph and Emma Married in Jan 1827

Fanny Alger Wife #2 — Age 16 Lived in Smith home as housekeeper

Under-age Wives

Joseph Smith, Jr.

Sarah Ann Whitney Wife #16 — Age 17

Other Polygamous Wives

Polyandry: When a [2] woman takes 2+ concurrent husbands.

Flora Ann Woodworth Wife #19 — Age 16

Louisa Beaman Wife #4

Agnes Coolbrith Wife #7

Sarah Lawrence Wife #24 — Age 17 — Sisters

Maria Lawrence Wife #25

Desdemona Fullmer Wife #30

"In the rise of poligamy i was warned in a dream Amy [Emma] Smith was going to poison me." [5] -Desdemona

Lucy Walker Wife #23 — Age 17

Deleena Johnson Wife #14

Eliza R. Snow Wife #15

Eliza, like many of the wives, went on later to marry Brigham Young

Helen Mar Kimball Wife #26 — Age 14 The youngest of the child brides

Emily Dow Partridge Wife #20

Eliza Maria Partridge Wife #21

Sisters

Nancy Winchester Wife #33 — Age 15

Martha McBride Knight Wife #17

Almera Johnson Wife #22

Joseph's [1] Legacy is 40,000+ fundamentalist Mormons living in Polygamy today

Olive Frost Wife #31

Melissa Lott Wife #32

Hanna Ells Wife #27

Fanny Young Wife #34

Rhoda Richards Wife #29

34 Wives Total

Polyandrous side:

Lucinda Morgan Harris Wife #3 — George W. Harris

Zina Huntington Jacobs Wife #5 — Henry Jacobs [3] Joseph sent Henry away on a mission

Sisters

Presendia Huntington Buell Wife #6 — Norman Buell

Patty Bartlett Sessions Wife #10 — David Sessions [4] Joseph sent David away on a mission

Mother Daughter

Sylvia Sessions Lyon Wife #8 — Windsor Lyon

Mary Rollins Lightner Wife #9 — Adam Lightner

Sarah Kingsley Cleveland Wife #13 — John Cleveland

Orson Hyde

Marinda Johnson Hyde Wife #11

Ruth Vose Sayers Wife #18 — Edward Sayers

Jabez Durfee

Elizabeth Davis Durfee Wife #12

Elvira Cowles Holmes Wife #28

Jonathon Holmes

Living Concurrent Husbands

[1] "Utah Struggles With a Revival of Polygamy", NY Times, 8/23/1998, James Brooke
[2] Polyandry Definition: http://en.wikipedia.org/wiki/Polyandry
[3] "Zina and Her Men", FAIR LDS Conference, 2006
[4] David Sessions mission call, wivesofjosephsmith.org, Patty Bartlett Sessions Biography
[5] D. Fullmer quote, wivesofjosephsmith.org, D. Fullmer Bio Marriage Details from: wivesofjosephsmith.org

MormonInfographics.com

"Freedoms"
is
Slavery

Freedom is the basic condition for you to touch life, to touch the blue sky, the trees, the birds, the tea, and the other person.

— Thich Nhat Hanh

INTERNATIONAL INCARCERATION RATES:

	Country	Per 100,000
1	USA	716
2	Seychelles	709
3	St Kitts Nevis	701
37	South Africa	289
90	Saudi Arabia	162
139	Italy	139
112	Australia	130
116	Zimbabwe	129
124	China	121
133	Canada	114
144	France	101
163	Netherlands	82
166	Germany	80
196	Japan	54

Data extracted from World Prison Brief, et al.; see http://en.wikipedia.org/wiki/List_of_countries_by_incarceration_rate

So the USA has the worst incarceration rate of any country, worse than any banana republic (my apologies to numerous beautiful and very sane islands). A good benchmark would appear to be Australia—listed 112 out of 224 countries—with 130 per 100,000. China is better than that benchmark, but the USA is 450% worse and almost 500% worse than China, the land of the unfree.

Now let's look a bit more closely at the USA.

LITERAL FREEDOM BY STATE:

Incarceration rate per 100,000

	Lowest Incarceration rates			Highest Incarceration rates	
1	Maine	151	1	Louisiana	1619
2	Minnesota	179	2	Alabama	735
3	Massachusetts	218	3	Oklahoma	661
4	New Hampshire	220	4	Texas	639
5	North Dakota	225	5	Mississippi	634
6	Utah	232	6	Arizona	567
7	Rhode Island	240	7	Florida	557
8	Nebraska	247	8	Georgia	540
9	Vermont	260	9	South Dakota	519
10	Washington	272	10	Arkansas	511
11	Iowa	291	11	Missouri	509
12	New Jersey	298	12	Kentucky	492

Data extracted from DOJ 2008; see http://en.wikipedia.org/wiki/List_of_U.S._states_by_incarceration_rate
There is a Wiki conflict in that the state numbers can vary, which I am putting down to older data.

—but it does appear as if U.S. incarceration rates are soaring, for fairly obvious reasons. Prisoners cannot vote (the criminal-record nightmare has already been discussed). Managing the prison system is big business; local politicians want to create jobs by building and running prisons. Privately run prisons have grown by 1600% (1990–2010); business lobbies lawmakers for more prisoners to improve the bottom line, and congressmen need money; thus, they listen to donors and not the voters (or excite the

voters with rabble-rousing tough-on-crime nonsense). Cracking down on immigration should be a real windfall, with 80% of that new business going to private companies. That is what happens when you sell democracy to the highest bidder.
http://finance.yahoo.com/blogs/daily-ticker/top-5-secrets-private-prison-industry-163005314.html

So the USA is almost 500% worse than China. Red states tend to be at least 100% worse than Blue. What does that say about being literally free in the USA? It should be noted that Stupidparty Disciples are totally uninterested in incarceration rates—preferring to end all thought with slogans such as THREE STRIKES AND YOU'RE OUT or back ludicrous gun laws such as STAND YOUR GROUND, a "get out of jail free" card for whites with guns.

If one has engaged in a debate with Stupidparty Disciples, and pointed out the lack of substance to their observations, they sooner than later spout out some bewildering comment about Freedoms, thus signaling the end point of their knowledge universe. This boundary is akin to a closed swing door to a dog; the door would open if the dog could just figure out (i.e., have the intellectual curiosity) how to give it a little nudge.

George Orwell wrote chilling novels about how the masses, the 99%, could best be controlled by the limited few. Characters in Orwell's *1984* loved to wax lyrical about the chilling notions of Freedom and its connection to Slavery: FREEDOM IS SLAVERY. (That was "Newspeak," the indoctrinating fictional language of *1984*.) The thing is, freedom is a double-edged sword. The world is not black and white; the notion of freedom is nuanced, and of course Stupidparty philosophy is simply not capable of nuance. Is Stephen Colbert with them or against them? They are nuance-blind.

Of course, there are many stupid laws. And of course, there is much waste. It is quite legitimate, and even vital to campaign against such. Here is an analogy. Imagine two neighbors closely situated. Close to the dividing line there is a large leaning tree that gives shelter to both properties, but the tree might fall, damaging the abutting property. Should the fearful neighbor tackle the subject by bringing out his semi-automatic to assist in the negotiation, or should he invite the neighbor out for a barbecue to discuss some way of sharing the cost of pruning the tree or replacing it?

With the Stupidparty owning some 30,000,000 semi-automatics, this simplistic, Neanderthal unnuanced attitude is how they prefer their representatives to behave in Congress.

Red states go on about the feds trampling on their Freedoms, but perhaps they should look closer to home. Let's take just one random Stupidparty state and check on some of their homegrown state-government freedom grabs.

Oklahoma
(as per stupidlaws.com):
This an entertainment site—info submitted by readers—so they may not all be correct.
Any person who leans against a public building will be subject to fines.
Location: Clinton, Oklahoma
Anyone arrested for soliciting a hooker must have their name and picture shown on television.
Location: Oklahoma, United States
Clothes may not be washed in bird baths.
Location: Wynona, Oklahoma

Dogs must have a permit signed by the mayor in order to congregate in groups of three or more on private property.
Location: Clinton, Oklahoma

Elephants are not to be taken into the downtown area.
Location: Tulsa, Oklahoma

Females are forbidden from doing their own hair without being licensed by the state.
Location: Oklahoma, United States

Fish may not be contained in fishbowls while on a public bus.
Location: Oklahoma, United States

Hotels must have sheets with an extra three feet of linen.
Location: Oklahoma, United States

If ones dog is run over by a car, the owner must pay for the dog's disposal.
Location: Bartlesville, Oklahoma

If you wear New York Jets clothing, you may be put in jail.
Location: Ada, Oklahoma

It is against the law to read a comic book while operating a motor vehicle.
Location: Oklahoma, United States

It is illegal for children to use towels as capes and jump from houses pretending to be Superman.
Location: Bromide, Oklahoma

It is illegal for the owner of a bar to allow anyone inside to pretend to have sex with a buffalo.
Location: Oklahoma, United States

It is illegal to cause "annoying vibrations" in the city limits.
Location: Bartlesville, Oklahoma

It is illegal to have sex before you are married.
Location: Oklahoma, United States

It is illegal to have the hind legs of farm animals in your boots.
Location: Oklahoma, United States

It is illegal to masturbate while watching two people having sex in a car.
Location: Clinton, Oklahoma

It is illegal to own a stink bomb.
Location: Oklahoma City, Oklahoma

It is illegal to tie a horse in front of City Hall.
Location: Yukon, Oklahoma

It is illegal to wear your boots to bed.
Location: Oklahoma, United States

It is unlawful to put any hypnotized person in a display window.
Location: Hawthahorne, Oklahoma

It's statutory rape for a man over 18 to have sex with a female under the age of 18, provided she's a virgin.
Location: Oklahoma, United States
Molesting an automobile is illegal.
Location: Clinton, Oklahoma
It is against the law to read a comic book while operating a motor vehicle.
http://www.stupidlaws.com/laws/united-states/oklahoma/

So evidently there is plenty to complain about back home. Plenty to complain about as the federal government went about its business through 2008. But then Obama becomes president, reduces virtually everyone's taxes before eventually allowing the George Bush tax cuts on those earning over $400,000 to expire well past the designated date. This is the time all those aging white guys from Oklahoma get on their bikes, waving their freedom (Confederate) flags, all because they want to be free of Obama in the White House—because that House is the White House. Get it?

When I see an aging white male frothing about freedom, the first thing that comes to mind is—well, if we were living in your ideal period, say 1760, you would most likely be dead by now. You can drink that glass of water, because you can be comfortable that it is clean. Same for the food you eat the air that you breathe.

Stupid Freedoms "I want my Freedoms,"
so what are they really asking for?
Bolded Freedoms will be discussed below.

1) **The Freedom to have a life expectancy of 35**
2) **The Freedom for (innocent) people to be put to death**
3) **The Freedom to start illegal Wars, killing U.S. troops, Civilians ….**
4) **The Freedom to invent your own "family values"**
5) **The Freedom to torture children (why stop at adults?)**
6) **The Freedom to enslave and then kill coal miners**
7) **The Freedom to rape**
8) **The freedom to tear up the Constitution**
9) **The Freedom to engage in institutional torture of livestock**
10) **The Freedom to demand vaginal probes**
11) The Freedom to be imprisoned for life based on three strikes
12) The Freedom to put prisoners in solitary confinement for life, i.e., torture
13) The Freedom for the U.S. government to default on its debt
14) The Freedom to racially profile
15) The Freedom to engage in voter suppression
16) The Freedom to refuse to serve black people, etc. (Ayn Rand, Ron Paul)
17) The Freedom to discriminate against homosexuals
18) The Freedom to cure homosexuals via conversion therapy
19) The Freedom to discriminate against women
20) The Freedom to be not allowed an abortion
21) The Freedom to ignore facts, science, or the experts
22) The Freedom to declare America to be a Christian country
23) The Freedom not to have access to healthcare
24) The Freedom to ensure others cannot get a living wage

25) The Freedom to be sexually harassed at work
26) The Freedom to harass in the bedroom.
27) The Freedom to treat corporations as people
28) The Freedom to overfish to extinction
29) The Freedom to pollute and decimate the oceans, lakes, and rivers
30) The Freedom to erode the fertility of the soil
31) The Freedom to use roads, bridges, and tunnels built by the government.
32) The Freedom to rabidly bite off the hand that feeds it, by not valuing:
    i) Social Security (presently protected from Wall Street greed)
    ii) Medicare, Medicaid
    iii) Benefit from the Affordable Healthcare Act
    iv) Benefit from public schools and universities
    v) Benefit from school buses
    vi) Benefit from the Food Stamp Act
    vii) Benefit from regulations ensuring your savings are safe, insurance claims are paid
    viii) Benefit from police protection, fire fighters
    ix) Benefit from assistance in case of natural disaster
    x) Benefit from libraries, postal services, especially in cut-off areas
33) The Freedom of a religious employer to prevent access to birth control.
34) The Freedom to pretend that you are not aiding and abetting bigotry.

Let's look at a few of the above in more detail:

1) The Freedom to have a life expectancy of 35.

Chart source data, when from Wiki, subject to being updated.

Stupidparty advocates love to dream about living free (from regulation?) and fantasize about colonial times. Well, back in 1760, it looks like you were lucky to reach 35. Today, life expectancy in the USA is 79.8. America comes in at 35 on that list.
On the other hand, according to historians E. A. Wrigley and Roger S. Schofield, between 1781 and 1851, life expectancy at birth rose from thirty-five years to forty years.
http://en.wikipedia.org/wiki/List_of_countries_by_life_expectancy

Here is the State Breakdown:

Best Life Expectancy		Worst Life Expectancy	
1 Hawaii	81.3	1 Mississippi	75.0
2 Minnesota	81.1	2 West Virginia	75.4
3 Connecticut	80.8	3 Alabama	75.4
4 California	80.8	4 Louisiana	75.7
5 Massachusetts	80.5	5 Oklahoma	75.9
6 New York	80.5	6 Arkansas	76.0
7 Vermont	80.5	7 Kentucky	76.0
8 New Hampshire	80.3	8 Tennessee	76.3
9 New Jersey	80.3	9 South Carolina	77.0
10 Utah	80.2	10 Georgia	77.2

http://en.wikipedia.org/wiki/List_of_U.S._states_by_life_expectancy

Mississippi is beaten by 60 other countries, including Bosnia, Ecuador, China, and Cuba, and ranked equal to Syria (before the war). Of course, places like Cuba have a better healthcare system and that helps.

Stupidparty Disciples have a life expectancy of around, say, 76 (as opposed to 80 for the other Americans). These individuals are forced to live twice as long as they would evidently prefer, because they benefit from stuff they supposedly hate—such as Social Security, Medicaid, clean air and water, food safety standards, workers'-injury compensation, vacation days to rest and travel, police to keep the peace, food nutrition programs.

2) The Freedom for (innocent) people to be put to death.

In 1977 only 16 countries had abolished the death penalty. By 2012 this number had risen to 97. In 2011 only 11 countries executed more than 5 people. These countries from Worst to Least Worse are China, Iran, Saudi Arabia, Iraq, USA, Yemen, North Korea, Somalia, Bangladesh, and Vietnam.

But the USA is somewhat unique, as it does not exactly have a unified approach—each state being free to decide its own policy.

18 states have abolished the death penalty. But the following are still pretty gung-ho.

	State	Executions Since 1976	# on Death Row
1	Texas	503	300
2	Virginia	110	11
3	Oklahoma	105	60
4	Florida	78	413
5	Missouri	68	48
6	Alabama	56	198
7	Georgia	53	97
8	Ohio	51	147
9	North Carolina	43	161
10	South Carolina	43	53
11	Arizona	34	122
12	Louisiana	28	88
13	Arkansas	27	38
14	Mississippi	21	48

http://en.wikipedia.org/wiki/Capital_punishment_in_the_United_States

Most people believe many of these individuals may not even be guilty, especially in the case of defendants who came up against a prejudiced jury and a plaintiff attorney or prosecutor significantly more skilled than the lowly public defenders. The following death row inmates have been exonerated—just to take two years, 2008 and 2009:

2008

*125. Kennedy Brewer Mississippi. Convicted 1995.

126. Glen Edward Chapman, North Carolina. Convicted 1995.

127. Levon "Bo" Jones, North Carolina. Convicted 1993.

128. Michael Blair, Texas.

2009

129. Nathson Fields, Illinois. Convicted 1986.

130. Paul House, Tennessee. Convicted 1986.

131. Daniel Wade Moore, Alabama. Convicted 2002.

132. Ronald Kitchen, Illinois. Convicted 1988.

133. Herman Lindsey, Florida. Convicted 2006.

134. Michael Toney, Texas. Convicted 1999. (Toney died in a car accident on October 3, 2009, just one month and a day after his exoneration.)

135. Yancy Douglas, Oklahoma. Convicted 1997.

136. Paris Powell, Oklahoma. Convicted 1997.

137. Robert Springsteen, Texas. Convicted 2001.

http://en.wikipedia.org/wiki/List_of_exonerated_death_row_inmates#2010.E2.80.932012
*125 means 125th exonerated death-row victim

New DNA technology, which is now used regularly, clears individuals of crimes they had been adjudicated guilty of. Also, minorities are more likely to attract the severe sentences. Various degrees of murder or manslaughter can make the outcome quite uncertain—but politically ambitious district attorneys love to buff their résumés against poorly represented and scary minorities, so when those grey areas emerge, the better lawyer will tend to carry the day.

3) The Freedom to tell countless lies, make misstatements, start illegal Wars, killing innumerable U.S. troops, Civilians, and "enemy" troops.

The Stupidparty succeeded in getting the country to accept that invading Iraq was essential, since Iraq was close to procuring weapons of mass destruction and was allied with al-Qaeda.

But:

1) In Bush's world view, the Iraq invasion was preordained—inconvenient facts would not get in his way.

2) There were no weapons of mass destruction.

3) The UN inspectors could never find any WMDs; they begged for more time.

4) Valerie Plame, a CIA agent with multiple contacts in Iraq, was treasonously exposed by Lewis "Scooter" Libby, and surely also by Vice President Dick Cheney. Thinking Libby, Cheney's chief of staff, was the scapegoat, the jury just wanted to know why Cheney had not been prosecuted.

http://abcnews.go.com/GMA/LegalCenter/story?id=2930733

5) Saddam Hussein was looking for an exit—but Bush and Co. wanted war.

6) There was no plan on how to proceed after Saddam Hussein had been removed.

7) The CIA always knew that there were no significant ties to terror. The scant evidence of any al Qaeda link was always debunked by the CIA and by "terrorism guru" Richard Clarke (the U.S. National Coordinator for Security, Infrastructure Protection, and Counter-terrorism, who had served Reagan, both Bushes, and Clinton and was the leading counter-terrorism expert).

This is the passage (and note the witnesses) in Clarke's book *Against all Enemies,* on page 32, where Clarke writes:

> Later, on the evening of the 12th, I left the Video Conferencing Center and there, wandering alone around the Situation Room, was the President. He looked like he wanted something to do. He grabbed a few of us and closed the door to the conference room. "Look, he told us, "I know you have a lot to do and all ... but I want you, as soon as you can, to go back over everything, everything. See if Saddam did this. See if he's linked in any way ...
>
> I was once again taken aback, incredulous, and it showed. "But, Mr. President, al Qaeda did this."
>
> "I know, I know, but ... see if Saddam was involved. Just look. I want to know any shred ..."
>
> "Absolutely, we will look ... again." I was trying to be more respectful, more responsive. "But, you know, we have looked several times for state sponsorship of al Qaeda and not found any real linkages to Iraq. Iran plays a little, as does Pakistan, and Saudi Arabia, Yemen."
>
> "Look into Iraq, Saddam," the President said testily and left us. Lisa Gordon-Hagerty stared after him with her mouth hanging open.

And that is how an illegal war percolated to the point of eventual fruition inside an unsuitable mind.

But Stupidparty Disciples don't care, because Stupidparty Disciples don't read (objectively) and they are not interested in facts, they just want to be FREE to turn Muslim nations into parking lots, FREE to be lied to:

IRAQ ON THE RECORD

The Bush Administration's Public statements on Iraq

prepared for Rep. Henry A Waxman [CA-D].

Number of Misleading Statements:

The Iraq on-the-record database contains:

237 misleading statements about the threat posed by Iraq that were made by President Bush, Vice President Cheney, Secretary Rumsfeld, Secretary Powell, and National Security Advisor Rice. These statements were made in 125 separate appearances, consisting of 40 speeches, 26 press conferences and briefings, 53 interviews, 4 written statements,

and 2 congressional testimonies. Most of the statements in the database were misleading because they expressed certainty where none existed or failed to acknowledge the doubts of intelligence officials. Ten of the statements were simply false.

Timing of the Statements:

The statements began at least a year before the commencement of hostilities in Iraq, when Vice President Cheney stated on March 17, 2002: "We know they have biological and chemical weapons." The Administration's misleading statements continued through

January 22, 2004, when Vice President Cheney insisted: "there's overwhelming evidence that there was a connection between al-Qaeda and the Iraqi government." Most of the misleading statements about Iraq—161 statements—were made prior to the start of the war. But 76 misleading statements were made by the five Administration officials after the start of the war to justify the decision to go to war. The 30-day period with the greatest number of misleading statements was the period before the congressional vote on the Iraq war resolution. Congress voted on the measure on October 10 and October 11, 2002. From September 8 through October 8, 2002, the five officials made 64 misleading statements in 16 public appearances. A large number of misleading statements were also made during the two months before the war began. Between January 19 and March 19, 2003, the five officials made 48 misleading statements in 26 public appearances.

Topics of the Statements:

The 237 misleading statements can be divided into four categories. The five officials made 11 statements that claimed that Iraq posed an urgent threat; 81 statements that exaggerated Iraq's nuclear activities; 84 statements that overstated Iraq's chemical and biological weapons capabilities; and 61 statements that misrepresented Iraq's ties to al Qaeda.

http://oversight-archive.waxman.house.gov/IraqOnTheRecord/

4) Freedom to invent family values.

Stupidparty leaders love to lecture about family values. They assume we will believe they are taking up the Sword of Christ, leading a Christian battle against evildoers or those whose lifestyles they disagree with. But these leaders, if they are to wield the sword, must be willing to be felled by their own arguments. Firstly, they cannot simply be allowed to talk the talk. If it turns out they are hypocrites, then they must be judged harshly by their own standards.

But what are these biblical values they keep thrusting down our throats? Surely they are not trying to promote slavery per St. Paul's instructions (Ephesians 6:5–9):

"Servants, be obedient to them that are your masters according to the flesh, with fear and trembling, in singleness of your heart, as unto Christ…"

Surely their family values allow women a vote, a voice—some equality? St. Paul did not simply promote slavery; he was by today's standards a bit of a misogynist (Ephesians 5:22–24: "Wives, submit to your husbands as to the Lord. For the husband is the head of the wife as Christ is the head of the church, his body, of which he is the Savior. Now as the church submits to Christ, so also wives should submit to their husbands in everything").

Surely they are not advocating genocide, as per Noah's ark, the final plague of Egypt, or the decimation of Sodom and Gomorrah?

How about the family goes out and enjoys a good stoning?

They cannot be suggesting stoning non virgins on their wedding night? ("Then they shall bring out the damsel to the door of her father's house, and the men of her city shall stone her with stones that she die"—Deuteronomy 22:13–21.)

They cannot be suggesting stoning for virtually any departure from their values—like, say, stoning livestock (if an ox gore a man or a woman, that they die: then the ox shall be surely stoned—Exodus 21:28), or likewise stoning for non-Christians, children who disobey their parents, those who break the Sabbath (Numbers 15:32–56) or for simply touching Mount Sinai (Exodus 19:13). Gandalf and Harry Potter must be stoned if you believe in Leviticus 20:27, and then sometimes stoning to death is just not enough—it must be followed by burning with fire (Joshua 7:1–26).

So even though Stupidparty pundits regularly suggest eradicating all and sundry, encouraging prisoner suicides to save taxpayer money (Ed Bolling on Fox News *The Five*), or immediately labeling as an enemy anyone who says, "Allah" (God)*—no, let us give them a break and presume that they have evolved and are actually referring to simple, easy-to-understand Christian values like pro-life, the institution of marriage, marriage between a man and a woman, and having a family with lots of happy, home-educated children to grow up as future consumers. But there are a few big problems in being so kind to our Stupidparty fellow Americans, who preach these supposedly Christian values.

(* John McCain had to give the presenters a little education on that one.)

The Bible is pro-choice.
The Bible simply does not have these so-called values.

Neither Jesus (nor the Bible) had anything to say about "straight" marriage or even about it simply being between one man and one women. Jesus had nothing to say about gays. Any supposed biblical arguments against gay marriage are unsustainable. The New Testament is pretty much silent on the institution of marriage. Not only that, but Jesus and his disciples were hardly good examples of such invented "family values." Were any of the disciples married? Did they have children? Yes, probably one, Peter—which in itself is odd, since he was the rock upon which the Christian Church was built. Yet centuries later, the papacy—for financial reasons unrelated to the teachings of Jesus—chose to become a male-dominated club. Jesus himself was quite comfortable consorting with Mary Magdalene, who many scholars believe had been a prostitute.

The Bible, Jesus—they had nothing to say about contraception. They had nothing to say on abortion. There is no pro-life biblical agenda. In fact, the reverse is true. The Old Testament God was clearly pro-choice, happy to choose genocide and other methods of terminating innocent life (as in Noah's flood, Sodom and Gomorrah, the tenth plague against Egypt, and let us not forget when God killed 14,000 people for complaining that God kept killing them).

5) Freedom to Torture Children, Freedom to torture, detain without representation.

Stupidparty tough on crime: Disciples seem perfectly content to allow the government the freedom to torture, thus to ignore the Geneva Convention and take away Freedoms without due process (Guantanamo Bay).

Well, they are only foreigners.

Back in America, "Joe Sullivan was sentenced to die in prison at age 13 for a sexual assault. He is physically and mentally disabled but remains imprisoned in Florida." http://www.eji.org/childrenprison/deathinprison/sentencedtodie/10

With the ever-increasing profit-fed incarceration rate, the massive lengths of time in solitary confinement come into greater focus. Worse is the issue of children spending months or longer under such conditions.

Artist, http://www.mattrotasart.com/

Many countries will not allow their citizens to be sent to the USA under extradition treaties—because of the death penalty. This trend is now exacerbated by growing concerns about due process and cruel and unusual punishment. Extended time in solitary—even life—would be considered by most thoughtful people cruel and unusual. As *The*

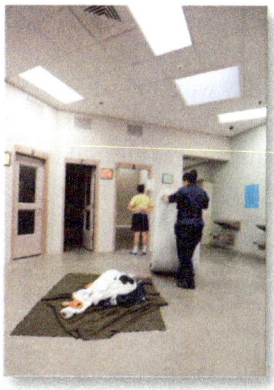

Guardian reports, "Thousands of teenagers, some as young as 14 or 15, are now routinely subjected by U.S. prisons to this psychological torture."

More from *The Guardian*

"One teen who participated in the Human Rights Watch report wrote that being in isolation felt like 'a slow death from the inside out.' Molly J said of her time in solitary confinement: 'I felt doomed, like I was being banished … Like you have the plague or that you are the worst thing on earth. Like you are set apart [from] everything else. I guess [I wanted to] feel like I was part of the human race—not like some animal.'

"Molly was just 16 years old when she was placed in isolation in an adult jail in Michigan. She described her cell as being 'a box … There was a bed—the slab. It was concrete … There was a stainless steel toilet/sink combo … The door was solid, without a food slot or window … There was no window at all.' Molly remained in solitary for several months, locked down alone in her cell for at least 22 hours a day.

"No other nation in the developed world routinely tortures its children in this manner. And torture is indeed the word brought to mind by a shocking report released by Human Rights Watch and the American Civil Liberties Union. 'Growing Up Locked Down' documents, for the first time, the widespread use of solitary confinement on youth under the age of 18 in prisons and jails across the country, and the deep and permanent harm it

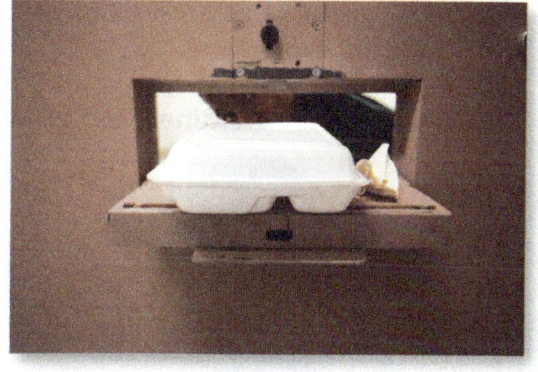

causes to kids caught up in the adult criminal justice system."

http://www.theguardian.com/commentisfree/2012/oct/10/children-solitary-confinement-america-prisons
http://www.wired.com/rawfile/2012/04/photog-hopes-to-effect-policy-with-survey-of-juvenile-lock-ups/#slideid-45201

6) The Freedom to Enslave and Kill Coal Miners.

Or divining what a John Galt (*Atlas Shrugged* by Ayn Rand) paradise might look like

Using the U.S. coal mining industry as an example serves a very useful tool in identifying the difference between the Stupidparty Disciples and the British working class (or what Americans rather euphemistically call middle class). In the UK, the working classes are not misdirected by hijacked religious claptrap; they are not confused about adherences to the Constitution or the vital need to own a gun. Although there probably may have been similar levels of fear and prejudice, such resultant bigotry would have not have run along party lines. No, the working class were not—are not—the intellectual slaves of the Asset Strippers.

In the UK, the National Union of Mineworkers, or NUM, once had great power; they voted solidly against the Conservative Party; they successfully overthrew the Ted Heath Conservative Party in 1974. Ted Heath had put Britain on a three-day working week to ration electrical consumption, as the country was fast running out of the coal necessary to run the coal-powered power stations. Even before Margaret Thatcher was elected in 1979, she knew she would have to defeat the NUM, and to do that, she had to initiate the timing of the coal miner strike; first, she had to build up coal stockpiles and second make sure the strike started in the spring and not the fall—as that would give her an additional year in any battle of attrition. The strike began March 1984.

So what happened?

1) In 1985, Thatcher defeats the miners, and massive coal mining closures ensue.

2) Coal miners get generous severance, and coal mining jobs are gradually replaced with far safer, healthier vocations as communities adapt (shrink) and slowly recover.

3) (In 1947, there were 700,000 coal miners.) In 1979, Britain had 170 underground mines employing about 190,000 people, producing 300m tons of coal, and as a result of orthodox Conservative policy by 2010 the number of mines had fallen to 3,000 employees, producing 17m tons. A reduction of about 95% or a 98% reduction in the workforce.

Coal mining is a very hazardous and unhealthy occupation. As seen above, the issue can be tackled and the long term implications for local communities do not have to be dire—assuming that one has relatively benign "conservative" governance aimed at preventing poverty rather than allowing Asset Stripping to the benefit of the 1%. But Margaret Thatcher (who came from the "working class") is not comparable to any Stupidparty leader. She was a scientist with a chemistry Bachelor of Science degree, a fact-based individual who had no tolerance for Myth. She was never a puppet of the 1%. It was not only all the social issues already mentioned, but economic issues, like fully supporting, say, the National Health Service or ensuring generous severance packages in hard times, which made her more progressive than even the U.S. Democrats. But most tellingly, and often forgotten, was the manner in which she sold off the nationalized industries and public housing in a manner strictly designed to disproportionately benefit the less well off or the small investor. She not working for the 1%. She was focused on the 99%. She was the polar opposite of Stupidparty.

Using the U.S. coal mining industry is also a useful example of how wealthy and empowered individuals in the U.S. oftentimes view their employees. It should be noted that coal mining in itself is a highly questionable activity in relation to Global Warming (which helps explain why so few tears were shed in the UK—there being no such thing as "clean coal." But that is somewhat off topic).

This industry also provides pertinent insight into Ayn Rand's idealistic John Galt paradise. One has to wonder how a total lack of regulations would pan out for anyone not invited to the Benefactor "country club," not able to untether themselves from the shackles of slavery that "Freedoms" have so kindly provided. Well, unlike H. G. Wells, we do not have to be quite so visionary; maybe we can get a glimpse into the not so distant future—by taking a closer look at present-day coal mining in the U.S.

Since the Stupidparty selected the homophobic high school bully, Asset Stripping Gordon Gekko "greed is good" twin, Mitt Romney, as their most recent standard bearer, we have a good place to start this analysis.

Coal Mine Owners—Benefactors to Stupidparty:

On August 14, 2012, Murray hosted Mitt Romney at Murray Energy's Century Coal Mine in Beallsville, Ohio. Robert Murray is the CEO of Murray Energy Corporation, one of the largest independent operators of coal mines in the United States

www.mywebface.com

You will Vote for Me and then you can drop dead.
Politico:

"If some of the coal miners standing with Mitt Romney in his new campaign ad don't look happy, it's probably because they're not. The campaign pulled the footage for its new 'War on Coal' spot from a recent Ohio rally; some coal miners complained they were forced to take a day off without pay to attend.

"Vote for me and the baby lives."

http://www.chrisweigant.com/

"The footage of Romney, flanked by coal miners, was taken at a Beallsville, Ohio, rally in August, where about a dozen employees have told WWVA-AM they were pulled out of the mine to join the Republican candidate. Murray Energy Chief Financial Officer Rob Moore told the radio station in an extended interview that the company shut down the mine because senior managers wanted to attend, and it could not remain open during a rally. 'We had managers that communicated [to employees] that the attendance was mandatory,' Moore said. 'But no one was forced to attend the event.'"

Read more: http://www.politico.com/news/stories/0912/81421.html

Encouraged by management, Murray workers have ponied up more than $120,000 to help elect Romney.

Alec MacGillis (in *The New Republic*) writes:

"The accounts of two sources who have worked in managerial positions at the firm, and a review of letters and memos to Murray employees, suggest that coercion may also explain Murray staffers' financial support for Romney. Murray, it turns out, has for years pressured salaried employees to give to the Murray Energy political action committee (PAC) and to Republican candidates chosen by the company. Internal documents show that company officials track who is and is not giving. The sources say that those who do not give are at risk of being demoted or missing out on bonuses, claims Murray denies."

http://www.newrepublic.com/article/politics/108140/coal-miners-donor-mitt-romney-benefactor

May 2012 Murray raises $1.7m for Mitt Romney during a single event.

http://en.wikipedia.org/wiki/Robert_E._Murray

Oct. 2012 Murray and his company are accused of violations of federal campaign laws. Citizens for Responsibility and Ethics in Washington (CREW) charge that Murray coerced its employees into giving 1% of their salary to Murray Energies Corporation Political Action Committee (PAC)

http://en.wikipedia.org/wiki/Robert_E._Murray

Three days after the 2012 presidential election Murray downsizes 156 workers, blaming Obama's supposed war on coal.

http://en.wikipedia.org/wiki/Robert_E._Murray

But I am not convinced that being forced to contribute to a political PAC, closing down the mine without pay and then intimidating individuals to act as backdrop, is the real reason these guys might be aggravated.

mine-safety_n_1165516.html

So what is really motivating Bob Murray:

As *HuffPost* reported, Murray has enlisted disgraced former senator Larry Craig* (SP-Idaho) to lobby for the coal industry, and mine safety regulations appear to be a hot topic.
*"Having left Congress after an embarrassing 2007 arrest, former senator Larry Craig (R-Idaho) has quietly reemerged in Washington as a lobbyist working on behalf of the coal industry. According to his federal filings, Craig has registered to wheedle his former Capitol colleagues on the obscure but critical issue of mine safety."
http://www.huffingtonpost.com/2011/12/22/larry-craig-lobbyist-

This unwillingness to implement safety standards is somewhat surprising, as safety should have been (and may have been) pretty much their top priority, especially when considering what had happened in the not-so-distant past:

Crandall Canyon Mine collapse: (Wiki)
Murray and his companies received national attention in August 2007 when six miners were trapped at the Crandall Canyon Mine in Utah, of which Murray Energy independent operating subsidiary Utah-American Energy had been a part-owner for 12 months. Prior to the collapse, the Crandall Canyon Mine had received 64 violations and $12,000 in fines, magnitudes similar to other mines of this size in the United States. He says that the safety violations were trivial and included violations such as not having enough toilet paper in the restroom. However, some news agencies reported troubling violations at other of Murray's operations. CNN specifically cited Murray's Illinois Galatia mine, which had almost 3,500 safety citations in the prior two and a half years.

Murray claims that the Crandall Canyon Mine collapse was triggered by a 3.9 magnitude earthquake, while government seismologists say the mine collapse was the cause of a coal mine bump. Richard E. Stickler, the government's top mine safety official, said, "It was not—and I repeat, it was not—a natural occurring earthquake."

Douglas S. Dreger, a seismologist at the University of California, Berkeley, said in the July 2008 issue of *Science* that his analysis strongly suggested that the mountain crumbled in two stages: After the pillars collapsed, giant, angled slabs of sandstone above the mine abruptly shifted. When the mine collapse finally occurred, it was so powerful that it registered as a 3.9 earthquake. Although the widely used industry practice of retreat mining is believed by some observers to be a cause of the mine's 2007 collapse, Murray insists the process was not responsible.

On July 24, 2008, the U.S. government's Mine Safety and Health Administration (MSHA) announced its highest penalty for coal mine safety violations, $1.85 million, for the collapse.

The Upper Big Branch: (Wiki)
This disaster occurred on April 5, 2010, roughly 1,000 feet (300 m) underground, in Raleigh County, West Virginia, at Massey Energy's Upper Big Branch coal mine located in Montcoal. Twenty-nine out of thirty-one miners at the site were killed…. The accident was the worst in the United States since 1970….

On May 19, 2011, the independent investigation team released a report which faulted both Massey Energy and the Mine Safety and Health Administration (MSHA) for the blast. Massey was strongly condemned by the report for multiple failures to meet basic safety standards outlined in the Mine Act of 1977. "A company that was a towering presence in the Appalachian coal fields operated its mines in a profoundly reckless manner, and 29 coal miners paid with their lives for the corporate risk taking," read the report. "The company's ventilation system did not adequately ventilate the mine. As a result, explosive gases were allowed to build up." Also detailed in the report are allegations that Massey Energy threatened miners with termination if they stopped work in areas that lacked adequate oxygen levels. Numerous other state and federal safety standards that Massey failed to comply with were detailed in the report.

Investigators also say that the U.S. Department of Labor and its Mine Safety and Health Administration were at fault for failing to act decisively at the mine even after Massey was issued 515 citations for safety violations at the Upper Big Branch mine in 2009. The report lambasts MSHA inspectors for failing to issue a flagrant violation citation which could have fined the company up to $220,000. Investigators claimed that this citation was entirely necessary given Massey's failure to meet basic safety protocols and the investigators found it "disturbing" that the violation was not issued. The failure to issue flagrant violation citations was attributed to MSHA which also failed to notify the miners and their families that they were working in a mine which had not met minimal safety requirements. As further evidence of MSHA's failures in the lead up to the UBB mine explosion, the report discusses how MSHA safety inspectors failed to enforce the safety protocols at Massey Energy's Aracoma Alma No. 1 mine. In 2007, a fire broke out at the Aracoma Alma No. 1 mine, killing two miners. The report described the fire as "preventable" and cites an internal MSHA review following the fire which found that inspectors "were shocked by the deplorable conditions of the mine" and that MSHA inspectors had "failed" to enforce adequate safety measures. Furthermore, the report outlines how in the lead up to the blast the UBB mine "experienced at least three major methane-related events." One in 1997, another in 2003, and a third in 2004. Instead of addressing these issues, "Upper Big Branch management elected to consider each methane outburst or explosion as an anomaly." Furthermore, MSHA officials "did not compel (or to our knowledge even ask) UBB management to implement," safety precautions following these events.

The report claims that Massey used its power "to attempt to control West Virginia's political system." The report cites how politicians were afraid of the company because it "was willing to spend vast amounts of money to influence elections." Massey intentionally neglected safety precautions for the purpose of increasing profit margins according to the report. Safety precautions in mines are "a hard-earned right paid for with the blood of coal miners," read the report's introduction.

Another source:

The report was produced by an independent team of investigators appointed by former West Virginia Gov. Joe Manchin and led by Davitt McAteer, a former federal mine safety chief who has investigated other mine disasters in the state.

http://www.npr.org/2011/05/19/136426906/report-blasts-massey-for-deviance-in-safety-culture

It was claimed [in the report] that the FBI had launched a probe investigating the possible bribery of federal officials overseeing mining industry regulation by Massey Energy.
http://en.wikipedia.org/wiki/Massey_Energy
additional sources:
http://www.npr.org/blogs/thetwo-way/2010/04/fbi_probing_fed_officials_and.html
http://www.reuters.com/article/2010/04/30/us-massey-fbi-idUSTRE63T39O20100430

and subsequently ... in 2011

"The security chief of Massey Energy's Upper Big Branch mine was arrested Monday and charged with obstructing the investigation into last year's explosion that killed 29 miners, the first criminal charges stemming from the worst U.S. mining disaster in 40 years."
http://www.washingtonpost.com/wp-dyn/content/article/2011/02/28/AR2011022803552.html?tid=nn_twitter

and subsequently ... in 2013

The former president of Massey Energy's White Buck Coal and the Green Valley Resource Group David Hughart, 53, has become the highest-ranking coal official to date to be sentenced to prison for violating U.S. mine health and safety standards. In addition to a 42-month prison sentence, Hughart was also ordered to serve an additional three years of supervised release, according to U.S. Attorney Beth Goodwin. Although Hughart never worked at the Upper Big Branch Mine in West Virginia—where 29 men were killed in April 2010 in the largest coal disaster in 40 years—he admitted that he and others at

Massey conspired to violate health and safety laws and to conceal those violations by warning mine operations when MSHA inspectors were arriving to conduct mine inspections.
http://www.mineweb.com/mineweb/content/en/mineweb-energy?oid=204647&sn=Detail

Black Lung Disease.

"Black lung" is a legal term describing a preventable, occupational-disease contracted by prolonged breathing of coal mine dust. In 1969 the U.S. Congress ordered the eradication of black lung from the industry. Today, it is estimated that each year 1500 former miners die

Healthy lung   Early stages   Late stages

an agonizing death, often away from the spotlight, in isolated rural communities.

"Eastern Kentucky and nearby areas of West Virginia and Virginia have seen a pronounced spike in cases of black lung, according to the National Institute for Occupational Safety and Health. In Eastern Kentucky, 9% of the miners screened in one NIOSH program between 2005 and 2009 had black lung. It was the highest prevalence of any state."
Read more here, http://www.kentucky.com/2013/08/22/2781347/us-rep-andy-barr-questions-need.html#storylink=cpy

As the Center for Public Integrity reports:

"After decades of decline, black lung is back. Its resurgence is concentrated in central Appalachia. Younger miners are increasingly getting the most severe, fastest-progressing form of the disease." The system for monitoring miners' exposure to the dust that causes black lung allows companies to cheat or exploit loopholes

From 2000 to 2011, the federal Mine Safety and Health Administration, MSHA, received more than 53,000 valid samples showing underground miners had been exposed to more dust than was allowed. Yet the agency issued just under 2,400 violations. This may be attributable, in part, to rules that allow samples to be averaged, potentially masking some miners' high exposures.

Even when companies get caught, they have little to fear. They can take five of their own dust samples to prove compliance, and an MSHA citation goes away.

The agency has routinely given companies extra time to fix cited dust problems, granting extensions in 57 percent of cases between 2000 and 2011.
http://www.publicintegrity.org/2012/07/05/9311/key-findings

Andy Barr, SP Rep. Kentucky 6th:
says, "Many members of Congress have questions about the rules, including whether they would add burden and cost on coal companies that would far outweigh any benefit to miners. If companies cut employment because of regulatory costs, it does nothing to advance the cause of workers' health."

"Worker safety is a top priority, but not at the cost of putting that family in a very precarious financial situation."
http://www.kentucky.com/2013/08/22/2781347/us-rep-andy-barr-questions-need.html

This is Orwellian speak for WORKER SAFETY MUST BE SACRIFICED FOR PROFIT.

***ThinkProgress* reports (Sept 20, 2012):**
"Coal has backed the GOP's political campaign with heavy spending on TV ads, lobbying and political contributions. Coal and dirty utilities have spent a total $66 million on lobbying since 2011. House Republicans have received $4.4 million in career contributions from the coal industry—nearly 5 times the amount Democratic members received.

"In 2012 alone, Republicans received 89% of the coal industry's campaign contributions."

Fred Upton, SP Rep. Michigan 6th, Chair of the Energy and Commerce Committee, has received $60,000 from both major utilities and the coal industry.

David McKinley, SP Rep. West Virginia lst:
Another supporter, he is the top recipient of coal cash for 2012, having received over $200,000.

"The coal industry has also waged a separate 'public awareness' campaign on pro-coal TV ads. The American Coalition for 'Clean Coal' Electricity has so far spent $12 million of its promised $40 million election-year [2012] budget on ads this cycle. So far, total fossil fuel spending has exceeded $153 million."
http://thinkprogress.org/climate/2012/09/20/873851/the-gops-war-on-coal-myth-brought-to-you-by-millions-in-coal-cash/

7) The Freedom to Rape.

(Examples from *The Daily Banter* and others)

Do not think that this laissez-faire free market attitude is down to a few Stupidparty reps. No, this is endemic within the Stupidparty. Let's see how many rationalizations for rape these misogynists can come up with:

Ron Paul, SP Rep. Texas 14th:
"If it's an honest rape, that individual should go immediately to the emergency room, and I would give them a shot of estrogen or—" I.e., in support of emergency contraception to prevent a rape pregnancy (February 3, 2012).
http://www.msnbc.com/rachel-maddow-show/ron-paul-and-honest-rape

Todd Akin, SP former Rep. Missouri 2nd:
"If it's a legitimate rape, the female body has ways of shutting that whole thing down."
http://www.nytimes.com/2012/08/20/us/politics/todd-akin-provokes-ire-with-legitimate-rape-comment.html?_r=0

"WELL, IN ONE SENSE, NONE OF THEM IS LEGITIMATE"

Paul Ryan, SP Rep. Wisconsin 1st, Chair of the House Committee on the Budget, VP choice:
He personally believes rape is "a method of conception" and not an excuse to allow abortion. Ryan also confirmed that he remained very proud of the Ryan/Akin–sponsored "forcible rape bill."
http://www.youtube.com/watch?v=KazMQGqX_dI

Steve King, SP Rep. Iowa 4th:
In the context of the House bill, he was asked, "what if someone isn't forcibly raped and for example, a 12-year-old who gets pregnant? Should she have to bring this baby to term?"

KING: "Well I just haven't heard of that being a circumstance that's been brought to me in any personal way and I'd be open to hearing discussion about that subject matter."

Steve King continues to spread nonsense about Planned Parenthood and voter fraud—all in the same breath:

"Harry Reid can defend those ghoulish and ghastly and gruesome practices that Planned Parenthood is advocating along with child prostitution and illegal immigration. He can play defense on that. They didn't do very well in the Senate when they tried to defend ACORN. I don't think they'll do any better this time."
http://www.motherjones.com/mojo/2011/02/rep-steve-king-pledges-smackdown-planned-parenthood

Maybe he should check out studies like from the Guttmacher Institute, which found at least half of all babies born to minors are fathered by adult men.)
http://www.thewire.com/politics/2012/08/steve-king-never-heard-anyone-getting-pregnant-statutory-rape-incest/56014/

Eric Cantor, SP Rep. Virginia 4th and House majority leader:
A reporter asks, "Is rape less heinous to some women?"

(Cantor threatened to kill efforts to remedy particularly high levels of rape on Indian reservations.)

"In other words, for Cantor, limiting the authority of tribal courts is more important than making sure rapists are prosecuted and women are protected from domestic violence. And now that the elections are over, and the GOP received the message that they need to do a better job of appealing to women and minorities, is good to get that clear"
http://www.examiner.com/article/cantor-rape-is-less-heinous-to-some-women
http://blogs.denverpost.com/opinion/2012/08/22/cartoons-day-todd-akins-legitimate-rape-comment/23978/7/

Richard Mourdock, SP Sen. candidate Indiana:
"I think even when life begins in that horrible situation of rape, that it is something that God intended to happen." October 23, 2012 (one day after being endorsed by Mitt Romney).
http://www.bbc.co.uk/news/world-us-canada-20054737

John Cornyn, SP Sen. Texas:
"Richard and I, along with millions of Americans believe that life is a gift from God"—coming to the defense of Richard Mourdock on October 24, 2012.
http://abcnews.go.com/Politics/OTUS/richard-mourdock-rape-comment-puts-romney-defense/story?id=17552263

Nikki Haley, SP Gov. South Carolina:
On her Facebook page she referred to the S.C. Coalition Against Domestic Violence and Sexual Assault as "special interests"; objecting to this, Rep. Bakari Sellers said battered and raped women are not "distractions."

John Koster, SP state candidate Washington:
says abortion should not be legal, even when it involves "the rape thing."
http://www.katu.com/politics/local/176665741.html

Roger Rivard, SP State Rep. Wisconsin:
"Some girls rape easy."
http://www.nydailynews.com/news/politics/paul-ryan-withdraws-endorsement-controversial-rape-statement-article-1.1181094

Linda McMahon, SP Sen. candidate Connecticut:
"It was really an issue about a Catholic church being forced to offer those pills if the person came in an emergency rape." October 15, 2012.
http://www.democraticunderground.com/1251150337

Rick Santorum, SP presidential candidate, angel candidate in waiting:
"I think the right approach is to accept this horribly created, in the sense of rape—but nevertheless a gift in a very broken way, the gift of human life, and accept what God has given to you … rape victims should make the best of a bad situation"—January 2012.
http://www.youtube.com/watch?v=hAZ5oNQqRl8

Tom Smith, SP Sen. candidate Pennsylvania:
Pregnancy from rape is similar to "having a baby out of wedlock."
http://www.businessinsider.com/tom-smith-rape-gaffe-out-of-wedlock-republican-senate-todd-akin-legitimate-2012-8

Larry Taylor, SP State Sen. Texas:
On the subject of rape and incest exceptions he stated "that he heard lots of testimony that amounted to 'making bad choices' and then wanting to 'walk away from them.'"
http://www.austinchronicle.com/blogs/news/2013-07-11/we-re-not-gonna-take-it-hb-2-passes-senate-committee/

Clayton Williams, SP gubernatorial candidate Texas:
"If it's inevitable, just relax and enjoy."
http://www.newrepublic.com/article/106317/five-other-politicians-whove-said-idiotic-things-about-rape

Chuck Winder, SP State Sen. Idaho:
"I would hope that when a woman goes in to a physician with a rape issue, that physician will indeed ask her about perhaps her marriage, was this pregnancy caused by normal relations in a marriage or was it truly caused by a rape. I assume that's part of the counseling that goes on"—March 2012
http://bobcesca.thedailybanter.com/blog-archives/2012/12/republican-partys-year-in-quotes-rape-edition.html

Scott Brown, SP former Sen. Massachusetts:
in 2005 sponsored legislation allowing doctors and nurses to turn away rape victims if they objected to emergency contraception.
http://www.alternet.org/story/145133/why_does_republican_senate_candidate_scott_brown_hate_rape_victims

Lawrence Lockman, SP State Rep. Maine:
"If a woman has [the right to an abortion], why shouldn't a man be free to use his superior strength to force himself on a woman?" Lockman wrote. "At least the rapist's pursuit of sexual freedom doesn't [in most cases] result in anyone's death."
http://www.huffingtonpost.com/2014/02/28/lawrence-lockman-rape-_n_4874586.html?utm_hp_ref=politics

Brian Nieves, SP State Sen. Missouri:
Most late-term abortions are not really undertaken to save a mother's life but are "a matter of convenience."
http://www.examiner.com/article/gop-sen-an-abortion-to-save-a-mother-s-life-is-simply-a-matter-of-convenience
http://thinkprogress.org/health/2013/07/24/2346621/missouri-lawmaker-abortions-to-save-a-mothers-life-are-a-matter-of-convenience/

Trent Franks, SP Rep. Arizona 8th:
Incidences of pregnancy from rape is "very low." (No scientific evidence supports this myth.)
http://www.washingtonpost.com/blogs/fact-checker/post/the-claim-that-the-incidence-of-rape-resulting-in-pregnancy-is-very-low/2013/06/12/936bc45e-d3ad-11e2-8cbe-1bcbee06f8f8_blog.html

Ryan Fattman, SP State Rep. Massachusetts:
Undocumented immigrant rape victims "should be afraid to come forward."
http://thinkprogress.org/politics/2011/06/09/240597/massachusetts-gop-immigrant-rape/

Kathleen Passidomo, SP State Rep. Florida:
"There was an article about an 11 year old girl who was gang raped in Texas by 18 young men because she was dressed like a 21-year-old prostitute."
http://videocafe.crooksandliars.com/heather/what-kind-sick-society-likens-11-year-old

Dennis Nolan, SP State Sen. Nevada:
was caught on tape allegedly offering to bribe the witness in a rape trial to change her story. (You can listen to the audio here.)

Sen. Nolan has now posted an open letter on his campaign website, claiming he feels "compelled to believe the sex was consensual" because the 16-year-old victim had been "very sexually active" prior to the rape, and because ("as a side note," he says) 42% of Nevada teenagers have been sexually active before age 16.
http://www.dailykos.com/story/2010/06/06/872990/-Outrage-Republican-Senator-blames-16-year-old-rape-victim#

SP House, Congressional Bill.
"GOP BILL WOULD FORCE IRS TO CONDUCT ABORTION AUDITS"
http://www.theatlantic.com/politics/archive/2011/03/gop-bill-would-force-irs-to-conduct-abortion-audits/72680/

8) The Freedom to tear up the Constitution.

It is usually-pretty galling to hear Stupidparty types lecturing President Obama on the Constitution, because they are so Stupidparty, while Obama is a constitutional law professor.

But these "critics" prove day after day that either they know nothing about the Constitution or they do not give a dam about the Constitution. To illustrate, I will focus on one event and one set of prognosticators, all from Fox—including Bob Beckel, the token non-Stupidparty devotee. Hosts and commentators such as Ed Bollings, Sean Hannity, Laura Ingraham, and Ann Coulter discussing the Boston bombers variously promoted the following ideas:

1) Ignoring Miranda Rights.
2) Trying "enemy combatants" in military tribunal.
3) Encouraging enhanced interrogation (evidently not torture, even though they had no idea what would happen).
4) Promoting FBI wiretap of mosques.
5) Disallowing Muslim students from entering the country.
6) Arresting bomber's wife for wearing a veil.

1, 2) Fifth Amendment through Eighth Amendment: constitutional right to a fair trial and the guarantee that no one should be compelled to self-incriminate. The Fifth provides an exemption regarding the requirement of a grand-jury indictment: "except in cases arising in the land or naval forces, or in the militia, when in actual service in time of war or **public danger.**"

But I just do not see how this remotely applies to the Boston bombers, especially once the younger one is caught, which by definition you are (caught) if you are facing a trial; the "public danger" escape hatch just does not cut it, because if so, then anyone could be seen a potentially a public danger, thus destroying our constitutional rights.

3) Eighth Amendment: no cruel or unusual punishment.
4) Fourth Amendment: no illegal search and seizure.
5) First Amendment: freedom of religion (prohibits the making of any law respecting an establishment of religion or impeding the free exercise of religion).

It is just amazing how cavalier Stupidparty advocates are with our Freedoms. One Boston bomber was a citizen, the other a legal resident with no apparent link to any international conspiracy or terrorist group. The justification for shredding the Constitution was made by Eric Bollings, who invented some Math on the spot to assert that 1,500,000 Muslims hate Americans enough to come to the USA and kill. Why bother with research, if you can figure it out, on the fly, in 15 seconds?

The only freedom that appears to be safe is the right to bear arms—which was put to good use on the night of the bombings. The police used 200 rounds of ammunition, most of it when the second brother was trapped with nowhere to go—quite odd when one considers that with one suspect dead already, it becomes all the more important to capture the other alive, and by sheer luck they accidentally succeeded. By way of comparison, the entire German police use less than 100* rounds a year.

*www.theatlanticwire.com/global/2012/05/german-police-used-only-85-bullets-against-people-2011/52162

9) The Freedom to engage in organized Torture of livestock.

Is your neighbor free to torture his pet Lab? Leaving it in unbearable heat, not feeding it, or chopping off body parts with an axe—or are you free to stop this cruelty. Yes, of course you are.

That'll do, Pig, that'll do:

Now let us just focus on one example. Pigs have cognitive intelligence greater than a three-year-old child, according to Cambridge University professor Dr. Donald Bloom, who explains that they can play video games and express preference for their desired temperature. They are actually clean, social fun-loving animals, capable of strong bonds and expressing pleasure and/or discomfort. The animal-right organization PETA explains below (the list is condensed quotations):

i. [Factory] mother pigs (sows) … spend most of their lives in individual 'gestation' crates. These crates are about 7 feet long and 2 feet wide—too small to allow the animals even to turn around…. Piglets are separated from their mothers when they are as young as 10 days old…. This intensive confinement produces stress—and boredom-related behavior, such as chewing on cage bars and obsessively pressing against water bottles….

ii. Every year in the U.S., millions of male piglets are castrated (usually without being given any painkillers) because consumers supposedly complain of 'boar taint' in meat that comes from intact animals….

iii. Piglets are prone to stress-related behavior such as cannibalism and tail-biting, so (factory) 'farmers' often chop off piglets' tails and use pliers to break off the ends of their teeth—without giving them any painkillers….

iv. For identification purposes, farmers also cut out chunks of the young animals' ears….

v. When they are transported on trucks, piglets weighing up to 100 pounds are given no more than 2.4 square feet of space, and farmers are warned that the piglets "probably will get sick within a few days after arrival." One study confirmed that vibrations like those made by a moving truck are "very aversive" to pigs….

vi. According to industry reports, more than 1 million pigs die en route to slaughter each year. No laws regulate the duration of transport, frequency of rest, or provision of food and water for the animals. Pigs tend to resist getting into the trailers, which can be made from converted school buses or multideck trucks with steep ramps, so workers use electric prods to move them along.

vii. No federal laws regulate the voltage or use of electric prods on pigs, and a study showed that when electric prods were used, pigs "vocalized, lost their balance, and to jump out of the loading area" and their "heart rate and body temperature was significantly higher [than] pigs loaded using a hurdle [movable chute]."

viii. A typical slaughterhouse kills about 1,000 hogs per hour. The sheer number of animals killed makes it impossible for pigs' deaths to be humane and painless. Because of improper stunning, many hogs are alive when they reach the scalding-hot water baths, which are intended to soften their skin and remove their hair, The U.S. Department of Agriculture documented 14 humane-slaughter violations at one processing plant, where inspectors found hogs who "were walking and squealing after being stunned [with a stun gun] as many as four times." An industry report explains that "continuous pig squealing is a sign of … rough handling and excessive use of electric prods." The report found that the pigs at one federally inspected slaughter plant squealed 100 percent of the time "because electric prods were used to force pigs to jump on top of each other."

http://www.peta.org/issues/animals-used-for-food/pigs-intelligent-animals-suffering-in-factory-farms-and-slaughterhouses.aspx

How is this OK? Humanity has to be better than this? What Stupidparty representative or Disciple gives a damn? It is all silly slogans: "read my lips," "no new…" "the government is bad," etc. Now, to be sure, I have just made a generalization, as obviously certain Stupidparty representatives have shown empathy to animals and may have a legislative record to back up that empathy—but is that enough? They are part of the party that will obstruct and mock any effort to reform. It you go about

Above Artist. http://www.mattrotasart.com/

life pandering to and exciting the mob that's screaming at any and all regulation, then you deserve to die by the sword so gruesomely unleashed by the lack of such legislation. Anyone supporting the Stupidparty infrastructure is not simply obstructing reform but actively part of a process that speeds up these repulsive and economically idiotic trends, ignoring cruelties on a massive scale. They want their Freedoms, for what?

Not only do factory farms get away with vile, inhumane activity, but they have decimated the family pig farms, the very farms that better understand the animals. They displaced farmers and their families who worked on real farms and understood how to practice stewardship of the land. The country would be better served if factory farms were not allowed to bypass basic standards

Female Elephant standing protective guard over dead friend wraps her trunk round the tusk as she says her final farewell.

of humanity to workers, to livestock, and to the environment. If anyone is remotely confused by this issue, here is my challenge. Go to the local zoo. Spend at least ten minutes staring into the eyes of a gorilla (he or she will stare back) and then ask yourself—what type of person am I—if I cannot feel shame at what we do to you?

Also for insight into the economics of factory farm v. family farm, read *Fast Food Nation.*
http://www.amazon.com/s/ref=nb_sb_noss_1?url=search-alias%3Daps&field-keywords=fast+food+nation&rh=i%3Aaps%2Ck%3A fast+food+nation

How about the Freedom to be a Consumer who gives a Damn?

Try harder; you never know what might happen:

The Land
The Farmer
The Animal
Your Health
Join the resistance…
http://www.youtube.com/watch?v=rEkc70ztOrc

10) The Freedom to demand vaginal probes.

Scott Walker, SP Gov. Wisconsin:
"Walker endorses mandating transvaginal ultrasounds and shutting down abortion clinics"
http://thinkprogress.org/health/2013/06/12/2141521/scott-walker-abortion-clinics-ultrasound/

Michigan—The Vaginal Probes are Back. "Michigan lawmakers are at it again. They just today introduced another vaginal probe bill in the House—HB 4187 of 2013."
http://www.democracy-tree.com/michigan-vaginal-probes/

"The Alabama legislature is considering a mandated vaginal ultrasound bill in an attempt to restrict safe abortion care, or as State Senator Linda Coleman (D-Jefferson) says, 'a state-sanctioned rape bill.' The bill explicitly includes mandated trans-vaginal ultrasound."
http://rhrealitycheck.org/article/2012/02/27/alabama-state-senator-colman-says-forced-vaginal-probe-bill-rape-0/

Mandatory Transvaginal Ultrasounds: Coming Soon to a State near You
—by Kate Sheppard, *Mother Jones.*
The following is a direct transcription:

Virginia's new law requiring every woman to undergo an ultrasound before she can get an abortion is still terrible, even if women can opt out of the trans-vaginal probe portion.

Most abortions take place within 12 weeks after a woman becomes pregnant. And if the woman has been pregnant for eight weeks or less, conducting an ultrasound generally requires the doctor to insert a probe in a woman's vagina in order to actually see or hear anything. Virginia is not alone in its desire to subject women to invasive probes before they are allowed to get an abortion, a legally protected medical procedure. Twenty states already have laws dictating rules for ultrasounds, according to the Guttmacher Institute. Here are seven other states that have advanced similar measures in the last year.

Alabama: State Sen. Clay Scofield offered his own ultrasound measure a few weeks ago, which included a penalty of up to 10 years in jail and a $15,000 fine if doctors don't carry out the procedure. But Schofield backed off a component of the bill that would have required doctors to stick a probe in women's vaginas, instead offering that a woman could undergo the "method of ultrasound that she would be more comfortable with."

Idaho: State Sen. Chuck Winder (R-Boise) has introduced yet another bill requiring an ultrasound before an abortion, expanding upon a law already in place in the state that requires doctors to offer an ultrasound by forcing them to do it and to show the woman the image. As one anti-abortion advocate in the state described it to the local press, the idea behind the law is to make women undergo the procedure because it "gives her a window into her womb."

Illinois: The House Agriculture Committee advanced a bill on February 22 that would require doctors to carry out an ultrasound and show it to the woman, unless she declines to view it in writing. And yes, you read that correctly: the Ultrasound Opportunity Act came from the agriculture committee. This prompted opponents to show up at the hearing wearing "Women are not livestock" T-shirts.

Kentucky: The state senate approved a new bill requiring that a woman undergo an ultrasound before she can get an abortion, and instituting criminal penalties if the ultrasound isn't carried out. The bill is not expected to advance in the House.

North Carolina: This law passed in 2011 was pretty much exactly like Virginia's, but as the local press pointed out, it didn't get nearly as much attention because people weren't talking about the "transvaginal" aspect. A federal judge ruled last October that doctors don't have to show women the ultrasound image, at least.

Pennsylvania: A pair of Republican state representatives introduced the Women's Right to Know Act, which passed out of committee last month before the uproar in Virginia prompted the majority leader to shelve it.

Texas: The Lone Star State was ahead of the curve on transvaginal ultrasounds, passing its bill in May 2011 under "emergency" status. A legal challenge to the law failed last month, and it became effective immediately

http://www.motherjones.com/mojo/2012/03/transvaginal-ultrasounds-coming-soon-state-near-you

Watch your vital Freedoms!
(What is Stupidparty jabbering on
about?)

Dana Rohrabacher, SP Rep. California
48th:
told town hall meeting attendees that
Global Warming is a "total fraud" designed to create a global government to
"control all of our lives."
Read more: http://dailycaller.com/2013/08/12/gop-congressman-global-warming-is-a-liberal-plot-to-create-global-government/#ixzz2cpEdZXL5

Ed Martin SP, candidate for Rep. Missouri:
Speaking "on the Gina Loudon radio program this afternoon, congressional candidate
told listeners that 'we have to be very, very aware' of policies pursued by Barack Obama
and Russ Carnahan that will 'take away' the freedom to be a Christian."
http://www.firedupmissouri.com/content/today-gop-extremism-martin-says-obama-carnahan-will-take-away-freedom-find-lord

Tim Donnelly SP Rep. California 33rd:
"They [guns] are used to defend our property and our families and our faith and our
freedom, and they are absolutely essential to living the way God intended for us to live."
http://www.mediaite.com/online/gop-legislator-guns-are-essential-to-living-the-way-god-intended/.

Louie Gohmert, SP Rep. Texas 1st:
Evidently, he opposes gun control because gay marriage leads to bestiality.
http://www.youtube.com/watch?v=eo1AHGEx7o4

Sarah Palin, SP 2008 nominee for Vice President, former Gov. Alaska: said she would
consider abandoning the Republican Party to create something called the "Freedom
Party" with conservative talker Mark Levin. (Responding to a Fox News viewer's Twitter
question June 2013.)
Read more: http://www.nydailynews.com/news/politics/sarah-palin-bolt-gop-create-freedom-party-article-1.1386434

Wayne LaPierre, NRA executive vice president and integral part of SP:
"The NRA is going to bring all of its knowledge, dedication and resources to develop
a model National School Shield Emergency Response Program for every school that
wants it. From armed security to building design and access control to information
technology to student and teacher training, this multi-faceted program will be developed by the very best experts in their fields."
http://nbclatino.com/2012/12/21/the-nra-speaks-14-quotes-from-wayne-la-pierre-a-week-after-sandy-hook-tragedy/

Bob Ney, disgraced former SP Ohio Rep.:
This is Bob "freedom fry" Ney. This is the idiot who forced the congressional dining
rooms to reprint their menus—changing French fries to "freedom fries" and French
toast to "freedom toast."
http://www.cbsnews.com/news/do-you-want-freedom-fries-with-that/

So how did they get these slogans, these backward notions of Freedoms, these economic
concepts that can only backfire on themselves?

The Freedom to pretend that you are not aiding and abetting Bigotry.

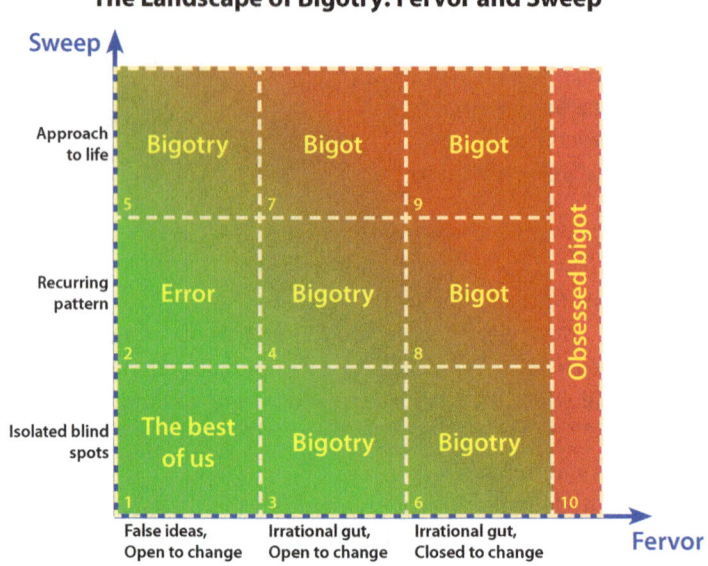

The Landscape of Bigotry: Fervor and Sweep

This chart works on the premise that we are all flawed to some degree, but while many of us may have some blind spots, we are willing to learn about our blind spots, while at the other extreme, all that matters is one's gut reaction; no amount of facts will create a change in heart.

So why do good people talk such nonsense? Why do people not speak out against bigotry? Why do good people vote for bigot panderers? Perhaps they are rationalizing their inability to accept personal responsibility for their role in passively accepting all these intellectual atrocities that continue daily under their very noses. Or more likely most people are easily distracted and allow themselves to be conned by all the false information that spews out as a result of the vast sums of money designed specifically for that purpose. That factor is all down to money and the ensuing corruption of democracy—which will be discussed later.

I believe it is a form of mass denial. It is human nature not to be bad, but to overlook details that might make us look foolish. We all do it. When the stock market is doing well, we love to think about our brilliant investment portfolios. But when the market tanks, we may not even open the pertinent monthly mailings. We think about other things.

People who support capital punishment do not want see the execution; they do not want to familiarize themselves with the accused. Likewise, the Stupidparty voter—why worry about facts, when gut judgments are so much more comforting? Stephen Colbert, on his first show, invented a new word for this flourishing trait: "truthiness." Denial of reality—it just feels better, especially if you are always going to be consigned to be on the wrong side of history. Better to create your own alternate reality. Talking of alternate realities, we will now move on to guns. Live free or die shooting at some self-made imaginary foe!

Artist http://www.mattrotasart.com/

CHAPTER 15

Guns and shooting yourself in the foot

SECOND AMENDMENT LOOPHOLE

I used to think it was possible for an artist to alter the inner life of the culture. Now bomb-makers and gunmen have taken that territory.

Don DeLillo, *Mao II*

I did not grow up in a "Gun Culture," but that does not mean that I am totally ill equipped to be firing off a few rounds. I was not exactly happy about being packed off to boarding school at the age of seven—but perhaps experimenting with various methods of venting my frustration or whatever, this unhappy camper seems to remember finding himself on the school shooting team, and quite capable of consistently hitting what seemed then at least a minute target with some type of rifle.

Since those days I have enjoyed quite a lot of clay pigeon shooting, paintballing, and more recently endured what was perhaps one the most uncomfortable and dull days of my life—glumly non-stalking apparently vacationing turkeys. Evidently, and much to my chagrin, one waits in absolute motionless silence for turkeys to come to you, rather than tracking turkey spoor to ascertain distance and estimated time of convergence. My one day of hunting being the polar opposite of my romanticized notion, globbed off my love of Wilbur Smith novels (which always involved epically long, energetic and death-defying big game chase scenes). But sullenly back to the car we walked, the blood once again circulating through my numbed and belatedly scratched limbs. And now—as we were turning onto the main road—there they were, a gang of notably harmless turkeys on the roadside, heading back home, chatting obliviously amongst themselves.

It is obvious that gun sports can be great fun and it is also obvious that some locations and individuals are more naturally suited to relaxed, happy, self-sustaining, and safe recreational gun activities than others. Just stating the obvious, one would hope.

The present-day gun (non)debate is absurd.

Stupidparty Myth #1.
The Constitution (Second Amendment in the Bill of Rights) guarantees virtually everything for the laissez-faire gun fundamentalists. Or does it?

There are several versions of the text of the Second Amendment, each with capitalization or punctuation differences, so people can argue interpretations. But more importantly:

The Supreme Court can and does tinker with, clarify, and amend the Second Amendment. Such changes are by definition constitutional.

By way of example:

In *District of Columbia v. Heller*, 554 U.S. 570 (2008), the Supreme Court ruled that the Second Amendment "codified a pre-existing right" and that it "protects an individual right to possess a firearm unconnected with service in a militia, and to use that arm for traditionally lawful purposes, such as self-defense within the home" **but stated that "the right is not unlimited. It is not a right to keep and carry any weapon whatsoever in any manner whatsoever and for whatever purpose." It also clarified that many long-standing prohibitions and restrictions on firearm possession listed by the court are consistent with the Second Amendment.**
Info from http://en.wikipedia.org/wiki/District_of_Columbia_v._Heller

So stop chanting and start debating. Some forms of gun control are allowable and if Congress accidentally steps over the mark, well, that is what the courts are for. Put that in your gun barrel and shoot it.

Now let us look some more Stupidparty myths:

Stupidparty Myth #2.
Violent TV leads to surging violence. But France, Germany, Australia, and England—they see a similar amount of violent content but have an average of 99% less gun fatalities than the USA. See charts below.

Stupidparty Myth #3.
Mental-health issues lead to surging violence. Clearly, that is nonsense, unless they are acknowledging Stupidparty adherence, as such, to be an issue. Nuance is not part of their thought process—so here is the nuance; yes of course mental health is an issue behind gun violence—as it would be in any country, but it does not explain why the USA has staggeringly different rates of gun violence than other countries. The only way this Myth becomes sustainable would be if SP support was deemed a mental-health issue. See charts below.

Stupidparty Myth #4.
Guns do not kill people—people do. No, gun proliferation kills people. See charts below.

Stupidparty Myth #5.
More guns make you safer. No they do not. See charts below.

Stupidparty Myth #6.
The government is trying to "take our guns away"
Show us an example of such draconian legislation.

THE REST OF THE WORLD COMPARED TO THE USA

COUNTRY/ TERRITORY	RANK BY RATE OF OWNERSHIP	GUNS PER 100 PEOPLE*	TOTAL CIVILIAN GUNS*	TOTAL HOMICIDES BY GUNS	HOMICIDES BY GUNS PER 100,000 PEOPLE	% OF HOMICIDES BY GUNS
United States	1	88.8	270,000,000	9,960	3.2	67.5
India	110	4.2	46,000,000	3,093	0.26	7.6
China	102	4.9	40,000,000			
Germany	15	30.3	25,000,000	158	0.19	26.3
France	12	31.2	19,000,000	35	0.06	9.6
Pakistan	57	11.6	18,000,000			
Mexico	42	15	15,500,000	11,309	9.97	54.9
Brazil	75	8	14,840,000	34,678	18.1	70.8
Russia	68	8.9	12,750,000			
Yemen	2	54.8	11,500,000			

COUNTRY/ TERRITORY	RANK BY RATE OF OWNERSHIP	GUNS PER 100 PEOPLE*	TOTAL CIVILIAN GUNS*	TOTAL HOMICIDES BY GUNS	HOMICIDES BY GUNS PER 100,000 PEOPLE	% OF HOMICIDES BY GUNS
Thailand	39	15.6	10,000,000			
Canada	13	30.8	9,950,000	173	0.51	32
Iraq	8	34.2	9,750,000			
Turkey	52	12.5	9,000,000	535	0.77	16.9
Italy	55	11.9	7,000,000	417	0.71	66.7
Spain	61	10.4	4,500,000	90	0.2	21.8
England and Wales	88	6.2	3,400,000	41	0.07	6.6
Switzerland	3	45.7	3,400,000	57	0.77	72.2
Australia	42	15	3,050,000	30	0.14	11.5
Serbia	5	37.8	3,050,000	45	0.46	33.1
Norway	11	31.3	1,400,000	2	0.05	8.1
Denmark	54	12	650,000	15	0.27	31.9
Netherlands	112	3.9	510,000	55	0.33	30.7
Northern Ireland	25	21.9	380,000	5	0.28	4.5

http://www.washingtonpost.com/wp-srv/special/nation/gun-homicides-ownership/table/
Listed: Countries with most guns, plus some European countries.

Comments:

1) Switzerland's gun culture is based on their history of being a neutral country and its citizens being trained to defend their country against an invasion. Though they have a mature and prevalent gun culture, your chance of being fatally shot in the USA is 400% greater than in Switzerland—and a lot higher than that if you live in a Stupidparty state.

2) England has an anti-gun culture, which bans fully automatic and submachine guns, etc. (private ownership of these weapons is totally prohibited). Semi-auto rifles over .22 and pistols are currently prohibited. England has 99.5% less gun fatalities than the USA.

3) Other countries with a high number of fatalities tend to be in South America, that have little control over drug cartels.

But surely Stupidparty Disciples, so enamored by the protective elements of a gun, must be safer?

UNSAFEST STATES

	State	Firearms Death Rate per 100,000		State	Firearms Death Rate per 100,000
1	Alaska	20.4	1	Hawaii	3.2
2	Louisiana	19.2	2	Massachusetts	4.1
3	Alabama	16.2	3	Rhode Island	4.6
4	Mississippi	16.1	4	New York	5.1
5	Wyoming	15.6	5	New Jersey	5.2
6	Montana	15.4	6	Connecticut	5.9
7	New Mexico	14.9	7	Minnesota	6.8
8	Arizona	14.6	8	Iowa	6.8
9	Nevada	14.5	9	California	7.7
10	Tennessee	14.4	10	Maine	7.9
11	Oklahoma	14.4	11	New Hampshire	8.2
12	Arkansas	14.4	12	Nebraska	8.2
13	West Virginia	14.1	13	Illinois	8.2
14	South Carolina	14	14	Wisconsin	8.6
15	Missouri	14	15	Washington	8.9

http://kff.org/other/state-indicator/firearms-death-rate-per-100000/

People living in the top ten Stupidparty states, have a 300% greater chance of being killed by a gun than people living in the top ten Blue states.

Okay, but surely possessing 270 million guns must have a positive impact on scary crimes; surely that will do the trick for our fearfully quivering Stupidparty Disciples?

VIOLENT CRIME RATES

Country	Murder and Non-negligent manslaughter (intentional homicide)	Forcible Rape	Robbery	Aggravated assault
Austria	1.5	9	61	47
Germany	3	9	64	188
England/Wales	2.6	23	157	—
UK, Scotland	2.66	20	60	117
USA	4.7	26.8	113	241

http://en.wikipedia.org/wiki/Crime_in_the_United_States, http://www.fbi.gov.

It should be noted that France and the U.S. do not count minor violence, such as punching or slapping, as assault, whereas Austria, Germany, and Finland do.

So the USA has twice as many aggravated assaults as the UK—in spite of the fact that there are 266 million more guns, which purportedly make you safer.

"Forcible" rape:

(Reminder to Stupidparty Disciples: women are not so keen on this and yes they can get pregnant.)

If one lives in the top-ten Stupidparty states, the odds of being raped are 94% higher than a top-ten Blue state and 400% higher than if you were to live in Austria or Germany—even though the chances of running into a gun in Austria or Germany are 1/3 compared to the USA.

RAPES PER 100,000			
1 New Jersey	11.4	1 South Dakota	60.2
2 New York	14.1	2 Alaska	58.1
3 Vermont	19	3 Colorado	44.5
4 Virginia	19	4 Michigan	44
5 Connecticut	19.2	5 Arkansas	41.3
6 California	20.3	6 New Mexico	41.2
7 Wisconsin	20.4	7 North Dakota	37.9
8 Maryland	20.5	8 Kansas	37.8
9 North Carolina	20.7	9 Nebraska	37.7
10 West Virginia	20.9	10 Oklahoma	37
11 Georgia	20.9	11 Montana	35.8
12 Missouri	21.3	12 Arizona	34.9
13 Massachusetts	24.7	13 South Carolina	34.5
14 Wyoming	25.7	14 Nevada	33.5
15 Pennsylvania	26.1	15 Kentucky	33.5

Source: Federal Bureau of Investigation, *Crime in the United States, 2011*, http://www.fbi.gov.
Crime Rate by State, 2011 | Infoplease.com http://www.infoplease.com/us/statistics/crime-rate-state.html#ixzz2cd9GMQWm

Gun advocates have their say:

In many cases, there is not much wrong in owning a gun. As far as I am concerned, living in a safe suburban setting, the fewer guns that we have in our neighborhood, the safer I would feel. Nevertheless, perhaps there are no doubt specific scenarios or environments where gun ownership might increase safety.

It is totally understandable why a peaceful rural community, totally removed from Washington DC, would resent undue interference in their way of life. If any government became silly enough to try take away their guns, effectively outlawing longstanding mainly peaceful passions, then it is understandable if unrest were to follow. Gun debates and actions should be locally appropriate.

Stupidparty Myth #7.

Gun advocates point out that violent crime has fallen significantly across the board since, say, 1990 and that this has happened at a time when gun ownership was increasing.

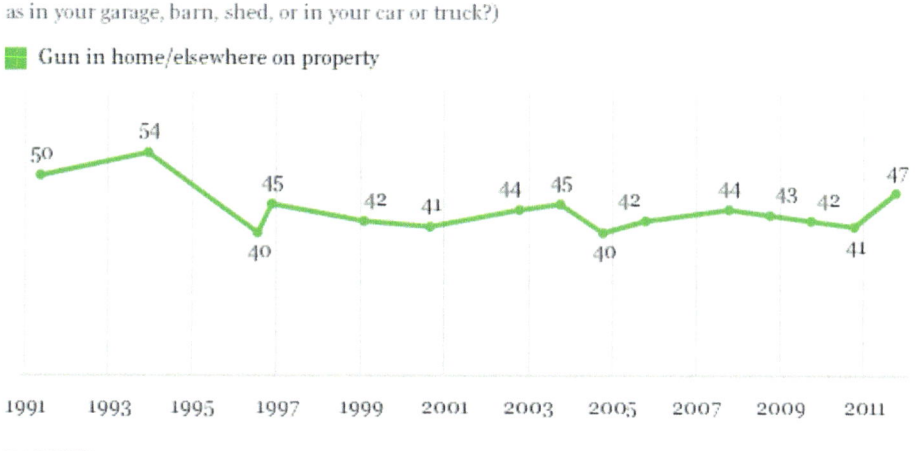

U.S. Gun Households, 1991-2011

Do you have a gun in your home? (If no: Do you have a gun anywhere else on your property such as in your garage, barn, shed, or in your car or truck?)

Gun in home/elsewhere on property

GALLUP

http://www.sangrea.net/free-cartoons/polit_guns-for-liberty.jp

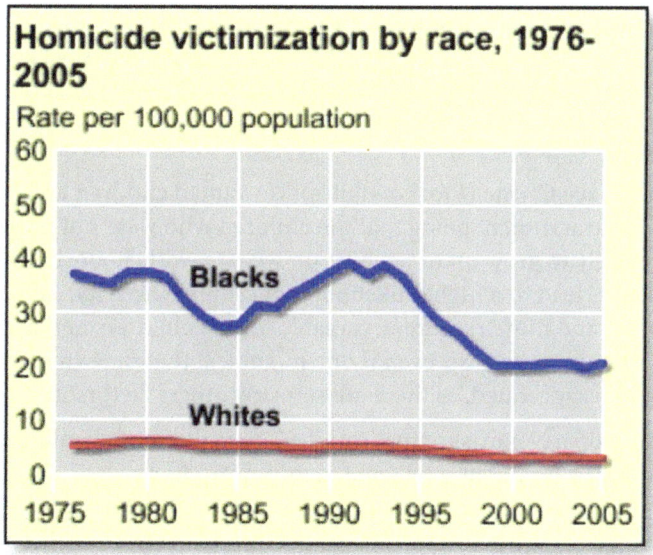

Google images "Homicide victimization by race, 1976–2005"

So, violent crime has fallen dramatically, by almost half since 1992. But the relationship to gun ownership apparently does not exist. Clearly, there has been something going on with the black population in particular.

Since "Increased Gun Ownership leading to reduced crime" is a myth, how do we explain the reduction in crime?

New York City: In 1990 there were 2,245 Murders and Non-Negligent Manslaughters. Stupidparty logic would have addressed this issue by saying, "Well, clearly the Bronx is an unsafe neighborhood, so give everyone a gun so that they can keep themselves safe.

Give taxi drivers a gun; shop owners a gun; teachers, students guns, so that will dissuade would-be thieves." Just give a gun to the good guys!

Clearly, such pearls of wisdom were ignored (well, the Stupidparty was not born until 2000).

So what happened in New York City?

2013 is on track to be close to 300 such deaths. These violent crimes have fallen by 85% since 1990. New York City is now one of the safest cities in the country, in the world. No one could say that this improvement was due to increased gun ownership, or vigilantes, or oozy waving superheroes dressed in Batman garb.

The city's dramatic drop in crime has been attributed by criminologists to the refocusing of policing tactics onto petty crime (based in the belief that graffiti, boom boxes, car-windshield washers all create an environment of lawlessness, conducive to crime); the end of the crack epidemic; and—controversially—the legalization of abortion approximately eighteen years previous, along with the decline of lead poisoning. There is a "growing body of research linking lead exposure in small children with a whole raft of complications later in life, including lower IQ, hyperactivity, behavioral problems, and learning disabilities. The mandatory installation of partitions in taxis, street-level security cameras, greater diversity of the police force, gentrification of neighborhoods, and infrastructure investment all helped reduce violent crime. Also, today it is a lot more difficult to steal a car, because of tracking technology, and those pesky experts argue that car theft is a gateway into a life of crime. Now back to that little titbit about the legalization of abortion.
http://en.wikipedia.org/wiki/Crime_in_New_York_City

Legal abortions reduce Crime (Freakonomics): Unwanted children are more likely to turn to crime—the argument being that the children who were not born after *Roe v Wade* were more likely to grow up in poverty, on welfare, with a poorly educated single mother. These factors lead to a higher likelihood of criminal activity. Add in less overcrowding in schools and more resources available for the children, and the researchers clearly have a very impressive case, even if one might feel that the extent of such impact might be somewhat exaggerated, as there are so many others factors in play.

So it was not a Stupidparty gun-slinging, aging white male Confederate wet-dream loud mob free-for-all that worked, but intelligent community efforts.

So do guns make you safer at home? Well, maybe some more ever-so-pesky science research stuff can help us.

"Risks and Benefits of a Gun in the Home":
David Hemenway, *American Journal of Lifestyle Medicine*, Nov./Dec. 2011—Abstract:

"This article summarizes the scientific literature on the health risks and benefits of having a gun in the home for the gun owner and his/her family. For most contemporary Americans, scientific studies indicate that the health risk of a gun in the home is greater than the benefit.

"The evidence is overwhelming for the fact that a gun in the home is a risk factor for completed suicide and that gun accidents are most likely to occur in homes with guns.

There is compelling evidence that a gun in the home is a risk factor for intimidation and for killing women in their homes."

Faith in America—Gods & Guns:

On the benefit side, there are fewer studies, and there is no credible evidence of a deterrent effect of firearms or that a gun in the home reduces the likelihood or severity of injury during an altercation or break-in. Thus, groups such as the American Academy of Pediatrics urge parents not to have guns in the home.
http://www.sciencedaily.com/releases/2011/04/110427101532.htm

After the Newton massacre, the White House comes up with some ideas—

Assault Weapons Ban:
Obama is seeking a reinstatement of an earlier federal ban, which expired in 2004.
Stupidparty says NO
"Impeach President Reagan retroactively for agreeing with Obama on the assault weapons ban"—John Fugelsang

Limiting High-Capacity Ammunition Magazines:
Advocates of a limit on high-capacity magazines believe it could slow down a shooter planning to carry out a massacre, such as the one at Sandy Hook. Obama's proposal would limit these magazines to 10 bullets.
Stupidparty says NO

Getting Rid of Armor-Piercing Bullets:
Although it is illegal to manufacture and import armor-piercing bullets in the U.S., the president is sending legislation to Congress that will ban the possession and transfer of the ammunition.
Stupidparty says NO

Gun-Trafficking Law:
A favorite of Mayors against Illegal Guns, a gun-control group with major backing from New York Mayor Michael Bloomberg, this measure would help prevent the trafficking of guns between states. This measure would make it easier for law enforcement officers to go after "strawmen" who buys guns for other people and transfer them across state lines.
Stupidparty says NO

Universal Background Checks:
Anyone who buys a gun at a store, a gun show, or through other private sellers would have to go through a criminal background check before purchasing the weapon, under this legislative proposal. Senior White House officials said there would be exceptions for transfers between family members, however.
Stupidparty says NO

Tougher Background-Check System:
The administration will give states $20 million in new incentives to share their information with a broader background-check system.
Stupidparty says NO

Review of Prohibitions on Gun Ownership:
The president will ask the attorney general to look into current laws that outline which people are prohibited from buying guns, and make appropriate recommendations to improve the system.
Stupidparty says NO

Nominate a New Head of the ATF:
Obama will nominate Todd Jones as permanent head of the alcohol and firearms bureau. The agency has been without a congressionally confirmed director in six years. Jones is a U.S. attorney in Minnesota and has been serving as acting head of the ATF.
Stupidparty says NO

Gun-Violence Research:
The president is seeking a resumption of research into gun violence by the Centers for Disease Control and Prevention through executive action. Congress halted the research because of lawmaker concerns that the agency was advocating for gun control. White House lawyers found that researching the cause of gun violence would not qualify as advocacy. The agency would be tasked with looking into the causes of gun violence, including a correlation between video games and violent behavior.
Stupidparty says NO

School Safety:
The administration, through executive order, will allow local communities to use money under the "COPS" initiative—which is aimed at putting more police officers on the street—to hire "school resource officers," who could help improve safety in schools. The White House would also make more money available to cities and towns to allow them to hire more mental-health workers for schools.
Stupidparty says NO

Combating Bullying:
Through the Health and Human Services Department, the administration will provide new resources aimed at reducing bullying.
Stupidparty says NO

Obamacare Regulations:
The administration will develop regulations for the Affordable Care Act aimed at ensuring comprehensive care for mental-health problems. This would include putting money toward new social workers and psychologists.
Stupidparty says NO
http://www.nationaljournal.com/whitehouse/what-are-obama-s-gun-control-proposals-an-easy-guide-20130116

But the response is also an indication that Boehner, who has an "A" rating from the NRA, is not going to lead one way or the other in the discussion and is certainly not going to rush any legislation to the floor.
http://www.rollcall.com/news/in_wake_of_tragedy_little_appetite_for_gun_control_among_house_republicans-220119-1.html

Sandy Hook:

Sandy Hook was an event waiting to happen. Why? Because a) this is America, b) this was a school, and c) this was Sandy Hook. Let me explain:

a) America, in spite of having only 270 million guns, seems to be the only country that has a material number of school shootings, and the only country where infantile political debate is tolerated when it comes to the safety of children. (There are no doubt some exceptions in countries undergoing civil war or drug-cartel domination of the police.)

b) Here is an illustration of how many school shootings there have been by decade.

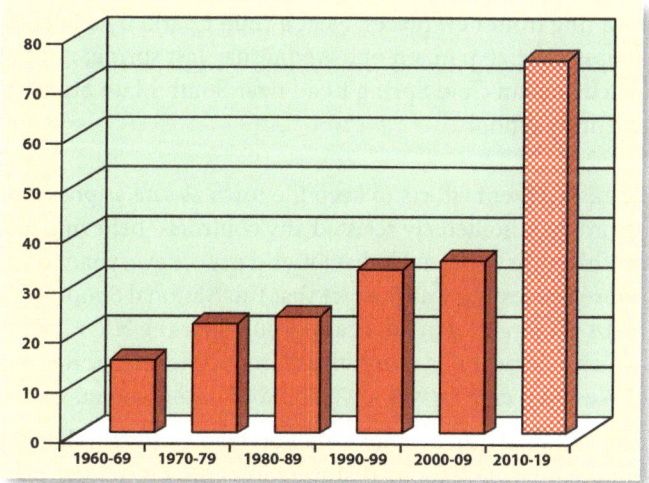

Here is the pattern for School Shootings by Year, since 2000

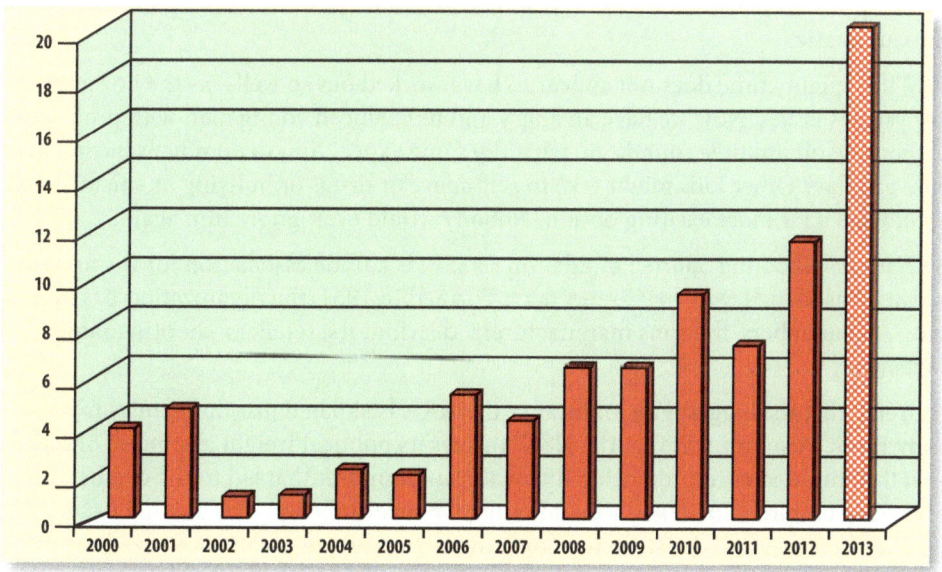

The checkered columns are prorated projections based on data through Aug 2013.

Stupidparty Myth #8.

Stupidparty Disciples will point to a few incidents abroad and suggest that Europe
is thus just as bad. They fail to figure out that while the USA, with less than half the
population of Europe, has had 167 school shootings since 1960, Europe has had 19. This
means that schools in America are 1,700% more likely to be hit than schools in Europe.

c) Newtown, Connecticut:
Newtown is no ordinary town. The inhabitants were quite used to the sound of gunfire.
As *The New York Times* reported:

"But in the last couple of years, residents began noticing loud, repeated gunfire, and
even explosions, coming from new places. Near a trailer park. By a boat launch. Next to
well-appointed houses. At 2:20 p.m. on one Wednesday last spring, multiple shots were
reported in a wooded area on Cold Spring Road near South Main Street, right across the
road from an elementary school."

http://www.nytimes.com/2012/12/17/nyregion/in-newtown-conn-a-stiff-resistance-to-gun-restrictions.html?pagewanted=all&_r=0

But in spite of law enforcement efforts to keep the town as safe as possible, there was
always a hard-core group who fiercely resisted any controls—believing it their birthright
to reenact eighteenth-century societal behavior and expect everyone to be comfortable.
Making matters more interesting was the fact that the National Shooting Sports Foundation (NSSF), perhaps the largest gun advocacy group after the NRA, had its headquarters in Newton, which I suspect had a significant impact on the local economy. Clearly, a
laissez-faire Wild West gun culture was alive and well in the saloons of Newtown.

Many of the more traditional gun owners were horrified by the fundamentalists,
complaining about the type of weapons that were intruding into their beloved pastime. The shooter in the Newton massacre, he liked guns. His mother was also passionate, evidently owning an impressive arsenal. So mother and son spent quality time
together practicing with a variety of weapons, including powerful hand guns and a
semi-automatic.

Sadly, this quality time does not appear to have worked out so well—as the boy grew to
have various issues. Now we have an angry and unbalanced young man with proficiency
for shooting off multiple rounds. So what does one expect him to do if he is having a
really bad day? Other kids might take to self-abuse or drugs or bullying or suicide—but
this kid had a far more exciting option. Nobody would ever ignore him again.

The National Shooting Sports Foundation (NSSF) is a trade association for the firearms
industry, based in Newtown, Connecticut. Formed in 1961, the organization has more
than 7,000 members: firearms manufacturers, distributors, retailers, shooting ranges,
sportsmen.

It is ironic that the biggest gun lobby after the NRA is situated just three miles from
Sandy Hook. Also ironic is that the NSSF throws its political weight around in order to
assist the Stupidparty in promoting the myths and mindset that led to the deaths of 20
very young children. In 2008 it went after the Obama campaign, threatening to sue; the
NSSF sent a "cease and desist" letter, objecting to the campaign's unauthorized use of its
"proprietary media letter," and sent a notification out to its members: "NSSF will not sit
idly by while its legal rights are harmed, particularly for partisan political gain," according to NSSF General Counsel Lawrence G. Keane.

So follow the dots. U.S. Gun Culture + U.S. tolerance for School Shootings + fundamentalist elements of the Local population + domicile of major Gun association + gun-loving Mother. Now throw into the recipe a troubled kid with gun skills and easy access to assault weapons.

No, Sandy Hook was not simply an accident; it was an accident waiting to happen.

"One failed attempt at a shoe bomb and we all take off our shoes at the airport. Thirty-one school shootings since Columbine and no change in our regulation of guns"—wrote correspondent John Oliver.

So how do Stupidparty representatives and Disciples react to this?

http://www.sangrea.net/freecartoons/polit_guns-for-liberty.jp

America needs fewer teachers and more guns. Ideas like this make sense only if you are Stupidparty.

And talking of Stupidparty:

Lamar Alexander, SP Sen. Tennessee: "I think video games is a bigger problem than guns, because video games affect people." (He must be oblivious to the fact that other countries play the same games.)
http://www.forbes.com/sites/davidthier/2013/01/30/senator-calls-video-games-a-bigger-problem-than-guns/

Phil Bryant, SP Gov. Mississippi: "When it's for self-protection, you need as much firepower as needed to protect your family"—quoted by the *Clarion Ledger,* saying he'll oppose President Obama's gun-control initiatives.
http://talkingpointsmemo.com/dc/mississippi-wants-to-secede-from-obama-s-gun-plans

Peter Kinder, SP Lt. Gov. Missouri: "Assault weapons is a misused term used by suburban soccer moms who do not understand what is being discussed here."
http://www.washingtonpost.com/blogs/the-fix/wp/2013/01/14/how-chuck-schumer-can-make-or-break-chuck-hagel/.

Joe Walsh, former SP Rep. Illinois: "We may have to shed blood every couple hundred years to preserve our freedoms"—quoted by *DNAinfo* Chicago.
http://thehill.com/blogs/ballot-box/house-races/276521-ex-rep-joe-walsh-we-may-have-to-shed-blood-to-stop-affordable-care-act-gun-control

Louie Gohmert, SP Rep. Texas 1st: "I refuse to play the game of 'assault weapon.' That's any weapon. It's a hammer. It's the machetes in Rwanda that killed 800,000 people, an article that came out this week, the massive number that are killed with hammers."
http://www.salon.com/2013/01/07/conservatives_demand_hammer_control/

Dan Dumaine, SP State Rep. New Hampshire: "A holstered gun is not a deadly weapon … But anything can be used as a deadly weapon. A credit card can be used to cut somebody's throat"— quoted by the *Concord Monitor,* opposing a move to ban guns for the chamber floor.
http://theweek.com/article/index/239628/the-10-dumbest-things-republicans-have-said-this-year

Jeff Duncan, SP Rep. South Carolina 3rd: "A national gun registry would be similar to a database used by the ruling Hutu tribe in Rwanda in the 1990s to locate and slaughter members of an opposing tribe in a genocide that killed up to one million people."
http://thehill.com/blogs/blog-briefing-room/news/293483-gop-rep-likens-gun-registration-to-rwandan-genocide

Louie Gohmert, SP Rep. Texas 1st: Gohmert says his office is drafting a measure to allow members of Congress to carry guns in the District of Columbia, including in the Capitol and on the House floor.
http://www.politico.com/blogs/glennthrush/0111/Gohmert_drafts_bill_to_allow_guns_on_House_floor.html

Stella Tremblay, SP State Rep. New Hampshire: "Just as you said would happen. Top Down, Bottom UP. The Boston Marathon was a Black Ops 'terrorist' attack. One suspect killed, the other one will be too before they even have a chance to speak. Drones and now 'terrorist' attacks by our own Government. Sad day, but a 'wake up' to all of us. First there was a 'suspect' then there wasn't. Infowars broke the story and they knew they had been found out"—on Glenn Beck's Facebook page
http://www.dailykos.com/story/2013/04/23/1204315/-NH-GOP-Rep-Stella-Tremblay-U-S-government-planned-Boston-bombings#

Larry Pratt, Gun Owners of America executive director: "Gun control supporters have the blood of little children on their hands. Federal and state laws combined to insure that no teacher, no administrator, no adult had a gun at the Newtown school where the children were murdered. This tragedy underscores the urgency of getting rid of gun bans in school zones. The only thing accomplished by gun free zones is to insure that mass murderers can slay more before they are finally confronted by someone with a gun."
http://www.salon.com/2012/12/15/gun_owners_of_america_gun_control_advocates_have_the_blood_of_little_children_on_their_hands/

Jim Sacia, SP State Rep. Illinois: "Here's an analogy folks, I ask you to think of this. You folks in Chicago want me to get castrated because your families are having too many kids. It spells out exactly what is happening here. You want us to get rid of guns."
http://cnsnews.com/blog/joe-schoffstall/incensed-illinois-lawmaker-compares-cutting-citizens-gun-buying-rights

Steve Stockman, SP Rep. Texas 36th: "If babies had guns they wouldn't be aborted."
http://thehill.com/blogs/blog-briefing-room/news/293601-rep-stockman-if-babies-had-guns-they-wouldnt-be-aborted

Ted Cruz, SP Sen. Texas, "called recent gun control proposals made in the wake of the Newtown shooting 'unconstitutional.'"
http://www.huffingtonpost.com/2013/01/06/ted-cruz-gun-control-unconstitutional_n_2420727.html

Pat Toomey, SP Sen. Pennsylvania, "blamed political polarization for the failure of the background-check compromise he reached with Democratic Sen. Joe Manchin; he said some in his party voted against the measure simply to prevent the president from winning a legislative victory: In the end, it didn't pass because we're so politicized. There

were some on my side who did not want to be seen helping the president do something he wanted to get done, just because the president wanted to do it."
http://politicalticker.blogs.cnn.com/2013/05/01/toomey-on-gun-laws-gop-didnt-want-to-be-seen-helping-obama/

Hence:

Senators Vowing to Filibuster Debate

Joining Kentucky Sens. **Paul and McConnell** are Sens. **Ted Cruz** (R-Texas), **Mike Lee** (R-Utah), **James Inhofe** (R-Okla.), **Richard Burr** (R-N.C.), **Mike Enzi** (R-Wy.), **Marco Rubio** (R-Fla.), **Jerry Moran** (R-Kans.), **Pat Roberts** (R-Kans.), **Ron Johnson** (R-Wis.), **Dan Coats** (R-Ind.) and **Mike Crapo** and **James Risch** of Idaho.
http://www.theblaze.com/stories/2013/04/08/these-are-the-14-republicans-who-have-vowed-to-filibuster-the-senate-gun-control-bill/

Conspiracy Theory #675,122

The government staged the massacre in order to confiscate guns.

Who is to blame for today's Gun Culture?

Americans are not the problem; gun owners are not the problem, and not even the members of the NRA are the problem. They overwhelmingly support background checks on gun sales. NRA members are open to all sorts of ideas. So what is the story? How are all of us being manipulated? Like everything to do with Stupidparty, the root cause can be narrowed to an extraordinarily small number of people inspired and/or financed by the Benefactors—using the standard strategies of the puppet master.

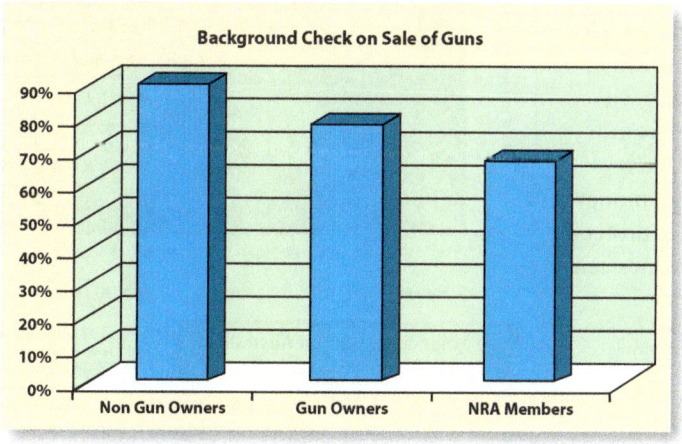

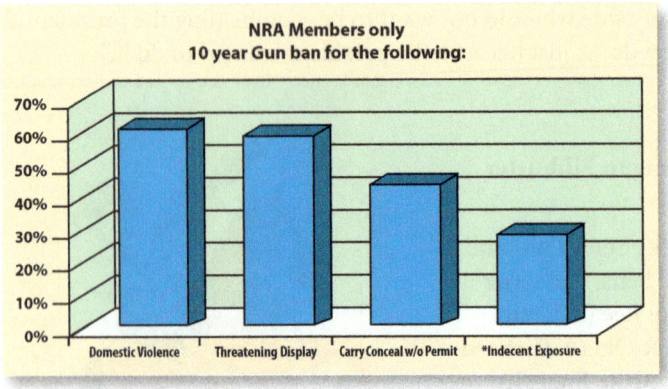

*I was wondering about carrying/concealing whilst at a naturist resort—how would they answer those questions?

The NRA:

Remember that conservative brain. The fear of your own shadow. Well, Wayne LaPierre, NRA mouthpiece, knows it—knows how to tap into it:

"After Hurricane Sandy, we saw the hellish world that the gun prohibitionists see as their utopia. Looters ran wild in south Brooklyn. There was no food, water or electricity. And if you wanted to walk several miles to get supplies, you better get back before dark, or you might not get home at all."

Or:

"Meanwhile, President Obama is leading this country to financial ruin, borrowing over a trillion dollars a year for phony 'stimulus' spending and other payoffs for his political cronies. Nobody knows if or when the fiscal collapse will come, but if the country is broke, there likely won't be enough money to pay for police protection. And the American people know it."

Or:

"Ominously, the border also remains open to agents of al Qaeda and other terrorist organizations. Numerous intelligence sources have confirmed that foreign terrorists have identified the southern U.S. border as their path of entry into the country."
http://thinkprogress.org/justice/2013/02/13/1592501/the-nine-most-insane-quotes-from-wayne-lapierres-apocalyptic-new-op-ed/

Or:

"Hurricanes. Tornadoes. Riots. Terrorists. Gangs. Lone criminals. These are perils we are sure to face—not just maybe. It's not paranoia to buy a gun. It's survival. It's responsible behavior, and it's time we encourage law-abiding Americans to do just that."

Why Does Stupidparty speak utter nonsense on gun issues?

One needs to understand the NRA.
http://dailycaller.com/2013/02/13/stand-and-fight/

The NRA Board (out-of-control Stupidparty Disciples with WMDs)

The NRA purportedly represents 4,000,000 members. But they do not, since we know that the vast bulk of the membership is open to a sensible dialogue about how to reduce the horrendous number of shootings caused by easy access to weapons of mass destruction. These weapons are not the weapon of choice to any type of hunter that the hunting fraternity would be happy to hunt with or especially be in a close proximity to.

So how does one explain the dichotomy? We need to look a bit more closely at the NRA board, who are supposedly elected by the membership. To be put up for election to the board you have to be nominated by the nine member **Nominating Committee**. The Nominating Committee has evidently nominated, selected, or endorsed 71% of the current board. While members' dues is the largest single source of revenue, in more recent years the NRA has significantly increased the amount of funds it receives from gun manufacturers—about $38m from 22 different manufacturers between 2005 to 2011.

George Kollitides, CEO of the largest gun manufacturer, the Freedom Group (Bushmaster and Remington), sits on that Nominating Committee. It appears that the rank and file never wanted such a figure to be on the board, let alone this nominating committee—but then the rank and file are not calling the shots.

According to the document below, obtained by *Mother Jones*, outsiders appointed to the current Nominating Committee include George K. Kollitides, Roger K. Bain, and Riley B. Smith.

Details regarding the Nominating Committee are quite obscure

NATIONAL RIFLE ASSOCIATION OF AMERICA

REPORT OF THE NOMINATING COMMITTEE

ARLINGTON, VIRGINIA   SEPTEMBER 17-18, 2011

TO: NRA Board of Directors and Executive Council

The Nominating Committee met at NRA Headquarters in Fairfax, Virginia on August 27, 2011, for the purpose of nominating individuals for election to the NRA Board of Directors in 2012. Members present were: Roger K. Bain; Matt Blunt; Patricia A. Clark; James S. Gilmore III; Graham Hill; Curtis S. Jenkins; Robert E. Sanders; and Committee Secretary, Edward J. Land, Jr. Committee members George K. Kollitides II and Riley B. Smith participated via telephone.

The Committee elected Patricia A. Clark as Chairman and Curtis S. Jenkins as Vice Chairman.

The Nominating Committee is a screening process designed to determine the most qualified candidates to be recommended to NRA voting members for election to the NRA Board of Directors. The Committee has made every effort to select the best possible candidates for nomination.

http://www.motherjones.com/documents/555419-nra]

Patricia Clark: "A record-holding shooter, Clark has been on the Board of Directors since 1999 and is currently the head of the NRA's nominating committee, which helps pick the majority of board members." She lives in **Newtown, Connecticut**. Named for a heroine of the American Revolution, the Sybil Ludington Women's Freedom Award was created in 1995. "She is also an instructor in the Eddie Eagle GunSafe program—heralded right after the Newtown tragedy on NBC's *Meet the Press* by Wayne LaPierre—but she has been on the NRA's governing board of directors since 1999, entrusted with ensuring that the NRA board's own ruling clique remains in power.
http://www.motherjones.com/politics/2013/01/nra-board-members-selleck-nugent

Frank Smyth reported: "I have spoken with numerous NRA members who complain about the obscure, Politburo-like governance of the NRA, which keeps ordinary members in the dark about how the organization is run and by whom." (Jan. 2013—Frank Smyth, a freelance journalist, has been covering the NRA and related groups since the early 1990s.)
http://www.progressive.org/what-judiciary-comm-should-ask-wayne-lapierre

Curtis S Jenkins, the vice chairman, "received the NRA legislative leadership award [and] is a Benefactor member"; he appears to be a remarkably one-track and rather obscure individual, holding a pivotal role. I could find little about him outside of guns, guns, guns, guns: he was a Georgia legislator interested in Conceal Carry guns laws (1976) and passionate about protecting Gun manufactures from lawsuits (1998), and was a force behind the license to commit murder—"stand your ground"—laws. Yet here is an individual with incredible power in the manipulation of who is chosen to be on the unelected NRA nominating board of nine. I find it very difficult to believe that such obscurity and single(simple)-minded devotion is not intended to scupper the democratic process that the NRA claims to promote, insisting that they represent NRA members. This smells—this individual smells like a guaranteed vote for an agenda. Imagine having one Supreme Court Justice (or two or three, for that matter) having been nominated by a small devout committee, who no longer represent present-day values, can never be removed and always vote for the interests of one group like, say, big business, the

Benefactors, regardless of any objective and equitable interpretation of the law—well, this what the NRA membership is forced to accept. But unlike the electorate, the NRA membership has a choice—they can resign.

The NRA claims to be bipartisan. (Perhaps if we lived in the Stupidparty parallel universe.)

One has only to look to the NRA's board of directors to discover that the organization is operated by a group that appears to be plagued with many individuals who promote racism, misogyny, homophobia, anti-immigrant animus, religious bigotry, anti-environmentalism, and insurrectionism. Some active board members have even had close relationships with brutal dictators in outside nations. Put simply, there are many members of the NRA leadership that no longer make for polite company.

"Moreover, while superficially bipartisan, the NRA is closely aligned with the most extreme elements in the Republican Party and has brought a number of the GOP's most influential operatives into positions of power within the organization. The GOP and NRA are now locked in a symbiotic relationship where Republican legislators advance the NRA's extreme agenda while the NRA musters its hardcore supporters to serve as attack dogs for a wide range of conservative causes."
http://www.meetthenra.org/about

So it appears that there are a couple of reasons why the NRA has become such an odious organization: a) It has become an advocate primarily for the gun manufacturers and b) the neocon extra-Stupidparty individuals took over control some time ago and have now fashioned the leadership, at least, into a thoroughly hopeless array of fundamentalist extremists who grow more like their stated adversaries (foreign, Muslim terrorists, etc.) every day. Because just as communism and unfettered capitalism end up in the same place, so do opposing fundamentalists.
http://www.theatlantic.com/business/archive/2013/01/new-evidence-that-the-nra-might-be-just-another-corporate-front/267244/

Meet some of the NRA Board Members
(who are not lucky enough to be on the Nominating Board)

Steve Hornady, president of Hornady Ammunition.

"Hornady is the son of Joyce Hornady, the founder of the company. Joyce began manufacturing ammunition because he was dissatisfied with the quality of surplus ammunition following World War II. Steve Hornady joined his father's business in 1970. Presently, Hornady Ammunition manufactures 'FMJ' armor piercing bullets for sale on the civilian market."
http://www.meetthenra.org/nra-member/steve-hornady

Ronnie Barrett.
"Barrett personally designed the first .50 caliber sniper rifle after observing a Browning machine gun mounted on a gunboat. This high-powered sniper

Honey I'm Home

rifle—available for sale on the civilian market—has an effective range of over a mile and can pierce armor.

"The virtually unrestricted availability of these firearms and ammunition, given the uses intended in their design and manufacture, present a serious and substantial threat to the national security."

http://www.meetthenra.org/nra-member/ronnie-barrett

Ted Nugent.

Stupidparty humor is discussed later, but Ted Nugent evidently likes to joke around, as a way to attack his perceived enemies. So he tells boastful stories about machine gunning wild feral hogs from a helicopter (an uncouth recreation) and then that leads him to speculating about crowd control in South LA—as people laugh. I just wonder at the type of person who tells these stories and those who find such images funny.

Mother Jones **reports:**

Ted Nugent

At the NRA's 2012 annual conference, **the Nuge** announced, "If Barack Obama becomes the next president in November again, I will either be dead or in jail by this time next year," prompting a **meeting with the Secret Service.**

Oliver North

"I love speaking out for the NRA in large part because it drives the left a little bit nuts," **says** the Iran-Contra conspirator and *Call of Duty* **pitchman**.

Marion Hammer

The former NRA president helped craft and implement Florida's **Stand Your Ground law**, which provided a model for similar self-defense laws in 24 other states.

David Keene

The current NRA president is the former chairman of the American. In 2003, his son was sentenced to 10 years in prison for firing at another driver during a **road rage incident.**

R. Lee "The Gunny" Ermey

Former Marine turned actor is best known for his turn as a drill sergeant in *Full Metal Jacket* (who is gunned down by a suicidal recruit). He's also a **spokesman for Glock**.

Wayne A. Ross

In 2009, Sarah Palin nominated the former NRA vice president to be Alaska's attorney general, but lawmakers **passed on him** after he was accused of making homophobic and **sexist comments**.

Carl T. Rowan Jr.

Formerly a cop, FBI agent, and vice president for the private-security firm Securitas. He is the son of columnist Carl Rowan Sr., who once caught a teenager swimming in his backyard pool and **wounded him** with an unlicensed handgun.

Larry Craig

The former Idaho senator sponsored a 2005 law **protecting gun makers** from liability in connection with their products being used by criminals. The NRA spent **$1.8 million** on lobbying Congress that year.

Grover Norquist

The president of **Americans for Tax Reform** is a NRA Life Member and member of the Fifty Caliber Shooters Association. After Newtown, he **echoed the NRA's line**: "We have got to calm down and not take tragedies like this, crimes like this, and use them for political purposes."

Robert K. Brown

The former Special Forces soldier and big-game hunter is the founder and publisher of *Soldier of Fortune*, which was sued in the late '80s for running **want ads for mercenaries and guns for hire.**

Roy Innis

The head of the Congress of Racial Equality, a civil rights organization now known as a **climate-denying AstroTurf outfit**. While representing the United States at a UN arms conference in 2001, **Innis explained**, "The Rwanda genocide would not have happened if the Tutsis had had even one or two pistols to fight back with."

Roy Innis has turned the former civil rights group Congress of Racial Equality (CORE) into his personal right-wing front group. *Mother Jones* says: "CORE is [now] better known among real civil rights groups for renting out its historic name to any corporation in need of a black front person. The group has taken money from the payday-lending industry, chemical giant (and original DDT manufacturer) Monsanto, and ExxonMobil." James Farmer, the founder of CORE, has accused Innis of running a "fraudulent" organization and called him "an American Idi Amin."

http://www.motherjones.com/politics/2013/01/nra-board-members-selleck-nugent (source for above)
http://www.meetthenra.org/board-list (source for below)

I will now use various snippets taken from the research done by **Coalition to Stop Gun Violence.**

I cannot help digressing for a moment to note that when well-meaning groups name their organization, the name describes the goal. When Stupidparty advocate groups come up with names, the goal is pretty much the opposite. Like, say, "Clear Sky" initiatives/laws: those groups assuredly mean the opposite—"let us pollute." Or "Giving workers the tools to compete" would mean cutting back training programs and "Citizens for … whatever" really means the Asset Strippers are covertly trying to screw people by leaning on Congress to enact self-enrichment laws. So if, by way of example, the Koch bothers funded a group called "The Coalition to Stop Gun Violence," we would all know that the objective of that group would be to encourage more people to buy guns, using the slogan SHOOT FIRST SO YOU CAN BE SAFE. Born to be disingenuous, their lazy propaganda efforts can be torn to shreds. These spongers, these spoilt silver spoon-fed Benefactors are far too intellectually lazy to come up with less transparently misleading titles. Money buys them whatever they want and their brain wilts. Just food for thought—as later these pages will gush with horribly self-serving and oh so predictably named captive groups with globs of money, as they lecherously ogle anything that has a spare dollar under the skirt, just begging to be stripped. Stupidparty Disciples—they strip easy.

The Coalition to Stop Gun Violence. This actually means what is says (and back on topic).
Who are they? (Wiki)
"In 1974, the United Methodist General Board of Church and Society formed the National Coalition to Ban Handguns, a group of thirty religious, labor, and nonprofit organizations with the goal of addressing 'the high rates of gun-related crime and death in American society' by licensing gun owners, registering firearms, and banning private ownership of handguns with 'reasonable limited exceptions' for 'police, military, licensed security guards, antique dealers who have guns in unfireable condition, and licensed pistol clubs where firearms are kept on the premises.' In the 1980s and 1990s, the coalition grew to 44 member groups. In 1989, the National Coalition to Ban Handguns changed its name to the Coalition to Stop Gun Violence, in part because the group felt that 'assault weapons' as well as handguns, should be outlawed. Today, the coalition comprises 48 member organizations."

While most Americans are not ready for the Coalitions ultimate agenda, the membership groups are diverse and impressive. This group is a font of information.

The Coalition writes:

Please note that for next six individuals (up to Ken Blackwell), I have selected a representative sample of quotes compiled from The Educational Fund to Stop Gun Violence, who are an affiliate organization of the Coalition to Stop Gun Violence

Cleta Mitchell (Board Member): "Mitchell served as an 'attack attorney' for many Tea Party Congressional candidates during the 2010 elections, including Sharron Angle, Christine O'Donnell and Joe Miller. She has suggested that the Democratic Party's 'tricks' include widespread engagement in voter fraud. Mitchell famously wrote a fundraising letter on behalf of Angle where she accused Senate Majority Leader Harry Reid of attempting to steal the election. Both Angle and Miller have been involved in high-profile controversies surrounding guns and the Second Amendment."

Pete Brownell (Board Member): "Brownell is the grandson of Brownells founder Bob Brownell and currently serves as the company's president. Brownells is the world's largest supplier of firearm parts, gunsmithing tools, equipment, and accessories. The company is part of the NRA's corporate giving program and has donated enough money to be included in 'The Ring of Freedom,' a designation reserved for NRA's largest corporate donors. Brownells contributed between $500,000 and $999,999 to the NRA between 2005 and 2010. During his campaign to join the NRA board, Brownell highlighted his company's close ties with the organization, saying, 'Having directors who intimately understand and work in leadership positions within the firearms industry ensures the NRA's focus is honed on the overall mission of the organization.' Brownell, however, has claimed that he has no financial interest in the positions of the NRA."

John Burtt (Board Member): Burtt has praised his fellow NRA Board Members by saying, "I am so impressed with the people I meet in that board room, who represent the firearms industry as well as the gun rights industry in America."

"During a 2010 interview with 'NRA News,' Burtt described efforts to ban civilian ownership of .50 caliber sniper rifles as the first step toward large-scale gun confiscation in the United States."

Bob Barr (Board Member): "In a June 20, 2012 oped for the *Marietta Daily Journal,* Barr wrote, 'I am a real fan of handguns manufactured by Glock. And, for many years I have known Paul Jannuzzo.' Paul Jannuzzo, former CEO of Glock, Inc., a firearms manufacturer, fled the country first to Mexico, and then Amsterdam amid allegations of embezzlement. He was arrested in Amsterdam and extradited to the United States. In March 2012, Jannuzzo was convicted for racketeering and theft. He was sentenced to seven years in prison and thirteen on probation. Barr also stated that he wrote a letter of support for Jannuzzo prior to his sentencing."

John Bolton (Chairman of the NRA International Affairs Subcommittee): The same John Bolton who likes to invade any country that even moves oddly. "During a speech at the 2011 annual National Rifle Association convention, Bolton said that President Barack Obama has 'disdain for the American people.' He also said that the President is 'using [the drug war] in Mexico, and the use of drugs in our own country, not to combat the illicit narcotic, but to use it as a foundation to argue for stricter gun controls at the federal level.'"

Pete Brownell (Board Member): "At the 2011 NRA annual meeting, Brownell criticized President Obama's position on gun rights but was unable to indicate anything that Obama has done to make gun laws more rigorous. He also claimed unnamed members of Congress are attempting to ban firearms."

Ken Blackwell (NRA Board Member & co-conspirator with Karl Rove in the 2004 Ohio election scandal). A quick reminder that the effort to steal? Ohio in 2004 was surely not reliant simply on voter suppression. Remember Rove's 2012 election-night meltdown on Fox?

Election night 2012 was not really that exciting, because the result was pretty much a foregone conclusion. The mainstream media was more motivated to create excitement with constant assertions of how close it would be. But really … take a moment to consider Princeton's Professor Sam Wang, a neuroscientist who in 2004 was one of the first people to aggregate polls using probabilistic methods, and let us not forget Nate Silver of the *FiveThirtyEight* blog (the 2012 *New York Times* polling guru)—these guys pretty much always get it spot on. Why do journalists keep touting specific polls or even specific sets of polls, as if they provide the answer? Single polls can be very wrong.

Many polls are third rate, and many are biased—more interested in driving a narrative than observing it—and these politically driven pollsters only make adjustments in the waning days so they can appear credible.

I should point out that one guy did even better than those master mathematicians, and that was Markos Moulitsas of *Daily Kos Elections,* who not only precisely predicted the 332–206 Electoral College result but outperformed Nate Silver in his popular-vote projection. Now, Moulitsas (and his blog *Kos*) are incorrectly labeled as left wing, when Moulitsas is simply a very rational and accurate prognosticator, who finds himself living in a fundamentally right wing universe.

But I digress … the fact is that any sound mathematical analysis had indicated for weeks what the outcome was going to be. And this takes us back to Karl Rove—who also really understands numbers—back to Karl Rove on election night 2012 at about 11 p.m. at the Fox News decision desk. Rove is now having a meltdown just after Fox and the rest have declared Ohio and thus the presidency for Obama. Rove is again focusing on Ohio. With 75% of the vote counted and many urban areas (Obama strongholds) still to report, the state was clearly going for Obama. But Rove says no and he just won't give up. Rove keeps insisting that those Ohio numbers are going to change. Witnessing this amusing event, many people could not help but hearken back to election night 2004, and Ohio at 11 p.m., a time when Karl Rove was actually in charge of the George Bush campaign strategy and thus must have been working closely with Ken Blackwell, Ohio's Stupidparty secretary of state.

At pretty much the same time, back in 2004, Kerry was clearly ahead in Ohio, and then at 11.14 p.m. the servers counting the votes crashed. But the powers that be in Ohio had a plan for just such an eventuality: they had contracted with a company called SmarTech to step in. Ken Blackwell was the individual who arranged that contract. The suspicious ties between SmarTech and Republican politics is documented by journalist Craig Unger in his book "Boss Rove," Without saying another word, I would just point out that suddenly after the system crash and against all expectations, Bush wins Ohio with some very suspicious numbers and thus secures his second term.

Back to election night 2012. Unfortunately for Rove, his role was now different. It was his world that was crashing and he could not find any aces up his sleeve, but instead he had to be slapped down by the tech-smart, number-crunching geeks in the

Fox news back office. If one could read minds "http://ronmwangaguhunga.blogspot.com/2012_12_01_archive.html" (see link to screen grab I have in mind), on that night Karl Rove's mind appeared to be quite transparent… Where was Ken Blackwell when he was most needed?

http://truth-out.org/news/item/12845-anonymous-karl-rove-and-2012-election-fix http://www.policymic.com/articles/21682/fox-news-lies-and-gaffes-the-5-biggest-blunders-of-2012 http://www.policymic.com/articles/21682/fox-news-lies-and-gaffes-the-5-biggest-blunders-of-2012

Ken Blackwell remains a major threat to the democratic process. He has no scruples. He presently meets weekly with other unscrupulous people such as Clarence Thomas's wife, Ginny; John Bolton (another NRA board member); Allen West, the former Stupidparty fundamentalist House member from Florida; Max Pappas, a top aide to Senator Ted Cruz (SP–Texas); and several journalists associated with the Breitbart News Network, Washington Examiner, and National Review. They plot not only how to turn Stupidparty stupider but how to keep making shit up—i.e., if Hillary runs, expect Benghazi to never stop; she will be called before Congress to testify, etc. Look at what Ken Blackwell says, and you get a good glimpse into what this bunch is capable of, whether it be by tapping into the huge funds of the Benefactors—or understanding that at least one member of the Supreme Court is beyond redemption, way beyond the fringe.

Also, there are careers to be made for black people willing to be a front for the Stupidparty—as Roy Innhas proven. The Stupidparty Benefactors desperately need these Trojan horses. So, yes, Clarence Thomas is right: sometimes affirmative action does put people in positions they do not merit. He is the poster boy for everything wrong with affirmative action.

is

Whether or not they are motivated by a very confused notion of Christian values or big bucks (for they are a strategic necessity for the Benefactors), or an entirely different incentive, people like Roy Innis, Clarence Thomas, Herman Cain, and Alan West have taken the ball, sprinted past the end zone, out of the stadium—all the way into a parallel universe where a black John Galt is running a paradise for opportunistic or merit-worthy black people who by accident or design fill a highly marketable niche.

We will spend a bit of extra time on Ken Blackwell because he is just so Stupidparty, and people like this get into positions of power—power that can dictate who actually gets to be president. Blackwell has been attributed with a seemingly near-infinite amount of fear-mongering, homophobic, ignorant, and bigoted material targeted to people who are most likely to resort to violence if their blood pressure gets much above 130/80. He spews out red meat to the 'zombie' believers.

As Coalition to Stop Gun Violence reports
(and all the following comes from that source):

In an October 22, 2010 op-ed for the *Patriot Post*, Blackwell wrote, "Today, tragically, nearly 40% of our children are born out-of-wedlock. And big government consumes nearly 40% of our Gross Domestic Product. I don't believe the 40/40 link is imaginary?"

In a May 31, 2010 op-ed for the Patriot Post, Blackwell wrote, "What's a dhimmicrat, you say? It's not the same thing as a democrat. A dhimmicrat is a person who, while not Muslim himself, nonetheless clears the path for sharia law to be adopted and incorporated into otherwise free nations … Eric Holder is a leading dhimmicrat in government today." In a December 17, 2010 op-ed for the *Patriot Post,* Blackwell urged the Senate to not ratify the Strategic Arms Reduction Treaty with Russia, because "President Obama has never disavowed his socialist convictions. Even *The*

http://www.chrisweigant.com/2011/02/15/cartoon-tuesday/

Washington Post refers to him as a socialist. Isn't it time we had a full airing of all of this before we ratify a treaty with the rulers of the Kremlin?"

In a November 2, 2010 op-ed for the *Patriot Post,* Blackwell—who does not believe in man-made climate change—claimed that "Cap and Trade" legislation would "nationalize all American enterprise."

Commenting on his support of Delaware Republican candidate for Senate Christine O'Donnell in a September 16, 2010 op-ed for the *Patriot Post,* Blackwell wrote, "It should not go without mention that [Stupidparty candidate Mike] Castle was the co-author of the Castle–DeGette bill. Under this measure, Americans would be taxed to create embryonic human beings. Taxpayers would then have to fund experiments upon those embryonic human beings, including cloning humans. Finally, the taxpayers would have to pay for the killing of these cloned humans and other embryonic human lives. This is a nightmare scenario for pro-life Americans."

In a July 28, 2010 op-ed for the *Patriot Post,* Blackwell claimed that the Obama Administration promotes abortion in Third World countries because the administration "wants fewer of them."

In an April 27, 2010 op-ed for the Patriot Post, Blackwell wrote, "When Mr. Obama bowed low before Emperor Akihito, it was a tacit apology for [the use of nuclear weapons against Japan during World War II]."

Commenting on his belief that the United States promotes abortion in Kenya in an April 16, 2010 op-ed for the *Patriot Post,* Blackwell flirted with "birther" rhetoric by writing, "The Obama Administration doesn't want to raise any questions about why it's pushing for fewer birth certificates in Kenya."

In a January 19, 2010 op-ed for the *Patriot Post,* Blackwell suggested that TWA Flight 800, which crashed in 1996 killing all 230 persons aboard, was downed by a terrorist attack. A FBI investigation revealed no evidence of terrorist involvement.

Blackwell authored an August 19, 2011 op-ed for the *Patriot Post,* criticizing President Barack Obama's role in the death of Osama bin Laden. He wrote that what was missing from the raid (ordered by President Obama) was "presidential leadership."

In a November 20, 2009 op-ed for the *Patriot Post,* Blackwell claimed "more than 90 percent" of Democrats "never go to church."

In an October 30, 2009, opinion piece, Blackwell attacked the Civil Rights Act of 1964—which prohibits discrimination on the basis of race, color, religion, sex, and national origin—by writing, "Would you rather not have a receptionist or customer service representative of your company who has tattooed his or her face with fierce Maori markings? You could be forced by the EEOC [Equal Employment Opportunity Commission] to make that hire."

Blackwell also worried about the EEOC's effect on "employers who would prefer not to hire or promote employees who dress as members of the opposite sex."

In a September 8, 2011 op-ed for the *Patriot Post,* Blackwell claimed that Congressman John Lewis (D-GA)—who spoke at the 1963 March on Washington where Dr. Martin Luther King Jr. delivered his "I Have a Dream" speech—intended to incite violence within the crowd with his original planned speech. In the actual speech Lewis delivered that day, he called for the crowd to nonviolently support the civil rights movement by "march[ing] with the spirit of love and with the spirit of dignity that we have shown here today." Blackwell's editorial portrayed a nonviolent, pro-union rally on Labor Day 2011 as "an incitement to riot."

In an October 20, 2011 op-ed for the *Patriot Post,* Blackwell claimed that the United States government's support of the ouster of Egyptian dictator Hosni Mubarak meant that, "American taxpayers [are] aiding the slaughter of Egypt's Christians." He went on to call President Obama "the most anti-Israel president in our history and also, de facto, the most anti-Christian." Blackwell's claim was based on a tragic October 2011 event where Coptic Christian protesters threw Molotov cocktails and fired weapons at the Egyptian military, which retaliated with deadly force

Writing about Iran, Blackwell authored a November 12, 2011 op-ed for the *American Thinker* in which he declared, "For three years, Mr. Obama has tried to appease the world's number one terrorist regime ... Even the anti-Semitic Richard Nixon was there for Israel, when the chips were down during the 1973 Yom Kippur War. Barack Obama's record makes him unmistakably the first anti-Israel president in our history."

In a November 4, 2011 op-ed for the *Patriot Post*, Blackwell made a number of unverified claims about President Barack Obama's policy towards Iran and claimed that the president "even sent Persian New Year greetings to the Iranian people and their dictatorial rulers." In fact, President Obama sent a greeting only to the people of Iran. In that greeting, he compared the political situation in Iran to populist uprisings in Egypt and Tunisia and stated, "Just as the people of the region have insisted that they have a choice in how they are governed, so do the governments of the region have a choice in their response. So far, the Iranian government has responded by demonstrating that it cares far more about preserving its own power than respecting the rights of the Iranian people."

In a December 24, 2011 op-ed for the *Patriot Post*, Blackwell wrote, "Nothing so threatens the middle class in America as Obama care."

In a December 8, 2011 op-ed for the *Patriot Post*, Blackwell wrote, "Mr. Obama and his administration keep Planned Parenthood in business—shoveling billions to their lethal efforts. Because of them, six in ten pregnancies in Harlem end in abortion. There is no hope in that dread change." In reality, only 3% of services provided by Planned Parenthood are related to abortion, with 90% of services aimed at preventing unwanted pregnancy.

In a February 26, 2012 web appearance on *The Daily Caller*, Blackwell said of Democratic President Barack Obama, "What you see is a president that ignores the Constitution, an administration that ignores the Constitution. And he wants to build a federal court system in his own philosophy and in his own image, and thereby give him, and his administration, unbridled power."
http://www.meetthenra.org/ties/conspiracy-theory

Before Stupidparty Birth

Earlier I inferred that sometime in the past the NRA was taken over by Stupidparty-type crazies—well before the actual birth of Stupidparty.

The Washington Post reports: In gun lore it's known as the Revolt at Cincinnati. On May 21, 1977, and into the morning of May 22, a rump caucus of gun rights radicals took over the annual meeting of the National Rifle Association.

The rebels wore orange-blaze hunting caps. They spoke on walkie-talkies as they worked the floor of the sweltering convention hall. They suspected that the NRA leaders had turned off the air-conditioning in hopes that the rabble-rousers would lose enthusiasm.

The Old Guard was caught by surprise. The NRA officers sat up front, on a dais, observing their demise. The organization, about a century old already, was thoroughly mainstream and bipartisan, focusing on hunting, conservation and marksmanship. It taught Boy Scouts how to shoot safely. But the world had changed, and everything was more political now. The rebels saw the NRA leaders as elites who lacked the heart and conviction to fight against gun-control legislation....

"We must declare that there are no shades of gray in American freedom. It's black and white, all or nothing," Executive Vice President Wayne LaPierre said at an NRA annual meeting in 2002, a message that the organization has reiterated at almost every opportunity since.
http://www.washingtonpost.com/politics/how-nras-true-believers-converted-a-marksmanship-group-into-a-mighty-gun-lobby/2013/01/12/51c62288-59b9-11e2-88d0-c4cf65c3ad15_story.html

The NRA has the financial muscle, the power over politicians, the ability to rally its supporters to pressure their congressmen—they have the power not only to suffocate debate but to keep advancing their insane agenda. They can send a message by targeting certain representative, throwing money at their opponents. In Sept. 2013 in Colorado they just completed such a coup.
http://www.huffingtonpost.com/2013/09/10/colorado-recall-results_n_3903209.html

This is enough to engender fear and buy subservience. "Stand Your Ground" laws are simply a device to allow armed people to shoot unarmed people at will. The gun manufactures and the freedom criers want everyone to be armed, to return us to the Wild West. Sure, people will get shot—but John Wayne or Clint Eastwood will ride in and save the day. "String 'm" high, all those bad guys, those immigrants, those gays, those damn Yankees. Safest for the womenfolk to stay inside—looking out through a veil.

So why do people fall for all this provable nonsense?

In an unfettered capitalist universe, money trumps everything. Money trumps facts. Money trumps common sense, money trumps humanity itself.

This will buy a lot of stupid.

The Benefactors are the Asset Strippers

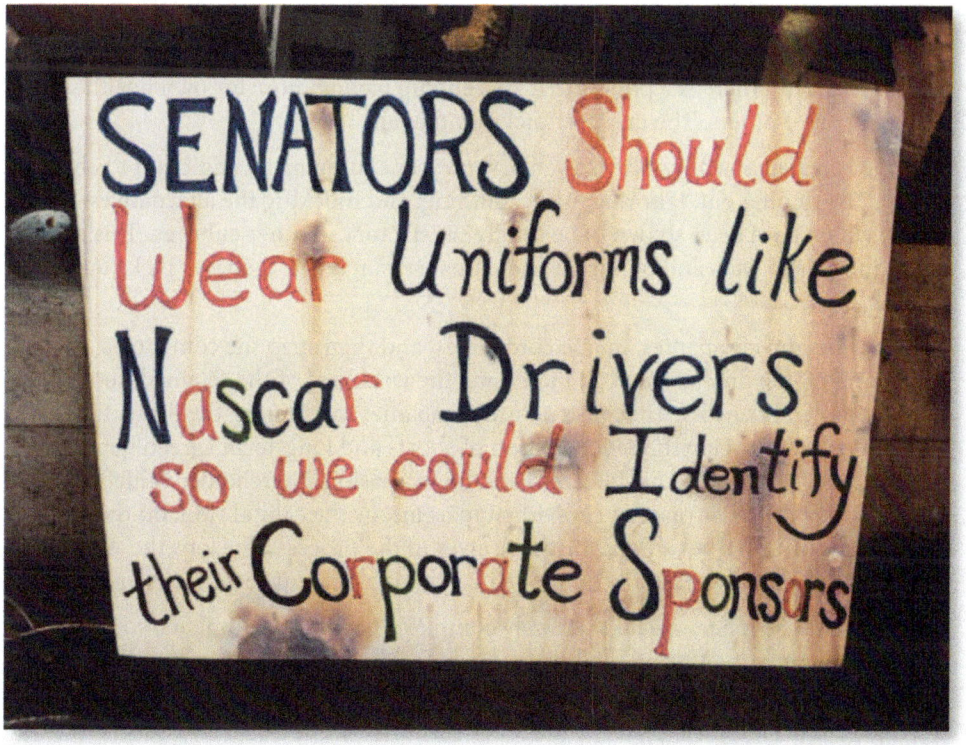

If your party serves the powerful and well-funded interests, and there's no limit to what you can spend, you have a permanent structural advantage. We're averaging fifty-dollar checks in our campaign, and trying to ward off these seven- or eight-figure checks on the other side. That disparity is pretty striking, and so are the implications. In many ways, we're back in the Gilded Age. We have robber barons buying the government.

—David Axelrod

The Asset Strippers:

The key point here is understanding how assets are flowing from one segment of society to a minute block of individuals—the argument about the overall economic benefits of Asset Stripping, if such a flow is not a one-way street, is more nuanced.

1) They create Factory Farms and Fast Food Restaurants, each dominated by four or five companies; simplify workers' skills to the point of Repetitive Disorder Syndrome (RSD, my own mashed-up terminology), thus stripping (enslaving), the ever-less-valuable worker, the livestock, and the environment. No time to actually cook a meal. To swaths of the population working ever harder for less, fresh produce becomes more expensive (i.e., unaffordable) than a burger and fries, and a supersized, 64-oz. bucket (which we must be "free to drink") as we ironically eat ourselves back into the factory chain we created. The taxpayer will pick up the tab.

2) But fear not. Sickness like RSD, depression, obesity, high cholesterol, allergies, and cancer—there is a pill for that. We end up paying more for own healthcare and that of others. The taxpayer picks up the tab.

3) They created an energy-dependent country, encouraging an addiction to cheap Oil, by ripping out, ignoring, bad mouthing, and mocking the alternatives—all of which have been shown to be totally satisfactory in other cultures. This addiction leads to wars and pollution and climate change. The taxpayer picks up the tab.

4) They buy up companies, merge companies, and then strip the companies by laying off the duplicated skill, increasing the workload of the retained, reducing salaries and benefits. They restructure companies by entering the protection of bankruptcy, forcing the renegotiation of short- and long-term agreed benefits, such as pensions and healthcare. Thus, by increasing "shareholder value," they walk off with their massive individual margins, or the capital gain, on the large stock blocks they leveraged for themselves in the process. The jobs the Asset Strippers create are usually barely self-sustaining. The taxpayer picks up the tab

5) The Asset Strippers create extremely complex financial instruments, so complex they are often barely understood even by the individuals trading them. Regulation if attempted gets swamped. Socially responsible investing by large institutions is virtually impossible because funds are indispensable to diversity and funds really need to compete using every tool available. Most people understand that this is a complex subject, beyond their grasp, and thus do not make an effort to really understand. The good news is that it can be explained in a very simple and fun way, as has been proved by John Bird and John Fortune in a brilliant nine-minute video on the subprime crisis. The taxpayer picks up the tab—as the "two Johns" explain. http://www.youtube.com/watch?v=mzJmTCYmo9g

6) The final trick for the Asset Strippers, how to reduce their taxes down to maybe zero, increase their tax loopholes, negate inheritance issues, further reduce worker benefits and safety, short circuit financial and environmental regulations, and basically rule

the country in ways that far exceed any historical precedent and certainly negate the intent of democracy. How to make a mockery of democracy. We will now analyze how this final coup is achieved.

French Spending on Elections:

"France's two 2007 presidential finalists spent a collective $54 million (out of a maximum legal limit of $49 million each). Individual contributions have a generous limit of $5,980, compared to the U.S. individual maximums of $2,500. But there are no Gallic versions of the unlimited gifts that can go to third-party groups, nor the super PACs which can spend the enormous amounts for candidates that so distend the American system. In France, companies, unions, and special interests are prohibited from funding favored French politicians. French campaigns are similarly regulated across all other areas."

Read more: http://world.time.com/2012/04/20/frances-stringent-election-laws-lessons-for-the-americas-free-for-all-campaigns/#ixzz2cv1NlaTF

British Spending on Elections:

Donations typically peak before elections. Between the 6th of April and the 6th of May 2010 (a general election campaign month) the Conservatives took £7,317,602, Labour £5,283,199 and the Liberal Democrats £724,000.

http://en.wikipedia.org/wiki/Political_funding_in_the_United_Kingdom#Donations

The UK has hardly any issues over gerrymandering and has no voter suppression issues
The UK hand counts the ballots, and the result is never disputed
The Courts have never had to decide an election.
Issues of Lobbying, undue business interference are a fraction of that in the USA

i.e. the total raised for the 2010 election was about £13.2 pounds or $20,000,000. The UK does not have a presidential system—so this is used primarily to elect 480 members of Parliament. To equate the UK population with the USA—it would be fair to say that $100,000,000 would be the prorated amount.

American Spending on Elections:

For the 2012 US election—the parties (basically two parties) spent $6,000,000,000. Yes, $6 billion. The USA spends 60 times more money on persuading (misleading) each voter.

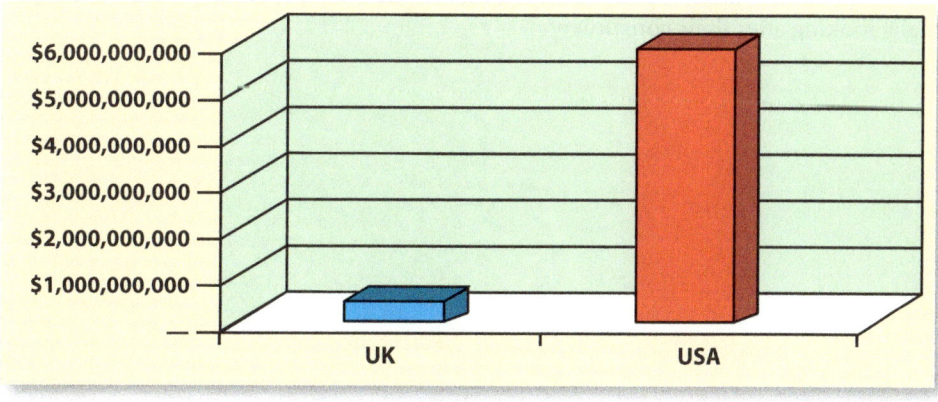

"Earlier this year, the Center for Responsive Politics estimated that the 2012 election would cost $5.8 billion—an estimate that already made it the most expensive in history—but with less than a week to go before the election, CRP is revising the estimate upwards. According to CRP's new analysis of Federal Election Commission data, this election will likely cost $6 billion."
http://www.opensecrets.org/news/2012/10/2012-election-spending-will-reach-6.html

But it even worse than that:

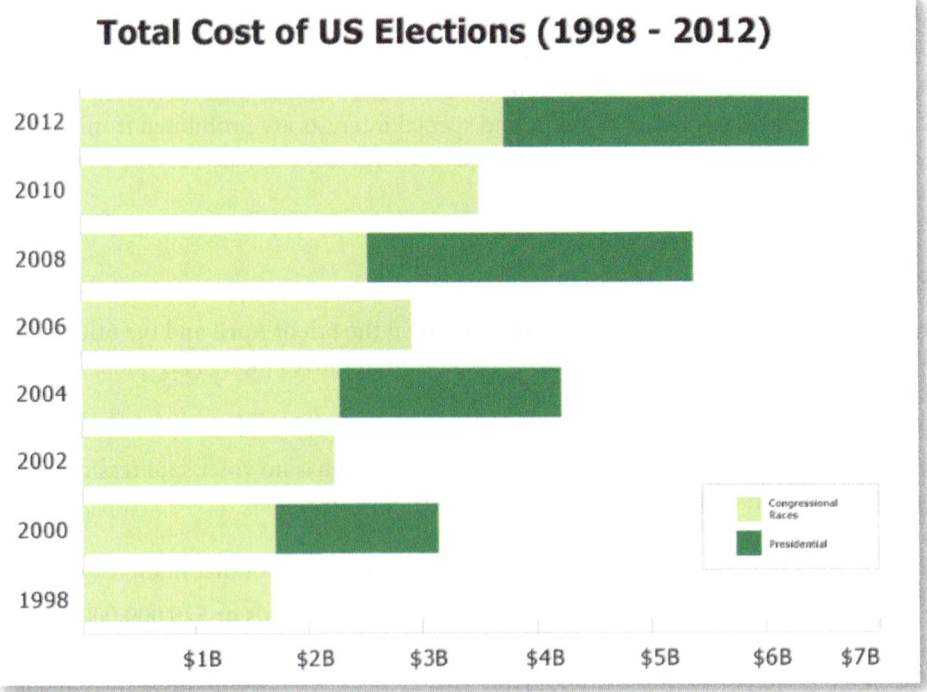

http://www.opensecrets.org/bigpicture/

It is worse than indicated because the USA presidential elections occur every four year (not five, as in the UK), plus the USA has critical congressional elections every two years. Midterm congressional elections cost more than 50% of the presidential cycle. So actually it is fairer to say that U.S. elections cost almost $10b, when they should only cost about $100m (that is, if you wanted a relatively uncorrupt system—or congressmen actually looking after their constituents).

$$$$ The Source of Corruption—however you slice it.

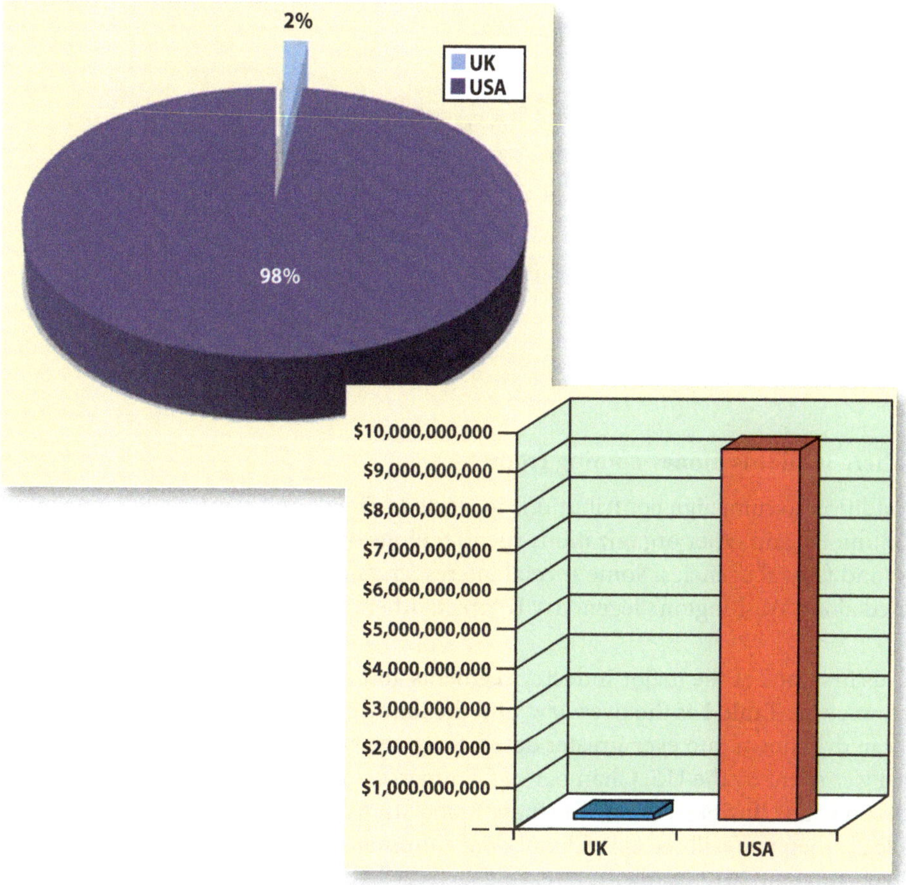

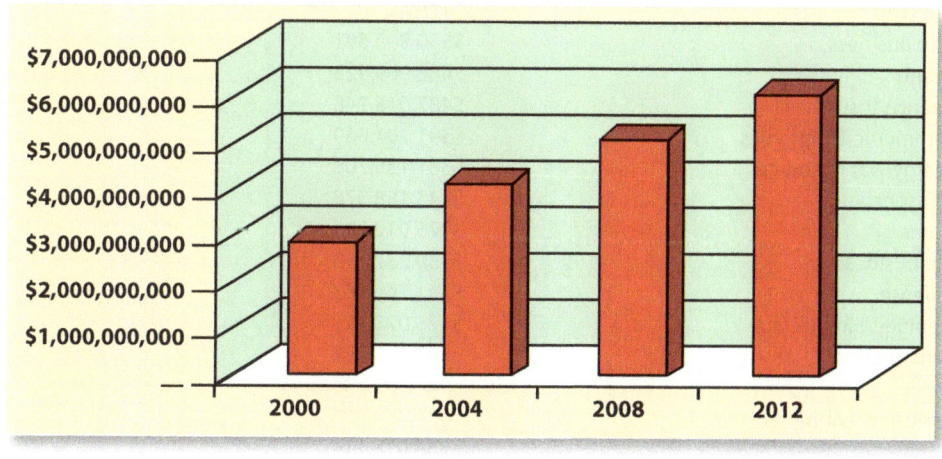

http://www.opensecrets.org/bigpicture/

And every cycle, it just keeps getting worse:

http://www.opensecrets.org/bigpicture/index.php?display=P

"I FEEL PERSECUTED and UNLOVED, YOU WORTHLESS PIECE OF CRAVEN LICKSPITTLE! MAKE IT BETTER WITH ANOTHER TAX BREAK OR WELFARE CUT."

So where is all this money coming from?

"In addition to campaign contributions to elected officials and candidates, companies, labor unions, and other organizations spend billions of dollars each year to lobby Congress and federal agencies. Some special interests retain lobbying firms, many of them located along Washington's legendary K Street; others have lobbyists working in-house."

http://www.opensecrets.org/lobby/

Let's us first look at the major industry segments and what they spent in the 2012 election cycle. **Table 1** is the overview, and the following three tables show you how you can drill down into ever-greater detail. So to see how much was spent by the U.S. Chamber of Commerce, one clicks on "Misc Business," then "Business Associations" (**table 2**); then you will see U.S. Chamber of Commerce at $136,000,000 for 2012 (**table 3**).

OpenSecrets.org
Center for Responsive Politics

TABLE 1

SECTOR	TOTAL
Misc Business	$550,893,691
Health	$488,969,423
Finance/Insur/RealEst	$487,648,748
Communic/Electronics	$391,201,069
Energy/Nat Resource	$381,135,708
Transportation	$243,188,578
Other	$225,010,186
Agribusiness	$139,232,313
Defense	$131,744,363
Ideology/Single-Issue	$127,073,117
Construction	$47,310,978
Labor	$46,195,734
Lawyers & Lobbyists	$24,414,806
	$3,284,018,714

http://www.opensecrets.org/lobby/top.php?showYear=2012&indexType=c

TABLE 2

INDUSTRY	TOTAL SPENDING
Business Associations	$173,243,690
Misc Manufacturing & Distributing	$110,283,326
Chemical & Related Manufacturing	$55,985,809
Retail Sales	$49,140,490
Business Services	$41,354,406
Casinos/Gambling	$34,012,668
Food & Beverage	$27,216,795
Beer, Wine & Liquor	$19,583,899
Lodging/Tourism	$9,077,575
Recreation/Live Entertainment	$8,113,689
Steel Production	$8,017,782
Misc Business	$6,985,717
Misc Services	$5,881,835
Textiles	$1,996,010
	$550,893,691

http://www.opensecrets.org/lobby/indus.php?id=N&year=2012

TABLE 3

CLIENT/PARENT	TOTAL
US Chamber of Commerce	$136,290,000
Business Roundtable	$13,890,000
Emergency Cmte for American Trade	$1,249,850
Employee-Owned S Corporations	$1,210,000
Organization for Intl Investment	$1,060,000
National Fedn of Independent Bus	$873,300
Natl Ass of Indstril & Office Prprt	$861,943
National Assn for Self-Employed	$827,94

http://www.opensecrets.org/lobby/indusclient.php?id=N00&year=2012

TABLE 4

INDUSTRY	TOTAL SPENDING
Insurance	$150,495,803
Securities & Investment	$99,849,633
Real Estate	$81,991,606
Commercial Banks	$61,599,445
Finance/Credit Companies	$36,390,053
Misc Finance	$31,653,605
Accountants	$15,180,000
Credit Unions	$9,802,353
Savings & Loans	$686,250
	$487,648,748

http://www.opensecrets.org/lobby/indus.php?id=F&year=2012

KEY SPECIAL INTERESTS:

Year	Total Contributions	Contributions from Individuals	Contributions from PACs	Soft/Outside Money	Donations to Democrats	Donations to Republicans	% to Dems	% to Repubs	
2012	$91,934,652	$54,824,492	$27,237,750	$9,872,410	$20,788,008	$60,811,987	25%	75%	Agri Business
2012	$124,333,923	$73,258,860	$15,920,789	$35,154,274	$25,354,177	$63,643,954	28%	72%	Construction
2012	$27,595,579	$9,445,930	$18,009,358	$140,291	$10,917,392	$16,447,547	40%	60%	Defense
2012	$141,554,322	$75,450,205	$37,999,372	$28,104,745	$22,507,542	$90,938,504	20%	80%	Energy&Resources
2012	$664,096,646	$431,147,056	$80,845,423	$152,104,167	$164,902,762	$346,260,080	32%	68%	Finance Ins Real Estate
2012	$262,664,098	$136,390,558	$65,104,009	$61,169,531	$89,188,023	$111,932,211	44%	56%	Health
2012	$465,190,112	$264,199,632	$45,796,576	$155,193,904	$124,578,166	$185,076,326	40%	60%	Misc business
2012	$77,876,586	$44,240,177	$26,549,802	$7,086,607	$16,886,150	$53,718,590	24%	76%	Transportation
2012	$209,615,262	$174,279,432	$16,877,711	$18,458,119	$134,597,283	$56,135,779	71%	29%	Lawyers law Firms
2012	$142,974,200	$1,304,730	$66,039,970	$75,629,500	$61,111,593	$6,114,347	91%	9%	Labor

SHOWING SUPER PAC RAISING > $3.5M

	Group	Independent Expenditures	Viewpoint	Total Raised
1	Restore Our Future	$142,097,336	Conservative	$153,741,731
2	American Crossroads	$104,746,670	Conservative	$117,472,407
3	Priorities USA Action	$65,166,859	Liberal	$79,050,419
4	Majority PAC	$37,498,257	Liberal	$42,121,541
5	House Majority PAC	$30,470,122	Liberal	$35,844,951
6	Freedomworks for America	$19,636,548	Conservative	$23,453,198
7	Winning Our Future	$17,007,762	Conservative	$23,921,705
8	Club for Growth Action	$16,584,207	Conservative	$18,253,913
9	Ending Spending Action Fund	$13,250,766	Conservative	$14,169,830
10	Congressional Leadership Fund	$9,450,223	Conservative	$11,286,590
11	Independence USA PAC	$8,230,454	Liberal	$10,004,235
12	http://www.opensecrets.org/pacs/indexpend.php?strID=C00513432&cycle=2012	$7,760,174	Conservative	$8,250,500
13	Women Vote!	$7,749,991	Liberal	$9,834,165
14	AFL-CIO Workers' Voices PAC	$6,331,541	Liberal	$21,855,151
15	Texas Conservatives Fund	$5,872,431	Conservative	$6,364,054
16	Service Employees International Union	$5,310,732	Liberal	$16,264,036
17	Planned Parenthood Votes	$5,039,082	Liberal	$6,446,014
18	Independence Virginia PAC	$4,921,410	Conservative	$5,173,500
19	YG Action Fund	$4,722,335	Conservative	$5,948,567
20	Make Us Great Again	$3,959,824	Conservative	$5,607,881
21	Endorse Liberty	$3,580,138	Conservative	$3,937,582

http://www.opensecrets.org/pacs/superpacs.php?cycle=2012$619,001,970

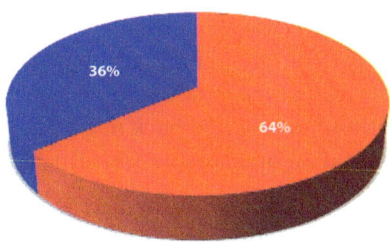

The vast bulk of this $10b does not come from the regular American. I would estimate that at least 85% of the $10b comes from wealthy Americans* or corporations. Obama raised about $233m from small donors ($200 or less), compared to Romney's $80m.

So the "people" are trying about 300% harder to be heard. But those numbers remain a drop in the bucket. And while the Blue team does get a portion (money likes to influence those in power), these funds are largely seeking conservative stances. The main exceptions being unions seeking to keep workers on a living wage, Hollywood concerned about humanity, and lawyers concerned abort too much tort reform.

*Wealthy Americans do not vote as a block; they merely lean Stupidparty. Occupy Wall Street's catchy 1% has a point in its effectiveness and simplicity. But in the real world, it is a bit more difficult to define wealth, and many wealthy people really do care about facts and the planet and have empathy for those who struggle. And yes, these individuals might well be voting against their own short-term economic interests by being prepared to accept equitable tax reform.

"Corporations are people too, my friend"

The interests of corporations are very different. People are looking for a comfortable living, while corporations must exact every ounce of effort they can. If slavery were legal, they would have slaves. If whipping slackers was legal, they would whip. If they could obtain a monopoly and charge usurious prices, they would do it. Capitalism, as opposed to unfettered capitalism, is designed to find an equitable balance.

So how does all this money Impact Congress?
Congressmen—Money, Money, Money........................

According to *The New York Times,* the committee that congressmen most covet is the one on financial services. This 61-seat committee has become so populated that extra nestled seats have had to be requisitioned to accommodate all those eager backsides drawn like magpies to the "30 pieces of silver"; well, actually that would not cut it, as it is more like $10,000,000 a year provided by the special interests, those titans of finance like Bank of America, Goldman Sachs and Co.—yes, those same special interests who are overseen by The Committee on Financial Services.

This would be like Exxon sponsoring a documentary on Global Warming (which I guess would be frowned on—since I can find no evidence of it). But it would be far worse, so perhaps it would be like the rules overseeing the conduct of priests being written by NAMBLA (yes gross, but we are discussing a gross subject). However, luckily, we, being of the twenty-first century, are a long way from that. So perhaps a better analogy would be that this would be like the tax policy of the USA being written by the Benefactors. Oh dear, what have I said? Do you see a can of worms? But we must temporarily set that thought aside and have our attention snapped back into re stiffened attention by absorbing a couple of examples reported on by *The New York Times*:

"Committee members don't seem particularly ashamed of the favors they do for those providing the cash. Andy Barr, a freshman [Stupidparty] from Kentucky, promised to protect a tax break worth $500 million to credit unions. (They gave him $15,000.) And he introduced a bill that would allow banks to give mortgages to people who cannot afford them, undoing a federal rule at the request of the big banks' lobbyists. (Banks have given him at least $47,000.)"

http://www.nytimes.com/2013/08/18/opinion/sunday/the-cash-committee.html?_r=0

From here on in, it is worth trying to ballpark what $15,000 might buy you.

Now we will compare a typical foreign politician with a U.S. congressman.

Day in the Life of a British MP: A British MP spends time meeting constituents. To understand how it works and British colloquiums, visiting one's MP is a bit like visiting the family doctor. You call or maybe just show up, and then one might sit in a waiting room until it's your turn; hence the phrase "surgery" below. Now better understanding his constituents, off to Westminster he goes. He then has direct access to the prime minister via the Prime Minister Questions sessions that take place every Wednesday.

Working in Parliament: When Parliament is sitting (meeting): "MPs generally spend their time working in the House of Commons. This can include raising issues affecting their constituents, attending debates and voting on new laws. Most MPs are also members of committees, which look at issues in detail, from government policy and new laws, to wider topics like human rights."

Working in their constituency: "In their constituency, MPs often hold a 'surgery' in their office, where local people can come along to discuss any matters that concern them. MPs also attend functions, visit schools and businesses, and generally try to meet as many people as possible. This gives MPs further insight and context into issues they may discuss when they return to Westminster."

http://www.parliament.uk/about/mps-and-lords/members/mps/

Or a less dry description: The BBC spends a day with a Member of Parliament.

His Wednesday starts at 9 a.m. with a two-hour-long Work and Pensions select committee.

He goes straight from there to Prime Minister's Questions and the big topic of debate is the government's decision to allow universities to charge tuition fees of up to £9,000. It's a difficult issue for the coalition as the Liberal Democrats pledged to vote against increasing tuition fees. He stays on in the chamber for a debate on the Bloody Sunday report.

After that he has a meeting with a local businessman about setting up an apprenticeship scheme in Eastbourne. That's followed by another meeting—this time with representatives from the charity Gingerbread.

He then meets up with his assistant Jack to look at what's coming up before catching up on some paperwork and his last meeting of the day—a meeting with fellow Liberal Democrats about Work and Pensions. There are no late night votes tonight so Stephen heads back to his constituency where he has another full day lined up. We catch up with Stephen again on Friday in Eastbourne. His first appointment is at a local printers celebrating its 20th anniversary in business. He places an order for his parliamentary Christmas cards.

Then it's onto a local residential care home which is also celebrating an anniversary—50 years providing care.

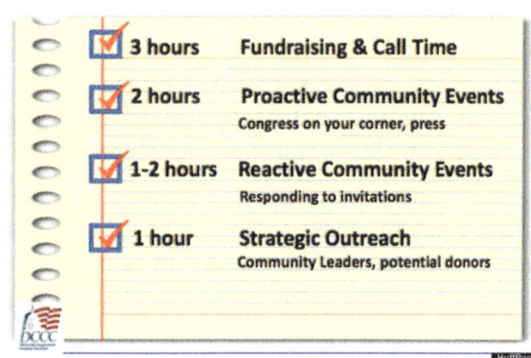

Later it's his weekly Friday surgery where he meets constituents worried about debt, changes to benefits and housing amongst other issues. It's a busy schedule but Stephen seems to particularly relish the chance to meet local residents.

http://www.bbc.co.uk/blogs/louisestewart/2010/11/day_in_the_life_of_new_south_e.html

A Day in the Life of a U.S. Congressman.
Or what happens when money takes over democracy

When Congress is in session (from a Power Point orientation presentation by Democratic Congressional Campaign Committee to incoming freshmen):

4 hours telephoning for money.
1 hour of strategic outreach (including fundraising and press)
1 hour recharge
3 or 4 hours for hearings,* votes, meeting constituents (i.e., donors)
*"Hearings: Congressional hearings and fundraising duties often conflict, and members of Congress have little difficulty deciding between the two—occasionally even raising money from the industry covered by the hearings they skip. It is considered poor form in Congress—borderline self-indulgent—for a freshman to sit at length in congressional hearings when the time could instead be spent raising money. Even members in safe districts are expected to keep up the torrid fundraising pace, so that they can contribute to vulnerable colleagues."

So basically it is all about fundraising. This might explain why congressmen often appear to end up talking so much nonsense.

As *The Huffington Post* reports: "One member of Congress said, 'The fundraising takes up so much time that members don't even have time to become experts on bills they sponsor. One thing that's always been striking to me is even the members playing a

MODEL DAILY SCHEDULE - DISTRICT

✓	3 hours	**Fundraising & Call Time**
✓	2 hours	**Proactive Community Events** Congress on your corner, press
✓	1-2 hours	**Reactive Community Events** Responding to invitations
✓	1 hour	**Strategic Outreach** Community Leaders, potential donors

*http://www.huffingtonpost.com/2013/01/08/call-time-congressional-fundraising_n_2427291.html

leading role on specific issues actually could not talk about the issues,' said the member, who didn't want to be quoted by name …

"Former Rep. Tom Perriello (D-VA), now a top official at the Center for American Progress, said that the four hours allocated to fundraising may even be 'low-balling the figure so as not to scare the new Members too much.'"

When back at home—the priorities are pretty much the same.

People Power.

The American people intuitively at least fully understand the insidious forces that they up against and they are trying as best they can:

In 2012 the Obama campaign raised \$733,000,000, compared to Romney at \$479,000,000.

A record 4,200,000 people contributed to Obama's presidential campaign. The Romney campaign does not appear to be anxious to reveal such info, but by looking at graphs provided by *The Washington Post,* we can guess that the number was about 1,500,000.
Data from: http://www.washingtonpost.com/wp-srv/special/politics/campaign-finance/

In spite of this massive 280% difference in people-powered support, Romney was only outraised by 50%. This is because 55% of Obama's donations came in amounts of less than \$200, compared to 22% for Romney.
Data from: http://www.nytimes.com/2012/10/26/us/politics/obama-and-romney-raise-1-billion-each.html

But however hard the people work to do the right thing, they are up against massive financial resources devoted to aiding the few at the expense of the many.

Corporate Power.

As consumers, we may not realize that the utilities we need, the services we desire, the medicines we rely on—most of our expenditures—go to companies that must maximize profits (which of course is totally legitimate), and the ways they find to do so have the potential to be against the public interest. Companies are not good or evil; they must squeeze every angle or die. Survival of the fittest.

The government, however, must act to protect the public interest and therefore find ways to equitably control activities that threaten that interest. We all know this, even Stupidparty Disciples, unless they are of the adolescent Ayn Rand variety.

Companies are regulated for a multitude of overwhelmingly important reasons. For capitalism to work, consumers must have faith in the product or service. When you hand over your cash to a bank, you must be comfortable that it's safe. The same regarding safety of everything from water to gas, from meat to vegetables. A capitalist system cannot work without regulations and oversight. The 2008 economic meltdown occurred as a consequence of unfettered capitalism.

Why did the Scorpion sting the Frog it was riding on as it was crossing the river? Because that is its nature. Therefore, companies must try and game the system. If they do not, their competitor will. How best to game the system? Get real close and personal with lawmakers. Money talks, money corrupts, and thus we can begin to see the endgame.

What does this mean? Well, imagine you are a coal miner's wife in the UK and you mention to your member of Parliament that you and your friends have noticed a spike in the number of miners feeling sick; your husband has an unremitting cough and his working days are numbered. Your MP will get right on the case; the prime minister might get quizzed on it next Wednesday during question time.

However, if you live in, say, West Virginia, first, you will never get an audience with your congressman, because he is far too busy raising money and undoubtedly getting hefty contributions from your husband's employer. So what is your poor congressman to do but a) send you back a form letter, b) get you agitated about a socialist in the White House coming to take away your husband's freedoms, and c) deflect by blaming immigrants coming for your job or the poor for being slackers/moochers?

It gets Worse.

But corporate power does not stop there—because corporations have leaders often worth billions, and corporations have shareholders, who as long as the dividends are paid and share prices increase, the last thing they care about or want to hear about is black lung disease.

Sociopaths are misunderstood.

This is the definition of a sociopath:

"A person with an antisocial personality disorder, manifested in aggressive, perverted, criminal, or amoral behavior without empathy or remorse."

You do not need to be a murderer to be sociopath. You can actually be quite likable and/ or capable of appearing very pleasant. We can even root for a sociopath, as many people do in the TV show *Dexter*. Sociopaths can be really useful in a pinch—especially in the Armed Forces.

By psychologist Martha Stout's estimate, in *The Sociopath Next Door*, as many as 12,000,000 people in the USA are sociopaths, or 4% of the population.
("Note: Other mental health experts put the percentage of sociopaths at 1–3% of the population, which is 3–9 million Americans.")

"Because sociopaths are ruthless and will squash their rivals and burn institutions to the ground in order to reach their goals—but are great at pretending that they care about people—they are incredibly destructive. Sociopaths would have been discovered very quickly in a small group. But in huge societies like ours, they can rise to positions of power and influence."
http://www.washingtonsblog.com/2012/08/as-many-as-12-million-americans-are-sociopaths.html

Sociopath and the CEO: Top executives have four times the incidence of sociopaths (10–16%) as the rest of us.

http://www.thestar.com/business/2012/07/05/psychopathy_and_the_ceo_top_executives_have_four_times_the_incidence_of_psychopathy_as_the_rest_of_us.html

I just thought that this would be a good time to mention this aspect of the human condition. I would suspect that one would get many more CEO sociopaths than politician sociopaths—as politicians tend to have yearning to be loved. Having said that, it would appear that perhaps one of the Stupidparty 2012 presidential candidates had all the hallmarks of a sociopath.

So we might well have been close to having a sociopath elected as president and we are surely close to having sociopaths select a president.

Super-Rich people power.

Some people are so wealthy that they are worth more that net worth of whole countries. One American family (the Walmart family) is so wealthy they have the same amount of wealth as 40 million American families combined. Some people are so rich that they believe they can select the leader of the largest supposed democracy in the world. There are many ways such people can try and influence events. One way is through the newly minted Supreme Court Citizens United super PACs. Here are the largest individual donations to super PACs.

2012 Top Donors to Outside Spending Groups:

"These are the top individuals and organizations spending their money to influence your vote. That is, these are the top DISCLOSED donors. Some categories of outside spenders, such as 501(c)(4) groups, are not required to disclose the identities of their contributors.

"In 2012, the top 100 individual donors to super PACs, along with their spouses, represent just 1.0% of all individual donors to super PACs, but 73% of the money they delivered."

Rank	Donor	Organization/Occupation	Total	Viewpoint*
1	Adelson, Sheldon G. & Miriam O. Las Vegas, NV	Las Vegas Sands/Adelson Drug Clinic	$92,796,625	C
2	Simmons, Harold C. & Annette Dallas, TX	Contran Corp	$26,865,000	C
3	Perry, Robert J. Houston, TX	Perry Homes	$23,450,000	C
4	Eychaner, Fred Chicago, IL	Newsweb Corp	$14,050,000	L
5	Bloomberg, Michael R. New York, NY	City of New York, NY	$13,672,973	L
6	Ricketts, John Joe Omaha, NE	Hugo Enterprises	$13,050,000	C
7	Simons, James H. & Marilyn New York, NY	Renaissance Technologies/Simons Fdtn	$9,575,000	L
8	Mercer, Robert L. East Setauket, NY	Renaissance Technologies	$5,409,354	C
9	Thiel, Peter A. San Francisco, CA	Clarium Capital Management	$4,735,000	C
10	Mostyn, J. Steve & Anderson, Amber Houston, TX	Mostyn Law Firm	$4,253,850	L

Rank	Donor	Organization/Occupation	Total	Viewpoint*
11	Childs, John W. Vero Beach, FL	JW Childs Assoc	$4,225,000	C
12	Perenchio, A. Jerrold Los Angeles, CA	Chartwell Partners	$4,100,000	C
13	Rowling, Robert B. Irving, TX	TRT Holdings	$3,635,000	C
14	Goldman, Amy New York, NY	Solil Management	$3,400,000	L
15	McNair, Robert Houston, TX	Houston Texans	$3,175,000	C
16	Ramsey, John Austin, TX	Student	$3,155,933	C
17	Katzenberg, Jeffrey Los Angeles, CA	DreamWorks Animation SKG	$3,150,000	L
18	Ellison, Lawrence Woodside, CA	Oracle Corp	$3,000,000	C
19	Singer, Paul E. New York, NY	Elliott Management	$2,815,316	C
20	Soros, George New York, NY	Soros Fund Management	$2,775,000	L

http://www.opensecrets.org/outsidespending/summ.php?cycle=2012&disp=D&type=V

The total amount for the top 20 is $241,000,000 of which 85% apparently helps the Stupidparty.

George Soros. Stupidparty enemy number 1, Myth # gazillion.

If ever you try and raise the issue of political corruption to Stupidparty Disciples, they seem to have one rebuttal. That the evil George Soros single-handedly creates a balance, thus justifying everything the Stupidparty Benefactors do. George Soros is a currency speculator and has worked tirelessly to further capitalism, especially in Eastern Europe.

So while Soros was most concerned about George Bush's sins against humanity, that illegal war, torture-detention stuff, he pretty much sat out the 2012 election.

And then …

"The news was greeted with a major sigh of relief in Democratic circles: philanthropist George Soros had decided to open his checkbook—to the tune of $2 million—to several liberal outside groups, the leading edge of what is expected to be $100 million in spending by the Democracy Alliance, a group of major Democratic donors."
http://www.washingtonpost.com/blogs/the-fix/post/what-george-soros-donations-tell-us-about-2012/2012/05/08/gIQAbeMfAU_blog.html

Perhaps he gave more in ways that are hard to investigate—just like all the individuals listed above. So call it $4m against $billions. The Stupidparty argument is a myth, but it is also revealing. The thing is that not only is George Soros a hard-core capitalist; he is also somewhat like an Asset Stripper or a hedge fund manager—occupations one might think are very far from humanistic. Perhaps George Soros recognizes the imbalance, because he happens to be one of the world's leading philanthropists.

Between 1979 and 2011, Soros gave away over $8 billion to causes related to human rights, public health, and education. He played a significant role in the peaceful transition from communism to capitalism in Hungary (1984–89) and provided one of

Europe's largest higher-education endowments to Central European University in Budapest. Soros is also the chairman of the Open Society Foundations. (Data from Wiki)

So while Stupidparty Disciples revile him, most of humanity would revere him—since
he has done so much work across the world to
fight poverty and bring capitalism and freedom to countries on the brink. That sounds like
Stupidparty Bush foreign policy—but without
the need to kill everyone. It sounds like charity—
but charity that does not simply involve giving to
one's own club (the Church) but rather to people
who actually need help. It sounds like giving
rather selflessly instead of trying to buy politicians, who will then vote to cut their tax rate or
the minimum wage, so that they can pocket more $billions.

That all is a good setup for—

Sheldon Adelson:

So having dealt with that evil *bête noire* Soros, who sits number 20 on the list of top
givers, we will look at a Stupidparty hero number 1, who contributed twenty-five time
more than Soros during the 2012 election cycle, an insignificant numerical difference if
you are that oxymoron—a Stupidparty mathematician.

"According to two GOP fundraisers with close ties to the Las Vegas billionaire Adelson
ultimately upped the ante and then some, spending closer to a previously unreported
$150 million, the fundraisers said."
http://www.huffingtonpost.com/2012/12/03/sheldon-adelson-2012-election_n_2223589.html

Like Soros, Adelson made his billions engaging in one of the more suspect forms of
capitalism, Adelson tapping into a recreation that many progressives and conservatives
view with concern—gambling. Progressives are concerned by its regressive nature,
exacerbating poverty, while those on the right worry about sinning (a bigger concern, it
seems, than poverty, which I find revealing).

Adelson did not used to be so Stupidparty. What might be the driving factors? His Las
Vegas casino holdings are under investigation by the Justice Department and the Securities and Exchange Commission, focused "on the casino company's operations in Macau,
the world's biggest gambling hub, court documents show. A former executive in Adelson's empire, whose allegations are believed to be central to the probe, cites potential
illegal dealings with a public official, as well as a tie to an organized crime figure."
http://www.reuters.com/article/2012/02/08/us-usa-campaign-adelson-idUSTRE8172DS20120208
http://campaignstops.blogs.nytimes.com/2012/08/06/embracing-sheldon-adelson/

"The legal headaches besetting billionaire Sheldon Adelson's Las Vegas Sands Corp. now
include a grand jury in Los Angeles, part of a federal money-laundering probe of his
Nevada-based casinos."
http://www.huffingtonpost.com/2013/06/05/sheldon-adelson-grand-jury-money-laundering_n_3381628.html

UPDATE: Aug. 2013: "Las Vegas Sands Corp. has reached a deal with federal prosecutors to pay more than
$47.4 million to the U.S. government in order to avoid criminal charges over alleged money laundering
activities."
http://www.reviewjournal.com/business/casinos-gaming/las-vegas-sands-return-474-million-avoid-criminal-charges

Adelson does not simply love money; he also has a passion for Israel. Since he is Jewish, that in itself is no surprise. He owns Israel's largest newspaper. One reason for this circulation triumph may be this newspaper is free. Boys will have their toys.

"In Israel, Mr. Adelson is better known as the force behind the five-year-old free newspaper, *Yisrael Hayom (Israel Today)*, which is seen by some as the Israeli print equivalent of Fox News. Touting Israeli patriotism, it is among the most widely read newspapers in the country and has a reputation for its fiercely loyal coverage of Mr. Netanyahu—and now Stupidparty presidential nominee Mitt Romney."

http://www.csmonitor.com/World/Middle-East/2012/0924/GOP-backer-Adelson-accused-of-commandeering-Israel-s-media-market

Adelson's Free Newspaper Sounds Just Like Fox News:

A study conducted by Moran Rada (Israeli Democracy Institute) showed that while competing newspapers' coverage of Netanyahu was "not especially fair," *Yisrael Hayom's* coverage was biased in favor of Netanyahu in most editorial decisions, that the paper chooses to play down events that don't help to promote a positive image for Netanyahu, while on the other hand, touting and inflating events that help promote Netanyahu and the Likud. Oren Frisco reached the same conclusion after the 2009 Knesset elections, writing that throughout the campaign, *Yisrael Hayom* published only one article critical of the Likud, and tens of articles critical of Kadima.

Data from http://en.wikipedia.org/wiki/Israel_HaYom

Mr. Adelson describes his paper as fair and balanced, which sounds suspiciously like you know who and is "Stupidparty speak" for not fair and not balanced. Well, of course an individual can pretty much believe what he wants. So what were Adelson (and his close friend Israeli Prime Minister Netanyahu) up to during to the 2012 election cycle? Initially, Adelson pretty much single-handedly kept Newt Gingrich's campaign afloat during the primaries.

Politico reports:

"Even as Newt Gingrich's campaign teetered on the edge of collapse in March, the wife of a casino mogul gave a pro-Gingrich super PAC another $5 million. The contribution brought the Adelson family's pro-Gingrich tally to $20 million—a figure Sheldon Adelson himself was floating in December. The Adelson's almost single-handedly funded Winning Our Future's (Gingrich's Super PAC) operations since its inception in December, but in recent days, Adelson has signaled he will put his wealth behind establishment Stupidparty candidates."

http://www.politico.com/news/stories/0412/75418.html#ixzz2d5bosbR5

This became Gingrich's platform on Israel:

• Gingrich thinks that the U.S. is setting up a confrontation with Israel.

• He thinks that Israel is in great danger and by not supporting Israelis, we're setting them up for a nuclear holocaust.

• He thinks that Israel has every right to maintain a blockade of Gaza in defense against Hamas.

• He believes there is no humanitarian crisis in Gaza but merely a political effort to undermine the safety of Israel.

http://2012.republican-candidates.org/Gingrich/Israel.php

After Gingrich implodes, Adelson then needs to be a real player for Romney.

Adelson's Romney-boosting support reportedly "limitless"
By MAGGIE HABERMAN
Via *Forbes*:

> A well-placed source in the Adelson camp with direct knowledge of the casino billionaire's thinking says that further donations will be "limitless."

> Adelson, will do "whatever it takes" to defeat Obama, this source says. And given that Adelson is worth $24.9 billion—and told Forbes in a recent rare interview about his political giving that he had been willing to donate as much as $100 million to his initial presidential preference, Newt Gingrich—that "limitless" description telegraphs potential nine-digit support of Romney.

> Adelson, this source continues, believes that "no price is too high" to protect the U.S. from what he sees as Obama's "socialization" of America, as well as securing the safety of Israel. He added that Adelson, 78, considers this to be the most important election of his lifetime.

http://www.politico.com/blogs/burns-haberman/2012/06/adelsons-romneyboosting-support-reportedly-limitless-126119.html

Romney Policies on Israel.

On his world tour in 2012, of basically insulting everyone, Romney was in Israel, naturally keen to keep the contributions flowing; it is not as if average Americans were rushing to contribute. So coincidentally, Romney would be much tougher on Iran. (Bear in mind that short of war, the international community already has an unusually cohesive and severe approach.) He would recognize Jerusalem as [Israel's] capital. For good measure, he insulted the Palestinians by declaring that cultural differences—not decades under Israeli occupation—are the reason Israelis are more successful economically. It's hard to say how this could affect policy if he were president, but it is not encouraging.

"The real audience for Mr. Romney's tough talk was American Jews and evangelical Christians, some of whom accompanied him on his trip. He is courting votes and making an aggressive pitch to donors, including Sheldon Adelson, the billionaire casino magnate with the hard-line pro-Israel views who is spending more money than any other American—$100 million—to defeat Mr. Obama."

http://www.nytimes.com/2012/07/31/opinion/mitt-romney-stumps-in-israel.html?_r=0

During Romney's infamous 47% moocher country-club talk, he confided that there was no point in seeking a peace process in Israel, since it was just too complicated, i.e., better leave it all up to Netanyahu to run the show.

Netanyahu.

Netanyahu's last bastion of international support really lies with the Stupidparty. People like Clinton and Obama and nearly everyone else on the planet (except Stupidparty) not only have some empathy for the Palestinian people, but also recognize that having America acting as a totally partisan broker in the Middle East is bound to energize terrorist support and other anti-Western activities.

Netanyahu interfered in the U.S. elections by trying to embarrass Obama and make him appear weak on Israel and Iran. This is how the Israeli opposition saw it. From Israel's *Haaretz* newspaper:

"Following U.S. President Barack Obama's victory in the American presidential elections, on Wednesday former Prime Minister Ehud Olmert accused Prime Minister Benjamin Netanyahu of blatantly interfering in favor of Stupidparty nominee Mitt Romney, adding that he did so in the name of Netanyahu and Romney-backer Sheldon Adelson.

"'This represents a significant breach of the basic rules governing ties between nations, made worse by the fact that these are allies like Israel and the United States,' Olmert said during a meeting with the heads of New York's Jewish community."

http://www.haaretz.com/news/u-s-elections-2012/olmert-netanyahu-interfered-in-u-s-elections-for-sheldon-adelson-1.475990

What is so ironic about this odd alliance between Netanyahu and the Stupidparty is that the evangelical wing of the Stupidparty merely sees Israel as the location for the end of times, that event will see the demise of all non-Christians. This odd alliance is more "the enemy of my enemy is my friend," even when such friend will never be invited to dinner.

It looks very much like Adelson would like to appoint the next president of the United States, and there appear to be two key motivating factors. His Jewish heritage is so deeply rooted within him that one has to wonder which country he's most loyal to—evidently, a key concern to all those "birther" Americans. He is clearly capable of massively influencing U.S. foreign policy in the Middle East by effectively buying up the presidency.

Regarding the assertions that Adelson is breaking the law and being investigated by the Department of Justice and the Securities and Exchange Commission—well, it is difficult enough for Obama appointees or any politician to pursue this, knowing that unlimited funds can be thrown to political opponents. As a general rule, the candidate with the most money wins. So if Obama is being massively intimidated, does anybody believe that a Gingrich or Romney appointee, or anyone in the Stupidparty, will have any motivation to enforce the law (assuming pertinent laws have not been gutted as payback for political contributions).

Bear in mind one other huge motivation. Romney never detailed his economic plans, as he knew if he did, not quite so many people would vote for him. But his plan was quite simple, and it was based on the debt argument. Simply put, there would be austerity,—paid for by everyone except the wealthy. The wealthy would carry on getting wealthier as a result of tax cuts for the wealthy. So Adelson's "unlimited" spending was actually a drop in the bucket, compared to amounts he would gain under Romney. From Adelson's point of view (and I believe he has admitted as such), gambling on Romney or any other Stupidparty candidate was a bet he could not possibly say *no* to.

So can we see the difference between Adelson and Soros? Can we see him as the polar opposite—if not, then simply turn back about four pages and start again?

Stupidparty Benefactor resources—it is worse than one can Imagine.

The Koch Bothers and a who's who of Stupidparty

The Koch family of industrialists and businessmen is most notable for its control of Koch Industries, the second largest privately owned company in the United States. The family business was started by Fred C. Koch, who developed a new cracking method for the refinement of heavy Oil into gasoline. David H. Koch and Charles G. Koch are the two brothers still with Koch Industries. Annual revenues for Koch Industries have been estimated to be a hundred billion dollars. (Wiki)

The Koch bothers do not even appear on the above lists. It is clear the Kochs play a massive role in influencing society, yet with little accountability. They are very secretive, which suggests that what they do in public is but the tip of the iceberg, both in terms of their own efforts and working in concert with other super wealthy people acting with similar motivations.

So how do we know that these brothers are Stupidparty? Because they bear all the intellectual prowess of the Stupidparty they have had such a crucial role in creating:

"Obama's a hardcore socialist," Koch told us, "and he's marvelous at pretending to be something other than that, but that is what I believe he truly is, a hardcore socialist. He's scary to me."
http://nymag.com/daily/intelligencer/2011/05/billionaire_conservative_david.html

"We have Saddam Hussein," declared billionaire industrialist Charles Koch, apparently referring to President Barack Obama (being a dictator) as he welcomed hundreds of wealthy guests to the latest of the secret fundraising and strategy seminars he and his brother host twice a year. The 2012 elections, he warned, will be "the mother of all wars."

During his welcoming remarks, Charles Koch warned his guests that the 2012 elections are nothing short of a battle "for the life or death of this country."
http://www.motherjones.com/politics/2011/09/exclusive-audio-koch-brothers-seminar-tapes

As *Mother Jones* reports: At a recent secret get together Charles Koch named 32 individuals and families who had donated more than $1 million over the previous 12 months, yet because of loopholes in federal campaign law, their donations do not exist in the public record.

But even though ever-greater portions of the press are owned by these types of individuals, we still do have a relatively free press, whose role is made much easier by the tools that go with the Internet. So word can get out. The question is, Who is listening?

Forbes has put the Koch brother wealth at $22 billion a piece. There is absolutely no evidence that this imaginary socialism is negatively impacting these guys.

To date, the brothers have spent more than $100 million supporting hard-right political campaigns and institutions. They are key funders of the movement to discredit climate science and sow doubt on the scientific consensus that human activities contribute to global warming.

The Kochs have tried to keep everything about the seminars secret: the content, identities of attendees and speakers—even meeting locations and dates.

The Kochs also bankrolled the fledgling Tea Party by making massive investments in right-wing political advocacy groups such as Americans for Prosperity, as detailed by Jane Mayer in *The New Yorker* last year. More generally, the brothers have dedicated a portion of their vast wealth—and that of their Benefactor circle—to influencing elec-

tions across the nation and swaying public opinion on everything from health care and fracking to labor policy and government spending.
http://www.motherjones.com/politics/2011/09/exclusive-audio-koch-brothers-seminar-tapes

At an Aspen get-together, guests were lavishly wined and dined under the stars as they cherished the mellifluous voice of Stupidparty superbrain and key puppet Glenn Beck, who told tales of life in paradise, where Asset Strippers can proceed at will—pursuing Life, Liberty, and unfettered freedom to take whatever they want … Actually, I have no idea why they would allow him in the gate (they must have a lot of free time) other than to humor him and his followers. But back to Beck's actual speech. As such, *The New York Times* reports:

"'Is America on the Road to Serfdom?' (The title refers to a classic of Austrian economic thought that informs libertarian ideology, popularized by Mr. Beck on his show.) The participants included some of the nation's wealthiest families and biggest names in finance: private equity and hedge fund executives like John Childs, Cliff Asness, Steve Schwarzman and Ken Griffin; Phil Anschutz, the entertainment and media mogul ranked by *Forbes* as the 34th-richest person in the country; Rich DeVos, the co-founder of Amway; Steve Bechtel of the giant construction firm; and Kenneth Langone of Home Depot."
http://www.nytimes.com/2010/10/20/us/politics/20koch.html?pagewanted=2

The brothers have held their twice-yearly seminars since at least 2003, endeavoring to keep almost everything about them a secret—not just the content but also the identities of attendees and speakers, and even the locations and dates. They've succeeded until recently. Last October, a leaked invite for the Kochs' January 2011 seminar was first obtained and published by the *New York Times.** … previous Koch seminars have featured "such notable leaders" as Rush Limbaugh and Glenn Beck, Sens. Jim DeMint (R-S.C.) and Tom Coburn (R-Okla.), and Reps. Paul Ryan (R-Wis.) and Mike Pence (R-Ind.). Supreme Court Justices Antonin Scalia and Clarence Thomas also have attended.

Several GOP governors made it to the Vail seminar in June, among them Florida's Rick Scott, Virginia's Robert McDonnell, and White House hopeful Rick Perry of Texas. News of the event slipped out after McDonnell put the trip on his weekend schedule; neither Perry nor Scott initially disclosed the trip to their constituents. A Perry spokesman acknowledged his attendance only after the Austin American-Statesman tracked the tail number of a plane belonging to one of the governor's top donors from Texas to Colorado. He described the summit as a "private gathering of business leaders."
http://www.motherjones.com/politics/2011/09/exclusive-audio-koch-brothers-seminar-tapes

The Koch Brothers—it gets worse and worse

All the horrifying numbers provided to date just scratch the surface. The more one digs, the deeper the hole gets. The Koch

bothers go to enormous lengths to hide the extent of their activities. But surely when you hear the words "freedom" or "America" or other Orwellian notions used in context of subversive secret groups—surely, the hair on your back must bristle.

Freedom Partners (pass the sick bag)
As *Politico* reports:

"An Arlington, Va.-based conservative group, whose existence until now was unknown to almost everyone in politics, raised and spent $250 million in 2012 to shape political and policy debate nationwide.

"The group, Freedom Partners, and its president, Marc Short, serve as an outlet for the ideas and funds of the mysterious Koch brothers, cutting checks as large as $63 million to groups promoting conservative causes, according to an IRS document to be filed shortly."

Freedom Partners is a 501(c)(6) business partnership. Such groups are not meant to be political—so what do they do? They assert that providing grants to other organizations—even if those groups spend some of their resources on political ads—is not political activity. So they do the following: They give the money away: $115 million—went to the Center to Protect Patient Rights (CPPR), a group that has no activities of its own other than giving grants to other politically active tax-exempt organizations. That's more than CPPR's budget in all the years combined since it was established in 2009. It's run by Sean Noble, a political consultant and Koch operative.*

CPPR has given grants to some of the same groups that—according to *Politico*—Freedom Partners gave funds to last year, such as the conservative seniors' group 60 Plus Association, which also has Koch connections. CPPR gave 60 Plus $14 million over three years

And 60 Plus—which has also received donations from the American Petroleum Institute, the Karl Rove-affiliated Crossroads GPS, and another Koch-connected group that does nothing but give out grants (TC4 Trust)—reported spending more than $4.6 million in the 2012 federal elections, much of it to support GOP presidential nominee Mitt Romney.

http://www.politico.com/story/2013/09/behind-the-curtain-exclusive-the-koch-brothers-secret-bank-96669.html

*Koch operative or not, he has been cited as a key Koch strategist

Update: "Now, however, according to three GOP operatives, Noble appears to have fallen out of favor with many in the Koch world. Even as he continues to leverage his 'dark money' ties with his private consulting business, Noble's center has become entangled in an ongoing California probe that a state election regulator has called the largest case of 'campaign money laundering' in California history."

http://www.huffingtonpost.com/2013/10/02/sean-noble-koch-brothers_n_4017578.html:

Getting too complicated? Maybe this will help.

Karl Rove American Crossroads—   -Raises $300. This was well known
Koch and cocktail chums—   -Raise $256m. This was not known

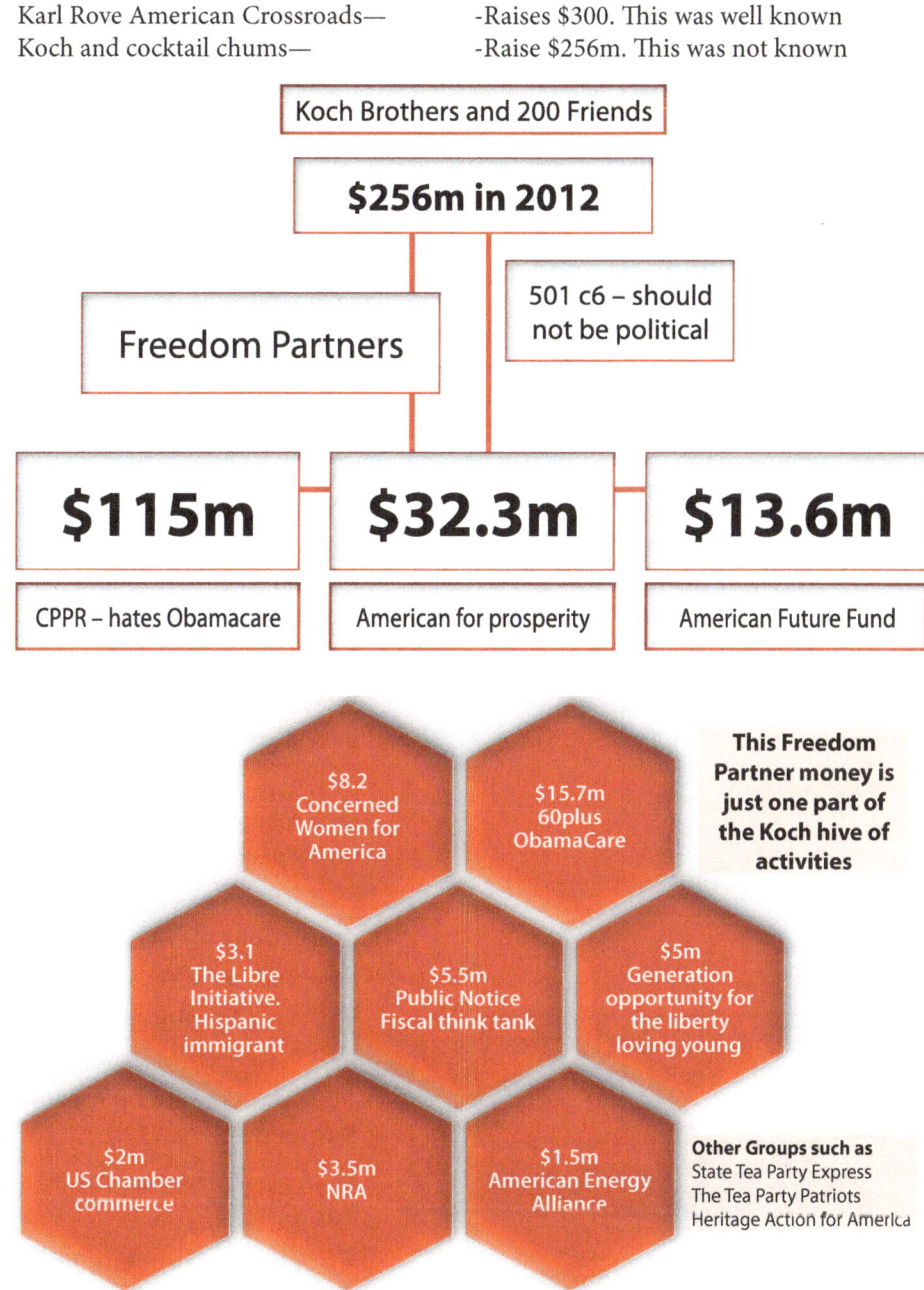

But there's much more Koch influence peddling than shown in the numbers so far:

Citizens for a Sound Economy was co-founded by David Koch in the 1980s. According to the Center for Public Integrity, the Koch Brothers donated a total amount of $7.9 million between 1986 and 1993.

Citizens for the Environment

Citizens for a Sound Economy becomes …

Americans for Prosperity (AFP). Creates …

Patients United Now fighting healthcare

FreedomWorks and Americans for Prosperity support for the

Tea Party movement

Cato Institute, libertarian Think tank—initial funding

Federalist Society—they are key donors

Institute for Energy Research

Institute for Justice

Foundation for Research on Economics and the Environment

Heritage Foundation

Reason Foundation

American Enterprise Institute

Heartland Institute

Yes, these Guys

The Charles Koch Foundation: provides grants to nearly 250 U.S. colleges and universities for "projects that explore how the principles of free enterprise and classical liberalism promote a more peaceful and prosperous society." A euphemism for

---

ORWELLIAN DICTIONARY

Citizens = middle class lackeys.

Prosperity = for us, less than minimum wage for you.

Freedom = Economic Slavery.

Peaceful = War & Guns

Tea Party = extra-silly branch of Stupidparty.

Research = Paying off 2nd-rate researchers to come up with non-peer tested papers.

Patients' Rights = No Insurance, emergency- room coverage only, and Assets Stripped.

Heritage = take us back to 1760

Reason = removal of facts and Science.

American = ignore any area where America underperforms.

Protect = remove all protections for middle class. (Struggling class)

Patriots = Immigrants, go home

Environment = to be Asset Stripped

Enterprise = No regs for Business.

Justice = for Corporations at expense of struggling- class lackeys.

Institute = Room and Board funded by Palm Beach Society of entitled moochers. (Benefactors)

interfering with the educational process and leaning on/bribing colleges to hire professors that they would not otherwise hire.
http://en.wikipedia.org/wiki/Political_activities_of_the_Koch_brothers

We will now look at just one of these many insidious organizations:

The Heritage Foundation: American conservative think tank based in Washington, DC. Heritage's stated mission is to "formulate and promote conservative public policies based on the principles of free enterprise, limited government, individual freedom, traditional American values, and a strong national defense." Considered to be one of the most influential conservative research organizations in the United States. (Wiki)

A Former Member/now columnist for *Salon*, Michael Lind, reports: "One of my next assignments was to write a policy paper justifying a forthcoming bill from the late Sen. Jesse Helms, a belligerent reactionary from North Carolina. When I met with the senator's staff, I was told to wait because Helms wasn't sure what he was going to put in the bill. After I failed to turn in the policy brief on time, I received an official reprimand from my supervisor, which I treasured until I lost it during a move. The reprimand said, in effect, that at Heritage we write policy papers first and add the facts later."

Rationalizing and promoting the thinking behind the 47% Moocher concept.
Lind explains: "The Heritage Foundation has published an 'Index of Dependence on Government' by William W. Beach and Patrick Tyrrell which seeks to bolster Mitt Romney's theme that at least 47 percent of Americans are parasitic, government-dependent 'takers' rather than 'makers' (hat tip to Thomas B. Edsall):

> Today, more people than ever before depend on the federal government for housing, food, income, student aid, or other assistance once considered to be the responsibility of individuals, families, neighborhoods, churches, and other civil society institutions. **The United States reached another milestone in 2010: For the first time in history, half the population pays no federal income taxes.** It is the conjunction of these two trends—higher spending on dependence-creating programs, and an ever-shrinking number of taxpayers who pay for these programs—that concerns those interested in the fate of the American form of government [bold emphasis mine].

"This is not just wrong. It is an error embarrassing enough to shame even a shameless propaganda mill like the Heritage Foundation. Heritage implies that a majority of Americans paid federal income taxes throughout American history, presumably back to the 1790s. Nothing could be further from the truth. For much of American history, one hundred percent of the population paid no federal income taxes, because there were none. And the federal income tax began to fall on the middle-class masses, not just the upper classes, only in the 1940s."
http://www.alternet.org/what-i-learned-conservative-think-tank-propaganda-now-facts-later

It is now all about Headlines and Fund raising—thus, it is simply a partisan attack machine.

They used to be fine with Obamacare, Here we can see Heritage scholar Robert Moffitt on the left among those present while Gov. Romney signed the Massachusetts universal healthcare law in 2006.

"Heritage has also notably flipped on immigration policy in recent years—from a long history of supporting higher immigration levels and legalization of immigrants, to the current posture of hostility."

Authored by Heritage scholar Robert Rector, the report argued that passing immigration reform would cost American taxpayers more than $6 trillion. An updated version of a similar Rector study released in 2006, the paper was widely blasted for its shoddy scholarship.
Heritage "made unwanted headlines in May, when one of the authors of a contentious immigration report, Jason Richwine, was found to have previously written a Harvard dissertation arguing that immigrants have lower IQs than white Americans, and that immigration policy should be based on the disparity. Richwine was fired; Heritage condemned the dissertation but stood by the report he'd coauthored. But that was problematic, too."

http://www.theatlantic.com/politics/archive/2013/09/the-fall-of-the-heritage-foundation-and-the-death-of-republican-ideas/279955/

But the vast majority of Americans Understand.

As reported by *Public Citizen:* Nearly 9 in 10 Americans agree that there is way too much corporate money in politics, and 51 percent strongly agree, according to a new poll released today by the Corporate Reform Coalition. The survey, conducted by Bannon Communications, found overwhelming support for strong, common sense reforms to ensure transparency and accountability for corporate political spending.

• 81 percent of Americans agree that companies should only spend money on political campaigns if they disclose their spending immediately; 80 percent agree that companies should only spend money on political campaigns if they get prior shareholder approval.

• Huge majorities of Americans across the political spectrum condemn corporate political spending and support strong reforms. For example, requiring corporations to get shareholder approval before spending money on politics is supported by 73% of both Republicans and Democrats, and 71% of Independents.

• 84 percent of Americans agree that corporate political spending drowns out the voices of average Americans, and 83 percent believe that corporations and corporate CEOs have too much political power and influence.

More than 8 in 10 Americans (81%) believe that the secret flow of campaign spending is bad for democracy, and 87 percent agree that prompt disclosure of political spending would help voters, customers and shareholders hold companies accountable for political behavior. Unfortunately the sources of corporate funds directed through third party intermediaries like the U.S. Chamber of Commerce remain largely hidden.

http://www.citizen.org/pressroom/pressroomredirect.cfm?ID=3748

Palm Beach, Florida: Best or Worst place in the USA?
Just call it Palm (not much of a beach)

So the American people overwhelming have a problem with what is going on. They try mightily to fight back with $10–$200 contributions. 280% more people gave to Obama than to Romney. Yet such Americans are up against overwhelming financial fire power from people who gather in locations that are designed to refuse entry to their Stupidparty Disciples, the very people that they are looking to disenfranchise, to Asset Strip. Whether this be the exclusive country clubs, the gated communities, the yachts, or private Jets, only landscapers, caddies, butlers, valets, chauffeurs, waiters and doorman need apply—and be grateful for a "good morning" or a kindly dispensed tip. Spa staff had better rub them the right way.

"Many of Palm Beach's residents are affluent. The town's affluence and its 'abundance of pleasures' and 'strong community-oriented sensibility' were cited when it was selected in June 2003 as America's 'Best Place to Live'" by *Robb Report* magazine.
http://www.announcemynews.com/announcement.php/?id=18755728

No place symbolizes entitled and insulated wealth better than Palm Beach—the heart of the Stupidparty powerbase. Ironically, nowhere could be more removed from Stupidparty heartlands.

"The island of Palm Beach is about as far from the gun club and the Tea Party as you can get," quipped Mark Alan Siegel, chairman of the Palm Beach Democratic Party. The county of Palm Beach, with more than 1.3 million residents, is actually heavily Democratic. But the town of Palm Beach, which sits on a barrier island east of the Intracoastal Waterway and has a year-round population of just 10,000 people, votes heavily Stupidparty.
http://www.nytimes.com/2011/08/22/business/media/palm-beach-draws-conservative-media-personalities.html?pagewanted=all

And then in 1996 Rush Limbaugh bought property there. After that Palm Beach and South Florida have become a magnet for conservative business leaders, both disgraced and otherwise; media personalities have all moved in over the years.

This beach is far too good looking and fun to be the beach at Palm

Rush Limbaugh	Stupidparty spokesman
Ann Coulter	Stupidparty spokeswoman
Lou Dobbs	Stupidparty spokesman
Neil Cavuto	Stupidparty spokesman
Matt Drudge	Stupidparty spokesman
Dick Morris	Stupidparty spokesman
Donald Trump	Stupidparty spokesman
Ivana Trump	
Rudy Giuliani	goes all Stupidparty on leaving NY
Conrad Black	convicted rightist media mogul
Don Black	White Supremacist
Tiger Woods	wanted Ari Fleischer as PR guy
Bernie Madoff	Ponzi scheme
Jeff Pillower	Madoff accomplice

Richard Fuld	Lehman Brothers
Jeff Epstein	Wall Street investor.
Jeff Atwater	GOP CFO,
Gaston E Cantens	convicted of running a Ponzi scheme.
Al Hague	would-be president
Bill Koch	drilling, mining; charged with domestic assault
Henry Kravis	barbarian at the gate; inspiration for Gordon Gekko?
Newsmax	a website and magazine popular with SP Disciples

Plus some more Billionaires:

Dick Ziff	publishing	$4.3b
Malcom Glazer	offshore gas	$3.6b
Isaac Perlmutter	Marvel	$2.3b
Wilbur Ross	various	$2.3b
Jeff Greene	real estate	$2.2b
George Lindeman	Southern Union (natural gas)	$2.2b
William Wrigley	Wrigley's	$2.2b
Kenneth Langome	Home Depot	$2.0b
Daniel Abraham	Slim-Fast	$1.8b
John Henry	hedge fund	$1.5b
Christopher Cline	coal mining	$1.2b

http://ftlauderdale.about.com/od/FtLauderdalePeopleInterviews/a/15-Wealthiest-People-In-Broward-And-Palm-Beach-Counties.htm

Palm Beach Donors to Presidential campaigns

If you go to OpenSecrets.org you can find out who donated to whom by zip code. So it is interesting to figure out just how Stupidparty Palm Beach is. Here are the individual donors, listed by size of individual donation. Even though this is public information, I have redacted info, out of respect for privacy. I find this list fascinating because..........

Something that is close to mathematically impossible happens: the first 55 are all Stupidparty. If Palm (Beach) were a balanced place, the odds of the below occurring would be 0.00000000000000555% or 20 trillion to one (by my math).

Candidate	Contributor	Employer	Date	Amount
Romney, Mitt	UMBACH PALM BEACH,FL 33480	INVESTOR	10/29/2012	$10,000
Pawlenty, Tim	ALLEN, MR PALM BEACH,FL 33480	RETIRED	6/14/2011	$5,000
Romney, Mitt	BURNS, PALM BEACH,FL 33480	PALM BEACH MORT	8/20/2012	$5,000
Romney, Mitt	CLARK, MR PALM BEACH,FL 33480		1/19/2012	$5,000
Gingrich, Newt	DEGU MR PALM BEACH,FL 33480	PRIVATE	1/31/2012	$5,000
Romney, Mitt	GAL MR PALM BEACH,FL 33480	MANAGEMENT	1/19/2012	$5,000
Romney, Mitt	HAM MR PALM BEACH,FL 33480	RETIRED	1/19/2012	$5,000
Romney, Mitt	HAME PALM BEACH,FL 33480	RETIRED	6/21/2012	$5,000

Candidate	Contributor	Employer	Date	Amount
Gingrich, Newt	HAN MRS PALM BEACH,FL 33480	RETIRED	1/31/2012	$5,000
Gingrich, Newt	HANE MR PALM BEACH,FL 33480	RETIRED	6/21/2011	$5,000
Gingrich, Newt	HEN MR PALM BEACH,FL 33480	INVESTMENT	3/22/2011	$5,000
Romney, Mitt	LEVI MR PALM BEACH,FL 33480	GOLD COAST	5/8/2012	$5,000
Romney, Mitt	MAT MR PALM BEACH,FL 33480	REAL ESTATE	12/2/2011	$5,000
Romney, Mitt	MEN MR PALM BEACH,FL 33480	RETIRED	1/18/2012	$5,000
Romney, Mitt	PLA MS PALM BEACH,FL 33480		1/18/2012	$5,000
Romney, Mitt	STO MR PALM BEACH,FL 33480		12/31/2011	$5,000
Romney, Mitt	COCH MS PALM BEACH,FL 33480		1/19/2012	$4,000
Romney, Mitt	GRU MR PALM BEACH,FL 33480	INVESTMENTS	11/1/2011	$3,500
Gingrich, Newt	FULL PALM BEACH,FL 33480	INVESTOR	1/20/2012	$3,000
Romney, Mitt	ABELL PALM BEACH,FL 33480	RETIRED	7/28/2011	$2,500
Romney, Mitt	ACK MR PALM BEACH,FL 33480	ASSOCIATES	10/8/2012	$2,500

It would appear that Palm Beach is impossibly Stupidparty.

http://www.opensecrets.org/pres12../search.php?zip=33480&amt=a&sort=A

First contributor for Obama kicks in at number 56.

We Care   **An Invitation to Palm Beach**
Please join us.   We work tirelessly for you

Let's talk about the needs of the Middle Class
You are all invited to our next Palm Beach Cocktail Party

Just drive up to the gate, honk your horn and wait for the gate to open.
$250,000 entrance if you are happy to join our friend Group.

Would you think $5,000 is enough for the purpose of securing a congressional vote on a discrete issue? Remember that $15,000 to "facilitate" a vote to allow banks to sell mortgages to people who cannot afford them? $100,000 for a Congressional Soul? $5m can get you Newt Gingrich in your back pocket? or $100m can get you a Romney? These guys are within a hair's breadth of controlling everything. Everyone has a price; politics as a profession is a magnet for unscrupulous behavior. I believe one might not have to wait for Black Friday to get a bargain. Every day is Black Friday.

Adelson would like to nuke Iran right now; these Iranian peace talks are driving him nuts. Gingrich and Romney have already shown how eager they were to please and appease Adelson. Now, I am not saying that they would be so infantile as to actually utilize nukes as the go-to foreign policy strategy, but they would be far more likely to Bomb, Bomb, Bomb Iran—and everyone in the Middle East would know that, and terrorism would flourish as a consequence. End of times Stupidparty-style.
http://swampland.time.com/2013/10/23/sheldon-adelson-nuke-iran/

Imagine being at a cocktail party in Palm Beach: Are these individuals giving any thought to income discrepancy, Global Warming, the minimum wage, the lives of the very people whom they con into believing that they actually give a damn about them—the Disciples? Yes, they fund the Tea Party, and Fox promotes the Tea Party. But they would not be seen dead rubbing shoulders with the Tea Party protestors they created: their expendable infantry in their battle to secure total domination of the process.

These entitled, pampered spoilt brats, these narcissists living off their inheritances or Assets Stripped from animal, vegetable, or mineral—they glibly advise and promote policies to nuke, to wage war, to pollute, to rip off consumers, whilst all the time also endangering those same consumers. They want to give less to employees by gutting the minimum wage, unions, worker safety, pension protections, and discrimination laws and sponsoring predatory loans. And by the way, they also pay too much in taxes, often forgetting that they already have enough loopholes to get their tax down to as low as zero anyway.

The people, the planet—we are all just fodder for their insatiable appetites. We have assets that they want to strip.

If these guys were smart (and I do not believe they are half as smart as they think, nuking Iran? Sheldon, really—the credit belongs to their accountants or CFOs), they would ask themselves how many yachts, private jets, and Lamborghinis and trophy wives does Palm Beach need? Figure that out and design an app for that—so all these toys could be available when they need them; auction off the rest and actually do some good with those redundant trophy assets. But please cut out the vanity projects; do not simply build another wing on the Lincoln Center—so that each visitor whose tickets seem remarkably far from subsidized in the first place (no Tea Party people here, please) has to worship before the altar of your false idol astride the front door.

With the raw financial and media power exhibited in just one rather small location, one can see the forces at play that will make reform a herculean activity. These individuals have the power to select the politicians and the presidency itself. They are used to getting their way. It is a brave person who will ensure they abide by the law, let alone suggest they pay reasonable taxes. Why would these people give up their power? The game is rigged in their favor, like owning a casino, the bank, and rigged roulette wheels, and the regulators all at the same time. The vast majority of politicians desperately either need a piece of their benevolence or at least must try to discourage them from supporting their opponent.

CHAPTER 17

What sound does a Fox make?

I could give a flying crap about the political process . . . We're an entertainment company.
                                        —Glenn Beck, Fox News *Forbes* interview, April 2010

The political spectrum is not a straight, bi-polar line. It's a circle.
                                        —T. Rafael Cimino, *Split... Civility for a Divided Nation*

Fox viewers are less informed than people who watch no news.

People who read, respect facts, science, and independent research—i.e., educated individuals—are by definition keen to be informed. But these very same people get mocked, vilified by the Stupidparty apparatus and their Disciples. In the repressive dictatorial countries of the twentieth century, they were persecuted as a priority by communist leaders like Stalin and Mao. That irony is too deep for Stupidparty Disciples.

It should be crystal clear by now that Stupidparty Disciples are staggeringly uninformed about issues they enthusiastically promote and vote on so reliably. It is mathematically impossible for people who are supposedly watching the news to get so many facts utterly wrong. If you are less informed than people who do not watch the news, then this suggests active misinformation is the agenda. Fox "news" is the PR arm of the individuals looking to hoodwink the more susceptible and desperate general public.

A study conducted in 2012 by Fairleigh Dickinson University in Madison, New Jersey, found that the average American was able to correctly answer 1.8 out of four questions on international news and 1.6 out of five on domestic. Fox News followers, however, only answered 1.04 domestic questions correctly, which is worse than those who said they watched no media at all—which stood at 1.22.

According to Ben Adler in *The Nation*, "This laziness, partisan hackery and lack of regard for basic accuracy is what separates Fox News from outlets that merely have opinions. And it is doing their audience a disservice. This Fairleigh Dickinson study is not the first to find that Fox News viewers are the most ill-informed of any news consumers. As of November 22, 2011, *ThinkProgress* had found seven studies showing Fox News's viewers to be the worst informed of all news consumers."
http://www.thenation.com/blog/167999/its-official-watching-fox-makes-you-stupider#

Another polling group weighs in.

A 2011 WPO poll found that "60% of daily viewers of Fox News believe 'most scientists do not agree that climate change is occurring.'"
http://suite101.com/a/watch-fox-news-and-get-misinformation-and-propaganda-a351659

WorldPublicOpinion.org "is an international collaborative project whose aim is to give voice to public opinion around the world on international issues. As the world becomes increasingly integrated, problems have become increasingly global, pointing to a greater need for understanding between nations and for elucidating global norms. With the growth of democracy in the world, public opinion has come to play a greater role in the foreign policy process. WorldPublicOpinion.org seeks to reveal the values and views of publics in specific nations around the world as well as global patterns of world public opinion."
http://www.worldpublicopinion.org/pipa/about.php?nid=&id=

According to the WPO poll, those who watched Fox News almost daily believe the following to be true:

1) most economists estimate the stimulus caused job losses (91%);
2) most economists have estimated the healthcare law will worsen the deficit (72%);
3) the economy is getting worse (72%);
4) most scientists do not agree that climate change is occurring (60%);

5) the stimulus legislation did not include any tax cuts (63%);

6) their own income taxes have gone up (49%);

7) it is not clear that Obama was born in the United States (63%).

http://thinkprogress.org/media/2010/12/16/135438/poll-fox-news-misinformation/

But it is worse than that, since the study shows that **the more you often you watch Fox, the more ignorant you get** on all the above topics. We will now look at one of the above in greater detail:

4) Most scientists do not agree that climate change is occurring (60%)

Whether you are in denial or not on this issue is not relevant. I have already proven that the vast bulk of scientists have concluded that climate change is occurring. This is an indisputable fact. But the more you watch Fox, the more ignorant, the more Stupidparty you get. Here are the numbers:

Most scientists think climate change is not occurring + views are divided evenly

	Never	Rarely	About once a week	About 2-3 times a week	Almost every day
Fox News	30	37	45	36	60
CNN	51	40	39	25	25
MSNBC	49	34	35	35	20
Network TV news broadcasts	59	37	41	36	35
Public broadcasting (NPR or PBS)	49	41	36	21	13
Newspapers and news magazines (in print or online)	48	43	41	24	40

http://www.worldpublicopinion.org/pipa/pdf/dec10/Misinformation_Dec10_rpt.pdf

But a picture of this mission to uneducate is worth a thousand words:

The higher the Number, the greater the Ignorance...... The More you watch Fox......

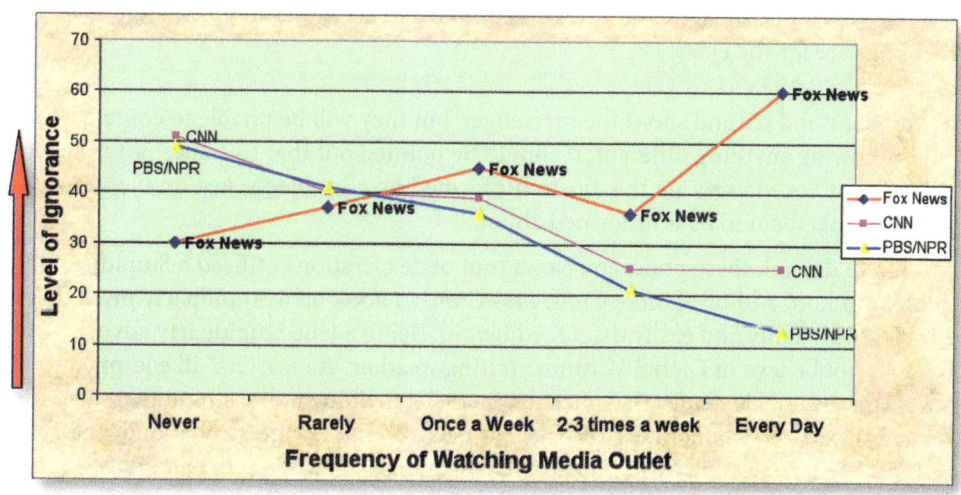

Fox News … investing in ignorance … Fox News … investing in ignorance …

A remarkable 60% of those who watched Fox News almost daily believe that "Most scientists do not agree that climate change is occurring," whereas only 30% who never watch it believe that. Only 25% of those who watch CNN almost daily hold that erroneous belief—and only 13% who listen to NPR or PBS almost daily.

As reported in *ThinkProgress:*

"WPO found one bright spot in its lengthy report: 'Those who had greater exposure to news sources were generally better informed. In the great majority of cases, those with higher levels of exposure to news sources had lower levels of misinformation.' However, there was one exception, Fox News...."

"This data coincides with results of previous surveys finding that Fox News viewers are more misinformed about public policy issues. An NBC/*Wall Street Journal* poll [in 2009] found that Fox News viewers were overwhelmingly misinformed about health care reform proposals. A 2008 Pew study ranked Fox News last in the number of 'high knowledge' viewers and a 2007 Pew poll ranked Fox viewers as the least knowledgeable about national and international affairs. And a 2003 study from the Program on International Policy Attitudes at the University of Maryland found that Fox News viewers were most likely to believe that Saddam Hussein had links to al-Qaeda, that coalition troops found WMD in Iraq, and that world public opinion supported President Bush's decision to invade Iraq."

http://thinkprogress.org/media/2010/12/16/135438/poll-fox-news-misinformation/

NBC News Poll 2009.

72% of self-identified FOX News viewers believe the health-care plan will give coverage to illegal immigrants,
79% of them say it will lead to a government takeover,
69% think that it will use taxpayer dollars to pay for abortions, and
75% believe that it will allow the government to make decisions about when to stop providing care for the elderly.

http://firstread.nbcnews.com/_news/2009/08/19/4431138-first-thoughts-obamas-good-bad-news

Fox will deny and try and shoot the messenger, but they will be unable to come up with studies showing anything different. It should be pointed out that this does not necessarily mean that Fox viewers are the most uninformed on all subjects, just on the subjects that Fox wants them to be uninformed about.

In trying to debunk these polls, Fox News (out of desperation) utilized a Stupidparty zealot, John Lott, author of *More Guns, Less Crime,* a book on a Stupidparty myth that has been thoroughly and easily dismissed herein. Being a true Stupidparty advocate, Lott does not believe in Global Warming (citing weather "forecasters" ill equipped to address the issue). He denies that after the financial meltdown, the stimulus created the jobs and dismisses statements by the CBO as biased. "The Congressional Budget Office (CBO) is a federal agency within the legislative branch of the United States government that provides economic data to Congress. The CBO was created as a nonpartisan agency by the Congressional Budget and Impoundment Control Act of 1974." (Wiki)

http://www.foxnews.com/opinion/2011/01/05/truth-fox-news-viewers/#ixzz2d8wf4rLb

In Chapter Five, I listed 26 polls illustrating how stunningly ignorant the majority of Stupidparty Disciples are. There is a pattern. Basically two-thirds of Stupidparty Disciples are dead wrong about issues that are vital to understand if they are to be qualified to contribute to the national debate. How can these people be so utterly wrong?

Well, they get their information from Fox News.

Bill O'Reilly: "If the Americans go in and overthrow Saddam Hussein and it's clean, he has nothing, I will apologize to the nation, and I will not trust the Bush Administration again, all right?"—on finding weapons of mass destruction in Iraq, March 18, 2003

http://politicalhumor.about.com/od/billoreilly/a/oreillyquotes.htm (numerous sources for all this stuff)

Bill O'Reilly to *Daily Show* host Jon Stewart, Sept. 22, 2004: "You know what's really frightening? You actually have an influence on this presidential election. That is scary, but it's true. You've got stoned slackers watching your dopey show every night and they can vote."

Bill O'Reilly: "If I'm the president of the United States, I walk right into Union Square, I set up my little presidential podium, and I say, 'Listen, citizens of San Francisco, if you vote against military recruiting, you're not going to get another nickel in federal funds. Fine. You want to be your own country? Go right ahead. And if al Qaeda comes in here and blows you up, we're not going to do anything about it. We're going to say, look, every other place in America is off limits to you, except San Francisco. You want to blow up the Coit Tower [San Francisco]? Go ahead'"—after San Francisco voted to ban military recruiters from city schools, Nov. 8, 2005

Sean Hannity: "Here you are, you're a liberal, probably define peace as the absence of conflict. I define peace as the ability to defend yourself and blow your enemies into smithereens"—Fox News host (October 2009)

Sean Hannity: "Halloween is a liberal holiday because we're teaching our children to beg for something for free … We're teaching kids to knock on other people's doors and ask for a handout"—Fox News host (October 31, 2007)

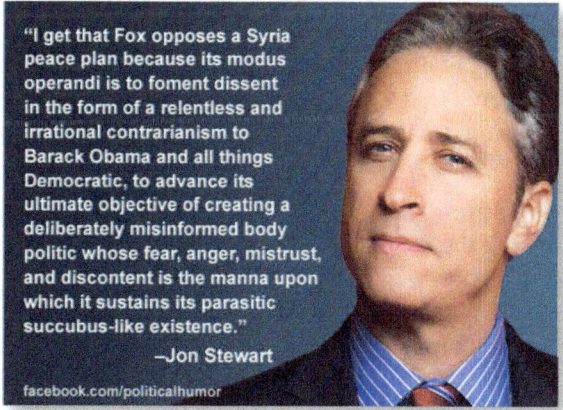

"I get that Fox opposes a Syria peace plan because its modus operandi is to foment dissent in the form of a relentless and irrational contrarianism to Barack Obama and all things Democratic, to advance its ultimate objective of creating a deliberately misinformed body politic whose fear, anger, mistrust, and discontent is the manna upon which it sustains its parasitic succubus-like existence."
–Jon Stewart
facebook.com/politicalhumor

Sean Hannity: "[Liberal rhetoric] now is so over the top, it's so vicious, it's so mean, it's so cruel, and I don't hear this coming from conservatives about liberals"—with a straight face

Glenn Beck on President Obama: "This president I think has exposed himself over and over again as a guy who has a deep-seated hatred for white people or the white culture … I'm not saying he doesn't

like white people, I'm saying he has a
problem. This guy is, I believe, a racist"—sparking an advertiser exodus
from his Fox News show, July 28,
2009

Glenn Beck: "I could give a flying
crap about the political process …
We're an entertainment company"—
Fox News, *Forbes* interview, April 2010

Bill O'Reilly and Megyn Kelly: Here
an exchange between Fox News hosts
that took place in November 2011,
in which they tried to downplay the
impact of pepper spray on student Occupy protesters at UC Davis:

O'REILLY: "First of all, pepper spray—that just burns your eyes, right?"
KELLY: "It's like a derivative of actual pepper. It's a food product, essentially."
ERIC BOLLING: "America was certainly safe between 2000 and 2008. I don't remember
any attacks on American soil during that period of time."

Rupert Murdoch, CEO of News Corp, which owns Fox News

"Keith Rupert Murdoch (born 11 March 1931) is an Australian American media mogul.
He is the founder, Chairman and CEO of global media holding company News Corporation, the world's second-largest media conglomerate.

"By 2000 Murdoch's News Corporation owned over 800 companies in more than 50
countries. In July 2011 Murdoch faced allegations in the UK that his companies, including the News of the World, owned by News Corporation, had been regularly hacking
the phones of celebrities, royalty and public citizens. He faces police and government
investigations into bribery and corruption by the British government and FBI investigations in the U.S. On 21 July 2012, Murdoch resigned as a director of News International." (Wiki)

Murdoch does not appear to have a huge respect for
journalistic standards or ethics. Notwithstanding
Murdoch's well-known reputation, the debacle that is
Fox may well be beyond his control. He has created a
Frankenstein that now has a life of its own. The brain
inside that Frankenstein is Roger Ailes, and only in
understanding Roger Ailes can we really fathom what
happened.

"**Roger Eugene Ailes** (born May 15, 1940) is president
of   Fox News Channel and chairman of the Fox
                Television Stations Group. Ailes was
                a media consultant for Republican
Roger Ailes   presidents Richard Nixon, Ronald
                Reagan, and George H. W. Bush

The mind manipulator

and for Rudy Giuliani's first mayoral campaign (1989). In 1996 Ailes was hired by Rupert Murdoch to create Fox News Channel for News Corporation to help with the new channel's launch, on October 7, 1996." (Wiki)

Because of Roger Ailes's huge success—in 2010 earning about $800m in profits—he can now pretty much do whatever he wants. Employees must be subservient to his agenda. Even Murdoch, who is very conservative, needs to be careful. He surely respects the profits but was quoted as saying, "You know, Roger is crazy," Murdoch recently told a colleague, shaking his head in disbelief, "He really believes that stuff."
http://www.rollingstone.com/politics/news/how-roger-ailes-built-the-fox-news-fear-factory-20110525#ixzz2d8RnLIov

Rolling Stone: June 9, 2011:

To watch even a day of Fox News—the anger, the bombast, the virulent paranoid streak, the unending appeals to white resentment, the reporting that's held to the same standard of evidence as a late-October attack ad—is to see a refraction of its founder, one of the most skilled and fearsome operatives in the history of the Republican Party. As a political consultant, Ailes repackaged Richard Nixon for television in 1968, papered over Ronald Reagan's budding Alzheimer's in 1984, shamelessly stoked racial fears to elect George H. W. Bush in 1988, and waged a secret campaign on behalf of Big Tobacco to derail health care reform in 1993. "He was the premier guy in the business," says former Reagan campaign manager Ed Rollins. "He was our Michelangelo."

Rolling Stone's Tim Dickinson goes on to discuss how Ailes would like the outside world to perceive his earlier years and that he is now different from his very partisan past. In a recent biography of Ailes, "*The Loudest Voice in the Room*," Gabriel Sherman "delivers a portrait of a manipulating, conniving, controlling, petty and fear-mongering man." This book, which interviewed 614 people, does indicate that Mr. Ailes has a fertile imagination when it comes to trying to shape his image. But "deception isn't the theme that knits together the key Ailes epochs documented in *The Loudest Voice in the Room*. Loyalty is." The more power you have, the more loyalty you can demand. "I see the most powerful man in the world is here," President Obama said, according to an "author interview with a person familiar with the matter." Moving to launch Fox News simply gave Ailes heretofore unknown megaphone methods of thrusting partisan propaganda on a public not equipped to recognize Fact from Fiction, especially when delivered as news under the guise of "fair and balanced."

As described in the article, he created one of the most "powerful political machines in American history," which took the helm in navigating Stupidparty—talking points and advancing the agenda of the far right. Fox News tilted the electoral balance to George W. Bush in 2000, prematurely declaring him president in a move that prompted every other network to follow suit. It helped create the Tea Party, transforming it from the butt of late-night jokes into a nationwide insurgency capable of electing U.S. senators. Fox News turbocharged the Stupidparty takeover of the House last fall, and even helped elect former Fox News host John Kasich as the union-busting governor of Ohio—with the help of $1.26 million in campaign contributions from News Corp. And by incubating a host of potential GOP contenders on the Fox News payroll—including Sarah Palin, Mike Huckabee, Newt Gingrich and Rick Santorum—Ailes seems determined to add a fifth presidential notch to his belt in 2012. "Everything Roger wanted to do when he started out in politics, he's now doing 24/7 with his network," says a former News Corp. executive. "It's come full circle."

Take it from Rush Limbaugh, a "dear friend" of Ailes. "One man has established a culture for 1,700 people who believe in it, who follow it, who execute it," Limbaugh once declared. "Roger Ailes is not on the air. Roger Ailes does not ever show up on camera. And yet everybody who does is a reflection of him."

http://www.rollingstone.com/politics/news/how-roger-ailes-built-the-fox-news-fear-factory-20110525#ixzz2d8RnLIov

How did Fox become such a threat to the truth?

Fox News managing editor Bill Sammon was widely condemned yesterday for an email telling the network's staff not to report on even the most widely accepted scientific facts without immediately challenging them, as reported here.

http://thinkprogress.org/romm/2010/12/16/207207/wattsupwiththat-foxgate-email-unequivocal-warming-of-the-climate/

Fox Box of Graphical Tricks:

What happens when Bush's tax cut on higher earners expires:

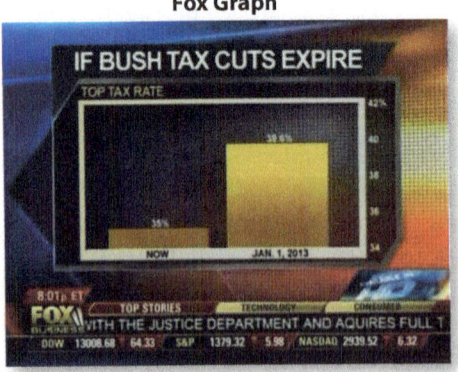

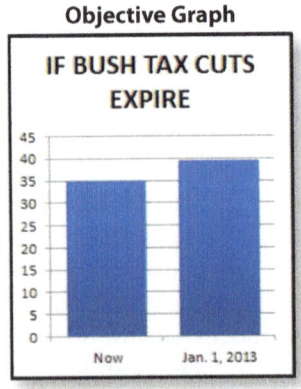

**Job losses will never stop
getting worse under Obama**   **or not**

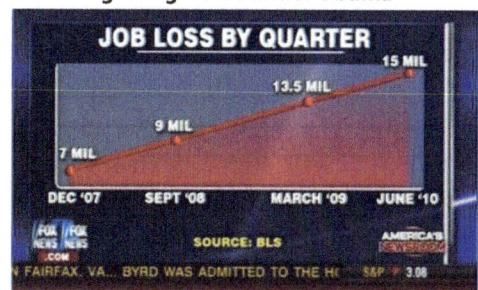

Fox Graph   **Objective Graph**

   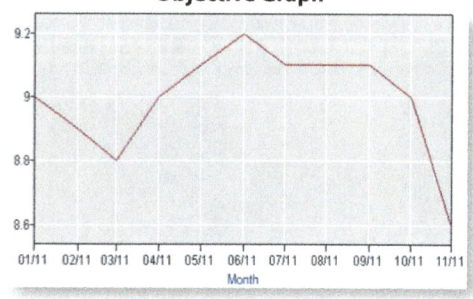

Evidently, 9% unemployment is the same as 8.6%

**Here it looks like Unemployment
doubled under Obama**   **Next day Fox is forced
to correct the graph**

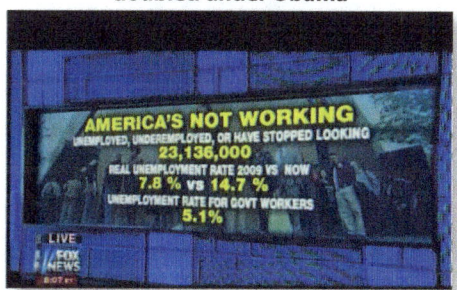   

In Reality, Fox conflates two Different Measures of Unemployment to distort Obama's jobs record.

Fox Graph numbers

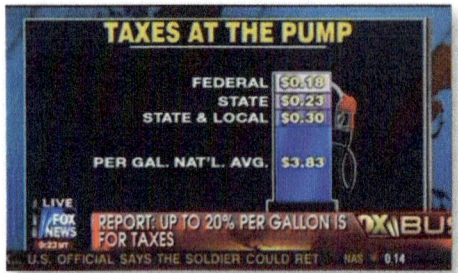

Objective Graph, plus

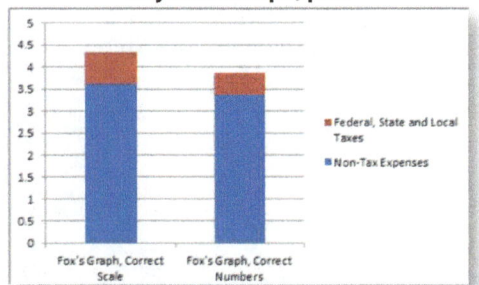

http://mediamatters.org/research/2012/10/01/a-history-of-dishonest-fox-charts/190225

Trying to Make the Government projections look silly

Correct Graph

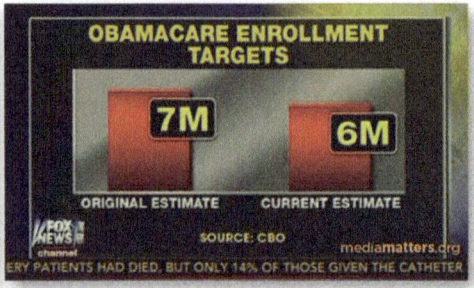

Truncating the Y axis

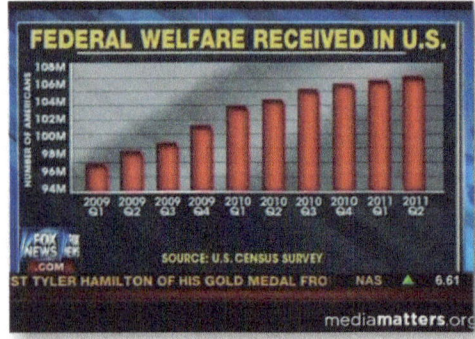

SP Math

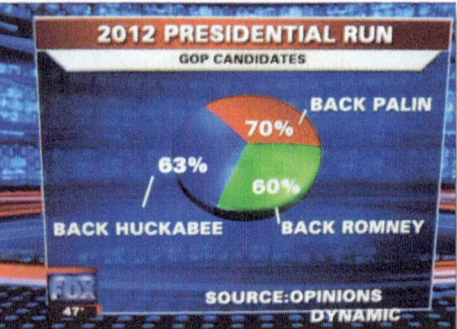

FOX SUBLIMINAL PROPAGANDA

ENERGIZING STUPIDPARTY BIGOT BASE

FOX GRATUITOUSLY DEMEANING THE PRESIDENT

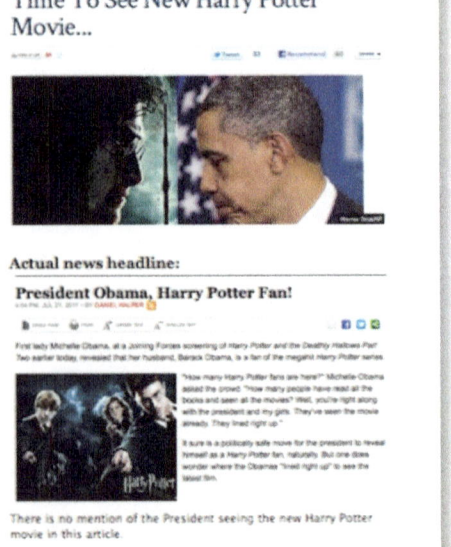

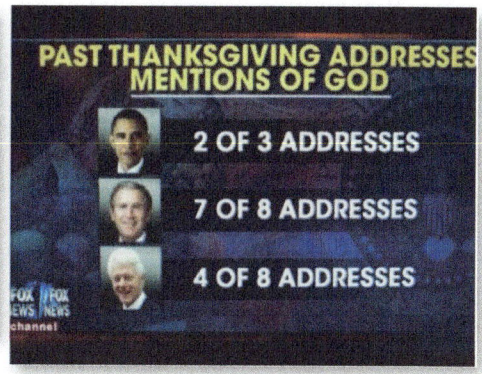

THE FOLLOWING HEADLINES CAN BE FOUND IN THE LINKED SCREEN GRABS

Fox undermining Facts, Science, and themselves

Chuck NorrisFacts: ARE THEY TRUE?
Fox Anchor Standing in front of snow: WHAT GLOBAL WARMING?
Fox Morning Gang: SPONGEBOB'S BIAS CARTOON BLAMES MAN FOR GLOBAL WARMING

Fox Creatively stretches to push Stupidparty agenda

Sarah Pain being interviewed headline UNIVERSAL NIGHTMARE
Fox Anchor: WILL HIGH GAS PRICES COST YOUR KIDS THEIR EDUCATION

Fox war on the Poor

Picture of Occupy Wall Street tented community: GOOD RIDDANCE.

Jon Stewart explains the game.
Note: While various individuals at Comedy Central keep the lights on (such as *The Daily Show, The Colbert Report* and *South Park*) during these dark ages, the brilliant and vital material that they produce to protect our Democracy is not so easily available—so this link comes with a 30 second advert which cannot be easily bypassed—so I regret the inconvenience.

But not all their propaganda should be dismissed without a closer look.

FOX BUSINESS CHANNEL PROMOTES FOX BUSINESS CHANNEL

FOX AND JOURNALISM—AND OXYMORON

Fox News will not be moving into Canada after all! (2011)

"The reason: Canadian regulators announced last week they would reject efforts by Canada's right-wing Prime Minister, Stephen Harper, to repeal a law that forbids lying on broadcast news. Canada's Radio Act requires that 'a licenser may not broadcast ... any false or misleading news.' The provision has kept Fox News and right-wing talk radio out of Canada and helped make Canada a model for liberal democracy and freedom. As a result of that law, Canadians enjoy high quality news coverage."

http://readersupportednews.org/opinion2/276-74/5123-fox-news-lies-keep-them-out-of-canada

Election Year 2012—Fox kicks it up a level
As reported by AlterNet / Stephen Hsieh

January 2012—Fox Peddles Racist "Food Stamp" Rhetoric.
Echoing Newt Gingrich's disgusting nickname for the president, several Fox person-alities peddled the misinformation that Obama is giving out more "freebies" than any other administration. As Media Matters reported, that's false. In actuality, George W. Bush oversaw the largest increase in food stamp usage. Evidently, coded racism doesn't bode well for credibility.

February 2012—Fox Pundit Says Military Women Should "Expect" to be Raped.
Fox News pundit Liz Trotta learned that Americans aren't too fond of victim blaming. Responding to news that women would be working closer to front lines, Trotta implied that women should "expect" to be raped more if they want to serve this country.

March 2012—Fox Pundit Claims "Hoodie" Killed Trayvon Martin.
Geraldo Rivera started a national movement this year when he suggested that Tray-von Martin died because of what he was wearing, not the overzealous vigilantism of a George Zimmerman or outrageous "stand your ground" laws.

April 2012—Fox Host Misinforms on the Environment.
Everyone knows Fox News has an appalling record on the environment. As the Union of Concerned Scientists revealed, Fox News has misled the American public in 93 per-cent of their climate change coverage. And in April, host Greg Gutfeld uttered a slew of environmental falsehoods, including the claim that the world plants more trees than it cuts down.

May 2012—Fox Appeals to Jingoism and Lies About Obama.
Media Matters reports a full on assault against President Obama for allegedly failing to express his gratitude to the Navy SEALs who killed Osama bin Laden.

June 2012—Fox Ignores Context of "Private Sector is Doing Fine"
"The private sector is doing fine." Remember when Fox News used this quote from the president to demonize him as an out of touch socialist without including the context that private sector jobs were in fact growing at a higher rate than the public sector?

July 2012—Fox Peddles Voter Fraud Myths.
Despite widespread reports on the rarity of voter fraud in this country, Fox's Patti-Ann Brown willingly referred to Pennsylvania's racist voter ID law as an "attempt to fight voter fraud."

August 2012—Fox Chooses not to Talk about Todd Akin.
In August, Rep. Todd Akin found a national audience when he claimed that women's bodies are biologically tuned to abort pregnancies resulting from "legitimate rape." As *ThinkProgress* reports, Fox News barely covered the story.

September 2012—The Polls Are Rigged …
When the polls weren't in Mitt Romney's favor, Fox News pundits joined conservative conspiracy theorists claiming that someone must've been cooking the numbers.

October 2012—So Let's Ignore Them …
At least one person paid the price for demonstrating supreme Stupidparty devotion

The now-terminated pundit Dick Morris predicted that Mitt Romney would win in a "landslide."
http://www.alternet.org/news-amp-politics/12-months-misinformation-explaining-fox-news-record-low-credibility

Romancing Petraeus: Fox News CEO Roger Ailes tries to recruit for the GOP.
"The Washington Post's Bob Woodward revealed that Fox News CEO Roger Ailes had dispatched a Fox News defense analyst to Kabul, Afghanistan to recruit Gen. David Petraeus as a GOP candidate for president. The notion of a news network soliciting candidates for political office is a perversion of the role journalists play in society." (Roger Ailes denies it—but audio proof exists. See link below.)
http://www.salon.com/2013/01/05/12_most_despicable_things_fox_news_did_in_2012/

Latinos being used for profit and politics.
"This has resulted in a flurry of disparaging articles on the Fox News flagship, while the same story is presented on the new Fox News Latino in a far less bigoted fashion. The pinnacle of this hypocrisy occurred during a Fox report on the election when it displayed video of illegal border crossers with a caption reading 'The Hispanic Vote.'"
http://www.salon.com/2013/01/05/12_most_despicable_things_fox_news_did_in_2012/

Fox lies about military access to voting in Ohio.
"This year Republicans in the state of Ohio sought to amend their early voting law so that only members of the military would be permitted to vote early in the three days prior to the election. Democrats objected to this as it discriminates against certain voters, and they filed suit to preserve the right of every Ohio citizen to vote early. Fox News picked up the story advancing the premise that Democrats were seeking to take something away from our military. Anchor Shannon Bream falsely declared that 'If President Obama gets his way, the special voting rights of some of America's finest will be eliminated.' The truth is that Democrats in Ohio were suing to ensure that nobody's rights were eliminated. The Ohio GOP was deliberately attempting to suppress the votes of citizens they presumed would vote Democratic. And Fox News helped them in that mission by brazenly lying about the substance of the debate."
http://www.salon.com/2013/01/05/12_most_despicable_things_fox_news_did_in_2012/

Fox Partisan hack posing as psychoanalyst.
"The in-house Fox News psychiatrist, Keith Ablow, has offered his embarrassingly ridiculous diagnoses on a number of occasions. Without ever having examined (or even met) President Obama, Ablow has declared him to be contemptuous of the judiciary and devoid of all emotion. He further assessed that Obama has 'got it in for this country' and doesn't like
Americans … Ablow's astonishing diagnosis was that Gingrich as president would make America stronger specifically because of his multiple infidelities. This is what passes for family values in today's GOP."
http://www.newscorpse.com/ncWP/?p=6237

When your primary goal is propaganda, you become unable to report the News.

Fox refuses to use their own polls when inconvenient.
"Fox was so determined to shut out anything that might challenge its narrative that it even failed to report its own Fox News polls if Obama was ahead. This was a part of a

broader effort to deceive its audience by castigating or ignoring polls when it didn't like the results and praising the same pollsters when their numbers were more favorable. They launched a campaign to demean professional pollsters and prop up disreputable charlatans with its 'unskewed' versions. Not surprisingly, this led to the unprecedented post-election state of shock experienced by those who were foolish enough to rely on Fox for information."

http://www.salon.com/2013/01/05/12_most_despicable_things_fox_news_did_in_2012/

When the economy looks better, they seek shelter in their Fox hole.

"Fox News cavalierly dismissed the October unemployment report showing a drop from 8.1 to 7.8 percent. Fox spent the whole morning trying to hatch skeptics. It brought in former General Electric CEO **Jack Welch** to explain his delusional Tweet: 'Unbelievable jobs numbers … these Chicago guys will do anything … can't debate so change numbers.' Fox's **Stuart Varney** concurred along with **Donald Trump** and a bevy of correspondents and guests. None of them could explain why an independent agency of career economists, without a single Obama appointee, would fudge the numbers for a president to whom they owed nothing."

http://www.salon.com/2013/01/05/12_most_despicable_things_fox_news_did_in_2012/

Fox not allowed to discuss banning assault weapons.

Fox opposes ban on assault weapons but imposes ban on talking about it. After the Newtown child massacre, talk on banning assault weapons was "met by Fox News as an attack on the Second Amendment and free enterprise. Its response was to slaughter the First Amendment by prohibiting any discussion of gun safety on the network. Sources told Gabriel Sherman of New York Magazine that 'David Clark, the executive producer in charge of Fox's weekend coverage, gave producers instructions not to talk about gun-control policy on air.' While Fox banned all talk of gun control, it did not banish talk of other explanations for the atrocity in Connecticut. Fox had no problem with laying the blame on mental illness, movies or video games. Fox host Mike Huckabee was permitted to go on the air and blame the killings on the absence of God in the classroom (which does nothing to explain similar shootings that have taken place in churches)."

http://www.salon.com/2013/01/05/12_most_despicable_things_fox_news_did_in_2012/

Fox Religious expert trumped by concept of a Muslim Historian.

"In this interview in 2013 Fox's religious correspondent Lauren Green, simply could not accept that a non-Christian professor, best seller Reza Aslan, with excellent credentials could possibly write an objective book about Jesus."

http://www.thedailybeast.com/articles/2013/07/30/lauren-green-the-woman-behind-fox-news-reza-aslan-interview-debacle.html

Fox News simply not able to report News.

Fox news is Roger Ailes, and Roger Ailes has a clear political agenda, that everyone must abide by. But that agenda is often based on utter nonsense. So this puts Fox reporters in an untenable situation when covering a wide variety of news. Take beach erosion in Florida; they can point to what is happening and the stopgap measures being taken, like transferring sand from other places or turning glass back into sand—but they cannot really talk about the causes (i.e., rising sea levels), because—well, Roger Ailes does not accept science, especially when it clashes with his agenda.

Fox Airs hour-long commercial for anti-Obama film on Hannity.

"In the heart of the presidential campaign season, Sean Hannity's program on Fox News devoted the full hour to a blatant infomercial promoting an anti-Obama movie by the people who brought us Citizens United. The program featured lengthy clips from the film as well as interviews with the film's creators, David Bossie and Steve Bannon. Bossie is the head of Citizens United, the organization that prompted the abhorrent Supreme Court decision that made it possible for individuals and corporations to donate unlimited sums of cash to political candidates and causes. Bannon is chairman of Breitbart News and was the director of the monumental flop, *Sarah Palin: Undefeated,* a movie that managed to fail miserably despite millions of dollars in free publicity courtesy of Fox News. What's particularly disturbing about this is that the producers freely admit that their purpose was not so much to promote the film, but to let their ads serve as disguised political messages aimed at disparaging the president and affecting the outcome of the election."
http://www.salon.com/2013/01/05/12_most_despicable_things_fox_news_did_in_2012/

More Fox Faux-mercial: Fox-produced anti-Obama video.

"Last May [2012] on *Fox & Friends,* the program's hosts introduced a video that purported to examine 'Four Years of Hope and Change.' What it was in reality was a four-plus minute campaign video that presented a variety of sound bites by President Obama accompanied by ominous graphics and eerie music that falsely implied his campaign promises were unkept."
http://www.salon.com/2013/01/05/12_most_despicable_things_fox_news_did_in_2012/

Over the course of his book, Sherman documents a number of such little fictions and embellishments propagated by Ailes and his associates, none more consequential than the one that took place at Fox News in May 2012. The media world blew up in outrage when the network's morning show "Fox & Friends" aired a four-minute anti-Obama video that had all the hallmarks of a GOP campaign spot. Under the gun, Fox News told the New York Times that Ailes wasn't aware of the video. Sherman reports that it was Ailes's "brainchild."
http://www.washingtonpost.com/opinions/book-review-the-loudest-voice-in-the-room-an-unflattering-portrait-of-fox-news-chief-ailes/2014/01/14/8671ab4c-7d49-11e3-9556-4a4bf7bcbd84_story.html

Fox News "Democrat" Kirsten Powers accuses Obama of sympathizing with terrorists.

This poser poses the notion that Obama is a terrorist sympathizer. Allowing her to spew that bile while posing as a Democratic analyst is part of how Fox distorts its presentation of fairness and balance.

http://www.newscorpse.com/ncWP/?p=8021

Atheists should leave the country already.

A conversation between Fox anchors.

http://www.rawstory.com/rs/2013/09/06/fox-news-host-tired-of-atheists-demands-for-freedom-from-religion-they-dont-have-to-live-here

Institutionalized False Information:

When individuals prattle on about how their religious values motivate them to seek public office, and how they receive divine assistance, so such people must be held to a higher standard. If you live by the sword, you should die by the sword. Thus, if you win support by using God's name or win votes by implying that your greater faith makes you better than your opponent, then when you slip up, the consequences should be greater. Being an adulterer need not be disqualify-

www.mywebface.com

ing, but a closet adulterer attacking an adulterer—perhaps that should be disqualifying. Using the same logic for the media, a small-time blogger does not need to be held to the same standard as the mainstream media. We expect, we demand a far higher degree of fact-checking, of objectivity from a news service. There must be severe penalties for news services who distort, mislead, and generally forget their 'raison d'être,' to faithfully report the news. Why have a news service if it cannot be trusted? Just because their viewers are trained to be oblivious is not an excuse. So if Fox employees are actively working to create a false news narrative, surely that is grossly unethical, bordering on and perhaps verging into criminal activity …

As Media Matters reports:

"NPR media reporter David Folkenflik writes in his forthcoming book *Murdoch's World* that Fox News' public relations staffers used an elaborate series of dummy accounts to fill the comments sections of critical blog posts with pro-Fox arguments.

"In a chapter focusing on how Fox utilized its notoriously ruthless public relations department in the mid-to-late 00's, Folkenflik reports that Fox's PR staffers would 'post pro-Fox rants' in the comments sections of 'negative and even neutral' blog posts written about the network. According to Folkenflik, the staffers used various tactics to cover their tracks, including setting up wireless broadband connections that 'could not be traced back' to the network.

"A former staffer told Folkenflik that they had personally used 'one hundred' fake accounts to plant Fox-friendly commentary:

On the blogs, the fight was particularly fierce. Fox PR staffers were expected to counter not just negative and even neutral blog postings but the anti-Fox comments beneath them. One former staffer recalled using twenty different aliases to post pro-Fox rants. Another had one hundred. Several employees had to acquire a cell phone thumb drive to provide a wireless broadband connection that could not be traced back to a Fox News or News Corp account. Another used an AOL dial-up connection, even in the age of widespread broadband access, on the rationale it would be harder to pinpoint its origins. Old laptops were distributed for these cyber operations. Even blogs with minor followings were reviewed to ensure no claim went unchecked. [*Murdoch's World,* pg. 67]

"In the book's endnotes, Folkenflik explains that 'four former Fox News employees told me of these practices.' It's unclear whether these tactics are ongoing."
http://mediamatters.org/blog/2013/10/20/
fox-news-reportedly-used-fake-commenter-account/196509

Fox—More Stupidparty than the Stupidparty:

97% of Fox viewers disapprove of Obama with 1% not having an opinion. I do not have the precise link for the pie chart but the 94% number is backed up by the link below: 94% of Fox Viewers vote Stupidparty—this, I believe, makes Fox viewers more supportive of the Stupidparty than the people who are registered Stupidparty supporters.
http://www.politicususa.com/2013/07/08/fair-balanced-fraud-exposed-94-fox-news-viewers-republicans.html

Mainstream Media Bias.

Stupidparty Disciples claim that the mainstream media has a liberal bias. They throw similar accusations at Scientists, Teachers, Fact checkers, College Graduates, Hollywood, all Europeans, New York City, Californians, Atheists—basically everyone but them.

Most journalists are employed by large corporations. These corporations must satisfy the appetites of their shareholders—thus, it is all about ratings. They must sell to their audience; therefore, the only natural bias would be to simply appeal to their audience. Even if Bill O'Reilly wanted to become more progressive, he could not do so without losing his ratings, and Roger Ailes would then have two reasons to have a meltdown. Bill O'Reilly's prognostications are preordained; he is a slave to his own success.

But journalists tend to be pretty well educated, pretty good at research, very careful about facts, are likely to travel and be exposed to different cultures. Thus, they tend not to be ignorant, and thus they are less likely to be bigoted. Most, therefore, would not have much respect for the Stupidparty. But this hardly makes them liberal. Being concerned about facts and about the truth does not mean you are a liberal. This does not mean to say that journalists do not have a price on their soul.

Most journalists get quite well paid. Senior writers and journalists typically earn a payroll of $200k or more per year. Not exactly starving, then. Food stamps, lack of health insurance, minimum wage, awful work conditions—these are not the most pressing items for our intrepid journalists. They are relatively comfortable. America is perhaps the most right wing capitalist country in the history of the planet, but they are not really jumping up and down screaming about income inequality or the lack of a public option—because they are not overly stressed about their own income or the healthcare situation. U.S, democracy has always favored the top echelons; journalists are part of that segment, and so they hardly kick and scream as the imbalance now goes to ludicrous extremes.

Journalists most often happily and unquestionably lap up jingoistic claptrap. Oh, to be entrenched with the invading troops or to interview the powerful, to wine and dine or travel with the newsmakers—not only makes a career but dampens the ability for objective independent analysis. By definition, to be comfortable with the status quo (which most journalists learn is the easiest route) makes one a conservative. For all these reasons, journalists have a conservative bias; they just happen to work in the most extreme conservative country on the planet (other than maybe Russia or Iran)—so those cave-dwelling fundamentalists may perceive journalists as being liberal, but they are wrong.

Obviously, journalists need to be seen as objective. To pick too deeply on the carcass of Stupidparty carries major risk—easier to just let stuff slide. So when Stupidparty says something silly like rape is okay (using code like dress attire or faux science, etc.), then journalists feel the need to balance such reporting by throwing in an off-kilter Democrat quote—like, say, from. Senator Chris Dodd, while on the campaign trail: "Eight more days and I can start telling the truth again."

But rarely are they equivalent. In fact, favorite Stupidparty gotcha moments and fake scandals are either untrue, like Al Gore saying he invented the Internet (he did not say that), or Bill Clinton: "I have never had sexual relations with Monica Lewinsky. I've never had an affair with her." Well, he never had intercourse (as to him and many/most other people, intercourse means penetration), plus he won two elections wherein the public knew full well his weaknesses on this front. But the nascent Stupidparty House, having failed in all their other trumped-up investigations, felt that it was okay for a bunch of known adulterers (Newt Gingrich, leader of the House; Henry Hyde, Chairman of the House Judiciary Committee; Bob right-to-remain-silent-about-wife-number-2 Barr, Judiciary Committee; and likely others) to pass judgment on the president.

The headline should have been the wasted taxpayer funds that Congress authorized for Ken Starr's witch hunt on Whitewater.

"The Whitewater controversy (also called the Whitewater scandal, or simply Whitewater) began with investigations into the real estate investments of Bill and Hillary Clinton and their associates Jim and Susan McDougal in the Whitewater Development Corporation, a failed business venture in the 1970s and 1980s. Decades of investigations stemming from politically desperate opponents—consistently yielding nothing." (Wiki)

This is not remotely the equivalent to Bush Jr. launching a war based upon false or contrived evidence. It is nowhere near the equivalency of Dick Cheney, though his lackey Scooter Libby, outing a CIA agent (which was one reason for the soured relationship between Bush and Cheney). Or compare the faux 2013 scandal whereby the IRS was supposedly targeting right-wing groups (a typically vacuous witch hunt to nowhere led by our friend Darrell Isa) with the actual Bush 2007 scandal of district attorneys being fired if they did not pursue voter-fraud (intimidation) campaigns.

Another example. Jerry Brown, governor of California, stated, "The conventional viewpoint says we need a jobs program and we need to cut welfare. Just the opposite! We need more welfare and fewer jobs." I think we can agree that no governor would campaign on eliminating jobs. So what he said was taken out of context. As it happens, he was way ahead of his time. What he was actually trying to discuss is now becoming a seriously considered economic theory.
http://www.nytimes.com/2013/11/17/magazine/switzerlands-proposal-to-pay-people-for-being-alive.html?_r=0

But Stupidparty would argue, Why not give Romney a break for saying he liked firing people (not a quote utilized herein)? However, there is a big difference between Romney and Jerry Brown. First and foremost, Romney (a stunningly dishonest human being) en- riched himself by Asset Stripping. If you can personally profit massively from downsiz- ing (say, to the tune $10,000 a person), not only does it prevent an objective analysis of what is best for the business, but it also means that you are likely to evolve into a person who doesn't mind firing people.

There is no general liberal bias in the mainstream media (although they might be a rath- er lame bias against stupidity). But when it comes to false equivalency, it is not only Fox, but the rest of the mainstream media that falls into that trap.

CHAPTER 18

False equivalency
destroys
reality

http://www.skepticalraptor.com/skepticalraptorblog.php/science-deniers-false-equivalency-pretend-debate/

[The Stupidparty] has become an insurgent outlier. It has become ideologically extreme; contemptuous of the inherited social and economic policy regime; scornful of compromise; unpersuaded by conventional understanding of facts, evidence, and science; and dismissive of the legitimacy of its political opposition, all but declaring war on the government. The Democratic Party, while no paragon of civic virtue, is more ideologically centered and diverse, protective of the government's role as it developed over the course of the last century, open to incremental changes in policy fashioned through bargaining with the Republicans, and less disposed to or adept at take-no-prisoners conflict between the parties. This asymmetry between the parties, which journalists and scholars often brush aside or whitewash in a quest for "balance," constitutes a huge obstacle to effective governance.

—Thomas E. Mann and Norman J. Ornstein, Washington Post op-ed. Mann is the author of *It's Even Worse Than It Looks: How the American Constitutional System Collided with the Politics of Extremism*

False equivalency

Now I have illustrated many stupid quotes and policies from the Stupidparty in order to demonstrate that they are Stupidparty. The Stupidparty may retort by saying that Liberals say stupid things and of course they have half a point. But progressives when they do say stupid things, the comments tend to be flaky, yet well meaning; they are fighting against Bigotry, Torture, Rape, Wars, environmental Catastrophe, etc. Progressives, by their very nature, are trying to make things better; they are not part of the odious promotion of dangerous nonsense. Rarely do the mistakes made by Democrats lead to the obvious conclusion of genuinely stupid, ignorant or bigoted. Here is a sample list of supposedly stupid things that Democrats say.

The top 15:

1. Sheryl Crow on environmentalism: "I propose a limitation be put on how many squares of toilet paper can be used in any one sitting."
Flaky? No, not even, as she explained she was just joking to draw attention to global warming.

2. Joe Biden on culturalism: "In Delaware, the largest growth of population is Indian Americans, moving from India. You cannot go to a 7/11 or a Dunkin' Donuts unless you have a slight Indian accent. I'm not joking."
Awkward, yes. Not mean-spirited or necessarily ignorant.

3. Whoopi Goldberg on 43-year-old Roman Polanski raping and sodomizing a 13-year-old girl: "I know it wasn't rape-rape. It was something else but I don't believe it was rape-rape. He went to jail and when they let him out he was like 'You know what, this guy's going to give me a hundred years in jail. I'm not staying,' so that's why he left."
I accept this was wrong. Not mean-spirited.

4. Joy Behar on economics: "Isn't it a little racist to call it Black Friday?"
No, Joy Behar was clearly not trying to be overly PC; she was simply having light banter with Whoopi Goldberg worthy of a slight cringe.

5. John Conyers on the Affordable Care Act, which he voted for: "I love these members; they get up and say, 'Read the bill'… What good is reading the bill if it's a thousand pages and you don't have two days and two lawyers to find out what it means after you read the bill?"
Impolitic. Not untruthful.

6. Former DNC Chairman Donald Fowler on possible delay of Republican National Convention due to Hurricane Gustav: "Plus, they think the hurricane's going to hit

[starts laughing] New Orleans about the time they start. The timing, at least it appears now, that it'll be there Monday. That just demonstrates God's on our side."

A very ironic and totally appropriate and deserved joke.

7. Barack Obama: "I've now been in 57 states? I think one left to go."

Obama is not Palin. Campaign fatigue. One suspects that if a Stupidparty Disciple knows how many states there are, in order to record this quote, we can presume Obama does.

8. John Kerry on the troops: "You know, education, if you make the most of it, you study hard, you do your homework and you make an effort to be smart, you can do well. If you don't, you get stuck in Iraq."

Kerry speech had prepared notes, and what he wrote on those notes was... "if you don't, you get <u>us</u> stuck in Iraq, <u>just ask President Bush</u>"—the underlined words, he accidentally dropped. (Wiki)

9. Howard Dean: "We know that no one person can succeed unless everybody else succeeds."

Clumsy but harmless.

10. Rosie O'Donnell: "Don't fear the terrorists. They're mothers and fathers."

Maybe she should have said, "One man's terrorist is another man's freedom fighter." Very carelessly spoken but not mean-spirited.

11. Al Gore: "During my service in the United States Congress, I took the initiative in creating the Internet." March 9, 1999.

Al Gore did not invent the Internet. What's more, he never said he did! However, his contributions to the development of the Internet as we know it were quite significant.

12. Congressman Hank Johnson on Guam: "My fear is that the whole island will become so overly populated that it will tip over and capsize."

Harmless and perfectly amusing observation. If it does not tilt, Global Warming will no doubt eradicate it soon enough.

13. Alan Grayson on healthcare: "The Republican health care plan: don't get sick... The Republicans have a backup plan in case you do get sick... This is what the Republicans want you to do. If you get sick, America, the Republican health care plan is this: Die quickly!"

This appears to be pretty accurate, since the Stupidparty position on healthcare is to let the uninsured rely on emergency rooms and charity.

14. Nancy Pelosi on the economy: "Every month that we do not have an economic recovery package 500 million Americans lose their jobs."

I think we know she meant 500,000.

15. Helen Thomas: Jews should "get the hell out of Palestine" and "go home" to Germany and Poland.

Very awkward vent, the only mean-spirited comment on this list, and certainly in no way connected to the Democrats in Congress or the party. (She was no doubt driven insane by the inability to have objective conversations on Palestine in the USA.) This has not stopped the Clintons and Obama from trying to be relatively honest brokers—in spite of the vast financial resources thrown against them.

http://thestir.cafemom.com/in_the_news/109417/50_Dumb_Liberal_Quotes

Bloomberg TV fact checks Bill Clinton's convention lecture on economics: "Not one claim was patently false." Fact checkers did, however, heavily criticize the Obama campaign for (supposedly) misrepresenting Romney on abortion; they did this based upon respected news articles from organizations such as CBS and *Time,* which stated: **"Romney's position on abortion is clear."** But such editorials show extreme naivety; they should have said **Romney's "position on abortion is clear today."**

This is an important distinction, because such journalists are acting as if Romney is not a sociopathic liar. I realize people can evolve and change positions, but... , but now please look at Romney's statements on abortion, **as reported by Patheos—a respected religious website:**

Romney Massachusetts Senate Campaign:
1994: Romney: "I believe that abortion should be safe and legal," and "I have since the time my mom took that position when she ran in 1970."
1994: Romney said he'd ensure abortion in Massachusetts was "safe, legal, and free for someone who can't afford it."
1994: Romney on *Roe v. Wade:* "I do not want to change it, overturn it, reverse it."

Governor's Race in Massachusetts: Making His Pro-Choice Values Clear
2002: Romney: "I've been very clear on that, I will preserve and protect a woman's right to choose, and am devoted and dedicated to honoring my word in that regard."
2002: Romney: "Let me make this very clear: I will preserve and protect a woman's right to choose."
2002: Romney: "I do not take the position of a Pro-Life candidate."

Finishing in MA and Looking National: Mr. Changing Sides
2005: Romney: "I am Pro-Life" except "in cases of incest, rape, and to save the life of the mother."
2006: Romney: "I'd like a state to have the choice to be Pro-Life," but "if another state wants to be Pro-Choice that would be its right."

Beginning of his 1st Presidential Run: Mr. Pander
2006: Romney later said he would sign a bill outlawing abortion, "even in cases of rape or incest."
2007: Romney said he would be "delighted" to sign a bill banning "all abortions."
2007: Romney said he supported a nationwide ban on abortion as part of the Republican Party Platform.

2nd Presidential Run: Mr. GOP Moderate
2011: Romney: "Abortion should be limited to only instances of rape, incest or to save the life of the mother."

Primary Romney Realizing Moderation Wasn't a Winning Strategy in the GOP Primary
2011: Romney: "The Supreme Court should reverse *Roe v. Wade.*"
2011: Romney said he "absolutely" would have supported amending the Massachusetts Constitution when governor (2002–2006) to define human life with all rights as beginning at conception.
2012: Romney: "I'm a Pro-Life Person and I'll be a Pro-Life President."

After Primary, Appealing to Swing Voters: Mr. Back to the Middle

2012: Romney: "There's no legislation with regards to abortion that I'm familiar with that would become part of my agenda."

Later that Same Day, After Backlash from Conservatives: Mr. Right Wing Again

2012 Campaign: "Governor Romney would of course support legislation aimed at providing greater protections for life."

2012: Romney: "I am a Pro-Life candidate, will be a Pro-Life president... I will take Pro-Life measures."

Courting Swing State Voters: Mr. Back to the Middle for Real This Time

2012: Spokeswoman: "Those [Romney campaign] ads saying Mitt Romney would ban abortions and contraception seemed a bit extreme. He thinks abortion should be an option."

Campaign spokesman (to swing voters in Ohio): *"Roe v. Wade* would be safe" in a Romney Administration and "remain the law of the land." (November 2012)

http://www.patheos.com/blogs/faithfuldemocrats/2012/11/romney-takes-stand-on-abortion-and-another-and-another-and/

Romney kept saying his position had never changed from last time—but what does that even mean?

Let us not forget, his VP choice, Paul Ryan, is a pro-life fundamentalist, most of the Stupidparty House is pro-life fundamentalist, and Romney as president would no longer be leading the sensible state of Massachusetts, but would be the leader of the Stupidparty. It is not simply humanity that Romney appears to be at least somewhat oblivious to, but evidently women in particular, judging by his refusal to condemn Rush Limbaugh's comments about Sandra Fluke or the advice he would dispense as a Mormon bishop. Mormon history is even more sexist than Catholicism, and Romney is a true Mormon thoroughbred. While his role as a bishop may have forced him to have some exposure to the problems faced by regular people, this role never appeared to cure him.

The New York Times **reports on how a group of Mormon Feminists** "demanding a greater role for women, found him condescending, doctrinaire or just plain bossy. He clashed with a married mother of four who sought to terminate a pregnancy; the incident made news years later, when Mr. Romney ran for United States Senate as a supporter of abortion rights—a position he has since abandoned.

"'Mitt is the type who liked to be called Bishop Romney or President Romney,' said Judy Dushku, a professor of government at Suffolk University in Boston and a Mormon feminist leader. 'He is very conscious of his place in the hierarchy, but not yours.'" Others found him "thoughtful and compassionate."

http://www.nytimes.com/2011/10/16/us/politics/for-romney-a-role-of-faith-and-authority.html?pagewanted=all

Even if during the campaign you could actually figure out his position on rape and incest exceptions, Romney has shown no ability to stand up on any position except protecting and enriching the 1%. I think the odds of him bucking the will of his Stupidparty base on this issue would have been minute—because [as demonstrated in his endless fluctuations] he just does not give a damn one way or the other.

Additionally, the Stupidparty platform at Aug 2012 does not exclude rape and incest.

Campaign ads have 30 to 60 seconds to get the message across. One simply cannot get close to fitting in all that disingenuous claptrap into that time frame. Long story short, those rape and incest exclusions were anything but safe.

Therefore, Obama's much-ma-ligned advert can hardly be called "pants on fire," when all it's trying to say is that if Romney became president, you have absolutely no reason to believe he would not change his twenty-fifth position on the rape-and-incest exclusions at least one more time.

Compare this to Romney's first 60-second campaign ad:

—showing a video of Obama apparently saying, "if we keep talking about the economy, we lose." But what Obama actually said was "Senator McCain's campaign actually said, and I quote, 'If we keep talking about the economy, we're going to lose.'"

Neither Romney nor his campaign apologized; they simply saw nothing wrong with this

strategy. This would appear to be a lie from an extraordinarily dishonest campaign that knew from Day One they could never win by being truthful. If the Stupidparty could win only by utter contempt for the truth, they had clearly picked the man for the job. To lie so absolutely without remorse is a symptom of a certain medical condition.

And Stupidparty politicians do not simply lie; they talk in code to tap into fears and ignorance. These efforts threaten the very fabric of society.

Only in an alternate reality can this happen:

This guy's war credentials . . . . .are deemed better than this guy's.

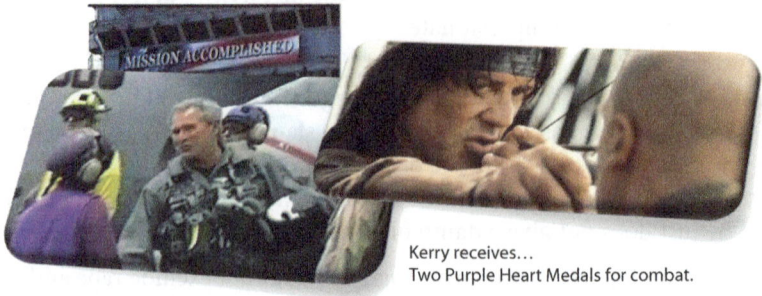

Kerry receives…
Two Purple Heart Medals for combat.

The issue here is not that George Bush Jr. was able to dodge the Vietnam War; many or most people would have been at least tempted. The issue is also not his extremely suspicious (non)activities whilst supposedly flying for the Texas Air National Guard (he may have had drinking issues, which should not be disqualifying). No, the issue here is that a Chicken Hawk with a hybrid Oedipus nomine Patris inferiority complex gets to successfully swiftboat a legitimate war hero. This might not be a great example of false equivalence because the press sort of did its job (yet evidently not enough), in that they established who was lying and who was telling the truth. But this is a good example of how money subverts the facts by promoting Myth, leaving open to debate a subject on which there should be no debate.

Swift Boat Veterans for Truth (SBVT) spent about $22,000,000 doing the exact opposite of their mission statement. Clearly, this money was not coming from a few bitter veterans (though many vets objected to Kerry's statements on "war crimes committed in Southeast Asia" in realization that perhaps the Vietnam War was misguided); no, this money was from the Benefactors. You might remember billionaire Bob Perry, the third largest contributor to the Stupidparty in 2012. Well, Perry Homes gave over $4,000,000 to the SBTV. Clearly, these guys do not age well. One of the big contributors to SBVT was Sam Fox who went on to become ambassador to Belgium, in spite of being blocked by the Senate (recess appointment). The PR Company behind the SBTV was an expert in Stupidparty dirty tricks.

http://www.sourcewatch.org/index.php/Swift_Boat_Veterans_for_Truth
http://www.opensecrets.org/527s/527events.php?id=61

"Dems voted for the Iraq War too."
The details behind the Bush lies and misinformation are discussed in the Freedom(s) chapter.

But people still come up with the "Dems voted for it to" line.

To allow this statement to be made without instantly reaching for a mallet would indicate a significant level of journalistic malfeasance. While on the face of it the statement is true, it reveals a high level of selective memory and lack of foreign-policy strategic thinking.

First, the context of the vote. The Bush team was arguing that Saddam Hussein was building WMDs and assisting al-Qaeda, amongst other significantly less important issues. The president had access to all the intelligence. If the elected president is willing to risk American lives, you have to have a level of trust that he is both competent and being truthful—as there can be no worse crime than misleading your country into a war. Who would do that?

Also, at the time the world community was bent on trying to get Saddam Hussein to co-operate with UN inspectors. The vote giving the president the authority to attack is not the same as actually voting to attack. By giving the president such authority, Congress gave Bush the leverage to force Saddam Hussein to the bargaining table and to cooperate with UN inspectors. Thus, if the inspectors were being unduly obstructed, it would be up to them to state that. But…

As Hans Blix, the chief UN inspector, wrote:
Blix (retired head of the International Atomic Energy Agency) was called back from retirement by UN Secretary General Kofi Annan to lead the United Nations Monitoring, Verification and Inspection Commission on Iraq.

"Rather, there seemed to be a prospect of an unimpeded inspection process—at least if the military pressure remained. I noted that Iraq 'has on the whole cooperated rather well so far' on process and that 'access has been provided to all sites we have wanted to inspect and with one exception it has been prompt.' The criticism I voiced was in relation to Iraq's failure to be 'proactive': either it should surrender WMDs, if there were any, or help to dispel the many unresolved issues. My comments were deliberately sharp, because I wanted to push Iraq hard to cooperate actively, as Security Council resolutions demanded. On point after point I explained what Iraq could do."
http://inside.org.au/iraq-2003-blix/

The leverage was bearing fruit. The inspectors were getting access; they were far from ready to assert otherwise. Only an incredibly myopic and incompetent president would authorize a war when the inspectors were making headway in a difficult mission—to find something that did not exist. And only an incredibly incompetent president would invade at the very time that Saddam Hussein was trying to flee the country and only an incredibly incompetent president would carry on asserting that Saddam Hussein had links to al-Qaeda—a charge that had been investigated and debunked numerous times by the CIA. British and Israeli intelligence had all come to the same conclusion before the attack was launched.
http://en.wikipedia.org/wiki/Saddam_Hussein_and_al-Qaeda_link_allegations
Bush was advised in no uncertain terms that there was no link. http://en.wikipedia.org/wiki/Against_All_Enemies

So while it was not criminal or even clearly wrong to vote to give the president the authority, it was a crime to actually authorize the war. It was a crime to fabricate evidence of WMDs, as had been figured out by Joe Wilson, a respected former U.S. ambassador sent to find such evidence, and it was a crime to out a CIA agent (Joe Wilson's wife), thus putting all her Iraqi contacts' lives at risk.

There's no equivalence between the bipartisan actions of Congress, intended to assist the president, and the actual decision to go to war made by Bush and his team—who should be designated war criminals, and one day history will surely make that judgment. I am convinced that no other political leader (other than Cheney) would have been that incompetent or made the decision to invade.

Nelson Mandela Dies:

A great man can still have a positive ripple effect. While evidently Rick Santorum believes his crusade to prevent people from getting healthcare coverage is akin to Mandela's fight against apartheid, individuals like Gingrich and Ted Cruz were willing to let bygones be bygones for at least a day. But this burst of truth and reconciliation did not sit so well with many of their Disciples. Ted Cruz's Facebook page degenerated into bile. But now even Cokie Roberts—a level headed contributing senior news analyst for National Public Radio, who also works as a political commentator for ABC News—falls into the false-equivalence trap. She says, "I'm sure the president is getting blowback for bringing Bush with him on the plane." (To Mandela's funeral.)
http://www.npr.org/player/v2/mediaPlayer.html?action=1&t=1&islist=false&id=249652844&m=249681401

No he will not, and yes people must stop saying such silly things. I tell you what—please find the equivalence for this:

False-equivalent pressure groups / Research Organizations:

As already referenced, one does not need to be a rocket scientist to figure out the difference between a Benefactor… or Citizens… or Freedom… pressure group and a legitimate Public or Citizens or Freedom pressure group. If you are at all confused as to what the real goal of such groups are just follow the money.

False equivalence: how "balance" makes the media dangerously dumb:
Bob Garfield, *The Guardian:*

"We've seen it in climate change reporting; we see it in shutdown coverage. Journalists should be unbiased, yes, but not brainless. Let us state this unequivocally: false equivalency—the practice of giving equal media time and space to demonstrably invalid positions for the sake of supposed reportorial balance—is dishonest, pernicious and cowardly."

Garfield uses the following editorial from *The Washington Post* (discussing the Stupidparty efforts to destroy the Affordable Care Act by closing down the government and defaulting on the debt) as a typical example of false equivalence:

"Ultimately, the grown-ups in the room will have to do their jobs, which in a democracy with divided government means compromising for the common good. That means Mr. Boehner, his counterpart in the Senate, Harry M. Reid (D-Nev), minority leaders Sen. Mitch McConnell (R-Ky) and Rep. Nancy Pelosi (D-Calif) and the president. Both sides are inordinately concerned with making sure that, if catastrophe comes, the other side takes the political hit. In truth, none of their reputations stands to benefit."

The Guardian then points out that this *Washington Post* editorial is full of it, completely wrong. The shutdown could not simply be the result of the two parties failing to agree on Obamacare, because that ship has already sailed. The Obamacare law had been passed, reviewed by the Supreme Court, and a national mandate received on the back of two elections. Yet Stupidparty House had redundantly attempted to repeal it 40 times (more since this article was written). So *The Guardian* concludes:

"No, the shutdown is the result of the divide between mainstream, center-right Republicans and Tea Party extremists. The latter are wrapped in suicide belts and perfectly willing to blow the GOP and the economy to kingdom come if they can: a) kill Obamacare (as if); or b) guarantee campaign windfalls from likeminded anti-government crackpots.

"This is not gridlock. It is a hostage situation."
http://www.theguardian.com/commentisfree/2013/oct/11/false-equivalence-balance-media

You are either with Stupidparty or you are a Liberal subversive:

Having established that there are different degrees of error, false statements, and lies, we realize that the water gets muddy and only objective insight will see or admit to the difference. Of course, the media makes a show of getting to the facts, and there are fact-checking websites. However, these efforts are massively constrained by the need to appear to be neutral—because if you consistently point out the nonsense from the Stupidparty, you get labeled a communist subversive. Not great for the image of a journalist simply looking to expose the absurd and support the truth. Also, there are individuals on the Democratic side who deserve ridicule—and various entities/respondents such as *The Daily Show, The Colbert Report,* and even MSNBC will happily expose such individuals.

Evidently, everyone in the USA is partisan; even the judges are identified with a party. One hardly needs to be a constitutional expert to know which Supreme Court justices will vote for what. This inability to find nonpartisan panels explains why electoral districting can often be so peculiar. The other problem being that experts, tending to be fact driven, are therefore not "Stupidparty," and thus, they are automatically labeled as liberals, along with Teachers, Readers, Journalists, Artists, Environmentalists, Scientists, Economists, Humanitarians, and Community Organizers.

So what to do? How can we get an objective take? Much to the chagrin of any Stupidparty Disciple, why not go abroad for an answer? The problem is that the Stupidparty has only one and a half countries overseas that might root for it. Pakistan being one (Obama has shown them up by the Bin Laden incident and those pesky drones)—the other half being the Netanyahu half of Israel and his death-wish alliance with American Evangelicals, who just know he will end up in hell anyway. But foreigners do represent 95% of humanity, so how can you discount them entirely? What is the most efficient country in the world? After the Swiss? The Germans?

***Der Spiegel* Article—Opinion Piece:**

Der Spiegel is a German weekly **news magazine** published in **Hamburg**. According to *The Economist, Der Spiegel* is one of **continental Europe's** most influential magazines. After the 2012 conventions—a time when the stars of each party have an opportunity to put their best foot forward on the national stage—it carried the following story by Gregor Peter Schmitz:

"Truth is in short supply. Both the Democrats and the Republicans have become more unabashed in their lies than ever before. With a mainstream media weakened by the appearance of partisan bias and editorial staffs that have been ravaged during the crisis, many of the whoppers won't be second-guessed."

The article then observed that, in the assessment of Politifact, Democratic misstatements pale when compared to the Stupidparty's "unscrupulous" tactics. The Pulitzer Prize–winning **PolitiFact.com** is, according to Wikipedia, a project operated by the *Tampa Bay Times*, in which reporters and editors from the *Times* and affiliated media outlets "fact-check statements by members of Congress, the White House, lobbyists and interest groups." (Wiki)

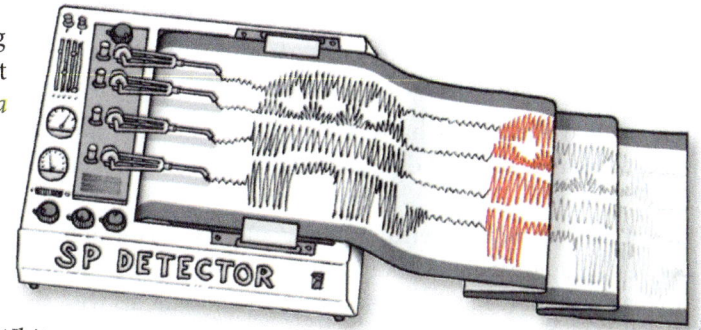

As *Der Speigel's* report (unsurprisingly) discovered, 10% of Romney's and other leading Republicans' statements were absolutely false, whilst Obama was totally incorrect 2% of the time. They do not see any sign that this situation will improve, despite the fact that Ryan's untruths have become legend. *Der Spiegel* thus rather incredulously ends with a quote from a Romney pollster:

"Despite all the debate over Ryan's most recent fibs, 'We're not going to let our campaign be dictated by fact checkers,' a defiant Romney pollster, Neil Newhouse, said at a panel hosted by ABC News at the Republican National Convention in Tampa last week."
http://www.spiegel.de/international/world/a-campaign-of-lies-us-candidates-unabashed-in-truth-stretching-a-853925.html

Therefore, not only are the Stupidparty lies worse, as demonstrated earlier in this chapter, but they lie 500% more often. But lies work, and this forces even the more honest politicians to stretch the truth more than they would otherwise feel comfortable. If you are playing a competitive game of golf with a blatant and repetitive cheat—and your very career depended on the outcome—I suspect the quality of your sportsmanship might suffer. I will take a mulligan too.

A *New York Times* op-ed reached the same conclusion:
Kevin M. Kruse, a professor of history at Princeton, is the co-editor, most recently, of Fog of War: The Second World War and the Civil Rights Movement.
http://www.princeton.edu/history/people/display_person.xml?netid=kkruse

This article takes a swing at the bulk of the news media, pointing out that fact-checking is fundamental to journalism but that it had become clear during the 2012 presidential campaign that most journalists were just going through the motions, presenting opposing arguments as if they had equal credibility. The article concludes:

"Fact-checking, once a foundation for all reporting, was now deemed the province of a specialized few. But as this campaign has made clear, not even the dedicated fact-checkers have made much difference. PolitiFact has chronicled 19 'pants on fire' lies by Mr. Romney and 7 by Mr. Obama since 2007, but Mr. Romney's whoppers have been qualitatively far worse: the 'apology tour,' the 'government takeover of health care,' the '$4,000 tax hike on middle class families,' the gutting of welfare-to-work rules, the shipment by Chrysler of jobs from Ohio to China."
http://www.nytimes.com/2012/11/06/opinion/the-real-loser-truth.html

A look at the graph below will help quantify what has happened as a result of the Stupidparty infrastructure being treated as if it should be worth listening to. Is it possible that the more you listen, the less informed you get? Well, I think we just demonstrated that in the previous chapter.

Not all Media are dopes—*The LA Times* now has a corrective policy:

"Letters that have an untrue basis (for example, ones that say there's no sign humans have caused climate change) do not get printed," Paul Thornton wrote.
http://www.cbsnews.com/8301-205_162-57606909/l.a-times-cuts-off-climate-change-deniers.

If it was not so sad and pathetic, and we could just do our jobs as voters and consumers, the extent of Stupidparty lies should simply be hilarious. But people who choose to vote Stupidparty (and now I am referring to those individuals who should know better) are allowing this black hole of lies to swallow up the light that would normally shine upon the truth—forcing the rest of us into their parallel universe, where the absurd rules over reason.

But the Stupidparty thinks it is just fine to deceive. Michael Steele (64th Chairman of the RNC) explains.
http://www.youtube.com/watch?v=O07V1N5CLhs

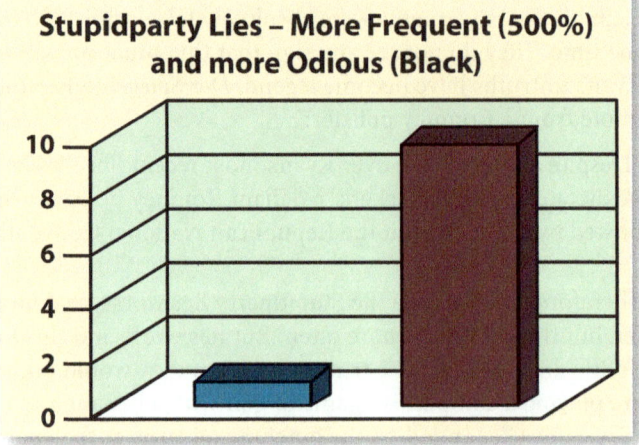

Stupidparty Lies – More Frequent (500%) and more Odious (Black)

CHAPTER 19

The quest for Ignorance-based humor

On the other hand, when you grow up, you will discover that some of the people in this world never passed beyond the stage of the cave-man.

—Hendrik Willem van Loon, *The Story of Mankind*

Let us look at a list of the most well-known Comedians operating in recent years.

Bee, Samantha
Behar, Joy
Bernhard, Sandra
Black, Jack
Black, Lewis
Borat
Carrey, Jim
Carroll, Steve
Carvey, Dana
Chappelle, David
Cleese, John
Colbert, Stephen
Crystal, Billy
David, Larry
DeGeneres, Ellen
Fey, Tina
Fox, Jamie
Garofalo, Janeane

Gervais, Ricky
Goldberg, Whoopi
Helms, Ed
Leary, Dennis
Letterman, David
Maher, Bill
Martin, Steve
Miller, Dennis
Murphy, Eddie
Oliver, John
Palin, Michael
Rock, Chris
Seinfeld, Jerry
Silverman, Sarah
Smith, Will
Stewart, Jon
Sykes, Wanda
Williams, Robin

Apparently, it is tough to find comedians that lean Stupidparty.

I was perhaps being generous putting Dennis Miller on the list, but back in the day his rapid-fire verbal jousting was pretty funny and he could hold an audience in his spell. But then 9/11 happened and possibly he learned all the wrong lessons. While most people around the world would have been comfortable with going after Bin Laden in Afghanistan, the incorrectly prioritized Iraq focus (driven by George Bush's personal defects) gradually changed all that. The September 11 tragedy had given the USA a great opportunity to strike a deep chord with many other countries, as the world community had been horrified by the event. But people like Dennis Miller allowed jingoistic outrage to trump introspection and the pursuit of a worthy foreign policy strategy. Having made that mistake and then voting Stupidparty in the 2004 election, thereby choosing to ignore the facts, Dennis Miller and the rest of Stupidparty supporters are forced to double down in order to rationalize that second Iraq war, which can now clearly be seen as having been undertaken only after a huge deception.

This doubling down, this entrenchment, this calcification of the brain, has a serious apparent side effect for Dennis Miller, in that he is no longer funny. He now apparently spends his time failing to add humor to various shows on Fox.

Comedy TV shows and Fox's Countereffort

Stupidparty advocates do not appear to have a coherent explanation. They blame Hollywood—forgetting that a comedian, to be successful, must simply make people laugh. If you can do that, you have a career. They point to Kelsey Grammer (more an actor than a comedian); he was funny on two famous sitcoms and decidedly unfunny when he undertook the Stupidparty attempt at comedy satire, *An American Carol,* in 2008 (in it, an anti-American filmmaker out to abolish the July Fourth holiday is visited by three ghosts, who try to change his perception of the country). This movie earned a Rotten Tomatoes rating of 0% from "Top Critics" and in spite of a well-known director and cast, it took in a rather pathetic $7m at the box office.

Stupidparty blogs try to come up with names of Stupidparty-supporting comedians, like Jeff Foxworthy, who appears to be a perfectly okay guy, with Christian "values," and I guess his humor is based on a Southern redneck shtick. But according to Wiki, "In 2012, Foxworthy endorsed Republican presidential candidate Mitt Romney, explaining, 'I avoided politics for 53 years of my life. I have been doing stand-up comedy for almost 30 and never wanted to be political. Selfishly, I wanted to make everyone laugh. But it got to the point that this is too important.'"

So what I read from that is that he has not made a living from advocating Stupidparty policies. How a Christian can vote for Romney is a different issue, but this oddity is not really relevant (since it apparently does not feature significantly in his public outings), and people living happily as rural hunters minding their own business—well, a dislike of any government intrusion is hardly an irrational philosophy.

But if Hollywood is liberal (a rather facile and misleading label), surely someone like Rupert Murdoch can tap into the massive business opportunity that must exist: 47% of the population are thirsting for good Stupidparty comedy.

Good Stupidparty Comedy

Jealous of the success of shows on Comedy Central in general and *The Daily Show* in particular, Roger Ailes is determined to counterpunch.

The 1/2 Hour News Hour. (Worst ever TV Show?) Starring comedians(?) Kurt Long, Jennifer Robertson, Manny Coto, Ned Rice, Dennis Miller.

Ran Feb. 18 through Sept. 23, 2007, created by Joel Surnow, a producer best known for his success with the serialized action show 24. His initial label was

"*The Daily Show* for conservatives"—later expanding upon that description by stating, "You can turn on any show and see Bush being bashed. There really is nothing out there for those who want satire that tilts right." Radio talk show host Rush Limbaugh had a recurring cameo role as the president, with conservative pundit Ann Coulter as his vice president.

The *Chicago Tribune* said, "The humor is so predictable and so stale that it fails to produce any laughs," while the…

The *Philadelphia Inquirer* commented, "The 1/2 Hour News Hour is slow torture all by itself."

MetaCritic's television division, which produces composite scores based on prominent reviewers' opinions of television pilots, other episodes, and/or DVD releases, gave *The Half Hour News Hour* pilots a 12 out of 100, making it the lowest-rated television production ever reviewed on the site. At the time the show was canceled, Bill Shine, the senior vice president of programming at Fox News, stated that "we are considering ways to re tool the show for future scheduling needs." The retooling continues. (Wiki)

STUPIDPARTY COMEDY MOVIES:
Since 1995

Movies attacking Stupidparty Values:

Title	Year	Rotten Tomatoes %	Comment
The American President	1995	95%	President—Polar opposite to Stupidparty
Bullworthy	1998	75%	Vital message about truth in politics
Bowling for Columbine	2002	96%	Targets NRS board members & others
Team America	2004	77%	Ironic take on Stupidparty Foreign Policy
Fahrenheit 9/11	2004	83%	Outing "evil doers" in the White House
Talladega Knights	2006	72%	Results of excess Consumerism etc.
Thank you for Smoking	2006	86%	How we are tricked into bad habits
Borat	2007	91%	Brutal takedown on Stupidparty values
Sicko	2007	97%	Even third-world countries have better healthcare
Idiocracy	2007	97%	The future is, we keep voting Stupidparty
Religulous	2008	69%	A case against Religion
The Campaign	2012	65%	Koch brothers making a mockery of Democracy
Total		**1003%**	

Movies supporting Stupidparty Values:

Title	Year	Rotten Tomatoes % Top Critics	Comment
An American Carol	2008	0%	An attack on Michael Moore. How to turn him Stupidparty.
No more			
No more			
No more			
Total		**0%**	

If a comedy is funny—which clearly, with one exception, the above are—and if it is also trying to send a message, then at the very least, the message is worth thinking about. We have zero % for Stupidparty compared to over 1,000% for attacks on Stupidparty. So I think we can actually say that Stupidparty humor is infinitely worse than real humor.

Stupidparty Comedy TV shows

None.

Every good comedy I can think of ultimately ends up about compassion, tolerance, and dealing with the realities of the world we live in. Shows that include bigoted characters like, say, Cartman in *South Park,* are there to assist in the narrative, to give us a benchmark from which we can all learn how to overcome ignorance and prejudice.

So if the top comedians and if movies and if TV shows cannot lend humor to the cause of Stupidparty, where else can we look for Stupidparty comedy, short of going to a KKK reunion or a Palm Beach cocktail party? Perhaps we should default back to major Stupidparty conventions, see how its leaders use comedy or how paid professionals can both support their agenda and be funny comedians—since comedy is a traditional way of starting a serious speech, or making points, and just simply getting the audience in a favorable state of mindlessness

Stupidparty leaders at their 2012 Convention

The following were told as jokes.

Romney: "President Obama promised to slow the rise of the oceans"—pause for laughter—"and to heal the planet." Audience laughs long and hard, evidently oblivious to science and George Bush's dreadfully incompetent response to Katrina.

Romney: "I thought about asking my church's pension fund to invest [in Bain], but I thought it was bad enough if I lost my investors' money, but I didn't want to go to hell too."

Pawlenty: He lists a bunch of Stupidparty-imagined Obama mistakes, ending with Joe Biden. The audience laughs at this excuse for a punch line.

(It should be noted that Mr. Pawlenty is a pretty wooden speaker, and thus timing and delivery of punch lines tends to be painfully awkward.)

Pawlenty: "Obama failed us, but that is understandable. A lot of people fail at their first job"—this gets almost a standing ovation.

Pawlenty: "And I will give Obama credit for creating jobs these last four years, for Golf Caddies." Even the Stupidparty audience appears to be getting bored at this point.

Pawlenty: "The president takes more vacations than that guy on the *Bizarre Foods* show."

John Thune said that he was a good [basket]baller and that he is still waiting on an invite from Barack Obama for a game of one-on-one. He added that it wouldn't be hard to defend Obama because he would always "go left."

Our inspirational Bobby Jindal gave humor his best shot.

Clint Eastwood and the empty chair: A terribly sad fiasco. But why was it so awkwardly unfunny? Remember the empty chair was Obama, and Obama's fictional comments were laced with venom and expletive language—tools never employed by Obama. If you are going to attack someone, make it based on that person, not your imaginary version of that person

Here is an explanation: punch lines should be clever, based on at least an element of truth. The fact is that there is Global Warming, Obama has had to achieve compromise by going to the right, and Obama at that point of time (August 2012) had overseen job growth for 30 months. It is really tough for Stupidparty to make jokes about jobs—since they have only one strategy: below-minimum-wage jobs created by the trickle-down effect (from the wealthy getting more tax cuts, paid for by stripping benefits and protections away from everyone else). It is just asking too much to expect that such jokes, when supporting such odious policies, would be funny.

Stupidparty pays for Professional Comedian

2012 CPAC
Bingo!—found a Stupidparty "comedian" to keep Dennis Miller company

The annual Conservative Political Action Conference (CPAC) is attended by conservative activists and elected officials from across the nation. More than 100 other organizations contribute in various ways. Heritage Foundation, Let Freedom Ring, the Young America's Foundation, and the National Rifle Association are some of the most prominent co-sponsors in recent years.

So plenty of money to burn, and they need humor to help liven up these wooden gatherings.

Right Wing Watch reported: "Conservative comedian Brad Stein (bet you have never heard of him) closed out day one of CPAC with a fifteen-minute set that consisted primarily of him railing against 'the Wussification of America' and screaming at a seventeen-year-old kid in the front row because kids today are, in Stein's view, representative of the very 'wussification' he detests… like requiring cars to have airbags or drivers to use seat belts and child safety seats."

But there's more

We have failed to find "good" Stupidparty humor from well-known comedians or partisan professional comedians—or in movies, TV shows, from Stupidparty leaders and celebrity advocates. Perhaps Stupidparty Disciples can fill the void. They certainly think they can. Here are some samples. I have avoided posting clearly hateful material.

Well, this might
be hateful

This seems to be Mad Hatter Tea Party
thought process

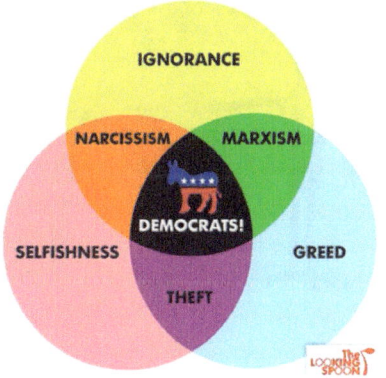

Zero objectivity. Assumes hedge funds are as useful as any other business
http://www.alternet.org/story/142556/over_100_million_americans have_smoked_marijuana_--_and_it's_still_illegal

Another tremendous leap into the absurd

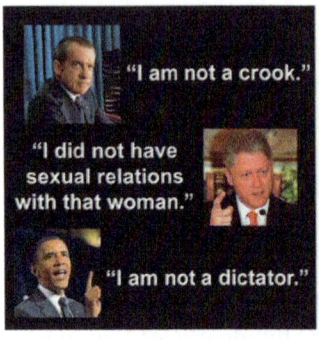

The dreams of the Stupidparty mind

Whatever floats your boat

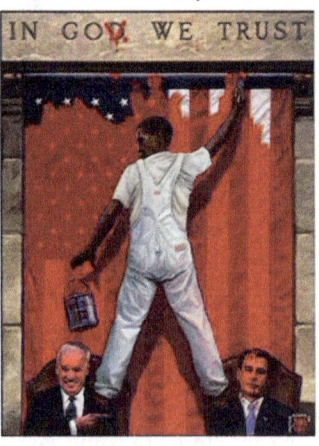

Could not have said it better

History Challenged

I have been unable to find good Stupidparty comedy. This doesn't mean that progressives cannot be mocked; of course, they can. The professional comedians listed at the beginning of this chapter go after anything that deserves mocking. Jon Stewart goes after silliness, regardless of party. The Occupy Wall Street crowd was mocked; it has failed to get traction, because they have so many diverse views—many flaky, many based on a total lack of economic fundamentals. This is not to say that if they had added substance and rallied around two or three cohesive themes, they would still have failed to gain traction—they are too easy to mock and discredit.

But comedy needs to be funny, based on elements of truth and not based on ignorance. Stupidparty cannot be supported by humor, because it is based on the opposite of those commodities. Bigotry and ignorance is just not funny to the vast bulk of humanity. Humor does not have left-wing bias—any more than truth and facts do. To blame the medium is just silly. We live in a free market country, and people will profit from good humor, but they will not profit from Stupidparty humor.

This is why Stupidparty humor is apparently impossible to find. This is also another reason why voting for Stupidparty is not remotely amusing.

Just for fun and to help negate some of the pitiful humor above...

CHAPTER 20

Postpartum uplift
or
letdown?

Life is like riding a bicycle, you keep moving or you fall off.

—Einstein

Looking at post-Presidential and post-Vice Presidential aspirations:

It is during the presidential campaigns that the best and the brightest take up the torch in promoting differing solutions and agendas regarding the problems of the day. Money flows in to numerous candidates, who then hire advisers, strategists, researchers, speech writers, and marketers. The candidates put their best foot forward. But as they age, these assets start taking more of a backseat, and the candidates' views are likely to become more adamant, more calcified, their character more transparent. So it is interesting see what these leaders or potential leaders do after they move on from either being president or planning to be.

Stupidparty matchups.

1) Reagan v. Carter:

President Ronald Reagan was probably suffering early onset of Alzheimer's disease by the end of his presidency; thus, retiring to the ranch was no doubt the best, most logical course of action. But one suspects that even if he had been healthy, President Reagan would have been totally content to spend the rest of his time with his beloved wife Nancy at the ranch.

President Carter, however, had so much more to offer. Within minutes of Reagan's taking office, Carter's much-criticized stance towards the Iranian hostages was vindicated, with the peaceful outcome. President Carter taught at Emory University, wrote numerous books, helped expand Habitat for Humanity to build affordable housing. He established The Carter Center to advance human rights, alleviate suffering, promote democracy, fight disease, to mediate and prevent conflicts. By way of illustration, The Carter Center is credited with reducing Guinea worm disease by 99%—an illness that impacted 3,500,000 people a year. He helped President Bill Clinton get North Korea to freeze and dismantle its nuclear program. This agreement fell apart under Stupidparty Bush Jr.'s brilliant foreign policy strategies of calcifying eternal enemies by deeming them "axis of evil" countries.

In 2002 President Carter received the Nobel Peace Prize. Although he is about 90 years of age, President Carter remains actively engaged in helping others. His inclusive and selfless activities seem to be in line with actual Christian teachings.

2) George Bush Sr. v. Clinton:

President George H. W. Bush rose to the top by a process of impressive diplomatic and political accomplishments and seniority and founded a family dynasty. His Gulf War was at least an honest one, and his efforts to be inclusive and compassionate were hit and miss, in a party moving in the other direction, as he sets up "a thousand points of light" and selected Stupidparty apostle Clarence Thomas to the Supreme Court—almost as awkward a choice as, but more damaging than, McCain selecting Palin as VP candidate. Although during his presidency the charity may have seemed somewhat expedient, he does stay involved after he leaves office.

After the presidency he basically retires to the ranch. He does some traveling (whilst in Iraq, there was an assassination attempt), becomes a chairman here and there, gets honored and makes various discreet appearances. He went into cruise control (in an August 2001 letter he told journalist Carl Cannon, "Now at 77, I find that I am perfectly content to let history be the judge of those things I got right, and of my mistakes as well"). Ironically, it was Bill Clinton's energy that would add more to George Bush's retirement. As their friendship and joint projects grew, President Bush wrote, "You cannot get mad at the guy. I admit to wondering why he can't stay on time, but when I see him interacting with folks my wonder turns to understanding, with a dollop of angst thrown in, Clinton is a fascinating character. He has opinions on everything—no matter what. He seems to have a great grasp of history's events and people."

http://politicalticker.blogs.cnn.com/2013/03/05/george-h-w-bush-on-bonding-with-bill-clinton/

President William Jefferson Clinton (paraphrasing and quoting Wikipedia):

President William Clinton does so much more than build the standard presidential library and write memoirs. In 2007 he released *Giving: How Each of Us Can Change the World,* which became a *New York Times* best seller and garnered positive reviews. In the aftermath of the 2004 Asian tsunami, U.N. Secretary-General Kofi Annan appointed Clinton to head a relief effort. After Hurricane Katrina, Clinton joined with fellow former president George H. W. Bush to establish the Bush–Clinton Tsunami Fund in January 2005.

Based on his philanthropic worldview, Clinton created the William J. Clinton Foundation to address issues of global importance. This foundation includes the Clinton Foundation HIV and AIDS Initiative (CHAI), which strives to combat that disease, and has worked with the Australian government toward that end. The Clinton Global Initiative (CGI) was begun by the Clinton Foundation in 2005 (and has raised about $74b through 2013, three times more than the Bill Gates Foundation). It attempts to address world problems, such as global public health, poverty alleviation, and religious and ethnic conflict. In 2005, Clinton announced through his foundation an agreement with manufacturers to stop selling sugared drinks in schools.

Clinton's foundation joined with the Large Cities Climate Leadership Group in 2006 to improve cooperation among those cities, and he met with foreign leaders to promote this initiative. The foundation has received donations from a number of governments all over the world, including in Asia and the Middle East. In 2008, Foundation Director Inder Singh announced that deals to reduce the price of antimalaria drugs by 30% in developing nations. Clinton also spoke in favor of California Proposition 87 on alternative energy, which was voted down.

In 2009, Clinton traveled to North Korea on behalf of Euna Lee and Laura Ling who had been imprisoned for illegally entering the country from China. Jimmy Carter had made a similar visit in 1994. After Clinton met with North Korean leader Kim Jong-il, Kim issued a pardon.

Since then, Clinton has been assigned a number of other diplomatic missions. He was named United Nations Special Envoy to Haiti in 2009. In response to the 2010 Haiti earthquake, U.S. President Barack Obama announced that Clinton and George W. Bush would coordinate efforts to raise funds for Haiti's recovery. Clinton continues to visit Haiti to witness the inauguration of refugee villages and to raise funds for the earthquake victims. These activities highlight a different attitude on Haiti than that of various Stupidparty leaders. In 2010, Clinton announced support of, and delivered the keynote address for, the inauguration of NTR, Ireland's first environmental foundation. At the 2012 Democratic National Convention, Clinton gave a widely praised speech nominating Barack Obama.

http://en.wikipedia.org/wiki/Bill_Clinton

One suspects that health permitting, Bill Clinton has many more chapters left in him.

3) George Bush Jr. v. Al Gore:

President George W. Bush. Retires to the ranch. Well, not literally. That rather ugly bit of land in Crawford where he would forever claim to be clearing scrub for no apparent reason other than pretending to be a cowboy. He moves to a suburb in Dallas where most notably he conducted the opening coin toss at a 2009 Dallas Cowboys game.

Okay—perhaps I am being a little unfair. In this context, keeping silent is impressive and as president he had at least meant well with his African focus; he has now been spotted doing stuff in Africa. But with any AIDS-related efforts, the more they are linked to abstinence, the more counterproductive they are likely to be.

President not-to-be Al Gore.
(Wherein I get to bask, benefit, and steal from all his glory)

Even though he won the popular vote and may have won Florida, a combination of Governor Jeb Bush, the overtly partisan Florida secretary of state (Kathleen Harris), and the Supreme Court, ended his ambitions in a highly questionable manner. Regardless and in spite of this crushing blow, Al Gore was far from done.

He continued to demonstrate that he has a very frustrating gift, that it was not only regarding the Internet that he is a man living ahead of his time. He was quick to see what was happening on the Bush Jr. Iraq war front, ahead of the curve on gay marriage; he refused to endorse his own VP choice and future Stupidparty convert, Joe Lieberman. He identified the dangers of Stupidparty religious zealotry, and he continued campaigning on the environment. He warned of the ever-increasing assaults on democracy:

In 2002—in a speech in California he lays out why he thinks that George Bush and Congress are far too much of a hurry to Invade Iraq. This criticism was prescient, since it was before the invasion and before it had become evident that the country had been misled.

In 2004—in a speech, Gore correctly accuses Bush of betrayal—by misleading the country—an analysis he is well equipped to deliver, since he had always been ahead of the curve anyway.

In 2004—Gore is honored to open the Democratic National Convention.

In 2004—Generation Investments Management is born; he is co-founder and Chairman. Later he launches the Alliance for Climate Protection (Note to Benefactors: this means protecting the environment, not raping it for personal gain.) He now also heads the climate change solutions group within the venture-capital firm of Kleiner Perkins Caufield and Byers. Gore also helps with the Live Earth benefit concerts.

In 2005—an ever-on-the-ball Gore warns of Religious Zealots, pretty much making the same points as I have been echoing in this book.

In 2005—no doubt horrified by the incompetence of Bush Administration, Gore discretely does a "heck of a job" in chartering two planes to evacuate almost 300 people from New Orleans after Hurricane Katrina.

In 2006—wins Academy Award for Best Documentary, *An Inconvenient Truth.* (As I've been on the case since around 1978, maybe I was ahead of his curve? Who knows?)

In 2007—writes a Stupidparty-type book, thus showing how remarkably ahead of the curve he is—but his book is called *The Assault on Reason*. He also argues that democracy is under threat but that the internet can help save us all. He clearly has a point, as anyone can see if they have been enjoying all the hyperlinks and hot links contained in this book.

In 2007—Gore receives the Nobel Peace Prize.

In 2008—again before public sentiment on the issue had fully taken hold Gore argued against the ban of same-sex marriage. He stated, "I think that gay men and women ought to have the same rights as heterosexual men and women to make contracts, have hospital visiting rights, and join together in marriage."
Data extracted from http://en.wikipedia.org/wiki/Al_Gore

4) Bob Dole v. Ted Kennedy: No clear winner here.

Presidential candidate Bob Dole had an impressive post-political career, adding to his military service to his country—concerned about lack of bipartisanship, world hunger, and erectile dysfunction. He is really a pre-Stupidparty individual, had a great sense of humor, and obviously capable of empathy.

Ted Kennedy kept fighting for reform to help the poor and the sick until his last breath.

5) Pat Robertson v. Jerry Brown:

Presidential hopeful Pat Robertson. This Stupidparty founding father (has been covered at some length already) and is surely massively ill-suited to living life outside of an asylum or apparently a jail cell, as *The Guardian* reports in "Mission Congo: how Pat Robertson raised millions on the back of a non-existent aid project":

"The televangelist claimed Operation Blessing was giving vital aid in response to the 1994 Rwandan crisis. A documentary opening at the Toronto film festival paints a less flattering picture. Some of the most damaging criticism of Pat Robertson comes from former aid workers at Operation Blessing.

"One of the stranger sights of the refugee crisis that followed the 1994 Rwandan genocide was of stretcher-bearers rushing the dying to medical tents, with men running alongside reciting Bible verses to the withering patients.

"The bulk of the thousands of doctors and nurses struggling to save lives—as about 40,000 people died of cholera—were volunteers for the international medical charity Médecins Sans Frontières (MSF) [Doctors without Borders]. The Bible readers were hired by the American televangelist and former religious right presidential candidate, Pat Robertson, and his aid organization, Operation Blessing International.

"But on Robertson's US television station, the Christian Broadcasting Network, that reality was reversed, as he raised millions of dollars from loyal followers by claiming Operation Blessing was at the forefront of the international response to the biggest refugee crisis of the decade. It's a claim he continues to make, even though an official investigation into Robertson's operation in Virginia accused him of 'fraudulent and deceptive'

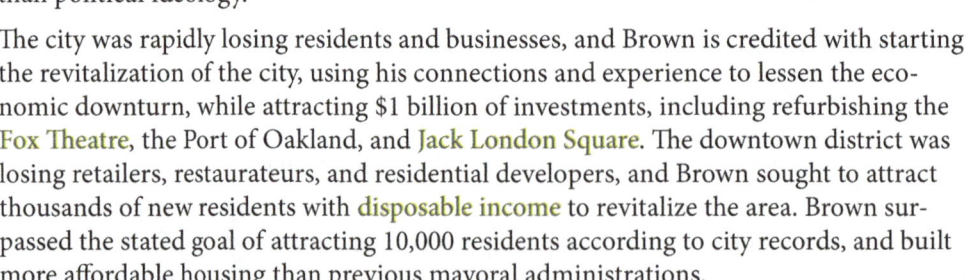

claims when he was running an almost non-existent aid operation."
http://www.imdb.com/news/ni56141651/

Presidential hopeful Jerry Brown.
Paraphrasing and quoting Wikipedia:

In 1999 after leaving the Democratic Party, disillusioned by the two-party system. Brown easily became mayor of the troubled, overwhelmingly minority city of Oakland. Brown was "more interested in downtown redevelopment and economic growth than political ideology."

The city was rapidly losing residents and businesses, and Brown is credited with starting the revitalization of the city, using his connections and experience to lessen the economic downturn, while attracting $1 billion of investments, including refurbishing the Fox Theatre, the Port of Oakland, and Jack London Square. The downtown district was losing retailers, restaurateurs, and residential developers, and Brown sought to attract thousands of new residents with disposable income to revitalize the area. Brown surpassed the stated goal of attracting 10,000 residents according to city records, and built more affordable housing than previous mayoral administrations.

Attorney General of California (2007–2011).

In June 2008, Brown filed a fraud lawsuit, claiming mortgage lender Countrywide Financial engaged in "unfair and deceptive" practices to get homeowners to apply for risky mortgages far beyond their means. The suit was settled in October 2008 after Bank of America acquired Countrywide. The settlement involved the modifying of troubled "predatory loans" up to $8.4 billion.

Governor of California (2011–present).

Through budget cuts and tax increases, it appears that California's dreadful economic performance under the previous Stupidparty Governor Arnold Schwarzenegger is on the mend.

http://en.wikipedia.org/wiki/Jerry_Brown

6) Alan Keyes v. Jesse Jackson:

Keyes ran for president in 1996, 2000, and 2008 and was a failed Republican nominee for the U.S. Senate in 1988, 1992, and 2004. Evidently, God must have changed his mind, as he only ran because "You are doing what you believe to be required by your respect for God's will, and I think that that's what I'm doing in Illinois."

Here is someone who sees stuff in Jesus's teachings unseen by anyone who has actually studied Jesus's teachings.

Paraphrasing and quoting Wikipedia:

In 2005, when his daughter Maya was twenty years old, she came out as a lesbian. There were reports her family threw her out of the house and stopped talking to her. Maya confirmed that her father "cut off all financial support."

Keyes asserted that he never cut her off and never would, because it would be "wrong in the eyes of God." He also said he would not be coerced into "approving of that which destroys the soul" of his daughter. He contended that he must "stand for the truth [Jesus Christ] represents," even if it breaks his heart.

During the 1992 election, Keyes attracted controversy when he took an $8,463/month salary from his campaign fund.

2004 news conference Keyes stated that Jesus Christ would not vote for Obama, because of votes that Obama—then a member of the Illinois Senate Judiciary Committee and a lecturer in constitutional law at the University of Chicago Law School—cast in 2001 against a package of three anti-abortion bills that Obama argued were too broad and unconstitutional.

2004 Illinois State Senate: Obama beats Keyes 70% to 27%. Keyes refused to make the call to congratulate, saying, "I'm supposed to make a call that represents the congratulations toward the triumph of that which I believe ultimately stands for . . . a culture evil enough to destroy the very soul and heart of my country? I cannot do this. And I will not make a false gesture."

Keyes defined homosexuality as centering in the pursuit of pleasure, literally "selfish hedonism."

When Signorile asked if Mary Cheney, Vice President Dick Cheney's lesbian daughter, fit the description and was therefore a "selfish hedonist," Keyes replied, "Of course she is. That goes by definition."

On December 12, 2007, Keyes participated in the *Des Moines Register*'s Republican presidential debate, televised nationwide by PBS and the cable news networks. He advocated ending the income tax and establishing state-sanctioned prayer in public schools.

On November 14, 2008, Keyes filed a lawsuit—naming as defendants California Secretary of State Deborah Bowen, President-elect Barack Obama, Vice President-elect Joe Biden, and California's 55 Democratic electors—challenging Obama's eligibility for the U.S. presidency. The suit requested that Obama provide documentation that he is a natural born citizen of the United States.

Following the inauguration, Keyes alleged that President Obama had not been constitutionally inaugurated, refused to call him president, and called him a "usurper" and a "radical communist." Keyes also claimed that President Obama's birth certificate had been forged and he was not qualified to be president.

In August 2003, Keyes came out in defense of Alabama Chief Justice Roy Moore, citing both the U.S. Constitution and the Alabama constitution as sanctioning Moore's (and Alabama's) authority to publicly display the Ten Commandments in the state's judicial building, in defiance of a court order from U.S.

In December 2009, Keyes authored a column for the *World Net Daily* critical of evolution and in support of Intelligent Design.
http://en.wikipedia.org/wiki/Alan_Keyes

Jesse Jackson.

Like Alan Keyes, he ran for president 1984 and 1988 and is religious—Jackson being a Baptist preacher—but there the similarity ends. His concerns, described below, about the 2004 election and specifically Ohio are in line with mine. *I was in Cleveland, Ohio (the 2004 swing state that determined the election), election night and witnessed the impact that the creation of massive lines had in people's ability to actually vote in that Democratic stronghold.

I also believe that Karl Rove had flown in to provide Ken Blackwell some "advice."

Paraphrasing and quoting Wikipedia:

Sometime after 1977 Jackson later adopted a pro-choice view that abortion is a right and that the government should not prevent a woman from having an abortion.

He ran for office as "shadow senator" for the District of Columbia when the position was created in 1991 and served as such through 1997, when he did not run for reelection. This unpaid position was primarily a post to lobby for statehood for the District of Columbia.

2002: Jackson was a target of a white-supremacist terror plot.
(Targets included the United States Holocaust Museum, the New England Holocaust Memorial; well-known Jews, including Steven Spielberg; and black leaders, including Rev. Jesse Jackson.)

*2004: Jackson gathered information and support to investigate the U.S. presidential election controversy, particularly the voting results in Ohio and its recount. He called for a congressional debate on the matter, asking for a fair count and national voting standards, saying that elections in the United States are each run with different standards by different states, with partisan tricks, racial bias, and widespread incompetence, and are an open scandal. He compared the voting irregularities of Ohio to those occurring in the 2004 Ukrainian presidential election, saying that if Ohio were the Ukraine, the U.S. presidential election would not have been certified by the international community. Jackson called Ohio Secretary of State Kenneth Blackwell inappropriately partisan and said that Blackwell may have been pressured by President George W. Bush and Vice President Dick Cheney to deliver Ohio to the Republican Party.

Based on information obtained in hearings held by Rep. John Conyers (D–MI) and discovered during a flawed recount of the Ohio presidential vote called for by Green Party candidate David Cobb and Libertarian Party candidate Michael Badnarik, Jackson suggested that the Ohio voting machines were "rigged" and that some African Americans were forced to stand in line for six hours in the rain before voting. When asked for evidence, Jackson replied, "Based on distrusting the system, lack of paper trails, the anomaly of the exit polls."

On June 23, 2007, Jackson was arrested in connection with a protest at a gun store in Riverdale, a poor suburb of Chicago. Jackson and others were protesting because of allegations that the gun store had been selling firearms to local gang members and was contributing to the decay of the community. According to police reports, Jackson refused to stop blocking the front entrance of the store and let customers pass. He was charged with one count of criminal trespass to property.
http://en.wikipedia.org/wiki/Jesse_Jackson

7) Dan Quayle v. John Kerry:

Dan Quayle, VP 1988–1992.

After leaving politics and failing to get any presidential traction, Quayle just decided to focus on making money.

Paraphrasing and quoting Wikipedia:

In 1999 he joined Cerberus Capital Management, a multibillion dollar private equity firm, and is chairman of the company's Global Investments Division. He has also been a member of the board of directors of Heckmann Corporation. Quayle is also a director of Aozora Bank, Tokyo. Quayle has also been on the board of directors of other companies.
http://en.wikipedia.org/wiki/Dan_Quayle

John Kerry, 2004, unsuccessful bid for president.

Like Jimmy Carter and like Al Gore, Kerry had to handle an absurd election outcome. This may have been worse than the Carter and Gore scenarios, for three reasons. By 2004 the country should surely have figured out that the Iraq war was built upon lie—but polling showed the 67% of Stupidparty voters remained clueless about the lack of a terror link or WMDs. Secondly, the impossible happened: George W. Bush, whose dad found a way to ensure that his son was safely engaged with the Texas Guard (and his record there is highly questionable), successfully swiftboated John Kerry, a certified was hero, where every investigation has corroborated his heroic actions during the Vietnam War, and thirdly, there were the shenanigans in Ohio, issues that John Kerry chose not to pursue—for the sake of national best interests, not to undermine the (rather sad) faith in the democratic process.

Since then, Kerry has continued serving in the Senate, focused on foreign affairs issues. He is presently Secretary of State and has revived the Middle East process—something that Romney had said (during his covertly recorded 47% Moocher gathering) was impossible, thus not worth trying. What Stupidparty foreign policy prognosticators fail to understand is that simply trying to be an honest broker in the Middle East goes a long way in mitigating hatred of the USA in the Middle East. They also fail to understand that hating foreign countries in general tends to undermine foreign policy.

8) Pat Buchanan v. Gary Hart:

Patrick J. ("Pat") Buchanan, after his unsuccessful bids in 1992 and 1996 to secure the presidential nomination, found that the still-gestating Stupidparty was just not really representing the "peasants with pitchforks" theme he had run his 1996 campaign on.

Paraphrasing and quoting Wikipedia:

In 2000, Buchanan won the nomination for the Reform Party. In his acceptance speech, Buchanan proposed U.S. withdrawal from the United Nations, expelling the UN from New York, abolishing the Internal Revenue Service, the Department of Education, the Department of Energy, and the Department of Housing and Urban Development; taxes on inheritance and capital gains and affirmative action programs.

In the 2000 presidential election, Buchanan finished fourth, with 449,895 votes, 0.4% of the popular vote. In Palm Beach County, Florida, Buchanan received 3,407 votes. (This confused many people, as Palm Beach County has a progressive Jewish slant and Buchanan is suspected of being an anti-Semite.) As a result of the county's now-infamous "butterfly ballot," he is suspected to have gained thousands of inadvertent votes. Bush spokesman and resultant serial liar Ari Fleischer tried to spin this as a "Buchanan stronghold." However, Reform Party officials strongly disagreed, estimating the number of supporters in the county at between 400 and 500. Appearing on *The Today Show,* Buchanan said:

"When I took one look at that ballot on election night . . . it's very easy for me to see how someone could have voted for me in the belief they voted for Al Gore."

In retrospect, Buchanan told *The Daily Caller* explicitly in October 2012 that "What cost Al Gore Florida in 2000, and the presidency, was the 'butterfly ballot.'" Prior to the 2004 election, Buchanan announced he once again identified himself as a Republican.

In September 2009, MSNBC removed a Buchanan opinion column from its website after it was urged to do so in a public statement by the National Jewish Democratic Council. Buchanan had used the occasion of the 70th anniversary of the German invasion of

Poland to argue that Britain should not have declared war on Germany. This revived charges of anti-Semitism and that he helped legitimize Holocaust denial.

In January 2012, Buchanan was indefinitely suspended from MSNBC as a contributor and MSNBC President Phil Griffin said he had not decided whether to let Buchanan come back. The minority advocacy group Color of Change had urged MSNBC to fire him over alleged racist slurs.

MSNBC permanently parted ways with Buchanan on February 16, 2012.

In a 2010 column, Buchanan expressed his disapproval of Barack Obama's nomination of Elena Kagan to the United States Supreme Court. Buchanan wrote, "If Kagan is confirmed, Jews, who represent less than 2 percent of the US population, will have 33 percent of the Supreme Court seats. Is this the Democrats' idea of diversity?"
http://en.wikipedia.org/wiki/Pat_Buchanan

The older he gets, the more fearful he becomes—and thus Pat Buchanan is truly the epitome of the Stupidparty Disciple and the trend line of the Stupidparty itself. These three quotes from his book *Suicide of a Super Power: Will America Survive to 2025?* are core values, and really help us get into the mind of Stupidparty:

> 1) Americans who seek stricter immigration control have been charged with many social sins: racism, xenophobia, nativism. Yet none has sought to expel any fellow American based on color or creed. We have only sought to preserve the country we grew up in. Do not people everywhere do that, without being reviled? What motivates people who insist that America's doors be held open wide until the European majority has disappeared?

> What is their grudge against the old America that eats at their heart?

> 2) What the above points to is a strategy from which Republicans will recoil, a strategy to increase the GOP share of the white Christian vote and increase the turnout of that vote by specific appeals to social, cultural, and moral issues, and for equal justice for the emerging white minority. If the GOP is not the party of New Haven firefighter Frank Ricci and Cambridge cop James Crowley, it has no future. And although Howard Dean disparages the Republicans as the "white party," why should Republicans be ashamed to represent the progeny of the men who founded, built, and defended America since her birth as a nation?

> 3) Perhaps some of us misremember the past. But the racial, religious, cultural, social, political, and economic divides today seem greater than they seemed even in the segregation cities some of us grew up in. Back then, black and white lived apart, went to different schools and churches, played on different playgrounds, and went to different restaurants, bars, theaters, and soda fountains. But we shared a country and a culture. We were one nation. We were Americans.

Gary Hart.

After his unsuccessful bids in 1984 and 1988 to secure the presidential nomination, the former senator remained moderately active in politics, serving on the bipartisan U.S. Commission on

National Security/21st Century, also known as the Hart–Rudman Commission, authorized on behalf of Bill Clinton in 1998 to study U.S. homeland security.

While for Buchanan it appears that the steam engine train has left the station, Hart is ready for the high speed train, or hyperloop future.

2001, a week before the 9/11 attack. Hart warned that the U.S. was at risk of a terrorist attack and also felt that the administration was ignoring such warnings. (Actually, there were numerous and quite specific warning prior to 9/11. All memos were aggressively ignored by Condoleezza Rice and the vacationing Bush—as their foreign-policy priorities were determinedly elsewhere.)

2003, he starts is own blog, which back in 2003 was pretty cutting edge, and of course he was the first prospective presidential candidate to do this.

2005 from May onwards, he has been a contributor at *The Huffington Post*. He is also member of the Council on Foreign Relations and is involved in the Advisory Board of Operation USA, an international relief and development agency. He is the author of *James Monroe,* in the Times Books series on American presidents.

2006, Hart earns an endowed professorship at the University of Colorado.

2007, *Huffington Post* publishes his warning letter to Iran. He is evidently concerned that the Bush Administration intentions are far from peaceful—no doubt irritated by Oilman Dick Cheney's never-ending warblings about American exceptionalism, which is Stupidparty code for being exceptionally good at bombing things and creating more terrorists.

2007, Hart says what must be said, by publishing an essay explaining how devastatingly absurd U.S. energy policy was—yes, I suspect he was trying to carry the torch that Carter was carrying in 1980, before being snuffed out by the first ripples of Stupidparty inception. He wrote, "In fact, we do have an energy policy: It's to continue to import more than half our oil and sacrifice American lives so we can drive our Humvees. This is our current policy, and it is massively immoral."

Yes—such a simple problem to have avoided, with just a tiny bit of critical thinking.

Massively immoral.

Hart is currently on the board of the Energy Literacy Advocates
Data extracted from http://en.wikipedia.org/wiki/Gary_Hart

CHAPTER 21

Strutting the States
for
Silly Stupidparty Stratagems

Welcome to Florida
Home of Disneyland
the Keys
&
Legalized Murder

(Senator John Kyle claimed that over 90% of what Planned Parenthood does is abortion.)
Over 90%, that is unbelievable... in that it is not true. Only 3% of what Planned Parenthood does is
abortion. Kyle just rounded it up to the nearest 90.

— Stephen Colbert

Basically, this chapter is All Quotes. If I have something say, it will be in Green. Normal quotation marks and guidances are not given in this chapter, but the usual links are still provided.

Oregon:

Art Robinson, SP State Chairman.

As reported by *Mother Jones:*

Healthcare:

After months of in-fighting, the beleaguered Oregon Republican Party elected a new chairman last weekend. His name is Art Robinson, and he wants to sprinkle radioactive waste from airplanes to build up our resistance to degenerative illnesses.

(His conclusion on the AIDS epidemic: Homosexuality might be a natural consequence of the gay lifestyle, and the federal government had cooked the books "as an excuse for all sorts of social engineering, especially in the public schools.")

Education:

"Public education (tax-financed socialism) has become the most widespread and devastating form of child abuse and racism in the United States. Moreover, people who have been cut off at the knees by public education are so mentally handicapped that they cannot be responsible custodians of the energy technology base or other advanced accomplishments of our civilization." (Robinson, a home-schooling activist, sells a DIY curriculum for $195.)

"My advice to home school parents is to teach geography, history, and government largely from books which were written in the 1950's and earlier, before it became popular to teach overt racism under the rubric of 'multiculturalism.'"

www.mywebface.com

Climate Change:

On climate change: "There is substantial scientific evidence that increases in atmospheric carbon dioxide produce many beneficial effects upon the natural plant and animal environments of the Earth."

Diversity:

The white-male imbalance at his alma mater, Cal Tech, Robinson argued, was due to the fact that "its

applicants are weighted toward those who seek severe, difficult, total-immersion training in science—an experience few women and blacks desire."
http://www.motherjones.com/mojo/2013/08/oregon-gop-art-robinson-nuclear-waste-airplanes

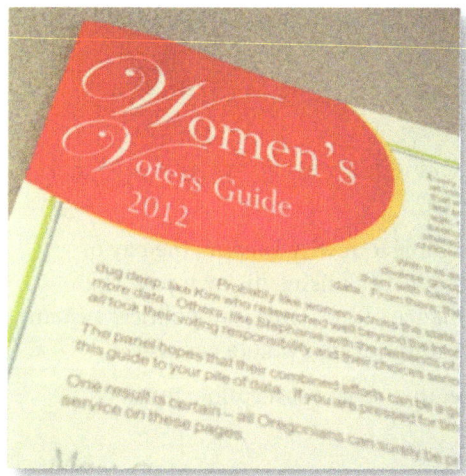

Oregon:

The Transformation Project:

In which Oregon's misogynists try putting on a skirt to appeal to women.

A mailing of *Women's Voters Guide* went out in Oregon.

Wondering who it's from? No, it's not the League of Women Voters; nor is it from by any group that works on women's issues. It's actually from a Republican-aligned group called the Oregon Transformation Project, which is almost entirely funded by money from Stimson Lumber.

How closely aligned are Oregon Transformation Project and the Oregon Republican Party? It's co-chaired by Allen Alley, chair of the Oregon GOP, and Rep. Dennis Richardson (R-Central Point). Its political action committee is run by Rob Kremer, treasurer of the Oregon Republican Party. None of them are well known as champions on women's issues.

Oregon Transformation Project has dumped hundreds of thousands of dollars into GOP candidate races.
http://ouroregon.org/sockeye/blog/halloween-comes-early

Alabama:

Alabama Stupidparty nearly boots 23-year-old college Republican from steering committee for calling same-sex marriage "reasonable because 'we're governed by the Constitution and not the Bible.'"

They reached a temporary compromise:

"If I didn't talk to any more press, or post on Facebook, or use any of my influence to talk about gay marriage, then they would not try to continue removing me from the steering committee," Petelos said.

… but one member of the group has suggested a change to the state party bylaws in response to the young-folk-having-opinions-these-days, wanting to boot any steering committee member who "publicly advocates" any opinion that is contrary to the national party platform stance.
http://www.buzzfeed.com/mckaycoppins/alabama-gop-trying-to-oust-college-republican-for-defending

Book Burning dreams:

In Arizona, GOP legislators want to ban swearing by teachers in classrooms or anywhere else on school property, and ban any profanity in any book or other material
used in the classroom, which means good-bye to a whole mess of great literature from
Catcher in the Rye to pretty much all of Shakespeare.
http://www.democraticunderground.com/1002314202

Alabama Sinks Deeper Into the Sea Of Stupid:

Alabama Republican State Senator Shadrack McGill is doing his godawful best to make
the State of Alabama the dumbest place in America.

His clever two-pronged attack involves using the Bible to justify keeping the pay of
teachers low, while using bogus logic absent fact to justify raising his own pay. The
world stares in silent, stunned wonder at the brilliance of the American political system
that continually fills its legislatures with these great minds of absolute genius.

> McGill said that by paying legislators more, they're less susceptible to tak-
> ing bribes.
>
> "He needs to make enough that he can say no, in regards to temptation….
> Teachers need to make the money that they need to make. There needs to
> be a balance there. If you double what you're paying education, you know
> what's going to happen? I've heard the comment many times, 'Well, the
> quality of education's going to go up.' That's never proven to happen, guys.
>
> "It's a Biblical principle. If you double a teacher's pay scale, you'll attract
> people who aren't called to teach."

http://grumpylion.wordpress.com/2012/02/02/alabama-sinks-deeper-into-the-sea-of-stupid/

Tough on crime, gun-wielding official caught stealing:

WASHINGTON—Dale Peterson, an Alabama Republican state official famous for flaunting
his rifle in campaign ads promising to be tough on crime, was arrested Wednesday and
charged with shoplifting a can of cashews. The arrest, first reported by YellowHammer-
Politics.com, marked the second time in six months that Peterson has been accused of
stealing.
http://www.huffingtonpost.com/2013/03/28/dale-peterson-gun-alabama-shoplifting_n_2968471.html

Jesse Lee Peterson, Alabama reverend and frequent Fox News guest:

"We should've never turned [the vote] over to women. And these women are voting for
the wrong people. They're voting for people who are evil, who agrees [*sic*] with them,
who are gonna take us down the pathway of destruction. They can't handle stress. They
can't handle anything….

"You walk up to them with an issue, they freak out right away. Especially if they can't get
the problem resolved right away. They go nuts. They get mad. They get upset, just like
that. They have no patience because it's not in their nature. They don't have love. They
don't have love," he said.
www.dailymail.co.uk/news/article-2141530/Fox-News-guest-Rev-Jesse-Lee-Peterson-says-women-shouldnt-a.

Mississippi:

Phil Bryant, SP Governor:

"There is no one who doesn't have healthcare in America. No one. Now, they may end up going to the emergency room. There are better ways to deal with people that need health care than this massive new program."

http://aattp.org/15-mind-numbingly-dumb-things-teapublicans-have-said-lately/

Googling Mississippi Stupidparty (first two pages) Oct. 2013.

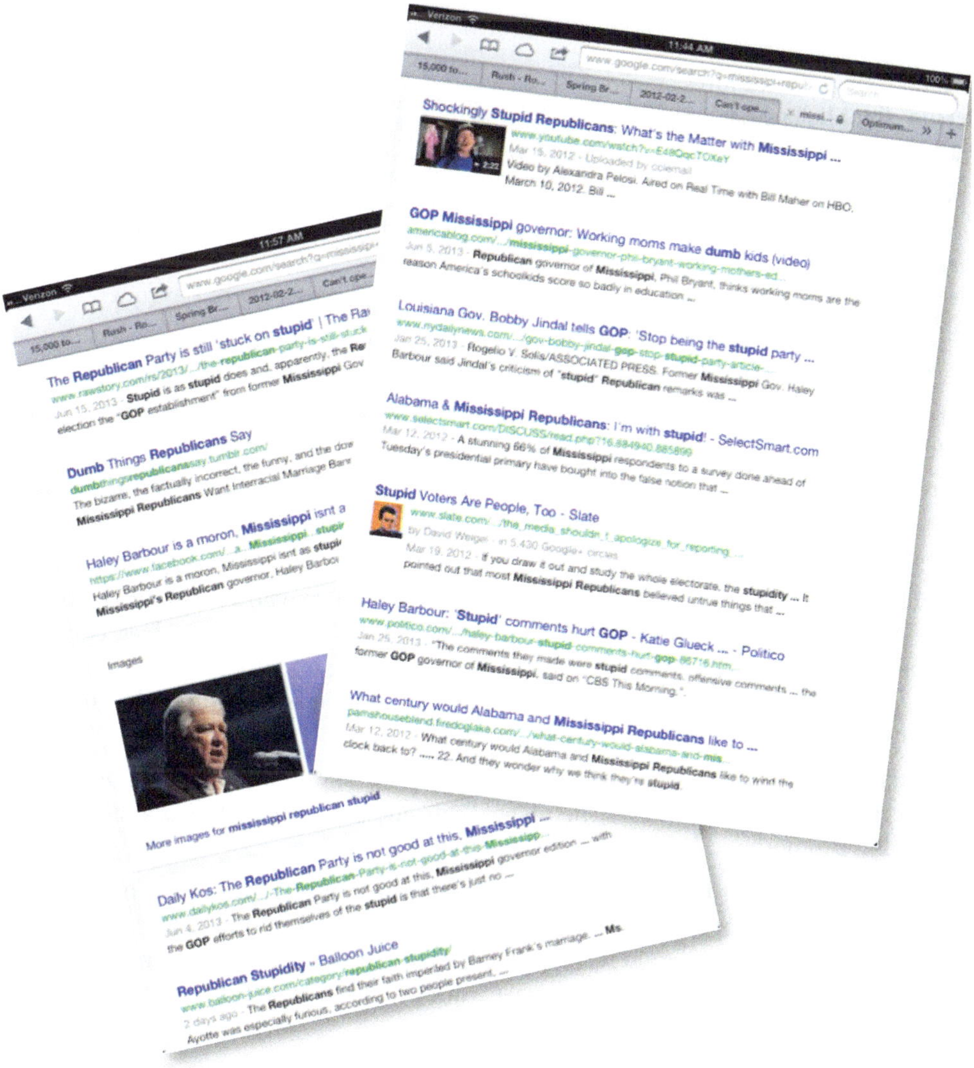

The South will rise up again:

Asset-Stripped Mississippi Disciples explain why they vote Stupidparty. Clue: half-breed Muslim president, following God, do not need the government, and the South will rise up again.
http://www.youtube.com/watch?v=yuanrYGnIOI

Ignoring Federal Laws:

Recently, many have watched in amazement as **Mississippi** legislators filed a piece of legislation that would establish a state committee empowered to decide which federal laws the state will agree to follow and which ones they will chose to ignore. According to these Mississippi state lawmakers, they possess the power to ignore any federal law they wish as a result of their state sovereignty—despite a United States Constitution that clearly says otherwise.
http://www.forbes.com/sites/rickungar/2013/04/03/north-carolina-lawmakers-introduce-law-to-establish-an-official-state-religion/

Tom Corbett, SP Gov. Pennsylvania.

"Republican governor hires crazy person" (by Michael Lazzaro, Aug. 20, 2013):

The decision by Pennsylvania Gov. Tom Corbett (R–Scandal Plagued, but I repeat myself) to hire a crazy person to be the "legislative liaison" for the Department of Revenue:

[Kitchen Table Patriots founder Ana Puig] is as tea party as they come. In recent years, she has promoted an event featuring topics including "The Muslim Brotherhood and creeping sharia law in America" and "Pro-Islamic bias and indoctrination in our public school textbooks."

There is no part of that that suggests "liaison" capabilities to anything, unless the Pennsylvania Department of Revenue is planning legislative negotiations with the saucer people. Which, I freely admit, is possible.

In 2011, she defended a member of her Kitchen Table Patriots who sold Nazi memorabilia, including German World War II military uniforms, medals and badges, edged weapons, flags, field gear and Hitler Youth accessories. Puig told the *Bucks County Courier Times* that the Nazi-enthusiast in their ranks "is, in essence, our media guy" and "concentrates on taping events, streaming them live."

Her Kitchen Table Patriots website also features a blog that promotes the "birther" conspiracy, refers to the President as a "petulant child," and says that Obama is a member of the Muslim Brotherhood.

So, how do Republicans find these people? There's clearly a Craigslist for insane Republican nutcases, is it open to everyone? Is there a membership fee? No matter how riddled with stupidity our politics would seem to be, the number of people founding their own groups claiming Obama is a secret Kenyan + Muslim + Marxist is still pretty damn low,

compared to the general population, and yet they keep popping up in Republican offices like little mentally unbalanced prairie dogs.
http://m.dailykos.com/stories/1232597

Virginia:

—"Children with disabilities are God's punishment." Or, sin causes birth defects (see up ahead).

Bob Marshall, SP State Rep. Virginia, spoke at a press conference against state funding for Planned Parenthood. He blasted the organization for supporting a women's right to choose, saying that God punishes women who have had abortions by giving them disabled children:

"The number of children who are born subsequent to a first abortion with handicaps has increased dramatically. Why? Because when you abort the first born of any, nature takes its vengeance on the subsequent children," said Marshall, a Republican.

"In the Old Testament, the first born of every being, animal and man, was dedicated to the Lord. There's a special punishment Christians would suggest."
http://thinkprogress.org/politics/2010/02/22/83337/disabled-abortion/

Virginia is for "Lovers": The commonwealth has a number of laws regulating lovers, including lewd and lascivious cohabitation, fornication, and crimes against nature—which is still maintained as a class 6 felony despite SCOTUS' Lawrence v. Texas ruling. Indeed, Attorney General Ken Cuccinelli gives law enforcement a green light to arrest gays under Virginia's statute, stating he believes it's appropriate to formulate public policy on the premise that homosexuals engage in behavior that is intrinsically wrong and offensive to natural law. As well, Cuccinelli advised Virginia universities to remove LGBT-specific provisions from their nondiscrimination policies
http://www.policymic.com/articles/21617/the-5-worst-states-for-lgbt-rights-in-america
* Cuccinelli—it appears he lost his reelection bid in 2013

E. W. Jackson, SP nominee for Virginia Lieutenant Governor, wrote in his 2008 book, *Ten Commandments to an Extraordinary Life,* that birth defects were caused because of sin He wrote the book when he was serving as a minister.
http://www.buzzfeed.com/andrewkaczynski/va-republican-lt-governor-candidate-said-birth-defects-were

North Carolina:

Carl Ford, SP State Rep., and Harry Warren, SP State Rep.: The primary sponsors of a bill introduced into the state's General Assembly that would clear the way for the state to adopt an official, state religion.

The proposed law, introduced earlier this week, [April 2013] states that the Establishment Clause in the First Amendment—which prohibits Congress from passing laws respecting the establishment of religion or prohibiting the free exercise of religion in America—simply does not apply to the states. The bill goes on to proclaim the sovereignty of the states in this matter while proclaiming that each state is free to make its own laws respecting an establishment of an official religion and that such an establishment cannot be blocked by either Congress or the judiciary.

http://www.forbes.com/sites/rickungar/2013/04/03/north-carolina-lawmakers-introduce-law-to-establish-an-official-state-religion/

Global Warming—coastal state solution:

Here's the NoCa (North Carolina) solution: pretend it's not happening. Pass a law saying it can't happen because we say it can't. Which is to say, ban any government agency from using the standard scientific tools like extrapolating data to figure out what's happening, and thus avoid all those scary, silly scientific facts and figures.

Global warming? Flooding seas? Not in North Carolina. Why? Because they say so, that's why.

News reports point out that businesses and local governments along the state's coast lobbied for the law, which declares that only data from years past can be considered in calculating future sea levels; essentially, if it didn't happen before, it can't happen, period. The pending law bans using real scientific techniques and formulas about rising sea levels because that could mean rising building costs, rising insurance rates and rising restrictions on coastal building. So instead, let's invoke wishful thinking and say it isn't so.

http://articles.latimes.com/2012/jun/05/news/la-ol-north-carolina-may-ban-global-warming-study-20120605

Hang'm high:

Larry Pittman, SP State Rep. North Carolina, wants to deter crime by reinstating public hangings, especially for "abortionists, rapists, and kidnappers."

http://www.democraticunderground.com/1002314202

Stop the Young from voting:

Using means now familiar in other states, North Carolina Republicans are proposing several ways of making it harder to vote. But one of the tactics is new to me. Republican State Senator Bill Cook wants to make voting harder for college students in particular, and to do that, he's pushing a bill that ties students' voter registration to their parents' taxes. If the student registers to vote at their college address, the parents would get a tax hike. They could no longer claim the student as a dependent, so the family would pay more in taxes.

http://freakoutnation.com/2013/05/02/your-april-gop-117-of-the-most-mind-boggling-insane-republican-moments-during-the-past-month-alone/

The legislation, the appropriately numbered S666 and its companion bill S667, would prohibit a parent from taking a personal exemption on their taxes for a child who registers to vote at a different address than his or her parents. The personal exemption ranges between $2,000 and $2,500 per child and, therefore, would constitute a significant incentive for parents getting their children not to register to vote when they go to college. In addition, the legislation would require that a registered voter have his or her car registered at the same address as they are registered to vote at, which would additionally discourage college students from registering to vote when they go to college if their car is registered at their parents' home.

http://www.addictinginfo.org/2013/04/06/the-gop-war-on-voting-continues/

Texas:

Jodie Laubenberg, SP State Rep. Texas:

"In the emergency room they have what's called rape kits where a woman can get cleaned out" … Laubenberg, on why there shouldn't be a rape or incest exception in Texas' sweeping anti-choice bills.

http://www.cosmopolitan.com/celebrity/exclusive/stupid-things-politicians-say#slide-1

Texas Stupidparty platform.

• We urge state and federal legislators to reduce spending.

• We urge Congress to adopt balanced budgets by cutting spending and not increasing tax rates.

• We recommend repeal of the Sixteenth Amendment of the U.S. Constitution, with the goal of abolishing the I.R.S and replacing it with a national sales tax collected by the States. In the interim we urge the income tax be changed to a flatter, broader, lower tax with only minimal exemptions such as home mortgage interest deductions.

• We favor abolishing the capital gains tax.

• State Tax Reform—We encourage: Abolishing property taxes … Shifting the tax burden to a consumption-based tax.

• Our founding fathers warned us of the dangers of allowing central bankers to control our currency because inflation equals taxation without representation. We support the return to the time tested precious metal standard for the U.S. dollar

It is not simply that the above indicates economic illiteracy when such policies are taken together during a recession, but also that every action above is regressive. The list was probably cobbled together at a Palm Beach cocktail party.

These policies would dampen demand: The top 20% of Americans spend 62% of their income (as compared to 87% for the rest). In other words, those who don't spend would be left with relatively more after-tax income than those who do, creating yet another drag on the economy. Note, too, that the second point above (regarding balanced budgets) is based on a false premise, i.e., that the federal government is budget-constrained (see "The Big Danger in Cutting the Deficit"). One of the least-understood economic facts today is that it isn't, the reason being that the entire debt is owed in something we and only we are permitted to print: US dollars. Nor is this inflationary except when the economy is near full employment—at which point there is no need for the government to continue deficit spending (see "Money Growth Does Not Cause Inflation").

Regarding those Founding Fathers, they had never heard of Keynes or had the chance to analyze the impact of an income tax or the Great Depression or understand the impact of trade agreements, outsourcing jobs, etc. So talking of the Founding Fathers in the context of twenty-first-century economic complexities is so very Stupidparty.
http://www.forbes.com/sites/johntharvey/2012/07/01/texas-gop-platform/

Texas Stupidparty Loves Hate:
As reported in *Burnt Orange Report,* or BOR for short, Texas's largest political blog:

Barry Smitherman, Texas Railroad Commissioner and Republican candidate for Attorney General, is upset. He's not bothered by the millions current Attorney General Greg Abbott has wasted on lawsuits he can't win, Abbott's dedication to voter disenfranchisement laws, or Abbott's near-release of thousands of Texans' Social Security numbers. No—he's distressed that certain hate groups are being labeled as hate groups.

Last year, Smitherman learned of study material used in his daughter's school to go along with the American classic To Kill A Mockingbird. The study material was provided by the Southern Poverty Law Center, which Smitherman claimed "has a more radical view of racism, hate, and intolerance."

The SPLC is an organization that has fought Southern racism for decades by identifying hate groups, publishing studies into institutional racism, and providing legal assistance to victims of racial discrimination. Rarely do even Republicans bring up complaints about the SPLC—that's reserved for the hate groups SPLC exposes.

Apparently, Smitherman thinks what the historic organization does is "radical"—and he's been working against it for the last year on behalf of some hideous groups. Smitherman wrote an email to his daughter's teacher laying out his complaints. "For example," Smitherman wrote in his email, "the group 'Crusaders for Yahweh' is labeled by the SPLC to be a 'Christian identity' group and is placed on the SPLC's 'hate map.' The same with the 'Evangelical Latter Day Saints' (Mormons), the Jewish Defense League, which SPLC calls 'anti-Arab,' and the Border Guardians, which is labeled by the SPLC as 'anti-immigration.'"

Let's look at those groups Smitherman came to the hearty defense of. Crusaders for Yahweh, as the Texas Observer explains, promotes "white supremacist language and Nazi imagery" on its websites. Its founder is a neo-Nazi named Paul Mullet "who's been in and out of prison and believes Obama is the anti-Christ."

The Jewish Defense League was deemed a "right-wing terrorist group" by the FBI in 2001 and has been "linked to beatings, bombings and assassination attempts, including Republican Congressman Darrell Issa, in the name of repelling anti-Semitism."

Smitherman got the name of the Mormon group wrong, almost certainly meaning the "Fundamentalist Church of Jesus Christ of Latter-Day Saints." FLDS' leader, infamous child abuser Warren Jeffs, is currently serving a life sentence in Texas on two separate child sex assault convictions. Border Guardians' leader "urged a leader in the neo-Nazi National Socialist Movement to undertake a campaign of harassment and violence against undocumented immigrants" in 2006.

The guy defending these hideous groups is calling the Southern Poverty Law Center "radical" for denouncing them? The radical's name is Barry Smitherman, and he shouldn't be allowed anywhere near the top attorney's office in Texas.

http://www.burntorangereport.com/diary/14219/republican-attorney-general-candidate-barry-smitherman-objects-to-identifying-hate-groups

Tennessee:

Scott DesJarlais, SP Rep. Tennessee 4th: [Bio] DesJarlais is a former physician and anti-choice crusader who was fined $500 by the Tennessee Board of Medical Examiners after it came to light that he had engaged in multiple extramarital affairs with female patients. When one woman became pregnant, the staunch anti-abortion conservative pressured her into terminating the pregnancy. Another patient charged that DesJarlais prescribed narcotic painkillers to her for recreational use and frequently smoked marijuana with her.

"I know God has forgiven me" for the transgressions, DesJarlais told a conservative radio hosting an interview in December of 2012….

During a question and answer session at the meeting, Molina stepped up to the microphone and, with a quavering voice, asked, "Mr. DesJarlais, I have papers, but I have a dad who's undocumented. What can I do to have him stay with me?"

Rather than make any attempt to assuage the girl's fears, DesJarlais said, "Thank you for being here and thank you for coming forward and speaking," but "the answer still kind of remains the same, that we have laws and we need to follow those laws and that's where we're at."

The tea party crowd whooped and applauded wildly as the little girl took her seat, head down. Progressive Populist reported that Josie Molina's father is currently in the process of being deported and that the girl is seeing a child psychologist in order to cope with the stress and anxiety.

http://www.rawstory.com/rs/2013/08/17/tennessee-republican-tells-girl-her-father-has-to-be-deported-as-tea-party-crowd-cheers/

"The Senate approved a bill Monday evening that deals with teaching of evolution and other scientific theories," the *Knoxville News-Sentinel* (March 19, 2012) reported, adding, "Critics call it a 'monkey bill' that promotes creationism in classrooms." The bill in question is Senate Bill 893, which, if enacted, would encourage teachers to present the "scientific strengths and scientific weaknesses" of "controversial" topics such as "biological evolution, the chemical origins of life, global warming, and human cloning."

Tennessee's top scientists, including Stanley Cohen, Nobel Prize winner in physiology of medicine, oppose "monkey bills": "By undermining the teaching of evolution in Tennessee's public schools, HB368 and SB893 would miseducate students, harm the state's national reputation, and weaken its efforts to compete in a science-driven global economy."

http://thinkprogress.org/climate/2012/03/20/448762/
anti-science-monkey-bill-passes-tennessee-senate/

South Dakota—explains how Obama is Hitler:
Reported by People for the American Way (PFAW), founded in 1981 by Norman Lear, the late Congresswoman Barbara Jordan, & a group of business, civic, religious, and civil rights leaders who were disturbed by the divisive rhetoric of newly politicized televangelists:
http://www.politifact.com/personalities/people-american-way/

Conference organizers recently announced that among the speakers will be Kitty Werthmann, the head of the South Dakota chapter of the Eagle Forum who produced a DVD called "Freedom to Dictatorship in 5 Years." Werthmann was 12 years old when Hitler came to power and conference co-chair Janet Porter makes the connection between Hitler and Obama abundantly clear:

She is 83 with a "vivid memory" of what happened in her homeland next. She witnessed the government take over the banks and the auto industry. Sound familiar? In the last nine months, Obama and the Democrats in Congress have successfully orchestrated the government takeover of Chrysler and General Motors along with countless banks.

She witnessed the "compulsory youth" service and indoctrination. That sounds a little like Obama's call for "mandatory volunteerism" for America's youth …

They had Joseph Goebbels; we have Mark Lloyd, the diversity czar, who is already poised to shut down private radio stations like his hero Hugo Chavez did threatening licenses and waging outrageous fines on stations (up to $25 million dollars) who say things he doesn't like …

"Each person was allotted ration cards like a pound of sugar per month." Werthmann said. "If your grandma died, and you used her ration card to buy sugar, the grocery store would report you. Then, the Gestapo showed up, but rather than arrest you, they recruited you as informant of your neighbors, boss, friends and family. You couldn't trust anybody, not even the mailman," Werthmann added. Weekly reports were required or arrests were made.

Sounds a little like Obama's recruitment of government informants, i.e. the "snitch program," to turn in offenders for "fishy" speech. No arrests just yet, but the Department of Homeland Security has already tagged pro-family Americans as "the most dangerous domestic terrorism threat in the United States." …

Werthmann said it took five years for Hitler to rise to a dictatorship, and is amazed at how fast history is repeating itself here. "It has to be done fast," she added, "so people won't catch on."

http://www.pfaw.org/rww-in-focus/why-are-gop-officials-embracing-extremists-upcoming-how-to-take-back-america-conference

Illinois:

Kyle McCarter, SP State Sen. Illinois:

"To redefine marriage is discriminatory towards those who hold the sincerely held religious belief that it is a sacred institution between a man & a woman"—Illinois state, in response to the state senate approving same-sex marriage.

http://aattp.org/15-mind-numbingly-dumb-things-teapublicans-have-said-lately/

Arizona:

Jon Kyl, SP Sen. Arizona:

Abortions make up "well over 90 percent of what Planned Parenthood does."

Bills Undermining Evolution in Public Schools: **Arizona's** Senate Bill 1213

Indiana's House Bill 1283
Missouri's House Bill 179 and House Bill 291
Montana's House Bill 183, and
http://ncse.com/news/2013/02/years-antievolution-legislation-so-far-0014699

Colorado just dodges Stupidparty bullet:

House Bill 13-1089 (PDF), which would have encouraged teachers in Colorado to misrepresent the scientific status of evolution and climate change, was rejected by a 7–6 vote in the House Committee on Education on February 4, 2013.
http://ncse.com/news/2013/02/
antiscience-bill-colorado-fails-0014701

Missouri:

Missouri Republicans are once again attacking women's health. The GOP controlled state Senate passed a bill on Thursday that would give pharmacies the option to refuse to stock drugs such as contraception. Pharmacies could also refuse to keep emergency contraception in stock.

The Senate approved SB 126 by a vote of 24–9 and it now heads to the Missouri House where Republicans are also in control.

If the bill were to become law, pharmacies across the state would be able to keep all forms of contraception off the shelves; meaning, even if a woman has a prescription from her doctor, a pharmacy could make the final decision regarding her health. For women who live in rural areas where pharmacies are few and far between, this legislation would force them to travel unnecessary distances to find a pharmacy willing to fill their prescriptions. Rape victims would be especially hit hard because pharmacies would be able to deny them emergency contraception.
http://brite.newsvine.com/_news/2013/04/07/17641931-missouri-gop-approves-bill-that-allows-pharmacies-to-decide-what-drugs-women-have-access-to-addicting-info

Kansas:

A Kansas legislator who last year led an effort to condemn the United Nations' sustainability agenda now wants to ban sustainability.

Dennis Hedke, State Rep., has introduced legislation that would ban Kansas state and local governments from spending public funds on sustainable development, Bloomberg reported on Tuesday. The move comes as conservative state lawmakers around the country—led by the John Birch Society—have introduced similar legislation to ban the implementation of the U.N. sustainability plan, known as Agenda 21. Hedke, who has ties to the oil and gas industry, did not directly mention Agenda 21 in his bill, but last year the lawmaker spearheaded a charge for legislators to speak out against the sustainable development initiative....

Other Kansas Republicans used the Agenda 21 debate to name the U.N. plan—which includes calling for bike paths—"radical" and "destructive to the American way of life." Democrats laughed off the GOP opposition, with then-state Rep. Mike Slattery (D-Kansas) saying that "stupid is as stupid does."
http://www.huffingtonpost.com/2013/04/09/kansas-sustainable-development_n_3045118.html

This and That:
As reported by the *Teamster Nation* blog (red font my emphasis):

Ban paid overtime in the United States:
U.S. House Majority Leader Eric Cantor wants to get rid of paid overtime. Reports *Daily Kos*: In Eric Cantors February 2013 speech, he said he wanted to propose Federal Law that would end overtime pay for hourly workers.

Give corporations the right to vote:
Montana Rep. Steve Lavin would give corporations that own property within a city to vote in a municipal election. *ThinkProgress* reports his bill would allow the president, vice president or designee to cast a ballot.

Eliminate child labor laws:
Utah Sen. Mike Lee thinks child labor laws should be illegal. So does former Missouri state Sen. Jane Cunningham, who filed a bill in the last session that would eliminate the prohibition on employment of children under age 14. Maine and Wisconsin's two wackadoodle governors, Paul LePage and job-killer Scott Walker, have both signed laws that roll back child labor protections.

Force unions to pay for non-union members' benefits:
Last year, Michigan and Indiana passed No Rights at Work bills that will weaken unions, increase poverty, lower their citizens' standard of living, and kill more people on the job. Republicans tried and failed to pass No Rights at Work in Kentucky and New Hampshire, but they're still at it in Missouri and Maine.

Raise taxes on everyone but the rich:
Republican governors in Ohio, Louisiana, Kansas, North Carolina, Oklahoma, and Nebraska are proposing tax hikes on the vast majority of citizens to cut taxes for the wealthy few.

Prohibit living wage and minimum wage laws:
Florida State Sen. Stephen Precourt filed a bill to overturn local laws in Orlando, Miami Beach, and Gainesville that require some employers to pay slightly more than the minimum wage. The bill has passed through committee.

Make it a crime to expose corporate crime:
A bill is now moving through the Indiana legislature that would criminalize the video or audio recording of unethical or illegal behavior on a farm or in a workplace. Similar laws passed already in Iowa, Montana, North Dakota, Kansas, and Utah.

Sell the national parks:
Utah Rep. Jason Chaffetz proposed selling off 3.2 million acres of public lands. Former **Florida** Rep. Cliff Stearns admitted on camera he wanted to sell off our national parks because we can't afford them anymore.

Make it a crime to make theft a crime:
Last year, the **Florida** House of Representatives passed a bill to overturn local laws that make it illegal for employers to steal wages from their employees. It failed in the Senate.
http://teamsternation.blogspot.com/2013/02/the-9-most-insane-laws-proposed-by.html

Banning Factual Terms:
As reported by *ThinkProgress.*

In **Virginia**, the Republican-led legislature commissioned a study to determine the impacts of manmade warming on the state's shores, only to ban terms like "climate change" and "sea level rise," deeming them "liberal code words." And **North Carolina Republicans** voted to ignore studies that predict rapid sea level rise due to global warming.

Allowing citizens to shoot at cops:
The NRA pushed Republicans in **Indiana** to pass a law that allows any citizen to open fire on a "public servant" for "unlawful intrusion." Police fear this means a citizen could shoot at a cop, then claim the cop was trying to enter his or her property.

Banning "Sharia Law."
Republicans in states like **Florida** and **Kansas** passed Sharia-law bans in their state legislatures. In Kansas, a spokeswoman for Gov. Sam Brownback (R-KS) went so far as to say that the ban meant that the state "will not consider the laws of foreign jurisdictions." The bans signified yet another year of the Republican establishment endorsing fringe Islamophobes.

Defining life as beginning before conception:
In **Arizona**, Republicans passed a new round of restrictive, anti-choice laws in the last year, chief among them HB 954. The bill, which one Republican defended by comparing women to cows and pigs, outlaws abortions after 20 weeks and actually starts the clock after a woman's last menstrual period.

Outlawing the dollar:
Washington state lawmakers introduced a bill that would have outlawed the paper dollar, because "only gold

and silver may be recognized as government legal tender." This is just part and parcel of the extreme right's continuing fascination with goldbuggery, a fascination to which the Republican Party's presidential candidates gladly pandered.

http://thinkprogress.org/politics/2012/12/27/1356311/the-craziest-republican-legislative-proposals-of-2012/

Don't let all this get you down.
Artist http://www.mattrotasart.com/

"When you don't fight your adversary, you become the coward in the sight of animalistic breeds, but they forget that your real strength stays in the whisper of your voice."

—Michael Bassey Johnson

CHAPTER 22

How far down the rabbit hole have you been led?

Scrabble®

WHAT IS YOUR SP QUOTIENT?
EVERY DAY IS APRIL FOOL'S DAY
THE ACTUAL FOUNDING FATHER HAVE THEIR SAY

When widely followed public figures feel free to say anything, without any fact-checking, it becomes impossible for a democracy to think intelligently about big issues.

—Thomas L. Friedman

How Stupidparty are you:

1) Was the earth created less than 100,000 years ago?
2) Is America a Christian Nation?
3) Was Obama born In Kenya?
4) Is Obama a Muslim?
5) Is Obama below average Intelligence?
6) For the 2012 election, was world opinion supporting Romney?
7) Without amendments, it is impossible for the Constitution to evolve?
8) Is Voter Fraud a significant Issue?
9) Is Voter Suppression unimportant?
10) Is Voter suppression a noble cause?
11) Should Adelson be allowed to choose the President?
12) Should we allow unlimited Corporate Funding of elections?
13) Should we allow anonymous Corporate Funding of elections?
14) Is the public option a terrible idea?
15) Is Obamacare a government takeover?
16) Was there credible evidence about Iraq's WMD?
17) Was there a credible link between Saddam and al-Qaeda?
18) Is it okay for a CEO's secretary to have a higher tax burden than the CEO
19) Should you assume that experts in a field know less than non-experts?
20) Do you know more about the climate than climatologists?
21) Is Global Warming a Hoax?
22) Is Austerity in a deflationary environment a good policy?
23) Is it good for Congress to focus on abortion over Jobs?
24) Is it good idea for America to default on its debt?
25) America defaulting on its debt would help its debt rating?
26) Is it a good idea to let the Auto Industry vanish?
27) Is it a good idea to allow the banking system to collapse?
28) Is it a good idea to allow big banks to take on ever-greater risk?
29) Do you constantly worry about your freedoms?
30) Is having 70m people without health insurance okay?
31) Should business owners be allowed to discriminate?
32) Is it okay to pay women less than men for the same skill set?
33) If Gay marriage is allowed, do you worry more about bestiality?
34) Does God decide where Hurricanes hit?
35) Is Rape a gift from God?
36) Was Jesus against Gay Marriage?
37) Was Jesus against contraception?
38) Was Jesus against abortion?
39) Was Jesus supportive of armed insurrection?
40) Did Jesus promote an eye for an eye?
41) Did Jesus treat the poor as moochers?
42) Did Jesus carry a weapon?
43) If you got seriously ill, would prayer trump expert medical advice?
44) If a category-five hurricane was imminent, would your #1 priority be praying?

45) Did the 2009 stimulus fail to create Jobs?
46) Do the Palm Beach Stupidparty Benefactors care about income discrepancy?
47) If you cannot get a job, should you starve?
48) If you cannot get a job, should your children starve?
49) If you are uninsured, broke and have cancer, should you be left to die?
50) Was Palin qualified to be president?
51) Was Bachmann qualified to be on the House Intelligence Committee?
52) Is Fox News fair and balanced?
53) Should you only get your news from Fox News?
54) Are Fox News viewers more informed than non-Fox viewers?
55) Should the news media give equal time to opposing views?
56) Should Myths be treated as Science in Public Schools?
57) Should we deregulate water, air, food, transport?
58) Is America a socialist country?
59) Does European-type socialism terrify you?
60) Does America have a healthcare system for all its citizens?
61) Does immigration hurt the economy?
62) Are non-Americans less smart?
63) Should there be more guns in schools?
64) Regarding crime, is it easy to spot the bad guys?
65) Should you be allowed to shoot an unarmed child in an open space?
66) Do you think anyone should have easy access to a machine gun?
67) Should members of the public have easy access to amour-piercing munitions?
68) Would it have been better to shoot to kill the Boston bombers?
69) Do you know that enhanced interrogation is not torture?
70) Should we dismiss the Miranda rights if we fear the accused?
71) Is it okay to allow income discrepancy trends to remain unchanged?
72) Should atheists leave the country?
73) Are you happy Zimmerman got acquitted?
74) Should the USA have the world's highest incarceration rates?
75) Should a fourteen-year-old disabled child be executed?
76) Should a fourteen-year-old child be executed?
77) Should a fourteen-year-old child be put in solitary confinement?
78) Should anyone be put in solitary confinement for life?
79) Should you assume that the mainstream media has a liberal bias?
80) Should you rely on your gut when analyzing a problem?
81) Do congressmen spend too little time fundraising?
82) Do congressmen spend too little time with lobbyists?
83) Do congressmen spend too little with special interests?
84) Do congressmen spend too much time studying the issues facing the nation?
85) Should congressional districting be determined by partisans?
86) Should taxpayers pay for environmental consequences of the Asset Strippers?
87) Should taxpayers have to pay for the social consequences of the Asset Strippers?
88) Should Asset Strippers pay even less taxes on profits from stripping?
89) Should billionaires be lauded for bankrolling laws reducing their taxes?
90) Should livestock be treated to cruel and unusual conditions?

91) Is the conservative brain less susceptible to fear?
92) Does disliking other countries, other races, indicate higher intelligence.
93) Do Stupidparty states have healthier residents?
94) Are the values of Stupidparty states better?
95) Does Massachusetts have the worst healthcare system?
96) Does Texas have the best healthcare system?
97) Would you rather be living in the pre-Civil War era?
98) Do people earning less than $25,000 a year work less hard?
99) Are Stupidparty states less reliant on the federal government's assistance?
100) The more money in politics, the less corrupt politicians will be?

FIGURING OUT YOUR SP QUOTIENT

	Yes	No		Yes	No		Yes	No		Yes	No
1			26			51			76		
2			27			52			77		
3			28			53			78		
4			29			54			79		
5			30			55			80		
6			31			56			81		
7			32			57			82		
8			33			58			83		
9			34			59			84		
10			35			60			85		
11			36			61			86		
12			37			62			87		
13			38			63			88		
14			39			64			89		
15			40			65			90		
16			41			66			91		
17			42			67			92		
18			43			68			93		
19			44			69			94		
20			45			70			95		
21			46			71			96		
22			47			72			97		
23			48			73			98		
24			49			74			99		
25			50			75			100		

Total

Total all your Yes answers

How black is your heart?
How well can your brain handle facts?

1	2	3	4	5	6	7	8	9	10

11	13	15	17	19	21	23	25	27	29

36	43	50	57	64	71	78	85	92	100

Connect the Fools puzzle. The Photo—to the Name—to the Lame comment.

April 1, 2014

April Fool's Day, but then every day is Fool's Day if you are living in Stupidparty land. In 2014 this special day falls rather ironically one day after the deadline for enrollment into the Affordable Care Act. So before we say our final adieu, let's have one last hurrah, one last game in unmasking the abundant low-hanging Fools so easily plucked from the pandemic vine that is choking the oxygen flow to the collective brain of the nation.

The Photos

The Names

Rep. Joe Barton @RepJoeBarton Nov 13
Sen. Ted Cruz ✓ @SenTedCruz
Speaker John Boehner @SpeakerBoehner
Rep. Steve Stockman @SteveWorks4You
Rep. Tom Marino ✓ @RepTomMarino
Rep. Todd Young @ToddYoungIN Nov 13
Rep. Renee Ellmers @RepReneeEllmers Oct 11
Chad Pergram @ChadPergram Nov 13

Rep. Jim Renacci @RepJimRenacci Nov 13
The Daily Caller @DailyCaller Mar 12
Rep. Brad Wenstrup @RepBradWenstrup Nov 13
Rep. Lynn Jenkins @RepLynnJenkins Nov 13
Rep. Bill Flores @RepBillFlores Nov 13
Rep. Steve Scalise @SteveScalise Nov 11
Rep. Tom Price @RepTomPrice Oct 3
Rep. Tom Cotton @TomCottonAR Nov 14

The Comments.
Note: Below are Twitter tweets, posted by the individuals listed above. Tweets by definition do not need to follow standard rules of writing. RT = Retweet, i. e., repeating someone else's tweet. # = hashtag, which is a way of classifying a tweet into a specific topic, and such a tweet will then show up in the thread of that Twitter topic. Quote marks or lack of quote marks simply reflect the actual content of the tweet.

    i. 106,185 people enrolled in Obamacare. 108,713 attended the 2010 NBA All-Star Game in Cowboys Stadium. #FullRepeal

    ii. "Enrollment in #Obamacare's federal exchange, so far, may only be in 'single digits.'"

iii. Putting #ObamaCare numbers in perspective: 106,185 people enrolled. 108,713 attended the 2010 NBA ASG in AT&T Stadium.

iv. Day four, and online enrollments of #Obamacare may be in single digits.

v. #Obamacare enrollees can fit inside Beaver Stadium. Comfortably.

vi. Seating capacity at Lucas Oil Stadium: 62,421. People who have been able to enroll in #Obamacare: Less than 50.

vii. If true, Obamacare enrollment numbers are pathetic: #NotReadyForPrimeTime

viii. Boehner on ACA enrollment numbers: This report is a symbol of the failure of the president's healthcare law. It is a rolling calamity.

ix. Shockingly low (and perhaps inflated) #Obamacare enrollment numbers further evidence that the law is a widespread failure. RT if you agree.

x. New enrollment numbers suggest #Obamacare is hurtling toward failure.

xi. Total October "enrollees" in the Obamacare Exchanges? 106,185. Capacity of OSU's Stadium, the Horseshoe? 102,329.

xii. These numbers are abysmal. The administration has not even met 25% of the #ObamaCare enrollment goal for the first month.

xiii. The low Obamacare enrollment numbers only further demonstrate the failure of this law. Enrollment falls short of target, less than 50,000 enrollees in private plans.

xiv. "Enrollment In Obamacare's Federal Exchange, So Far, Is In The 'single digits.'" Only 27k signed up for #Obamacare using the federal insurance website, not even enough to fill up Razorback Stadium. Pic.twitter/8AMyjEKIVc

https://twitter.com/jesseclee44
http://talkingpointsmemo.com/livewire/white-house-mocks-conservatives-obamacare-enrollment

Some background context.

Back in 2013 President Obama pointed out that the Affordable Care Act was not simply a website. But this simple truth was always going to be too complex for Stupidparty. So now on April 1, 2014, we can look back in the rear-view mirror to that Stupidparty heady month of glory—November 2013—where Stupidparty was given a free pass to reveal themselves, with the idle mainstream media just lapping it up, because the mainstream media barely has a sufficiently progressive bone to support a viable spine. The media in general is not biased in favor of the imagined "left," but they are not exactly diligent either. It is the path of least resistance, the quickest sale and the highest ratings for them. Enlightening the audience takes effort, entails risk, threatens dimming attention spans—thus why bother?

Interested in Math rather than Myth? Well one blogger, Charles Gaba was and he and his diligent sources worked tirelessly to get a grip on the facts, and as a result he has become the go-to resource on enrollment statistics. The pertinent website is http://acasignups.net/graph, and there you can find a graph that was always been available, tracking the facts.

So now we have engaged in crossword puzzles, Scrabbled fun, a level-of-ignorance test, hidden clues in cartoons, and "Easter egg" videos. This last puzzle has a simple catch-all answer.

The answer to the connect Fool's-name-to-comment puzzle.

The answer is that it does not matter; they are all much the same, talking the same insidious cultlike nonsense, rooting for failure, and all as if being puppet mastered by a more powerful force, conning the same target group, the Disciples. It does not matter, because virtually all SP reps were saying pretty much the same thing, all oblivious to the consequences of having zero reform. These Fools, these SP members one and all, appear not simply content to having the USA come in at #46 on the international healthcare table, but their plan is evidently to maintain a strategy of allowing the USA to freefall further toward the bottom.

We love to love a Fool—but not these ones. These Fools, these SP members, are a threat to everyone except to the Asset Strippers. If you have any asset, including your health, they want it. One day we will be able to look back and see not only what progress all these Fools stymied, but all the things that they stopped us from achieving. We will see not only all the damage they have wrought on us but what an existential threat they were to all of humanity—because America has great power, power that must be yielded with wisdom. We will not be remembering these Fools fondly, with any tears in our eyes.

Note: Polls will likely show continued trends toward public approval for Obamacare, but these polls are always somewhat misleading because of people like me. I believe that Obamacare is very far from satisfactory because Obama was forced to drop the public option. Thank you, Joe Lieberman (reborn again SP convert), who as a solid Blue state senator (Connecticut) had no excuse. Without the public option Americans will continue to pay approximately 50% more than necessary, business will continue to be responsible for unnecessary and costly burdens, and individuals and doctors' offices must continue to waste countless resources agonizing about payment, coverage, and deductible issues.

All is not lost. There may be cases where a logical approach will be able to take hold on a state basis—and once that happens, the approach will likely flourish and one day force other states to follow suit. For when the public option is adopted, Math will triumph over Myth. The Math will then most likely determine that a single-payer system (but with the option to buy additional insurance) will evolve that can best allow the American healthcare system the prospect of offering a product that can compare with other developed nations. I never heard a coherent argument against the public option. The Benefactors won, big money won, and they won by successfully promoting Myth.

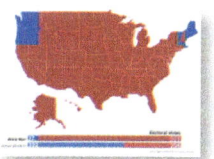

Supremely Stupidparty—(Thomas Jefferson lays out his nightmare.)

THE 5
FOR THE 1%

These five guys—Big Business must win every time—they are fine with unlimited funds for the Asset Strippers to buy politicians. The Supreme Court justices are not chosen on merit; money chooses the justices. The more money in the political process, the less the newly selected justices will reflect the will of the ever-more-suppressed and -uninformed electorate. Belief in Myth is ignorance, and the ignorant can be easily manipulated. Money will use an outmoded and ever-more-moribund Constitution to further its own agenda and not the agenda of the people. The Constitution had a history of evolving, but that is history now.

James Madison (Father of the Constitution?)

"Knowledge will forever govern ignorance and a people who mean to be their own governors must arm themselves with the power which knowledge gives."

Thomas Jefferson in 1804 predicted that this day would come.

"To consider the judges as the ultimate arbiters of all constitutional questions; a very dangerous doctrine indeed, and one which would place us under the despotism of an oligarchy.... their power [is] the more dangerous as they are in office for life and not responsible, as the other functionaries are, to the elective control. The Constitution has erected no such single tribunal, knowing that to whatever hands confided ... its members would become despots. It has more wisely made all the departments co-equal and co-sovereign within themselves.... When the legislative or executive functionaries act unconstitutionally, they are responsible to the people in their elective capacity. The exemption of the judges from that is quite dangerous enough."

Thomas Jefferson, letter to Thomas Ritchie, December 25, 1820

"A judiciary independent of a king or executive alone is a good thing; but independence of the will of the nation is a solecism, at least in a republican government."

The Asset Strippers, the Beneficiaries, they have taken control. They are the oligarchy in waiting; the democracy we think we see—it is just a mirage.

CHAPTER 23

Time for the 33.333% to stand up and be counted

All that is necessary for the triumph of evil is that good men do nothing.

—Edmund Burke

Now is the time to Stand up and be Counted
Now is the time to do the Math and to dispatch the Myth Sayers
For Stupid is really dangerous.

How stupid can we get? On July 16, 1945, this became an existential question. That was the day of the first successful atomic explosion, the day when we demonstrated the technology to destroy ourselves. Professor Stephen Hawkins asks, "In a world that is in chaos politically, socially and environmentally, how can the human race sustain another 100 years?" He advises that we need to explore space and be quick about it.

The Search for Extra Terrestrial Intelligence, SETI, has been frantically and fruitlessly studying the skies—and concluded that very few planets could sustain life and only 1% of such planets might have intelligent life. There are a number of reasons for such scarcity, one being: intelligent life may well have existed on other worlds but does not currently exist. There may be billions of planets, but the average lifespan of a civilization may be just a few thousand years, or even less. Possibly most intelligent civilizations wipe themselves out before developing spacecraft technology...

Since that atomic explosion world population has grown from about 2.4 billion to about 7 billion, projected to grow to 10 billion by 2050. These numbers are simply not sustainable.

Eminent Australian scientist Professor Frank Fenner, who helped wipe out smallpox, predicts humans will probably be extinct within 100 years because of overpopulation, environmental destruction, and climate change. Imagine a gigantic five-mile-wide one-mile-high combine harvester ripping though the planet's resources with gay abandon, spewing poisonous waste in its wake—and yet this is the only planet that can sustain life that is not many light years away. That is the definition of insanity. Our behavior is so myopic. Here is the thing: if we do not find some answers, then answers will be found on our behalf. Which option do you prefer?

This is such a vital question, but I fear it is like water running off a duck's back to anyone who cannot even get a grip around relatively simple stuff like evolution. Why is this so difficult? Religious doomsday numb nuts have had their chance. How many times must they be proved wrong? Below illustrates the numerous the times they've been proved wrong. That's about 150 times. Of the 26 predictions with the end of

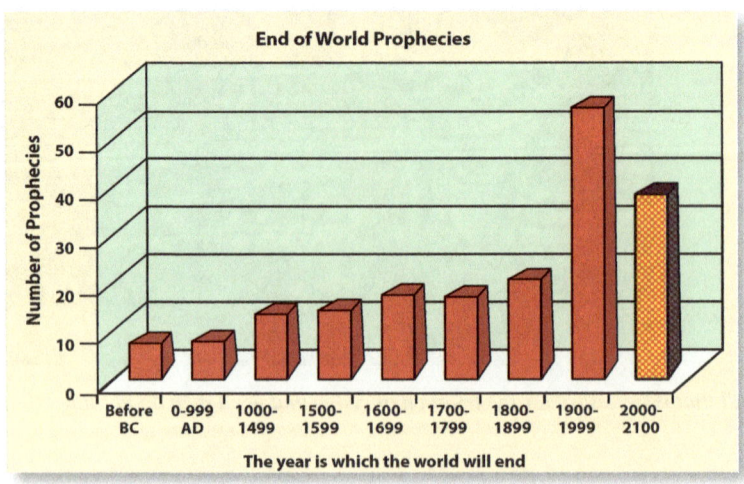

the world occurring on various dates in the twenty-first century, 21 one of those have already proved wrong.

The end of the world will not happen as described by Michelle Bachmann and her crowd. There will be no four headless or two-headed or hydra-headed horsemen riding down some random main street for no apparent reason or maids a-milking or partridges in pear trees. It will not happen as a result of misinterpreting some ancient text, written by or interpreted by some guy with an agenda living in a cave or a devout Christian exiled to the Greek Island of Patmos—whose fully headed, vengeful horses were more likely headed to slaughter the Emperor Nero, sworn enemy of Jerusalem, than people sipping coffee at Starbucks.

But it might well happen as a result of man's stupidity. It will happen by giving power to people like Bachmann and numerous other characters who have been discussed in this book. As the world nears a crisis, a crisis that they created (Stupidparty thinking) and have refused to address, they will just say it is God's will (or Allah's will, Yahweh's will—for they are all the same), and what will they do? They will pray. Bastards!—for they just killed us. They preached the crass pillaging of the planet, the enmity towards others, the lack of "respect for all living creatures," the need for short-term profit to trump long-term strategic thinking, and the assault on reason, nuance, and critical thinking. And now, as the world ends, they pray. The final irony; the bliss of Ignorance.

If the end of the world happens in the short term, the facts tell us it will likely happen as a result of war, disease, climate—because we now have the capability of destroying ourselves, and actually it will not be the end of the world, but it will be the end of us, of you, your children. Yes, other less-immediate threats beyond our control can get us too. Planetary apocalypse has already happened and it will happen again, and yes, the fact is that eventually the sun will expand and get too hot, and after that the universe will collapse. But you and I can only be concerned about what we can control, our odds of maintaining a civilized, livable planet over the next hundred years. To do this, we must get a grip; we must renounce Stupid—and revive Party.

I have just one question for Stupidparty Disciples. If America were no longer a place you could tolerate, what country would you move to? What country could you tolerate? What country could tolerate you?

Two-thirds of Stupidparty Disciples are temporarily lost, and nothing that can be said can penetrate these skulls—for unless the information comes from Fox News or the much-admired "hate radio" programs/talk shows—or unless it comes from Ann Coulter, Glenn Beck, Hannity, some paramilitary nut case author, or even worse from one of the faux Christian leaders discussed—these 67% are not at this moment open to listening, not to factual political news. It would seems that this 67% live in an information bubble induced by carefully sponsored paranoia. We have a large segment of society that are hiding in their caves.

But we have established that about one-third of Stupidparty Disciples still function with high critical thinking skills. And we have not only common ground but we probably agree on the vast majority of issues. We all accept that the earth is round, that Jesus did not walk with Dinosaurs, that the Planet is Warming, that Obama was born in America and is not a Kenyan Communist Muslim Terrorist mole. We mostly recognize that traveling to other countries is both educational and fun, that fact-based education is important. We mostly accept that whites are not inherently better than nonwhites, Americans not better than non-Americans or straights better than homosexuals.

This one-third recognizes that religion should not be hateful, that Jesus did not believe in genocide or war or simply helping the wealthy, that religion should fight poverty and disease rather than fostering environments in which poverty and disease flourish—such religious individuals must surely accept that God blessed humanity with a brain, and thus this brain should be exercised, not exorcised. Neither the pope nor the archbishop of Canterbury has ever suggested that science and facts should be ignored. These pillars of the Christian faith do not preach creationism or anti-science fervor.

This 33.333% understand that it is okay to discuss gun control; it is not okay to keep allowing more money into the democratic process. It is okay to discuss living sustainable lives in a sustainable society, and torture of any living creature is unacceptable.

Yes – you can be rational

In spite of all this, the 33.333% keep voting with Stupidparty and thus empowering the 67.677%—perhaps in the provably erroneous belief that their relative or delusional moderation will act as a moderating force. But the exact opposite has happened. You (the 33.333%) are being used. Your passivity has empowered the bigotry and stupidity that rages across the nation, threatening democracy at home and humanity across the globe.

Why? Why allow this?

Perhaps all you care about are your short-term taxes?

Perhaps you are personally struggling financially as a result of the shrinking "Middle Class"?

(Morphing into the Struggling class.)

Perhaps you hold onto the (mistaken) belief that the Iraq war was justified.

Perhaps you simply have a conservative brain and are terrified out of your wits of not getting a supersized discount for the gallon of Coke you drink at the movie theatre?

Perhaps you believe in cutting taxes? (Which, by the way, is fine when done correctly.)

Perhaps you just want to be a Republican and you feel embarrassed about being Stupidparty?

But the problem is—all the problems discussed in this book—well, you own them, and it is time to take a stand. Without your 33.333%, the 67.677% do not form a cohesive, singular unit capable of making Congress totally and destructively incompetent. You want the Republican Party back? First, you must leave it. It has to be rebuilt on new foundations, and this will only happen when the path of least resistance is no longer available.

Blaming both sides is just wrong, not only on the facts of the matter but also strategically. Blaming both sides is the same as saying, "Let's keep the status quo"—because by simply and incorrectly blaming both sides to an equal degree, you will end up with the status quo, which is actually the definition of being a conservative. By unreflectively blaming both sides to an equal degree, you are being conservative, and at present that means you are Stupidparty. By blaming both sides, you are in effect playing a game of chess, each player left with their king and not much else, which would be a stalemate other than for the fact that you have a spare pawn and are too set in your ways to realize that this pawn can be converted into a queen. You do not have to be stuck in that stale rut of always being The King of your intellectual domain. Let your mind travel: you could become a Queen for a day—and you might even have some fun, as it is the journey not the destination that adds color to our otherwise preprogrammed actions.

Time to change your strategy:

To move forward, we must have a winner. Then the loser must evolve to regain its self-respect.

You want lower taxes? Okay, but only if the overall economic package tackles income- discrepancy trends.

You want less government? Okay, but only if the overall reform package tackles safety, security, education, pollution, poverty, infrastructure, proper people-financed democracy, guards against unfettered capitalism, etc.

You want the Republicans to win? Okay, but only if they stop winning by cheating, lying, and being the tool of the corrupting power of money.

You want to be free to practice you religion? Okay, but you are already free to practice your religion.

You want to be free to pollute? Okay, but you must pay for the true cost of your activities.

You want America to have a strong, assertive foreign policy? Okay, but you must respect other nations. Without such respect you cannot have an effective foreign policy.

You want to have a debate? Okay, but stop the hostage taking, demand the truth, and respect facts.

What else could you possibly want?

We are all fallible, we all make mistakes—I am not inclined to list my worst mistakes, and I am not overly quick to own up to them. I have my own forms of denial. I have had my head in the sand about some of the issues discussed in this book. I am not totally free from prejudice and I realize that the only way to change that might be to get out there (travel) and live amongst the issues that confound me. Economically if you had asked me about the French twenty years ago, I would have thought that while they may enjoy a significantly superior quality of life—with their food, climate, architecture, liberated culture, benefits, and work and play lifestyles—I would have predicted that to be unsustainable. I still predict that, but so far they have sustained it. I just do not really understand how.

I have evolved massively in the last fifteen years. Many Americans have. Just look at the sea change on the issue of gay marriage over the last ten years; the same seems to be happening regarding smoking pot—so we can change, and change fast. Suddenly we have become more enlightened. While I have always been the same on the climate is-sues, I personally have changed simply by being exposed to the total idiots we see in the House, or because of the religious leaders that I have discussed. When you see a group of really stupid people, you just want to walk in the opposite direction—don't you?

So back to voting Stupidparty. Whatever your reason for voting Stupidparty, it is not working. It is backfiring to a stupendous degree. You have accidentally brought this country down to its intellectual knees—because you have delayed taking responsibility.

For the 33.333%, I really hope that you can ponder the road we have been on that has led us up to this moment and that the status quo is simply not acceptable. I guess you might choose to double down, have more of the same. But I doubt that, because you care about others besides yourself (well, except for the sociopaths that have been dis-cussed). The facts are just too overwhelming. The Stupidparty is not a force for good—and voting Stupidparty is a vote for bad, a vote for corruption and a vote for bigotry. There is nowhere to hide from the light of the facts.

You must abandon the 67.67%. Only this way can the sustenance that makes it into their caves be brought to a halt. Starved of this sustenance, the 67.67% will be forced out into the open. In the light of the day this segment will soon realize what has happened and that they have been conned—and will turn their fury upon the Stupidparty Benefactors. Once the billions of $$$$$ flowing from the Benefactors start falling on barren soil, only then can you plant and sow the seeds of a fertile and productive democracy that re-sponds to the needs of the people rather than the needs of the Asset Stripping Benefac-tors. Only then can we all come together and engage in intelligent debate—yes, plenty of different ideas but ideas based upon Math, Science, Justice, and Knowledge.

Be aware of the company you keep, as that is how you will ultimately be judged. It is not good enough to say, "Well, my congressman is a decent person." It is not enough because that very same congressman will vote with the economic terrorists, vote to mock fact-based research; that congressman was voted into power by a carefully cultivated bigot base, winning as a result of Benefactor largesse, and therefore will vote for dysfunctional government against the economic interests of the vast majority of Americans. These politicians will vote to tolerate, pander to, and promote the obnoxious ignorance illustrated in this book. They know that only by cheating can their party win. So they will vote for self-survival; they will actively obstruct efforts to get Congress answerable to the needs of the people. Your needs.

Before voting Republican again, demand more from your own party. Demand that true democracy should not be for sale to the highest bidder. Demand the truth, demand decency, demand research-based solutions. Demand tolerance and an equitable society. Demand sustainable polices, demand respect for humanity across the globe.

If your party leaders are saying God tells them to do this or that, then demand that these leaders are as good as people like Gandhi or Mandela, and by the way, ask them to describe the cadence of this divine voice: Does Perry's God have a Texas drawl? We all have a right to know about this ever-so-special knowledge that is not derived from this planet. If a politician is suggesting that God supports his or her campaign, then make that politician walk barefoot on hot coals.

The Republican Party is in a coma. By all accounts, the Stupidparty has taken possession. The only people who can revive the patient are the 33.333% supporters who are not delusional, who can read a chart. The only way to save the patient is to disown what the patient has become. The only way to stage an intervention is to walk away. If you walk away, I can guarantee that only then will the patient awaken and come looking for you. The patient will apologize to you. The patient needs you in order to survive.

Abandon the 67% in order to save the 67%, and they will be forced to stop watching the bigot panderers; they will leave their information bubble and start demanding more from their representatives, their preachers, and their friends. And you, the 33.333%, will have brought the nation from the brink; the tidewaters of absurdity will recede, and the end of times will no longer be an imminent, probable self-fulfilling prophecy.

It is time to stand up and be counted.

I am asking you to save the Republican Party by abandoning the Stupidparty.

Scrabble ®

Solution to Crossword Puzzle – Chapter 7

Across

2.	…Rules	(MONEY)
3.	Recreational group radicalized by a coup	(NRA)
6.	Romney owns, Bush plays, evangelicals await	(HORSES)
8.	Profiting off the labor of struggling people	(MOOCHER)
10.	…Is peace	(WAR)
12.	…Is Slavery	(FREEDOMS)
13.	Removed on entry into Stupidparty	(IQ)
15.	House committee meeting room	(VACUUM)
16.	Nonexistent in Stupidparty land	(COMEDY)
17.	Supreme Court was its midwife	(STUPIDPARTY)

21. Supreme Court's wet dream to facilitate them   (OLIGARCHS)
22. ...United against the interests of the people   (CITIZENS)
24. Feeling superior based on tribal birth   (RACISM)
26. The food fed to Disciples to trigger allegiance   (FEAR)
28. No child, adult or animal is left behind   (TORTURE)
29. 280 million in the USA   (GUNS)

Down

1. Helped the poor, the sick and admonished the rich   (JESUS)
2. Foundation of facts   (MATH)
4. Watch in order to see less   (FOX)
5. The puppetmasters   (BENEFACTORS)
7. Salivating over your Assets   (STRIPPERS)
9. Disciples' wet dream   (APOCALYPSE)
11. Dislike born out of Ignorance   (BIGOT)
14. Mental condition of "cutting" and self harm   (REDSTATE)
18. Supremely safe ancient Mythical horse   (TROJAN)
19. Freedom fighters for Willy, Watergate for Dick, Disciples for ...   (KOCH)
20. True believer of Benefactor Mythical claptrap   (DISCIPLE)
23. ...Up might be better than down   (TRICKLE)
25. Like Garlic to a vampire, these are to a Disciple   (FACTS)
27. Foundation of Stupidparty   (MYTH)

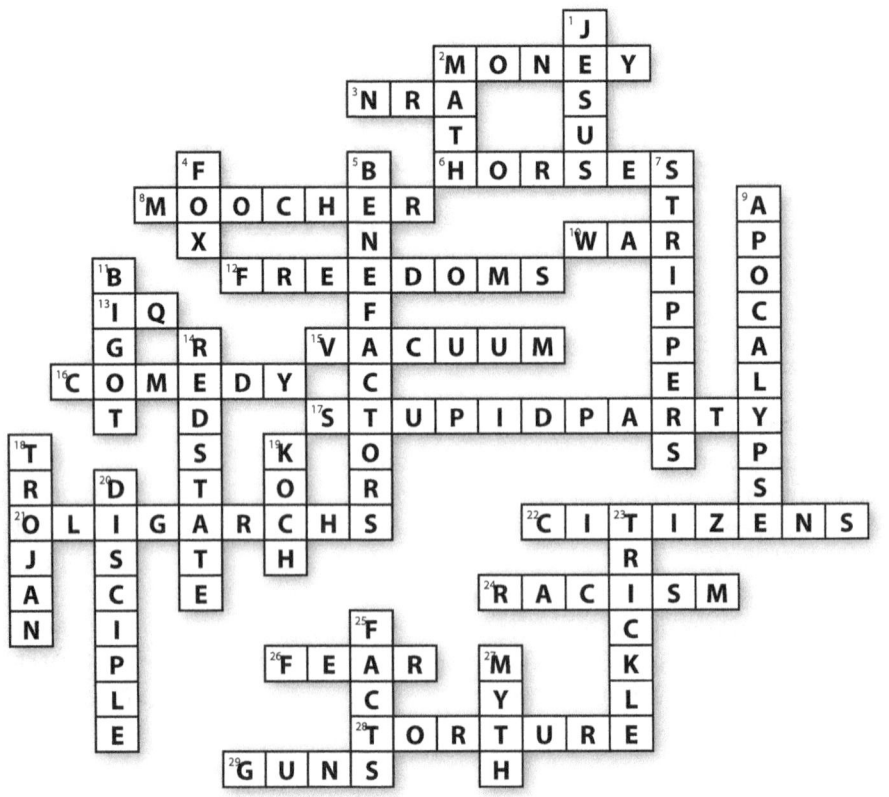

Acknowledgments

J. Longo
The artist retained for the book.   http://jlongoart.com/

Plus others.

Copyright permission for Albrecht Durer, Four Horsemen of the Apocalypse - Stock Image purchased by Jason Longo from IStock.
http://www.istockphoto.com/

Matt Rota
A different artist retained for the book   http://www.mattrotasart.com/

Also much thanks to the following artists for their assistance:

George Trosley   www.georgetrosley.com

Mark Howard   http://www.newscorpse.com/

Ron Miller   http://www.black-cat-studios.com/

Tim Whyatt   http://whyatt.com.au/cartoons/

Clay Bennett   http://www.claybennett.com/

The Union of Concerned Scientists
   for giving permission to reproduce.   http://www.ucsusa.org/

The Facts are coming by…Brian Narelle   http://www.narellecartoons.com/

Some Guy on Twitter…Hugh Macleod   http://macleodcartoons.blogspot.com/

HIs sound bite eating our data…S.M.   unknown

Pollution creating Healthcare jobs…John Klossner   http://www.jklossner.com/

Sydney Harris

   ScienceCartoonsPlus.com   For the following:
   Darwin at a Turning point
   1+1 =
   Miracle Occurs
   Church of Divine Healing
   Second Amendment Loophole.

Royalty-Free Cartoons   http://free-cartoons.sangrea.net/

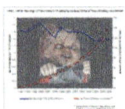    

Chris Weigant   http://www.chrisweigant.com

The Skeptical Raptor Blog

For the Words on the False Equivalency Cartoon   http://www.skepticalraptor.com/

Various political Cartoons

Purchased from   https://www.politicalcartoons.com/

Hazmat suit, The Ryan Bludgeon, Digging for the grass roots, One day this will be yours, Zimmerman arrested again.

And by Pat Bagley

Texas deregulation. Freedom. Legitimate Rape. Voter Suppression. The lies of Fox.

Mother Jones   http://www.motherjones.com/

Mother Jones has been nominated for the industry›s highest honor—the National Magazine Award for General Excellence—in each of the past four years, and has won twice. *MoJo* has also garnered a slew of other awards for its reporting, illustration, and photography

Think Progress and Climate Progress   http://thinkprogress.org/

THINKPROGRESS

In 2008, *Time* magazine named *Climate Progress* as one of the «Top 15 Green Websites».[4] In 2009, Thomas L. Friedman, in his column in *The New York Times,* called *Climate Progress* «the indispensable blog»,[5] and in 2010, *Time* included it in a list of the 25 «Best Blogs of 2010».[6]

Alternet   http://www.alternet.org/

AlterNet, an award winning project of the non-profit **Independent Media Institute**

Eric Sapp–Contributor to Patheos   http://www.patheos.com/

The site is listed as 10th out of the 50 best spirituality blogs ranked by Online Christian Colleges. On January 3, 2011, *Newsweek* listed Patheos as one of «21 Ways To Be Smarter in 2011»

Farm Sanctuary   http://www.farmsanctuary.org/

Stop Factory Farms   http://www.stopfactoryfarms.org/

Mormon Infographics   http://www.mormoninfographics.com/

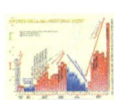 

http://jimcgreevy.com/gvdc/Natl_Debt_Chart.html
http://www.you-can-be-funny.com./VeryFunnyCartoons.html

Various Clipart (purchased)

Clipartof   http://www.clipartof.com/

Shutterstock   http://www.shutterstock.com/

Slidesharecom

http://www.slideshare.net/sorourkewalker/why-be-a-vegetarian-13113914?from_search=6
http://www.slideshare.net/shivanggupta94/soil-pollution-seminar-1?from_search=6

In the Public Domain
No known restrictions on publication

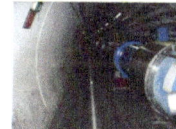

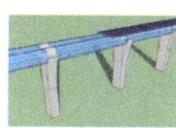

http://commons.wikimedia.org/wiki/File:Large_Hadron_Collider_dipole_magnets_IMG_0955.jpg

http://commons.wikimedia.org/wiki/File:Hyperloop.jpg

http://commons.wikimedia.org/wiki/File:Olivehurst,_Yuba_County,_California._Child_of_parents_who_were_migratory_workers,_now_settling_in_Ol_._._._-_NARA_-_521604.jpg

http://commons.wikimedia.org/wiki/File:Scene_at_the_Signing_of_the_Constitution_of_the_United_States.jpg

http://commons.wikimedia.org/wiki/File:Carracci,_Annibale_-_The_Stoning_of_St_Stephen_-_1603-04.jpg

http://commons.wikimedia.org/wiki/File:Government-Vedder-Highsmith-detail-2.jpeg

http://commons.wikimedia.org/wiki/File:CastingoutMoneyChangers.jpg

RUSTY RED LINKS
Funny or Sad

CPSIA information can be obtained at www.ICGtesting.com
Printed in the USA
BVOW10s2004080914

366001BV00001B/1/P